NOMOS

NOMOS

Essays in Athenian law, politics and society

edited by
PAUL CARTLEDGE
PAUL MILLETT
&
STEPHEN TODD

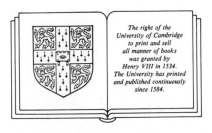

The right of the
University of Cambridge
to print and sell
all manner of books
was granted by
Henry VIII in 1534.
The University has printed
and published continuously
since 1584.

CAMBRIDGE UNIVERSITY PRESS

Cambridge
New York   Port Chester
Melbourne   Sydney

Published by the Press Syndicate of the University of Cambridge
The Pitt Building, Trumpington Street, Cambridge CB2 1RP
40 West 20th Street, New York, NY 10011, USA
10 Stamford Road, Oakleigh, Melbourne 3166, Australia

First published 1990

Printed in Great Britain at the University Press, Cambridge

British Library cataloguing in publication data
Nomos: essays in Athenian law, politics and society.
1. Greece. Athens. Law, ancient period
1. Cartledge, Paul 11. Millett, Paul 111. Todd, Stephen
343.8′5

Library of Congress cataloguing in publication data applied for

ISBN 0 521 37022 1 hard back

OCLC: 20593912

To the memory of Moses Finley

Contents

Notes on contributors

PAUL CARTLEDGE is University Lecturer in Ancient History and Fellow of Clare College, Cambridge. He has published widely on Greek history and historiography, and is the author of several standard works on Spartan history, most recently *Hellenistic and Roman Sparta: A Tale of Two Cities* (1989) (with A. Spawforth).

DAVID COHEN is Associate Professor of Rhetoric in the University of California at Berkeley. He has written *Theft in Athenian Law* (1983), and a range of articles on Athenian legal and social history. He is at present preparing a study of *Law, Violence and Community in Classical Athens* for Cambridge University Press's Key Themes in Ancient History Series.

NICK FISHER is Lecturer in Ancient History at the University of Wales, Cardiff. He is the editor of *Social Values in Classical Athens* (1976), and is at present writing a book on *Hybris*.

DAVID HARVEY is Lecturer in Classics at Exeter University. He has written widely on many aspects of Athenian social and political history, and was joint editor with Paul Cartledge of *CRUX. Essays presented to G.E.M. de Ste. Croix on his seventy-fifth birthday* (1985). He is currently preparing an edition of Herodotus' Lydian *Logos*.

PAUL MILLETT is University Lecturer in Ancient History and Fellow of Downing College, Cambridge. He has written several articles on Athenian social and economic history, and is at present preparing a book for Cambridge University Press on *Lending and Borrowing in Ancient Athens*.

OSWYN MURRAY is Fellow and Tutor in Ancient History at Balliol College, Oxford. He is an authority on archaic Greek history, well known as the author of *Early Greece* (1980); he is at present undertaking a major study of the Greek *Symposium* during his tenure of a British Academy Research Readership.

ROBIN OSBORNE is Tutorial Fellow in Ancient History at Corpus Christi College, Oxford. He is the author of *Demos: the Discovery of Classical Attika* (1985), of *Classical Landscape with Figures* (1987), and of a number of articles on Greek art, archaeology and history.

TREVOR SAUNDERS is Professor of Greek at the University of Newcastle upon Tyne. His particular interest is in the *Laws* of Plato, a translation of which he has published in the Penguin Classics series (1970), and on which he has written extensively. He is at present writing a book, *Plato's Penal Code* (to be published by Oxford University Press).

STEPHEN TODD is Lecturer in Classics at Keele University. An earlier version of 'Evidence in Athenian Courts', his first published paper, was awarded the George Grote Prize of the University of London for 1988. He is now preparing a book on *The Shape of Athenian Law* (Oxford University Press).

Preface

This is a book about legal texts, and how they may be used as documents in writing a history of society. It has its origin in a series of seminars on 'Law and Society in Classical Athens', organised by Paul Cartledge and Paul Millett under the auspices of the Faculty of Classics at Cambridge in 1986/7. The scope of the book is roughly that of the seminar-series, but inevitably there have been some changes, both losses and gains. John Davies had hoped to present a paper on the proto-history of Greek law, but other commitments prevented this. Douglas MacDowell delivered a paper on the Athenian *oikos*, which has since been published elsewhere (1989). Trevor Saunders, on the other hand, was unable to take part in the seminars because of sabbatical leave in the United States: we are pleased that he has agreed to publish his paper in this volume.

The chapters which make up the book were for the most part delivered as independent papers. The exceptions were those on sykophancy by Robin Osborne and David Harvey, and on *hubris* by Nick Fisher and Oswyn Murray. In each of these cases both papers were delivered at the same meeting, with one speaker presenting a point of view to which the other responded.

The articles in this collection, then, were conceived as separate entities; and they are intended to be accessible as such. Nevertheless the book has (or so we hope) a unity as a whole. It does not claim to be a systematic treatise, covering all or even all the main aspects of Athenian law; it is rather a series of case-studies of method, outlining different ways in which the available Athenian legal texts can be read. It will soon become clear to the reader that the contributors do not hold identical opinions. In some cases, indeed, the papers present very different viewpoints: Harvey, for instance, argues that Osborne's 'sanitised' picture of the sykophant remains at best not proven. But this sort of disagreement in a book of this kind should be seen as a merit rather than a defect.

There are however two presuppositions which all the contributors share;

and it is these which lend an underlying unity to the book. Both are implicit in our subtitle. In the first place, this is a book about the relationship between law on the one hand and society and politics on the other: historians of ancient Greece have in the past tended to treat these as two separate issues; but we believe that the two subjects are inter-related, so that the study of one should illuminate the study of the other.

Secondly, the book focuses on 'classical Athens' rather than on 'ancient Greece'. This arose partly out of convenience: when the organisers originally invited contributions to a series of seminars on 'ancient Greek law and society', the response was overwhelming. From the United Kingdom alone, almost thirty scholars replied with offers of papers, revealing a general perception that this was an important combination of topics. Confining the series to classical Athens, from which the bulk of our evidence is derived, restricted the material to manageable proportions. But there is a second, more significant reason for the concentration on classical Athens. All our contributors believe that classical Athenian law is best studied in its own right, as the legal system of a unique social and political entity, rather than as part of a general study of the development of Greek legal doctrines. This is a contentious issue, and some of its implications are considered in the first chapter, which itself serves as an introduction to the main themes of the book. For the moment, it is enough to say that recent work on Greek legal doctrines has tended to become abstract; and our contributors share a bias towards the concrete. We possess in fact more evidence for the workings of the legal system of classical Athens in the century 420–320 than for any other place or period in the ancient Greek world, with the possible exception of Graeco-Roman Egypt. That is not to say that any of our contributors would wish to 'let the sources speak for themselves': Athenian legal texts require as careful interpretation as any of the literary sources which the ancient historian has to use; some of the problems involved are discussed in the course of this book. But with such a wealth of material available, it seems perverse not to use it.

Our use of the term 'legal text' is deliberately broad. We have not restricted our attention to the texts of legal statutes: few of these survive from classical Athens, and their importance within the legal system is debatable. Instead, the term is used to denote any text which has legal significance. Most notable of course is oratory; but other genres cited throughout the book include philosophy, constitutional history, tragedy, comedy, lyric poetry and inscriptions. It has to be admitted that these can all pose problems of accessibility to those without systematic knowledge of the classical world. Similarly, legal terms and concepts tend to be unfamiliar even to classical scholars. In order to assist readers across a range of disciplines, the contributors have adopted a deliberate policy of providing background information where it seemed necessary. All passages of Greek are translated, and transliterations are given for words and phrases for which there is no precise English equivalent. All words, phrases and concepts that seemed to pose potential problems have been gathered in a glossary at the end of the book; page references have been added, to enable this to serve as an index. But the glossary is intended to have a value of its own, independent of its function within this book: we hope that it will prove helpful to readers who may be baffled by the technical terms in books and articles about Athenian law. For this reason, several important terms which (as it happens) are not mentioned in the text of the book nevertheless receive entries in the glossary.

Many people have helped in the conception and production of this book, to whom the editors are most sincerely grateful. Individual debts are acknowledged by the various contributors, but as editors we would like to thank in particular a number of lawyers who gave us advice on matters outside our specialist knowledge: Graham Davies on ancient Near Eastern law; Neil Duxbury on legal history and philosophy; Katherine de Gama on legal anthropology; Jenny McEwan on English procedural law; and Ted Powell on the law and its enforcement in medieval England. They should not be held responsible for legal errors on our part.

Two people deserve our gratitude in a more general way. The inspiration for the theme of law and society came from the work of John Crook, whose *Law and Life of Rome* may be taken as a model for what the organisers of the seminar hoped to achieve. Our other principal debt is to Sir Moses Finley. He received the idea of a seminar series revolving around Athenian law and society with enthusiasm, agreed to deliver the opening paper, and advised us on the form that any resulting publication should take. Sadly, his death during the summer of 1986 deprived us of his promised paper. It is therefore fitting that this book should be dedicated to his memory.

P.A.C., P.C.M., S.C.T.

Abbreviations

Note: Abbreviations of periodicals follow the conventions of the relevant volume of *L'Année philologique*, the scholarly annual of record which regularly devotes a section to 'Loi, grecque'.

CAF	KOCH, T. (1880–8), ed., *Comicorum Atticorum Fragmenta*. 3 Vols. Leipzig
CGFP	AUSTIN, C., (1973) ed., *Comicorum Graecorum Fragmenta in Papyris Reperta*. Berlin & New York
DK	DIELS, H. & KRANZ, W. (1951–2, 1954), eds., *Die Fragmente der Vorsokratiker*. 5th–7th edns. Berlin
ESS	SELIGMAN, E.R.A. & JOHNSON, A. (1930–5), eds., *The Encyclopedia of the Social Sciences*. 15 vols. New York
FGH	JACOBY, F. (1923–58), ed., *Die Fragmente der griechischen Historiker*. Berlin & Leiden
IESS	SILLS, D. (1968–79), ed., *International Encyclopaedia of the Social Sciences*. 18 vols. London & New York
IJG	DARESTE, R., HAUSSOULLIER, B. & REINACH, Th. (1891–8), eds., *Recueil des Inscriptions Juridiques Grecques*. 2 vols. Paris
Kleine Pauly	ZIEGLER, K. & SONTHEIMER, W. (1975), eds., *Der Kleine Pauly*. 5 vols. Munich
LSJ	LIDDELL, H.G., SCOTT, R. & JONES, H.S. (1940), eds., *A Greek–English Lexicon*. 9th edn. Oxford (with Supp. 1968)
OCD	HAMMOND, N.G.L. & SCULLARD, H.H. (1970), eds., *The Oxford Classical Dictionary*. 2nd edn., Oxford
OCT	Oxford Classical Text

PCG   KASSEL, R. & AUSTIN, C. (1983–), eds., *Poetae Comici Graeci*. Berlin & New York

RE   PAULY, A.F. VON, WISSOWA, G. & KROLL, W. (1894–1972), eds., *Realencyclopädie der classischen Altertumswissenschaft*. 66 vols. in 34

Law, society and Athens

STEPHEN TODD AND PAUL MILLETT

THE STUDY OF ATHENIAN LAW

In what turned out to be his last book, Moses Finley (1985: 99–103) devoted several pages to 'the problem of Greek law'. In doing so, he was returning to one of the earliest interests of his career (cf. Finley 1951 and 1952). It would perhaps be fair to describe Finley, along with the classicist and sociologist Louis Gernet,[1] as pre-eminent among the very few exponents of the 'law and society' approach to Greek law for which we are pleading. It is striking, therefore, that both Gernet and Finley in major works lamented the lack of attention which the subject has received from the scholarly world. In the introduction to his first volume of essays, Gernet (1955: 1) complained that Greek law was studied by two groups only: philologists, who took no interest in questions of law; and Roman lawyers, who were constrained by inappropriate categories of thought. Borrowing an apt phrase from Hans-Julius Wolff, Finley (1985: 99) described Greek law as 'notoriously a stepchild in modern study'.

One might perhaps take Finley's point, and also the metaphor, a stage further. The problem of Greek or, to be more precise, Athenian law (see section II of this chapter) is that it is not simply a stepchild, but a stepchild overawed by several overbearing (not to say ugly) sisters. It is not just that more work needs to be done, though it has to be admitted that the Attic Orators, the central source for Athenian law and legal procedure, remain relatively under-researched.[2] Rather, the relationship between Athenian law and other kindred subjects needs to be re-examined. Indeed, part of the reason

---

[1] For a convenient introduction to Gernet's work, see Humphreys (1978: 76–106).

[2] Absence of interest in the Orators is symptomatic of a wider neglect of the fourth century B.C. as compared with the earlier centuries of Greek history. As a recent illustration, there is Garner 1987: despite its title, *Law and Society in Classical Athens* (i.e., fourth century as well as fifth), the concluding chapter on 'The Fourth Century' is restricted to a mere fourteen pages (see the reviews by Osborne 1987 and by Cartledge 1988). A glance at Garner's table of contents gives a correct impression of the very limited overlap between his book and the present volume.

for the low scholarly profile of Athenian law may be that it has traditionally been studied on the basis of questions and categories of thought derived from inappropriate disciplines. This point deserves to be discussed in more detail, considering the relationship of Athenian law first with Roman law, then with Greek law, and finally with law in general.[3]

I   ROMAN LAW AND ATHENIAN LAW

The legal systems of the modern west are divided broadly into two groups: the civil-law systems of France, Germany and the bulk of continental Europe; and the common-law systems of England and the United States. There are of course exceptions: Scots law for instance is a hybrid, containing elements of both systems (Robinson, Fergus & Gordon 1985: 258–79, 377–405).

The influence of Roman law in continental Europe is not surprising. Civil law, after all, derives its name from the *ius civile*, the 'law that pertains to citizens', of ancient Rome. The connecting link between Roman *ius civile* and modern civil law is the codification of Roman law in the name of the emperor Justinian in the sixth century A.D. The body of texts issued under Justinian is described collectively as the *Corpus Iuris Civilis* (corpus of civil law), although it was never as complete and systematic as the name suggests. Most important was the Digest, also commonly known as the Pandects, issued in 533, an authoritative compilation of excerpts from the leading classical jurists of the second and third centuries A.D. The Institutes (also 533), an introductory textbook for law students, was likewise made up of quotations from similar but older works; and the *Corpus* was completed in 534 by the promulgation of a second Code of imperial constitutions (i.e., statute law), superseding an earlier Code of 529 (see Wolff 1951: 158–76; Nicholas 1962: 38–45). Roughly half a millennium later, in the eleventh and twelfth centuries, the Digest began to be adopted as the basis of study by the emerging law schools of northern Italy, most notably that of Bologna; and the prestige of these law schools attracted students not only from Italy itself but from the whole of northern Europe, in particular Germany and France. University-trained lawyers, therefore, studied law according to categories of thought derived from Justinian. They took what they had studied back to their own kingdoms, where it seemed so much more sophisticated than the local customary law that they applied it in their pleadings and their judgements. This process culminated in what is called the Reception, by which a revived Roman law was 'received' (accepted) as the basis of national law in place of local custom.[4]

---

3 In what follows, emphasis has been placed on citation of more recent work on Athenian law. For a comprehensive list (but without comment) of materials available down to *c*.1925, see Calhoun & Delamere (1927). A further list, covering the years *c*.1925–*c*.1965, may be found in Berneker (1968: 697–770), although the organisation of this bibliography is rather confusing.
4 For details of the Reception of Roman law in medieval Europe, see Vinogradoff 1909, with Wolff (1951: 177–206), Nicholas (1962: 45–54) and Robinson, Fergus & Gordon (1985:

In England on the other hand the situation was different. Romanist ideas were not unknown (Vinogradoff 1909: 97–118; Nicholas 1962: 46), but there was no Reception. Instead, it was customary law, extended and made uniform ('common') throughout the country, that formed the basis of English (and indirectly American) common law (Robinson, Fergus & Gordon 1985: 208–58). Nobody has ever satisfactorily explained why the Reception should have happened throughout Continental Europe but not in England; but it should be emphasised that the spread of Romanist thinking was a gradual process, and its progress was determined by complex factors (Wolff 1951: 183–206; Nicholas 1962: 48–50). Reception took place more easily within the Holy Roman Empire than outside it, because the Digest presupposed the jurisdiction of the Emperor. Where customary law was already perceived to be sufficiently sophisticated to meet the needs of society, this will have reduced the pressure for change. The way in which the law was taught may also have played a part: English lawyers have traditionally been trained by practising lawyers at the Inns of Court rather than by academic lawyers at universities or law schools.

It was therefore predictable that Roman law would have traditionally had a firm hold on the legal scholarship of continental Europe. What is at first sight more surprising is that Roman law has had a considerable impact on English legal thinking also. This may in part derive from the sheer dominance of Roman law as an effort in systematic thinking: whether we agree or disagree with it, we cannot get away from it. Roman law remains a traditional though declining component in law degrees in English universities.[5] But the dominance of Roman law may also be connected with its own inherent ambiguities: different sides in the same dispute can both look back on Roman law as their spiritual progenitor. Thomas (1968: 1–3) for instance uses Roman law of the classical period before Justinian in order to attack the Reception: he praises it as a creative system in which rulings were made to meet practical problems, rather than a fossil in which doctrines are expanded with ruthless logic to cover future eventualities. This is the language in which the case-based common lawyer berates his code-based civil-law colleague; and it is done by appealing to Roman law.

The dominance of Roman law in Anglo-American as well as Continental legal scholarship therefore helps to explain the traditionally low profile of Athenian law as an intellectual discipline. This was by implication the thrust of Finley's lament: the study of Greek law is a 'stepchild' in the sense that it

---

71–121). For a comparative perspective, examining the reception of systems other than Roman law, see Watson 1974.

[5] Roman law in England has traditionally been studied from a strictly theoretical perspective, almost as a form of jurisprudence, because its relevance to English law is purely intellectual. The jurisprudential tradition has been particularly strong at Oxford, as suggested by several of the books in the Clarendon Law Series: Hart 1961, Sawer 1965, Raz 1980. The relationship between modern jurisprudence and Athenian law is discussed further in section III of this chapter.

has had that of Roman law as a stepmother. The strength of this link can easily be demonstrated, in terms of the restricted opportunities for the former both in employment and in publication. The number of scholars studying Greek law has never been large; and many of these, at least on the Continent, have held posts in departments of Roman law. Hans-Julius Wolff, for instance, the most distinguished German scholar of his generation in the field, was Professor of Roman and Civil Law at Freiburg; Arnaldo Biscardi, the most eminent contemporary Italian expert, is Professor of Roman Law and Director of the Istituto di Diritto Romano in Milan. The context in which a scholar works will necessarily have implications for his methods of study.

The restricted opportunities for publication are even more striking. There are perhaps four journals which might be expected to show a specialist interest in articles on Greek law: none of these, we note with regret, is published in an English-speaking country.[6] Of the four, the Belgian *Tijdschrift voor Rechtsgeschiedenis* (*TR*: sometimes known by its alternative French title as the *Revue d'histoire du droit* or *RHD*) and the French *Revue historique de droit français et étranger* (*RDFE*) are both concerned with legal history in general; the latter contains few articles on Greek law with the exception of a very useful critical bibliography of the subject, which appears annually, edited most recently by Alberto Maffi. The other two journals however do specialise in ancient law: these are the French *Revue internationale des droits de l'antiquité* (*RIDA*) and the German *Zeitschrift der Savigny-Stiftung für Rechtsgeschichte* (*ZSS*: sometimes *ZRG*). For the Greek lawyer, *RIDA* would at first sight appear the best prospect. Each issue is divided into three or four sections: the ancient Orient; classical and hellenistic Greece (combined or separated in different years); and Rome. But the relative size of each section is striking: we conducted a rough survey of the thirty-three volumes of the third series available to us (1954–86); we counted both number of articles and number of pages, and the two sets of figures varied by only three or four percentage points in each case. During that period the ancient Orient filled roughly 25–30 per cent of the whole; Rome filled 55–60 per cent; and Greece (even adding classical and hellenistic together) was confined to a mere 10–15 per cent. The picture becomes even sharper with *ZSS*, which does indeed publish work on Greek law. But *ZSS* is divided into three simultaneous series, independently edited, with one volume of each appearing annually: Roman law, German law, and Canon law. If an article on Greek law is published, it will appear in the *Romanistische Abteilung*. This has a powerful symbolic significance.

The dominance of Roman law therefore helps to explain the 'stepchild' status of Greek law. But it has also had an effect on the way in which Greek law is studied. As Gernet (1955: 1, cited above) complained, when Roman lawyers study Greek law, they tend to impose inappropriate categories on it.

---

[6] This is of course an oversimplification, because it ignores the willingness of general classical and even legal journals, both in Britain and in the United States, to publish work on the subject. But the point remains: it is impossible to name a specialist journal published in this country.

This is best illustrated by examining the structure which authors of systematic textbooks have given to their work.

Sir Henry Maine, who introduced to this country the comparative study of ancient law,[7] observed in a famous phrase that in the early stages of legal development 'substantive law [is] secreted in the interstices of procedure' (Maine 1883: 389; see further n.12 below). To the modern mind, this may seem surprising: we would tend to assume that substantive law ('what are my rights and my duties?') has a logical priority over procedural law ('how do I go about defending my rights?'); after all, you need to know what your rights are before deciding whether to go to court to protect them. This, however, has not always been so. In Athens, so far as we can tell, procedural law held both a chronological and a logical priority: the reason for example why the Athenians had no proper concept of a distinction between ownership and possession is that they had no procedure whereby absolute ownership could be asserted; instead, they had only a series of procedures by which you could assert a better right than a particular opponent.[8] Procedures came first, and a substantive right could only exist where there was a procedure available to create that right.

Now this of course has implications for the structure of textbooks and general works of reference. If we are correct in applying Maine's dictum to Athens, then a general textbook on Athenian law should give priority to legal procedure rather than to substantive law. There are not very many such textbooks;[9] a total of seven may be listed. These, are, in chronological order: Beauchet (1897),[10] Lipsius (1905–15), Vinogradoff (1922), Bonner & Smith (1930–8), Harrison (1968–71), MacDowell (1978), and Biscardi (1982). Vinogradoff and Bonner & Smith are to some extent attempting a different

---

7 The influence on Maine of Savigny and the historical school of German lawyers is an important topic; but it is beyond the scope of this chapter, and it does not substantially detract from Maine's own originality: for details, see Kuper (1988: 20–3).

8 This is a disputed point: it is rejected by Kränzlein (1963), who devoted his work on the law of property to a search for the concept of ownership. Harrison (1968: 205 n.2) appears to agree with Wolff that this search has proved ultimately unsuccessful. Harrison himself (1968: 201 n.2) suggests that the absence of a concept of ownership was the reason for the limited nature of the remedies available to a would-be Athenian claimant of property; but this is surely to mistake cause for effect.

9 We leave on one side here a number of very useful short introductions, many of them articles in encyclopaedias or general introductions to the Classical world (Wyse 1916, cf. n.26 below; Weiss 1933; MacDowell 1988); because of their brevity, these do not have to face the problem of organising their material in the same way as do the full-scale textbooks. Also deserving of passing reference are the entries on specific legal topics in the standard Classical dictionaries. The articles in the *OCD* (2nd edn, 1970) are useful for immediate reference, but they are generally too brief to be of great significance. The entries in *RE* (1894–1972) are for the most part highly technical, though normally comprehensive and often definitive. Perhaps the most penetrating, though inevitably the most dated, are the pieces in the French lexicon edited by Daremberg & Saglio (1875–1919): many of these were the work of Exupère Caillemer, himself the author of a series of important short studies (Caillemer 1865–72; cf. Caillemer 1879).

10 Beauchet was not the first writer to be interested in the subject, but no earlier work has the comprehensiveness and accessibility required of a textbook. Even the great manual by Meier & Schömann 1824 is better described as a work of legal antiquities.

sort of exercise; and discussion of their work will be postponed until section III of this chapter. This leaves us with five books to consider.

Lipsius' interests at first sight appear to be procedural, but he was in fact writing not so much a work on procedural law as a catalogue of legal procedures: the second volume, which itself appeared in two parts (1908–12) and together is longer than the other two volumes combined, consists of a separate study of every attested type of prosecution, catalogued in terms of the presiding magistrate. As Gernet complained (1938a: 266–8), the result is brilliant on questions of detail but conveys no unified conception of how Athenian law hangs together.[11]

The remaining authors all adhere more or less closely to a pattern derived not from Athenian but from Roman law. Beauchet indeed confines his attention ruthlessly to 'private law', a category unknown in Athens, and one which he himself found it increasingly difficult to sustain throughout four volumes (Harrison 1968: vi–vii). Biscardi's introduction (1982: 6) protests against his predecessors' use of inappropriate Roman categories; but he then devotes 19 pages to sources of law, 37 to public and 159 to private substantive law, with only 19 pages allowed for legal procedure and a further 36 for the early history of criminal law. Similar priorities are displayed by Harrison: substantive law takes up the first of his two volumes, and was originally intended to fill the first half of the second volume also (Harrison 1971: v–vi). Much of Harrison's vocabulary is similarly derived from Roman law, which at times results in a certain obscurity. The work is indispensable to the specialist, but rarely consulted by more general readers.

A reaction against Harrison's uncompromising austerity came from Mac-Dowell, who had himself been the literary executor for Harrison's posthumous second volume. MacDowell's own book studiously avoids the technical terminology of Roman law: it is admirably lucid and accessible to the non-specialist. Indeed, MacDowell (1978: 9) virtually rejects on principle the use of other legal systems for comparative evidence, preferring to devote his attention to Athens itself. But we may doubt whether such a manifesto can really be maintained. Historians who reject the explicit use of comparative evidence tend in practice to use it implicitly and subconsciously; and for a British legal historian, the natural starting-point is an amalgam of English, possibly Scots, and a bit of Roman law. The plan of MacDowell's work is indeed very similar to that of Harrison's: the only major change is the addition of an introductory section on the development of the courts (57 pages); substantive law (136 pages) once again fills the bulk of the book, and is again considered ahead of procedure (57 pages).

To sum up: our society's emphasis on substantive and in particular private substantive law should not be regarded as somehow 'natural' and therefore

---

[11] Lipsius' second volume (1908–12) is itself based on his 1883–7 revision of Meier & Schömann 1824. He may, as Gernet (1938a: 266) suggests, have been to some extent a prisoner of this earlier work of legal antiquarianism (cf. n.10 above).

intrinsically correct; it is an assumption derived indirectly from the priorities of the Roman jurists. The historian of a legal system earlier than, and consequently independent of, classical Roman law should perhaps look instead to other ancient societies to gain an understanding of other possible categories of thought. The immensely creative work of Maine (esp. 1861) on ancient law, though by no means as unsophisticated as some of his modern critics seem at times to imply, is now rather dated.[12] Much the same must now be said of other early scholars in the comparative tradition: Fustel de Coulanges (1864, with Momigliano & Humphreys 1983) and Glotz (1904, 1906, 1928). The most recent extensive work, that of Diamond (1971) is weakened by a certain economic determinism; and for our purposes it focuses on communities considerably more 'primitive' than any of the Greek *poleis*. But it would perhaps be worth strengthening the links between Greek law and the legal systems of the ancient Near Eastern kingdoms, about which we are relatively well-informed (Driver & Miles 1952–5; Boecker 1980). Indeed, as a corrective to the Romano-centricity of European legal thought, the perspective of independent modern systems such as Islamic (Pearl 1979) or Communist (Hazard 1970) law should not be ignored. Islamic law for instance consciously and deliberately seeks to impose a particular social and religious framework upon society; and in Communist law the court has an overtly political rôle. Both cases may supply closer analogies for an ancient Athenian court than does modern European law (at least in the eyes of modern European lawyers). Similarly our understanding of the law-code of Solon may be illuminated by consideration of ancient Near Eastern codes: such codes were 'interstitial' rather than 'exhaustive' (Sawer 1965: 58); their rôle was to fill in gaps in pre-existing customary law rather than to replace it. Their function was therefore far closer to that of statute in a common-law system than to that of a modern civil-law code.

II GREEK LAW AND ATHENIAN LAW

The study of Greek law, as a discipline distinct from Athenian law, was invented by Ludwig Mitteis at the end of the nineteenth century. Before that date, attention had been focused on Athens, as the source of virtually all our literary evidence. During the nineteenth century, however, two new bodies of non-literary evidence began to come to the attention of ancient legal his-

---

12 Particularly questionable, when viewed from an Athenian perspective, is Maine's emphasis on the concept of legal evolution (see Stein 1980: 69–98). For its unsuccessful application to one aspect of the law in ancient Greece, the origins of the putative concept of 'crime', see Calhoun 1927 (more generally, Calhoun 1944). Maine himself had strikingly little to say about ancient Greece, in spite of an interest in legal and social systems that ranged far beyond ancient Rome (e.g. Maine 1871; 1875; 1883). It may be that the democratic aspect of classical Athens proved uncongenial to his essentially conservative temperament (see Maine 1885, with Feaver 1969: 227–50). On the other hand, Maine's emphasis on the importance of procedure in early law has often been wrongly criticised: but what has been refuted is Maine's belief that such procedure was formalistic, not that it was important (see generally the discussion in Sawer 1965: 62–4).

torians: inscriptions[13] and papyri.[14] Of Greek inscriptions, only a few are of much legal significance in the narrow sense, and the majority even of these came from Athens itself; but the picture was different with the papyri. For reasons of climate, virtually all the papyri that have survived have been found in Egypt, a country which was first opened up to Western scholars by the campaigns of Napoleon; by the end of the nineteenth century, scholars had begun to be deluged by Greek documentary papyri, recording the activities of the non-native population of Egypt during the millennium that it was under Graeco-Roman rule.[15] Mitteis was one of the first legal historians to realise the possibilities of this material; and it was he who revealed a very striking phenomenon. Just as Greek rather than Latin remained the normal language of the immigrant population of Egypt (indeed, of the eastern Mediterranean in general) even under the Roman empire, so the law which was there applied at ground level showed far greater conceptual affinities with what was known of Athenian law than with the civil law of Rome itself. Mitteis (1891) described this as the survival of Greek *Volksrecht* ('popular law') in the face of the official Roman *Reichsrecht* ('imperial law'). Mitteis and his followers[16] concluded that Greek law should therefore be seen as an entity in its own right, ranging in time from Homer to the Arab conquest, and covering the whole of the Greek-speaking world; differences between the law in Homer, in classical Athens and in the papyri should be seen as local variants at particular stages of development.

Mitteis' thesis was persuasive and, for more than half a century, commanded very wide if not total acceptance. It formed the basis of many important works, including for instance Fritz Pringsheim's book on the law of sale (Pringsheim 1950). It was, indeed, in an extended review of Pringsheim's book that Finley (1951) mounted one of the first serious challenges to the validity of the concept of Greek law. Finley's major objection was that statements about Greek law were of two kinds: those which had to be qualified

---

[13] There are a number of standard general collections of inscriptions (for details see Woodhead 1981: 94–107); specifically juridical texts are collected in *IJG*.

[14] A good impression of the range of surviving documentary papyri can be gained from the Loeb selection edited by Hunt & Edgar (1932–4: two vols. of a promised five-vol. collection, of which only three were ever published; the third vol., edited by Sir Denys Page, contains literary poetic texts).

[15] Egypt was ruled by the Ptolemies (a Graeco-Macedonian dynasty) from soon after the death of Alexander in 323 B.C. until the death of the last Kleopatra in 30 B.C. From then until the Arab conquest in the seventh century A.D., it remained part of the Roman or Eastern Roman empire. By the end of this process, the law applied in the papyri appears to have consisted of a multiplicity of layers: Roman imposed on Graeco-Macedonian imposed on native Egyptian law.

[16] Mitteis himself was cautious, and fully aware of the perils of his thesis: 'Indeed, there is the danger that we may carry too much over from the papyri to ancient Greek law, that is to say, that we date back to ancient Greek law phenomena which are the products of a later development. Further, in using such later sources, we must always reckon with the possibility of local or temporary legal variations.' This passage was cited with a certain irony by Finley (1952: viii), but his bibliography here is incomplete and we have not been able to identify the quotation.

out of existence to allow for exceptions to the rule; and those which were of such a general nature that they became banal (see further Finley 1986: 134–46). Either way, Greek law was a concept of no analytical utility.

The issue is still contentious. Scholars have divided along broadly national lines, with the Anglo-American world generally following Finley (thus Harrison 1968: vii; and see further the comments of Millett in chapter 8 below) and most German and Italian scholars continuing to speak of Greek law (thus cautiously Wolff 1979: 31 n.72, and more outspokenly Biscardi 1982, criticised by Stroud 1985). But there have been many exceptions.

Nobody would wish to deny the close relationship between the legal systems of the various Greek *poleis*. After all, as Wolff (1979: 31 n.72) pointed out, they did speak the same language. And much valuable comparative work has been done. On the question of marriage, for instance, it is notorious that a woman in classical Athens (or at least, the sort of woman who is mentioned in our sources) had far less control of her property than did either her Homeric predecessor or her Hellenistic successor. The details of this are well set out by Schaps (1979: cf. Ste. Croix 1970), and some of the underlying reasons are explored by van Bremen (1983). But an important further contribution has been made in a paper by Modrzejewski (1983), a firm believer in Greek law, who has done much to isolate those features of the law of marriage which remained constant throughout the Greek world from those which did not.

It is certainly a valid and often a fruitful exercise to undertake a comparative study of a legal institution in different parts of the Greek world. But it is dangerous to go further than this, for two reasons. In the first place, there is a great temptation to use what we know about Graeco-Roman Egypt to fill in the considerable gaps in our knowledge of classical Athens, and *vice versa*; this point is well made at the outset by both Harrison (1968: vii) and MacDowell (1978: 8). But classical Athens and Graeco-Roman Egypt are the two areas about which we are relatively well-informed: if we wish to discuss the legal systems of other *poleis*[17] or the early law of Athens,[18] we are dependent almost

---

[17] After Athens, the classical *polis* about which we know most is of course Sparta, and Spartan law has been the subject of a recent book by MacDowell (1986). This book represents a brave attempt, but it ultimately founders on the lack of evidence. MacDowell is finally driven to do what he has himself sharply criticised elsewhere (1978: 8): he fills in the gaps by declaring that 'as a working hypothesis, it would really be better to assume that Spartan law was much the same as Athenian law on all topics . . . on which we are not told that it differed' (1986: 152). See the criticisms by Cartledge (1986: 142–3).

[18] Early Greek law has recently been the subject of an important book by Gagarin (1986, with forthcoming rev. by Todd 1990b). This is full of pertinent and provocative observations, most notably concerning the relationship between the early history of writing and the origins of law. But since Gagarin has to rely for his information on a few chance references in Homer, on a fifth-century Cretan text which is deemed to be 'primitive' in outlook, on a fifth-century Athenian inscription that purports to repeat a seventh-century text, and on such etymological speculations as *Ath.Pol.* 3.4 (cf. Gagarin 1986: 56), the book remains something of a *tour de force*, and his ideas can never have a status higher than that of attractive suggestions. Gagarin's previous work on the origins of *dikē* (Gagarin 1973; on *dikē* see further n.25 below) confined itself to a specific problem; and given the nature of our evidence for early law, this may be a more secure approach. The alternative is to follow MacDowell (1963) in his outstanding study

entirely on a combination of snippets of information and guesswork-by-analogy.

A second problem concerns the relationship between law, society and politics. For those who accept the proposition that 'law' is an entirely autonomous activity, there is no difficulty here: it becomes perfectly legitimate to assume, in default of hard evidence to the contrary, that the function of a named institution in a democratic *polis* like Athens will have been essentially the same as its function in a dynastic state like Ptolemaic Egypt. But the moment we admit that law has an organic relationship with its social and political context (see the discussion of the word '*nomos*' in section III of this chapter), then we must admit also that the practical differences between places and across time were probably greater than the continued use of the same legal vocabulary might imply. Classical Athenian law for instance appears to have paid more attention to ways of calling to account public officials (for details, see Roberts 1982) than to ensuring the orderly devolution of property-rights. For this it has been extensively criticised; but the Athenians would presumably have replied that the function of law in a democracy is to protect the weak against the excesses of the strong, and to prevent socially indefensible concentrations of landed property. Are we really to assume that the same applied in an oligarchy such as fifth-century Thebes, let alone in a monarchy such as the Ptolemaic kingdom?[19] The changing social context of a single legal concept (*hubris*) in archaic and classical Athens is examined in the papers by Fisher and Murray which together make up chapter 6 of this volume.

The question of Greek law and its conceptual validity has tended to divide English and American scholars working in the subject from their continental European colleagues. But their methods and interests have divided them still further. English and particularly American scholars have traditionally shown a great interest in the legal ramifications of inscriptions, stemming in part from the work of the American School at Athens in excavating the Agora, with regular publications in the journal *Hesperia* and its Supplements. Another major American speciality has been constitutional history, with important recent publications by Stroud (1968), Ostwald (1969, cf. n.23 below; 1982; 1986) and Sealey (1987).[20]

of Athenian homicide law, and to restrict any attempt at a general synthesis to the age of the Orators (*c*.420–320 B.C.), the only period for which we have adequate information.

[19] It was, in our opinion, precisely this diversity which inspired a man like Theophrastos to write his *Laws* (*c*.320), a work which appears from the surviving fragments to have comprised a comparative study of those different legal systems which were known to him, after the model of Aristotle's comparative study of different *poleis* in the *Politics*. Szegedy-Maszak 1981, in his useful edition and commentary on the few surviving fragments, nevertheless argues from the existence of the *Laws* that Theophrastos believed there was sufficient common ground between the legal systems of the Greek *poleis* to justify modern use of the term 'Greek law'. But one of the legal systems which Theophrastos discussed is that of Carthage: are we to suppose that he believed this to be a Greek *polis*?

[20] It is perhaps significant that the impulse behind Sealey's book arguing that (1987: 146) 'Athens was a republic, not a democracy' should have come from (1987: ix) 're-reading H. S. Maine's *Ancient Law*' (see above, n.12). For Sealey's work, see further n.31 below.

A fair impression of the work now being done by continental scholars may be gained by consulting the *Symposion* volumes. These contain the proceedings of a conference on Greek and Hellenistic legal history, held at roughly triennial intervals since 1971 at a range of venues in Germany, Italy, France, Greece and Spain. Four volumes have so far appeared (Wolff 1975a, Biscardi 1979, Modrzejewski & Liebs 1982, and Dimakis 1983): they reveal a considerable interest in Homer and in the papyri, and much attention is also paid to legal concepts and doctrines; but relatively little is said about the social context of Greek and *a fortiori* classical Athenian law.

The discontinuity between English-speaking and continental European scholarship is, fortunately, by no means complete. There are a few English-speaking scholars who work on the law of the papyri: Naphthali Lewis for instance is both an expert papyrologist (Lewis 1983), and also (it is interesting to note) one of the few English-speaking scholars to have contributed a paper to one of the *Symposion* volumes (Lewis 1982). Similarly, there are a few Continental scholars interested in fields which have traditionally attracted their English and American colleagues: Eberhard Ruschenbusch for example is a specialist in among other things constitutional law (e.g. Ruschenbusch 1966, 1978). And there are one or two scholars who are equally at home in both intellectual worlds: Mogens Hansen, for instance, has published in both German and English in addition to his native Danish. But it is striking, and a matter for regret, that only three of the eighty-four papers in the four published volumes were delivered by English-speaking scholars;[21] it is even more regrettable that no *Symposion* volume has ever been reviewed in an English-speaking journal.[22]

III   ATHENIAN LAW AND THE STUDY OF LAW

The final relationship to be discussed is that between Athenian law and law as an intellectual discipline. The word 'law' is notoriously difficult to define, and jurisprudents from Austin to Hart have bartered rival analyses for generations. (For discussion of the theories of Austin, Kelsen and Hart, see Raz 1980; a useful introduction to the thought of Hart and his predecessors is found in MacCormick 1981.)

For the ancient Greek world, the problem is compounded by the cluster of meanings that hang around the word *nomos*. Although the common rendering of *nomos* as 'law' is often appropriate, alternative translations offered by the

---

[21] The statistics are *Symposion 1971* – 5 French, 10 German, 3 Italian; *Symposion 1974* – 5 French, 3 German, 11 Italian; *Symposion 1977* – 2 English, 11 French, 10 German, 3 Italian; *Symposion 1979* – 1 English, 7 French, 8 German, 5 Italian; giving a grand total of 3 English, 28 French, 31 German, and 22 Italian. There is some indication that the picture may be beginning to change: two papers were delivered by English-speaking scholars in 1982 and four in 1985 (as yet unpublished, but see notices in *RDFE* 60 (1982) 548–9 and 63 (1985) 463–4).

[22] This tendentious assertion is based on negative evidence (that of *L'Année philologique*), and there may therefore be exceptions.

great lexicon of Liddell, Scott & Jones (LSJ) range from 'usage' and 'custom' to 'ordinance' and 'statute', with the apparent underlying sense of 'that which is in habitual practice, use or possession'.[23] *Nomos* also has the sense of 'tune' or 'melody': a favourite source of puns in Plato's *Nomoi* or *Laws* (700b, 722e, 734e, 775b, 799e). In fact the *Laws* gives a powerful impression of the range of activities in the *polis* potentially under the control of *nomos* in one sense or another (Saunders 1970: 5–14). As one of the characters in the dialogue is made to remark (714b), 'some people say that there are as many kinds of laws (*nomon eidē*) as there are of political systems (*politeion*)'; and this finds a practical expression in the tendency for words compounded with *nomos* to be adopted as slogans by opposing political groupings at times of conflict: the *isonomia* ('equality of *nomoi*') of the democrats was matched against the *eunomia* (lit. 'good *nomoi*', but with the overtones of 'law and order') of the oligarchs. Needless to say, it is this meeting of law, society and politics in the idea of *nomos* that makes it an appropriate choice as the title of this collection of essays.

For the moment, however, we are concerned with law not so much as an entity in its own right but as an intellectual discipline: should we study Athenian law in the way that a modern student of law evaluates his own legal system, or does such an approach raise misleading questions? The questions raised by lawyers in this context are broadly speaking either normative or jurisprudential. Jurisprudence in the modern sense is the philosophy of law; and this has made up a major strand of modern work on Athenian law, reaching back at least as far as Dareste (1893). The central interest of Vinogradoff (1922), as indicated by his title *The Jurisprudence of the Greek City*, lay in discussing Greek attitudes to law as revealed in the works of the philosophers.[24] He was followed, perhaps less successfully, by J. W. Jones (1956). It is however always difficult to answer the question, when is a philosopher speaking for himself and when is he reflecting the values of society (cf. Harrison 1957)? The majority of English lawyers and judges have at least

23 For a discussion with respect to modern jurisprudence of the semantic distinctions between law, norms and rules, see Christie 1982. There is an enormous bibliography on the meaning of *nomos* and the significance of its possible shifts over time. Some recent items are referred to by Garner (1987: 19–26); for a more detailed exposition see Ostwald (1986: *via* the index *s.v.* *nomos*; on this book see further n.31 below). Ostwald's earlier book (1969) *Nomos and the Beginnings of the Athenian Democracy* deserves special mention here: Ostwald believes that the use of the term *nomos* (with its overtones of 'custom') to denote a legal statute, in place of the earlier *thesmos* ('that which is laid down'), was a deliberate act of political policy, perhaps to be attributed to the late sixth-century reformer Kleisthenes. This thesis is highly contentious, but few would deny the close relationship between politics and the law which is implicit within Ostwald's title.

24 Vinogradoff dedicated the book (for which see the detailed review by Adcock 1923) 'to the memory of Rudolphe Dareste'. It was the second in a projected multi-volume treatment of the *Outlines of Historical Jurisprudence*. Volume One (1920) had dealt with *Tribal Law*; a third volume was promised (1922: frontispiece), to cover *The Medieval Jurisprudence of Western Christendom*, but this had not appeared by the time of Vinogradoff's death in 1925. Vinogradoff was writing in an attempt to reconcile the approach of Maine with the objections of at least some of his critics (see n.12 above); as such, the *Outlines* (if completed) would have constituted the high-water mark of the evolutionist school (for details, see Stein 1980: 115–21).

some familiarity with the ideas of Bentham or Austin; but though Plato's views on the nature of justice are interesting in their own right, they are a radically unsafe guide to the attitudes of Athenian jurors. The relationship between Plato's ideas and the realities of Athenian justice is examined by Saunders in chapter 4 below; there is here a distinction which many scholars (Jones in particular) have failed adequately to maintain.

Later work has to some extent avoided this problem by focusing on epic and tragedy as a source for more widespread views of the nature of justice. This has resulted in a series of thought-provoking studies, focusing in particular on the meaning of the term *dikē*. Although conventionally seen as the Greek equivalent of 'justice', the word is almost as many-sided as *nomos* (cf. above). 'Right', 'punishment', 'court-case' and 'law court' are all possible renderings, depending on the context.[25] Although our appreciation of the subtlety of the Athenian concept of justice has been enhanced by these studies, again the question arises: in a society where there are no specialist judges, to what extent are values and attitudes shared at different levels of society (Dover 1974 with the reactions of Adkins 1978)?

There has also been a search for jurisprudence in its older sense of ancient legal textbooks. One of the notable features of Athenian law is that our most valuable evidence consists of published versions of speeches delivered by litigants in court: we do not normally hear the other side of the case, and consequently any statement of fact or of law is at least potentially unreliable (for the problems involved, see Todd 1990a forthcoming). The most perceptive critic of rhetorical misrepresentation has been William Wyse, in his monumental commentary on Isaeus (1904); Wyse was rightly suspicious of Isaeus' honesty, if perhaps too confident of his own ability to disentangle the truth behind the orator's lies.[26] Cartledge in chapter 3 of this book explores the limits of legitimate inference in a case which at first sight appears particularly unpromising because of the fragmentary nature of the text concerned.

Because of the difficulties involved in interpreting the orators as sources of law, some scholars have yearned for a clear, unbiased statement of the law of Athens; and the publication in 1891 of the newly discovered Aristotelian treatise on the *Athenian Constitution* (*Ath.Pol.*) seemed at first to have answered their prayers. But the *Ath.Pol.* is a curious work. It divides into two parts: a summary of the development of the constitution is followed by an analysis of contemporary constitutional administration (which here includes the lawcourts). The first half appears to be derivative, and combines in a fairly

---

[25] Again, the modern bibliography is massive: for a selection, see Garner (1987: 4–10). The full-length study of the idea of justice by Havelock (1978) is perhaps too preoccupied with the evolution of ethical thought, in the same way as other scholars (cf. n.12 above) have been preoccupied with tracing the supposed evolution of Athenian law. The sense of continuity is greater in the studies by Adkins (1960; 1972). Particularly rewarding is the brief but wide-ranging discussion of *dikē* by Goldhill (1986: 33–56).

[26] Wyse should also be mentioned as the author of perhaps the best short introduction in English to Athenian law, in Whibley's *Companion to Greek Studies* (Wyse 1916).

random fashion some important new information with gross errors of fact. The second half is probably the author's own work, and is generally reliable and of considerable historical value.[27]

Bonner & Smith (cf. section 1 of this chapter) appear to have based their textbook, consciously or otherwise, on the *Ath.Pol.* Their first volume (1930) is an extended meditation on the stages by which the constitution developed. In choosing this approach, they appear to have been strongly influenced by the *Ath.Pol.*, the discovery of which was sufficiently recent for it still to be idealised. The first half of the *Ath.Pol.* consists of a series of eleven successive constitutional changes, culminating in the democratic restoration at the end of the fifth century – a pattern which Bonner & Smith follow closely. But, as already noted, most of our detailed information about Athenian law comes from the Orators of the fourth century, and the first half of the *Ath.Pol.* says nothing about this period. As a result, the space devoted by Bonner & Smith (1930) is in approximately inverse proportion to the amount we know. Their second volume (1938) would seem at first sight to have overcome this problem: rather than a chronological sequence, it is organised as a series of topics, in much the same way as part two of the *Ath.Pol.* But there the resemblance ends: whereas *Ath.Pol.* was concerned with fourth-century institutions, Bonner & Smith begin virtually every chapter with Homer, and trace the development of each institution down to the fourth century. To a large extent, therefore, they are repeating the pattern of their first volume and simply filling in some gaps. Bonner & Smith is an important and still a useful work; but for a general book on Athenian law its perspective is distorted.

Those modern lawyers who believe that law should be normative have traditionally regarded Athenian law with great distaste, on the grounds that the courts did not do their job properly – and the job of a court, as we all know, is to enforce the law as it stands. An attempt has been made to defend Athenian law from this criticism, by arguing that the courts did in fact adhere to the strict wording of their statutes (Meyer-Laurin 1965, followed by Wolff, e.g. 1975b: 11); but in our opinion this attempt has proved unsuccessful (see the criticisms by Finley 1985: 102). It seems better to accept with Gernet (1955: 67, first published in 1937) and Paoli (1933: 66–72) that Athenian courts were more concerned with dispute-settlement than with the enactment of justice in our objective sense (thus, recently, Osborne 1985).

The mention of dispute-settlement brings us perhaps to the heart of the matter. For the phrase 'dispute-settlement' belongs to the terminology of the anthropologist; and one of the central themes of this book is a plea for the

---

[27] The leading authority on the *Ath.Pol.* is Peter Rhodes, who has produced both a magisterial commentary (1981) and a very useful translation with notes in the Penguin Classics series (1984). Since the authorship of the *Ath.Pol.* is disputed (Aristotle or a pupil), we have referred to the text throughout either by its title or as [Aristotle].

study of Athenian law to loosen some of its links with 'law' and to strengthen its links with legal anthropology.[28] This is not the place for an extended survey of the history of legal anthropology as a discipline. Neither of us would have the specialist competence to perform that task; and several excellent introductions to the subject are available elsewhere.[29] Nor is this book an appeal to anthropology as the answer to all our problems: that would be starry-eyed. But it is an attempt to shift the perspectives from which Athenian law has traditionally been studied. Law and legal process in Athens were embedded in society, so that questions about Athenian law are in the last resort anthropological questions about the Athenians. Throughout much modern work on Athenian law there runs the implicit or expressed assumption that the fifth-century comic poet Aristophanes was right in his critique of Athenian democratic justice in the *Wasps*[30] (422 B.C.), and that the Athenian legal system was indeed inherently flawed (cf. the quotations assembled by Powell 1988: 299–300). And yet the Athenians seem to have been happy to retain it with only minor alterations until at least the end of the democracy, more than a century after the production of the *Wasps*.[31]

Instead, this is a plea for co-operation. We believe that the study of Athenian law has much to gain from an awareness of the questions which anthropologists ask about law; and that anthropologists in their turn may benefit by considering material from past as well as from contemporary societies. We end this section with a few illustrative suggestions of the benefits which might be gained by both sides in this relationship.

One of the notable perspectives of recent legal anthropology is the insistence

---

[28] The term 'legal anthropology' here should be taken to include also legal sociology. Strictly speaking, legal anthropology should cover the legal systems of contemporary 'primitive' societies, and legal sociology those of 'advanced' societies. But the distinction is in many ways an unreal one (Goody & Watt 1968: 27–8). Sawer 1965, in his standard introduction to legal sociology, ranges over both legal anthropology (1965: 27–47) and also ancient legal history (1965: 48–69). There is a useful collection of articles in Aubert 1969, who himself stresses that the task of the legal sociologist is essentially descriptive, whereas the lawyer's rôle is always to some extent normative (Aubert 1969: 9–14).

[29] Perhaps the clearest general introduction to legal anthropology as a discipline is that by Simon Roberts 1979. Also to be recommended are two short surveys of the historical development of the subject, both of which introduce a collection of articles on legal history: Roberts again in Bossy 1983 and Sally Humphreys 1985b in Humphreys 1985a. Humphreys is one of the few contemporary classical scholars to have held a joint appointment in Classics and Anthropology; and her work on Athenian law combines the two disciplines in a particularly fruitful way. *History and Anthropology* (Humphreys 1985a) is unfortunately a very difficult periodical to lay hands on.

[30] There is an important commentary on the *Wasps* by MacDowell 1971, himself (perhaps significantly) a major legal historian (cf. MacDowell 1963; 1978).

[31] There is clear evidence for constitutional change in Athens at the end of the fifth and during the fourth centuries B.C., but there is no sign that the Athenians collectively repudiated their democratic legal system before the suppression of the democracy itself. For the evidence and details of the changes, see Rhodes (1980); their significance is discussed by Ostwald (1986: 497–524), Hansen (1987: 94–124) and Sealey (1987: 134–8), but none of these three impressive but very different interpretations has yet commanded general acceptance.

that law and politics are not separate areas of activity but poles of a continuum: a clear and recent exposition is given by Moore (1978: 181–213). In Western political theory, on the other hand, ever since Montesquieu formulated his theory of the tripartite separation of powers in the eighteenth century, there has always been a strong sense that the legislature (in British terms, parliament), the executive (the government), and the judiciary ought to be independent bodies. There have even been attempts to read this doctrine back into the ancient Greek world (e.g. Friedrich 1934), relying most heavily on Aristotle's distinction between *ekklesiazein* (being an assembly-member), *arkhein* (being a public official) and *dikazein* (sitting as a judge).[32] But it should be remembered that ancient political theorists had no reason to regard Montesquieu's theories as normative;[33] moreover, Aristotle's purpose in this passage lies in classifying the functions that go to make up a full citizen, and nowhere does he suggest that these powers ought to be exercised by different people. Nevertheless, the influence of Montesquieu remains as an unstated premise in much modern criticism of Athenian law. The Athenian assumption, that their lawcourts did and indeed should play a political rôle, is explored throughout the essays in this book; but all too often, scholars have assumed without argument that the use of a prosecution for political ends was somehow a misuse.

A second perspective concerns the decision to prosecute and the choice of procedure. These are important questions even in a modern state: Moore (1978: 54–81) discusses the use of legal rights as a bargaining-counter, where the threat to prosecute may itself be used against the potential defendant to elicit concessions which are not formally connected with the case. The papers in Nader & Todd (1978) consider the reasons which govern the would-be prosecutor's choice of procedure: is this determined by the nature of the resources which form the subject of the case, or by the relationship between the participants, or by more complex factors? Questions like this acquire particular point when applied to the society of the Athenian *polis*, which was seen by its members as a *koinonia* – a community of interests. In order to preserve that sense of community, disputes arrived in court only after

---

[32] Arist. *Politics*, IV, 1297b37–98a3 (who however uses the periphrasis *to peri tas arkhas* alongside *to bouleuomenon* and *to dikazon*). For discussion, see Johnson 1984.

[33] The danger of forcing Aristotle into the categories set by Montesquieu was stressed most forcibly by Hansen (1974: 11–12). More recently, however, Hansen 1981 has himself argued on other grounds that fourth-century Athenians did adhere to a doctrine of separation of powers: he believes that those bodies charged with taking decisions (the assembly and the courts) were rigidly differentiated from those whose function was to propose initiatives (the *arkhai* or public officials, and the *boulē* or council). In this Hansen is followed by Sealey (1987: 146–8). In our opinion this is mistaken: whatever the formal distinction between bodies of government, effective separation of powers requires rigid separation of persons; but the personnel of the Athenian *boulē* was simply a (restricted) selection of those already entitled to attend the assembly. But even if Hansen is correct here, his doctrine of separation is wholly different from that of Montesquieu. Hansen is not arguing that the Athenians distinguished between political and judicial decision-making: 'keep politics out of the lawcourts' is a distinctively modern slogan.

attempts at arbitration, formal and informal, had failed (see Finley 1985: 102–3); and yet prosecutions, even for offences against the community, were normally undertaken only at the initiative of private individuals.

The function of conflict is a third area in which anthropology has much to contribute to the study of Athenian law. Should disputes be seen as a pathological symptom – something wrong with society – or is conflict necessary in order to maintain social equilibrium? This question has been posed in a very striking manner by Simon Roberts (1979: 11–16), and applied to the enforcement of law in late medieval England by Powell (1989). It lies at the centre of the dispute (not, we hope, itself a pathological symptom!) between Osborne and Harvey in their papers in this book.

These are simply three illustrations of the ways in which recent work on legal anthropology may help to illuminate our understanding of Athenian law and society. But the anthropologist too may stand to gain from considering the law of past societies; and we hope that this volume may prove useful in this context, together with two other recent collections of papers, those edited by Bossy (1983) on a range of western societies, and by Davies & Fouracre (1986) on medieval Europe. Two areas in particular may be noted.

One of the perennial problems faced by anthropologists concerns the relationship of the researcher and his informants: if you ask people questions, they will tend unconsciously or otherwise to give you the sort of answers they think you are looking for. Perhaps the first anthropologist to recognise this problem was Malinowski (1926), himself the second founder of legal anthropology after Sir Henry Maine. Malinowski attempted to counter the problem by using not simply informants but extended fieldwork and observation. At first sight, the ancient historian appears to be at a disadvantage as regards sources: unlike the anthropologist, we cannot cross-question our informants to obtain the information we want. But paradoxically, this can itself be an advantage. Published lawcourt speeches are by no means transparent sources, but they are aimed at their original hearers or readers, instead of being repeatedly extemporised for our benefit; and one type of distortion is thereby removed. There are of course corresponding difficulties: a written speech cannot contradict any false inferences we may draw from it; and the relationship between what is said in court and what is done in society raises a further complexity, which is examined by Cohen in chapter 7 of this book. But the contrast between the two types of informant may itself be instructive.

The second problem concerns translation, a question which is discussed by Todd in chapter 2 below. Even in a society like Athens, where there was relatively little technical legal vocabulary and the language of the street was itself the language of the law, words nevertheless had connotations which are not necessarily carried by superficially similar terms in other societies or other languages. The problem of translation is in many ways closely connected with that of the informant. When Llewellyn & Hoebel (1941) pioneered the use of the 'trouble-case' (i.e. the study of individual cases of dispute-settlement) as a method of research, they were trying to get away from the danger of directive questioning, based on a legal framework which would make sense to a modern lawyer rather than to a Plains Indian, and which would tend to elicit precisely those answers which the Plains Indian thought that the modern lawyer wished to hear. Llewellyn and Hoebel were by no means wholly successful. They tended to romanticise their subject, and at times their attitude to their informants is curiously unsophisticated: for instance, they insist that adultery was uncommon among the Cheyenne on the grounds that their informants seldom referred to it, without raising the possibility that there might be reasons for either the community or the husband to turn a blind eye (Llewellyn & Hoebel 1941: 169–211). Nevertheless, the book remains a classic in legal anthropology. The study of trouble-cases is now widely accepted; and the success of their book, and in particular the fact that Hoebel was an anthropologist and Llewellyn a jurist, did a great deal to make legal anthropology an intellectually respectable subject among both anthropologists and lawyers.

More recently, the problem of translation has become sharply focused as a central issue of anthropological method, in the course of a long-running disagreement between Max Gluckman and Paul Bohannan. Bohannan (1957) first raised the question, when he criticised Gluckman (1955) for his use of Western legal categories to interpret African tribal law: in Bohannan's eyes, Western law was as much a 'folk system' as was tribal law, and the former should not be given privileged status as the 'analytical system' used by the anthropologist to interpret the latter. There is a striking parallel here to the problem of legal history raised by Maitland in his seminal study of early medieval English law (Pollock & Maitland 1968: 229–32): if we organise our discussion of a past legal system according to the categories which made sense to its own contemporaries, we are in danger of rendering it incomprehensible to ourselves; if we re-organise it according to the categories with which we ourselves are familiar, we may very likely miss the priorities which its practitioners thought important. But that perhaps brings us back in a circle to the question of Roman law from which we started.

2

The purpose of evidence in Athenian courts[1]

STEPHEN TODD

I

Perhaps the greatest danger which faces the student of any foreign legal system is that of assimilation. To some extent, indeed, this problem is inherent in the need to translate. For instance, Athenian law has an institution called the *dikasterion*, which for convenience we describe as a 'lawcourt'. Those who man the *dikasterion* are called *dikastai*; but here the semantic leap is more obvious, for we have a choice between two possible English equivalents: 'judges' (but with a footnote to say that in many ways the *dikastai* were closer to a modern jury), or else 'jurors' (again with a footnote to explain that they also performed the functions which we would associate with the judge).

Now the difficulty of translation is an obvious point; and of course no professional Classicist is likely to forget that there is no precise English equivalent of the *dikastes*. But the problem runs deeper than this: indeed, the more obvious the translation, the more insidious the tendency to assimilate. It is easy enough to remember that the *dikastes* is neither precisely a 'judge' nor a 'juror'. But every time that we translate *dikasterion* as a 'court' (and it would be insufferably pedantic never to do so) we thereby imply that an Athenian court was essentially similar to our own, not only in appearance but also (and this is the important point) in function. This is a false assumption, and it is wasted criticism, based on modernising assumptions, to blame the Athenian *dikasterion* for failing to achieve that supposedly objective enactment of justice for which it was never designed.[2]

---

[1] A range of people have read successive drafts of this paper, and offered criticism and suggestions: the participants in the Cambridge Ancient History Seminar, and particularly my fellow-editors Paul Cartledge and Paul Millett; Jenny McEwan, Douglas MacDowell, Peter Rhodes and Gerhard Thür; and the anonymous referees of Cambridge University Press. My thanks are due to them all, even when I have disagreed with their advice.

[2] For a typical example of such criticism, see Lämmli 1938: 79, 85; see also Bonner 1905: 12–13. Against the belief that Athenian law was designed to secure the 'objective enactment of justice', see further section IV of this paper (on the use of laws as evidence) and the discussion of Meyer-Laurin 1965 in section III of chapter I above.

The purpose of this paper is to question one of these modern assumptions: that Athenian *martures* were the equivalent of modern witnesses, and that therefore their function was to tell the truth. This assumption is in my opinion incorrect, or at least over-simplified; and it has led either to misinterpretation or else to frank incredulity when faced by the apparent irrationality of Athenian practice. For most of the time, I shall be concentrating on the use of witnesses; but something will be said about other forms of evidence as well.

To help us identify some of the assumptions which we shall be meeting, I begin with a brief summary of modern practice. There are of course certain differences in the treatment of evidence between civil-law and common-law countries, and therefore between the assumptions of Franco-German and of Anglo-American scholars. Nevertheless the differences are not great; and for convenience I shall therefore concentrate on English law, although noting characteristic differences where they appear.

The function of evidence in English law is to enable the court to get at the facts. In a case for breach of contract, for instance, it is the substantive rules of the law of contract which determine what are the facts 'in issue' (that is, what points either side needs to prove in order to win: only what is relevant to these points may be produced as evidence); the law of evidence determines how these facts are to be proved (Phipson & Elliot 1987: 15; Cross, Wilkins & Tapper 1986: 2).

It would not be true to say that every assertion produced in court needs to be proved by means of evidence. The court takes 'judicial notice' of any point of law; the judge is presumed to know the law already, and he never hears evidence on the subject. Some issues of fact may also be the subject of judicial notice, in particular 'notorious facts': for instance, a court in 1857 decided – perhaps rashly – that it was a matter of common knowledge, which therefore did not require evidence, that one of the purposes for which the University of Oxford exists was the advancement of learning (Oxford Poor Law Rate Case, 1857, cited by Cross, Wilkins & Tapper 1986: 45). In addition to judicial notice, facts which neither side wishes to contest can be proved by 'formal admission' of the parties. And there are certain facts which it would be difficult or impossible to prove directly, but which may be proved by means of 'presumptions' or inferences that are deemed to be legitimate: for example, if in civil proceedings I can prove that you have been convicted of a crime, then the court will infer that you committed that crime, until and unless you can prove that you were wrongfully convicted (Civil Evidence Act 1968 §11, cited by Phipson & Elliot 1987: 78). With these qualifications, however, it would be reasonably accurate to say that any contested fact needs to be proved by producing evidence (Cross, Wilkins & Tapper 1986: 20–1).

The law of evidence deals with four questions: the burden of proof, the level of proof, the method of proof, and the weight of proof.

The phrase 'burden of proof' is shorthand for the question, which party has the job of proving each contested fact? In a civil court, the rule is that whichever side wants the court to act must persuade it to do so, and whichever side produces an assertion must justify it. In a criminal court, the general rule is that the prosecution has to prove everything; but there are some statutory exceptions to this: for instance, if a defendant pleads not guilty by reason of insanity, it is his job to prove that he is insane, rather than the prosecution's job to disprove it.

The level of proof required to sustain that burden is different in civil from in criminal cases. In a civil case, matters must be proved on a balance of probabilities; in a criminal case, they must be proved 'beyond reasonable doubt'. The question, 'has the evidence reached this level?' is the question of the weight of evidence, to which we shall shortly return.

There are in English law five main methods of proof: testimony (the evidence of a witness, delivered orally, on oath, and subject to cross-examination); hearsay (the quoted statements of those who are not formally witnesses and cannot therefore be cross-examined: hearsay is generally excluded in criminal cases because these are heard by a jury); documents (which may themselves be either hearsay, if used to prove the truth of the contents of the document, or else real evidence, if used to prove that such a document exists); things (physical objects produced in court, sometimes called 'real evidence'); and circumstances (forensic evidence in a criminal trial is usually circumstantial). Testimony has in this country traditionally been regarded as by far the most important of these five: Bentham for instance (cited by Honoré 1981: 172) described witnesses as 'the eyes and ears of justice'. The reason behind the high status of testimony is simple and significant: lawyers believe that (with appropriate safeguards) it is the most reliable way of getting at the truth. The oath provides a sanction which turns dishonesty into perjury (Murphy 1988: 410); cross-examination is 'a powerful and valuable weapon for the purposes of testing the veracity of a witness and the accuracy and completeness of his story' (Lord Hanworth, Master of the Rolls, quoted by Phipson & Elliot 1987: 117); and the main objection to hearsay is that it deprives the court of the opportunity to examine the demeanour of the witness during his evidence (Cross, Wilkins & Tapper 1986: 107). English law has always assumed that oral evidence is the most reliable method of getting at the truth. Recent criminological research has indeed cast considerable doubt on this assumption, particularly in the area of identification: the tests available to forensic science have been shown to be vastly more reliable (see Cornish 1968: 173–9, and more generally Greer 1978). Nevertheless, the status of witnesses in English legal procedure has in practice remained almost as high as if their reliability had never been challenged: it is little more than a decade since the Court of Appeal first issued rules limiting the use of unsupported testimony as evidence of identification (Devlin 1979: 188–93).

There are of course certain types even of oral evidence which are notoriously untrustworthy, and which a trained lawyer or experienced judge learns to treat with scepticism. The jury however in a criminal trial consists of lay-people. Rather than take the risk that the jury might be swayed by untrustworthy information, English courts have preferred to prevent the jury hearing such information altogether. This is thought by certain scholars (Cornish 1968: 87; Phipson & Elliot 1987: 4–5) to be the main reason behind what are called the 'rules of evidence': in other words, exclusionary rules laying down the sort of evidence which the jury must not be allowed to hear. These rules deal mainly with categories of information (such as previous convictions) or categories of evidence (how that information has been transmitted, e.g. hearsay and opinion); some of the rules however are personal, and impinge upon groups of witnesses who are thought likely to be unreliable (for instance, courts have traditionally not been permitted to convict on the basis of the unsworn evidence of young children, unless this evidence was corroborated; and even when children were on oath, judges have had to warn juries that it was unsafe to accept their evidence without corroboration).[3]

The weight of the evidence is for the jury (or in a civil case the judge acting as the judge of fact) to decide. Nevertheless, within the limits of the substantive rules of law appropriate to the case, it is the evidence which is decisive. If the side charged with the burden of proof produces insufficient evidence (in the judge's opinion) to support a *prima facie* case, then as a matter of law he will stop the trial. The importance of evidence in English law, and particularly of the examination of witnesses, can be shown by three observations. First, we should notice the amount of space dedicated to it in the standard advocates' handbooks: Lord Justice Wrottlesley (as he later became) spent an entire book on *The Examination of Witnesses in Court*; and Richard Du Cann devoted three of the twelve chapters of his *Art of the Advocate* entirely and a further two substantially to this subject (chapters 6, 7, 8, and 5, 9, respectively). Secondly, there is the order of events in a case: the advocate should not normally state a fact until he has proved it by means of evidence.[4] Thirdly, one of the favourite tactics of defence lawyers in criminal trials is to attack the personal credibility of the prosecution's chief witness: Devons (1978: 157–9) recounts a case in which a defence lawyer successfully needled an 'officious bureaucrat' into patronising the court; and it is a standard defence tactic in rape cases to suggest that the complainant brought the attack upon herself.

In French and German law, the relative position of the various forms of evidence is slightly different. There is no formal system of cross-examination, as there is in English law where a barrister is obliged to cross-examine opposing witnesses on each and every point which conflicts with the version of the facts that he or she is presenting in chief: if you fail to do this, you are taken

---

3 Both requirements have now been formally abolished by §34 of the 1988 Criminal Justice Act, but it is still too early to see what effect the changes will have in practice.

4 Du Cann (1964: 69) points out that, when the advocate introduces his case, he does so without calling evidence; but that even at this stage, he should not make any assertion which he will not call evidence to support.

to have conceded the point. Consequently there is in both French and German law a greater readiness to admit hearsay; and there is a general preference in both countries (and in France a statutory preference) for documents ahead of witnesses (Honoré 1981: 181–5): a French court may decline to order testimony to be given if it feels that the written evidence is sufficient. There is no lay jury in either country, and so the court allows itself considerably wider discretion: it can hear – or rather 'call', because civil-law countries use the inquisitorial system of justice in which it is the judge and not the advocate who examines witnesses – whatever evidence it chooses. For our purposes however we can ignore the differences of detail: it is enough to say that in both common- and civil-law countries the function of evidence is identical, to get at the truth; the difference is one of method: how best to achieve this aim? And in practice the differences are often not that great: it is only in very unusual circumstances, for instance, that a French or German court would accept hearsay without independent corroboration (Honoré 1981: 189).

II

Traditional interpretation of the Athenian law of evidence rests on the unstated assumption that an Athenian witness had the same primary function as a modern witness: to tell the truth. But it is clear even on a cursory examination that Athenians did not use witnesses in the way that we do.[5] Cases in Athens are won and lost not on the quality of your witnesses but on the quality of your speech (Leisi 1907: 113). The order of events within the speech is significant: whereas an English barrister examines his witnesses and then builds their evidence into his case, an Athenian litigant gives his own version of events, periodically calling witnesses to corroborate what he has said so far (Bonner 1905: 54). Indeed, out of 404 occasions in the extant speeches on which witnesses are produced, there is only a handful of cases in which discussion was preceded by testimony.[6] Moreover, while English advocates' handbooks devote themselves to the techniques of cross-examination, an Athenian witness was not normally examined, and indeed after approximately 380 B.C. he could not be examined at all: before that date,

[5] This point has been recently and powerfully made in an important paper by Sally Humphreys (1985c), which is in my opinion by far the best available work on Athenian witnesses. Humphreys begins from the observation that an Athenian witness is primarily a supporter of his litigant; she sees the main reason for this in terms of the attempt to perpetuate, in a society in transition from village to city, the means of proof appropriate to a village community; and this general thesis is supported by a detailed analysis of the different types of people who appear as witnesses in Athenian courts. The starting-point of my paper is the same as that of Humphreys: the witness as supporter; and although I have developed this observation in different directions, I owe a great deal to her article. I hope that our perspectives will prove complementary and not contradictory.

[6] The only certain case is Dem. xxxiii.30–1. Several other examples are possible (Andok. 1.112–16, Dem. xxvii.8–9, and perhaps Lys. xx.26); in each instance testimony is followed by a discussion which looks as if it may be based on deduction from what the witness had said. But in the absence of the witnesses' statements, certainty is impossible.

he delivered an oral statement; after it, he attested to a written deposition prepared either by himself or by the litigant on his behalf.[7] Furthermore, although in English courts personal attacks on witnesses are common, there are in the Attic Orators very few attacks on the credibility of the opponent's witnesses, or attempts to defend your own witnesses against such attacks. In several cases a witness is named as the real instigator of the opponent's case (Melas in Isaeus v.7–8, Hierokles in Isaeus IX.22–5, and Kriton in Dem. XL.57–9), and frequently the opponent is attacked for having suborned false witnesses (e.g. Lys. XXIX.7, Isoc. XVIII.52–7, Dem. XIX.216). But otherwise personal attacks on witnesses are rare indeed (excluding for obvious reasons *dikai pseudomarturion*, actions for false witness, in which the former witness has now become the defendant, there are only three possible examples: Lys. XII.87, Dem. XXXIV.18–20, and perhaps Dem. XXVII.51). Character-assassination is aimed either at the opponent himself or against the *sunegoroi* who make speeches on his behalf.

The traditional responses to these differences between Athenian and modern practice have ranged from the *a priori* to the incredulous (the exception, above, is Humphreys 1985c). Let us consider the former first. It is the duty of an Athenian litigant to produce his own witnesses, and the court gives him no powers to do so. Nobody has been able to find the equivalent of a *subpoena* in Athenian law. This is not, admittedly, for want of trying: several scholars (Leisi 1907: 48–56; Bonner & Smith 1938: 136) have argued that there must have been a *subpoena* somewhere, because no system of justice can function without one. Bonner & Smith try to discover the *subpoena* hiding behind either the *exomosia* or the *dikē lipomarturiou*. But neither of these procedures enables a litigant to force an unwilling witness into court.

By using the *exomosia* ('oath of denial') you could compel a reluctant witness to make one of three choices: either to testify to a text you had prepared, or to deny knowledge on oath,[8] or else to pay a fine of 1,000 *drakhmai* (Lyk. 1.20 with Harrison 1971: 139–40). This threefold choice is closely related to the process of *kleteusis* (summons), but it is not clear whether *kleteusis* is the name of a separate procedure or (more probably) the method of imposing the fine on a man who refuses either to witness or to deny knowledge. The procedure of *exomosia* and/or *kleteusis* is used with some frequency by Demosthenes and his contemporaries, but in the vast majority of cases it appears that the potential witness is already present in court: even when this is not made explicit (as it is in Lyk. 1.20), the speaker clearly expects the situation to be immediately resolved (e.g. Dem. LIX.28), in a way that

---

[7] The implications of this change are discussed further in section III of this paper.

[8] These alternatives are of course incomplete; but that is no reason to argue *a priori* that the witness could instead say, 'I do know, but the facts are not as you allege' (thus Leisi 1907: 67 and MacDowell 1978: 243; Harrison 1971: 144 is rightly cautious). Thür (1983: 334–5) discussed an inscription from Stymphalos outlining parallel regulations: the witness has a similar choice, and it is clear beyond doubt here that his alternatives are incomplete. The significance of this point is discussed in section IV of this paper.

would be impossible if the witness was not present.[9] But if this impression is correct, then it suggests that *exomosia/kleteusis* was not used, and perhaps could not be used, to force an absent witness to attend court.[10]

The *dikē lipomarturiou*, on the other hand, was apparently used to punish a witness who had failed to attend. The details here are obscure, because we know of only one case where its use was attempted, and that unsuccessfully and probably unlawfully (Dem. XLIX.18–21); indeed the evidence for the *dikē lipomarturiou* is so poor that Gernet, the Budé editor of Demosthenes' speeches, could argue plausibly that the procedure never actually existed (Gernet 1959a: 19 n.2). But even if Gernet is wrong here, it seems likely that the *dikē lipomarturiou* could only be used against a witness who had first promised to appear and then gone back on his contract. This at least is how the ancient lexicographer Pollux (VIII.36) interpreted the term. Apollodoros in Demosthenes XLIX certainly takes trouble to emphasise that Antiphanes the defaulting witness had previously and repeatedly (*phaskon aiei*) promised to appear; so there seems no good reason to reject Pollux's statement here.[11] Concerning the possible use of a *dikē blabes* (private action for damages) against a defaulting witness, our information is even more scanty. Apollodoros claims that he instituted such a case in the aftermath of his *dikē lipomarturiou*; but it sounds as though he did not have a very good case, and it is by no means clear that the alleged 'damage' rested on anything more substantial than Antiphanes' breach of his putative agreement to give evidence. What is clear, at any rate, is that none of these procedures could be used in the way that we use a *subpoena*.

At the other extreme, the response is incredulity. Athenian law, like English law, had clearly-defined exclusionary rules of evidence; but whereas our rules are concerned with categories either of evidence or of information, the Athenian rules were concerned with categories of people: slaves, women and

---

9 The only apparent exception to this rule is Dem. XXXII.27–30, where the speaker threatens to summon one Protos, who has apparently absconded from Athens; but although Protos is described as a witness in §29, he is also in another context a potential defendant (§27); and it is not clear in which capacity he is to be summoned.

10 It is clear that in some situations an Athenian witness could be compelled to give evidence. A man who had been twice convicted by *dikē pseudomarturion* of giving false witness could refuse to testify on any subsequent occasion (Hyp. *Philippides* §12), because a third such conviction would lead to automatic *atimia* (loss of citizen rights): the implication is that witnesses could not otherwise refuse. But this may of course refer only to those who can be compelled by *exomosia* and/or *kleteusis*: i.e. (if the preceding argument is correct), those who are already present in court.

11 Bonner & Smith (1938: 139–43) do reject this statement by Pollux, and assert that the *dikē lipomarturiou* was available against any witness who had received a summons to give evidence, whether or not he had made any promise to do so. In this they may have been over-influenced by their previous *a priori* insistence that any decent judicial system needs to be able to compel witnesses to attend (1938: 136). MacDowell (1978: 243) follows Bonner & Smith here, citing also Harrison (1971: 141–2), who however does not appear to commit himself so definitely. More recently Humphreys (1985c: 321) appears to follow Bonner & Smith and MacDowell, but she doubts the practical impact of these formal means of compulsion: 'in practice litigants had to provide themselves with witnesses who could be trusted to appear' (Humphreys 1985c: 321 n.27).

children could not be witnesses.[12] (I should add here that Athens did have a rule forbidding hearsay; but the reason behind this rule was not in my opinion the same as our own, and will be discussed later.) If the function of a witness is to tell the truth, then the exclusion of women does not make sense, particularly because women were not debarred from giving evidence: they were, if challenged, permitted to take an evidentiary oath (although this did not make them witnesses). The fact that this oath was taken in public weakens MacDowell's suggestion (1978: 243) that the reason women cannot be witnesses is that it would be socially improper for them to appear in court.[13] Children similarly could not be witnesses; and superficially here the reason might be that they could not be trusted to tell the truth. But an adult could apparently be a witness to what had occurred during his minority (inferred by Lipsius 1915: 874 n.32 from Dem. XLIX.42); and it seems an unnecessarily tortuous explanation to say that a child could be trusted to perceive the truth but not to describe it (as Leisi 1907: 12 followed by Harrison 1971: 137 n.2). Slaves also could not be witnesses, but their statements were admissible as evidence if delivered under torture with the consent of both parties. Mac-Dowell (1978: 245) suggests that the reason for the torture is that the slave would normally belong to one of the litigants and would therefore be afraid to testify against his owner, and that the need for consent was that a slave was valuable property. Both parts of this explanation are I believe incorrect (see section IV below). Astonishment if not incredulity is the final reaction of the two standard English textbooks on Athenian law: Harrison (1971: 137) describes the Athenian rules of evidence as an 'unresolved paradox' which 'must sometimes have spelt substantial denial of justice to litigants'; Mac-

---

[12] It used to be thought that women and slaves could be witnesses, at least for the prosecution, in homicide cases; but this is now considered doubtful. Lipsius argued that both categories were permitted: slaves on the basis of several passages in Antiphon (1915: 873 n.29); and women on the basis of Dem. XLVII.68–73 (1915: 874 n.30). Leisi followed him on both counts, admittedly with some hesitation (women 1907: 12–18; slaves 1907: 20–6). Bonner however showed conclusively that the passages in Antiphon do not bear the weight which Lipsius had placed upon them (in Ant. v, for instance, *marturein* used of a slave is clearly a non-technical synonym for *menuein* 'to denounce', Bonner & Smith 1938: 223–9); Bonner himself on the other hand believed that women were admissible (Bonner 1906, Bonner 1912, summarised in Bonner & Smith 1938: 221–3). More recently however MacDowell (1963: 106–7) has shown that Dem. XLVII is at best inconclusive, and in this he is followed by Harrison (1971: 136). (On the inability of slaves and others to witness in homicide cases, see now Carey 1988.)

It is possible that slaves were allowed to appear both as witnesses and even as litigants in *dikai emporikai*, cases concerning maritime trade, in the later fourth century; and this may indeed provide a striking indication that traditional status-distinctions were beginning to break down, if only in this restricted area of law (Gernet 1955: 162–3, first published as Gernet 1950; cf. more generally Gernet 1938b). But this deduction depends solely on the case of Lampis, described as an *oiketes* in Dem. XXXIV.5; and it is at least possible that the word here means 'ex-slave'. If so, the right of a slave to witness and sue in such cases, and also the argument for the decline of status-distinctions, falls to the ground. On *dikai emporikai* see further n.23 below.

[13] For the regular appearance of women, children and slaves in court 'in a capacity only technically distinguishable from witnesses', see Bonner (1905: 27, cf. 32–4).

Dowell (1978: 243), with a certain characteristic dryness, describes the rules as 'remarkable'.

III

In order to resolve this paradox, I suggest that we should re-examine the function of a witness. Witnesses clearly do play an important rôle in Athenian law: they are cited on more than four hundred occasions in the one hundred forensic speeches, at an average frequency of six sets of witnesses per hundred sections of text. It is a rationalisation of the problem when Leisi (1907: 112) says that witnesses were unimportant – and still more so when he offers as an explanation of this 'the notorious duplicity of the Athenians' (Leisi 1907: 112, cf. also 114).

I have spoken of the rôle of Athenian witnesses; but this term is perhaps misleading. Athenian witnesses fulfil two rôles. One of these roughly corresponds to that of a modern witness: his job is to tell the truth, and the court is interested in what he says. But the second rôle is to us a more alien one (to describe it as 'more primitive' would be to beg the question, below): the function of a witness is to support the litigant for whom he appears, and the court is interested in who he is (Humphreys 1985c).

Even outside the lawcourt, there is a strong idea that the *martus* is not simply an observer but in some sense a partisan. In the work of the historians Herodotus and Thucydides, *martus* and its cognates are used in a consistent and striking way: they are regularly found with the meaning 'somebody (or something) which supports my argument at this point' (e.g. Hdt. II.18.1; Thuc. 1.8.1); but the term is not used to describe 'sources of information' in a neutral context. For this purpose Herodotus uses *akoē*, 'word of mouth', 'oral tradition'; and when Thucydides discusses his methods of research, he speaks of cross-examining *ton allon*, 'other people' (1.22.2). The Penguin translates this as 'eyewitnesses', which is the word which we would naturally use in this context; but Thucydides like Herodotus appears to have thought that *martus* was the wrong word to describe someone who was not at that moment supporting anybody.

In his paper on Athenian methods of proof, Soubie (1973: 226) has made the interesting observation that the torture of slaves is not so much a legal as a socio-political problem. This can be applied more widely. Witnessing in Athenian law is a ritualised socio-political act of support. (I use the term 'political' here in a broad sense, because it is clear that this was a privilege open also to metics and even to foreigners.)[14] That it was an act of support, we have already seen; each litigant produced his own witnesses, and there was no

---

[14] A list of examples is given by Leisi (1907: 7). Even if we discount his two sets of Olynthian witnesses, on the grounds that at this date (343 B.C.) they were probably in possession of citizen-rights at Athens (Aesch. II.154; Dem. XIX.146), there are still enough clear cases to prove the point (a Tanagran in a public case, Dem. XXV.62; and in private cases, Argive ambassadors in Isoc. XVI.16, and a metic in Hyp. *Athenogenes* 34).

subpoena. That it was in some sense a political act is clear from Isoc. XVIII.51–2, where the fact that Kallimakhos has acted not only as prosecutor but as witness is used to demonstrate that he is a sykophant; from Aristophanes *Ekklesiazousai* 561–2, where Praxagora treats the verb *marturein* as a comic synonym for *sukophantein* (on which see the papers by Osborne and Harvey in this volume); and from the existence of several lead curses, dedicated by prospective litigants, which call down destruction not only on the writer's opponent but also and by name on his witnesses (e.g. Jordan 1985: no. 9). Like all political acts, witnessing is a privilege, and therefore carries a risk – the risk that you may be punished by *dikē pseudomarturion* if you are found to have given false evidence. The orators and the rhetorical theorists repeatedly associate the act of witnessing with words describing 'risk': *kindunos* (Ant. *Tetr.* II.d.7, Dem. XXXIV.19, cf. Arist. *Rhet.* I, 1375b27–9), *hupodikos* (Isaeus XII.4), and *hupeuthunos* (Dem. XLIII.30, XLV.13).

The element of risk is presumably the explanation behind the rules of exclusion: it is not that women and slaves cannot be trusted to tell the truth; but that they cannot sustain the privilege of witnessing because they do not have the capacity to be sued by *dikē pseudomarturion*. This is clear from the fact that women can take an evidentiary oath (not subject to *dikē pseudomarturion*); and also from Plato (*Laws* 937), who suggests, presumably as a reform of current Athenian practice, that women and slaves should be permitted to witness, provided they could supply sureties to appear at a subsequent *dikē pseudomarturion*.

What a witness is doing is supporting his principal by offering to share in the dangers which the latter faces. This may help to explain two further peculiarities of the Athenian law of evidence. In the first place, Athenian law like English law excludes hearsay; and both allow certain exceptions to this rule, for instance in the case of statements made by people who have since died. The reason for the English rule is that hearsay is untrustworthy: the author of the original statement is not on oath and not subject to cross-examination. An exception is permitted in the case of dying declarations, because (or so it is conjecturally believed, Greer 1978: 165) people speak the truth at death. It has often been suggested that the rationale behind the Athenian rule was the same (thus Bonner 1905: 20–3, in the course of a general attempt to match Athenian to Anglo-American rules of hearsay). But dying declarations in English law are very tightly defined: in a case in the last century, a young woman with her throat cut dashed out of a room in which she had been alone with her boy-friend, and exclaimed, 'O, dear aunt, see what Harry has done for me!' before expiring (*R. v. Bedingfield*, 1879, cited by Phipson & Elliot 1987: 229); the court ruled that this was inadmissible as evidence, because the girl had not had a 'settled hopeless expectation' of death. In Athenian law, on the other hand, any statement made by a deceased person is admissible; this can hardly reflect a belief that people speak the truth because they are going to die at some time in the future! Presumably, therefore, the reason behind the Athenian rule is that where possible the original author of the statement should run his own risk.

But secondly, it is important not to over-emphasise the witness's initiative: his offer to share his principal's danger remains only an offer, and it is for the opponent to decide whether to take that offer up. It is often claimed that Athenian witnesses could not be cross-examined. Like most generalisations, that is not quite true; and in this case the truth is more revealing. In the period before approximately 380 B.C., the formal possibility existed to cross-examine witnesses. We only hear of one real instance when this right was exercised, however, and that over an entirely non-controversial matter (to attest a document, Andok. 1.14). There is also one parallel in comedy (Ar. *Wasps* 963–6), where Bdelykleon, acting on behalf of the silent defendant (a dog), interrogates the cheese-grater. Here again the evidence elicited is hardly controversial; indeed, it adds nothing to the plot, and its comic purpose is presumably that of incongruity. Around 380, the right of cross-examination was effectively abolished by the switch from oral to written evidence.[15] And nobody, it seems, felt that they were losing anything by the change. This is a significant point: it implies that the right had not previously been extensively used (Bonner 1905: 56, against the implicit suggestion of Thür 1977: 319). At

---

[15] The shift from oral to written evidence at Athens was first discussed by Bonner (1905: 46–8). He was interested primarily in the date at which the change took place; and his conclusion, that it occurred around 380, has been generally accepted. Bonner was not himself particularly interested in the reason for the change, but he accepted the claim of Dem. XLVI.6 that it was intended to prevent dispute about what the witness had said in case of a subsequent *dikē pseudomarturion*. Various additional reasons have since been suggested: for instance that it will have saved the court's time (Lämmli 1938: 112; MacDowell 1978: 243). A similar and roughly contemporary reform obliged litigants to submit their initial formal statements of accusation or denial in writing. Calhoun (1919) has even suggested that both reforms are to be dated to the same year, 378/7; but this cannot be proved.

At first sight, it might appear attractive to suggest that a rapidly increasing concept of the value of writing was affecting the way in which Athenians viewed some of their court-proceedings. Peter Brown (1975) has suggested that such a change in twelfth-century Europe was in part responsible for the decline in the use of the ordeal; and this might provide an attractive parallel for the non-use of torture or of the oath in fourth-century Athens (below, section IV). But I am not convinced that this explanation should be pressed too far. Brown's picture of the twelfth century is that of a society with a rapidly changing attitude to literacy; but one of the notable features about the use of writing in Athenian courts was the very slowness of change. One of the very few things that we almost certainly know about the early reformer Solon (c. 590) is that he introduced the form of prosecution known as the *graphē* (*Ath.Pol.* 9.1). This is a very significant name ('piece of writing'): it implies not simply that the indictment was written (whether by the plaintiff or by the magistrate's clerk, Calhoun 1919), but that even at this date it was possible to conceive of an indictment as a document. At the other end of the scale, Athenian juries throughout our period remained consistently and deeply suspicious of unattested written documents, even after the introduction of privileged status for written contracts in *dikai emporikai* (see n.23 below). Humphreys (1985c: 322) rightly emphasises the marginality of documents in Athenian courts, even in the fourth century. In the field of literacy at least, Athenian law seems to have been more static than is sometimes supposed (see n.19 below).

the trial, the witness has only offered himself as a potential adversary, and the person to attack is the opposing litigant. If you want to take up the witness's offer, you do not cross-examine him or assassinate his character; instead, you bring a *dikē pseudomarturion*.

Now I should say at this point that the model I am attempting to construct is neither wholly new nor wholly revolutionary. The rôle of the witness as supporter has recently been explored by Humphreys (1985c); even before that, Pringsheim (1951) had suggested that the original function of the witness in both Greece and Rome was not to hear, see and say, but to act and intervene; and a resemblance had at times already been noted between the idea of the witness as supporter and the mediaeval concept of the oath-helper or compurgator, a witness who swears not to the facts of the case but that his principal's oath is 'clean'.[16] Scholars have occasionally suggested that something like compurgation had existed in the primitive stages of Athenian law:[17] Gernet (1927) had argued that this might help us to understand the procedure called *diamarturia*, widely used in fourth-century inheritance-cases; this was a special plea, in which the defendant produced a formal witness to block the plaintiff's claim. An explanation in this form, however, tends towards the 'myth of the primitive survival'.[18] When you describe a procedure or an institution in Athenian law as 'primitive', you tend therefore to imply that it had lost much of its importance, was perceived to be anachronistic, and would soon be abolished. As a supporter, the witness was indeed playing an ancient rôle; but he is not a 'primitive survival'. Indeed Humphreys (1985c: 322 and n.33) doubts the relevance of oath-helping to Gernet's thesis here. She rightly points out that there is no evidence that oath-helping as such had ever existed at Athens; and she strongly criticises the use of explanatory models based on 'primitive survivals', preferring to speak instead of the co-existence of alternative methods of proof.

It would be going far too far to claim that the modern concept of the witness played no part in Athenian law. Instead, I would suggest that the two functions ('who you are' and 'what you say') continued together in tandem throughout the classical period, often in harmony, sometimes in opposition; and that where there was opposition, it was often the 'alien' (to us) concept which proved the stronger. There does not seem to me to have been much of a development from a 'primitive' to an 'advanced' view of the witness during our

---

[16] Admittedly the parallel is not very close, because, except in cases of homicide, an Athenian witness was not normally on oath: see further section IV of this paper.

[17] Or that it existed in other Greek *poleis*: Bonner & Smith (1938: 174–91) find a possible instance at Kyme.

[18] Note that legal anthropologists are particularly critical of explanations based on 'primitive survivals': see Roberts (1979: esp. 184–91; 1983), and Humphreys (cited below).

period. But then, I believe in a generally static rather than a developmental model of Athenian law.[19]

IV

In what remains of this paper, I should like to outline some possible developments of what I have said, in three areas: the frequency of witnesses; the classification of evidence; and the rôle of the *dikē pseudomarturion*.

From what has already been discussed, it will be clear that we cannot simply add up the number of witnesses in a speech and use this as a test of the speaker's veracity. Harvey (1985: 92) suggests that 'the production (or non-production) of witnesses' should be used to test the strength of allegations of bribery. But it is rarely clear what a witness is witnessing to: depositions are not normally quoted in the speeches, but are represented by a lemma such as *marturia* ('evidence'); and in the standard introduction *kai moi kalei touton marturas* ('call me witnesses of these things') the word *touton* ('of these things') may have referred to anything or nothing of what has just been said. Moreover, Athenian law has no rule that evidence must be relevant to a fact in issue, presumably because 'who you are' matters more than 'what you say'. Indeed, a speaker with a weak case might well try to bolster it by producing large numbers of witnesses to confirm uncontested points. This may be the reason why witnesses in Isaeus IX appear more than twice as frequently as they do in any other speech of Isaeus:[20] William Wyse, the great editor of Isaeus, was a captious critic; but he regarded the speaker's case in Isaeus IX as weak even by Isaeus' own standards (Wyse 1904: 626).

On the other hand, there are some constructive things to be said about the relative frequency of witnesses in different speeches. There is a striking difference between the use of witnesses in public and in private disputes. The following figures are very crude, and are subject to all possible qualifications; but they are I think nevertheless significant. In the various impeachment-procedures (*eisangelia, euthunai* and *apophasis* – fifteen speeches), witnesses are called on 3.3 occasions per hundred sections of text; in the two procedures used against illegal proposals (*graphē paranomon* used against decrees, and *graphē nomon mē epitedeion theinai* used against laws – six speeches in all), this figure falls to a mere 0.4. In both types of case the level of witnesses is low, perhaps because potential supporters would normally appear as *sunegoroi*; in

---

[19] That is, I tend to believe that the changes in Athenian law from the archaic period to the end of the democracy were considerably less drastic than the majority of scholars (following Glotz 1904) have believed: archaic Athenian law was less 'primitive', and late classical law less 'advanced' than has been claimed. To that extent – but only to that extent – my reading of Athenian legal institutions is similar to that of Sealey (1987: 1–4). A low level of development was detected by Hansen (1976) in the procedure of *apagogē* or summary arrest; and a similar picture appears in the relationship between literacy and the law (see n.15 above): I hope to develop this argument at greater length in the future.

[20] Isaeus IX contains 40.5 witnesses per hundred sections: the next most frequent are Is. VII with 17.4 and Is. V with 17.0. For the figures which follow, see p. 39 below.

the procedures against illegal proposals it is extremely low, perhaps because the place of witnesses is taken by laws and decrees (6.7 per hundred sections). Of the private speeches, on the other hand, the frequency in contractual disputes (thirteen speeches) is 8.2; and in the twenty-five speeches concerned with family property it reaches 13.8. Humphreys (1985c: 325–49) has examined the types of witnesses who are used in disputes; she has considered in more detail elsewhere (Humphreys 1986) the use of kin as witnesses in those disputes which directly involve family relationships: one of the things you are doing by producing relatives (often named) as witnesses is seeking to convince the jury that the family consensus is on your side.

Of the whole corpus of forensic speeches, only one was written for a non-Athenian court. That is Isoc. XIX, in which the speaker is trying to prove a will before a court in oligarchic Aigina (on the legal problems of this speech see Wolff 1979: 15–34). But Isoc. XIX, uniquely among fully preserved speeches in family–property disputes, contains no witnesses whatever. I have no certain explanation of this fact; but it may be that the socio-political institution of the witness played less of a rôle in an oligarchy than in a democracy.

To speak of the Athenian classification of evidence is perhaps misleading. Ancient rhetorical theorists spoke of *pisteis*, and to translate this as 'evidence' or as 'proofs' is to beg the question: a better term might be 'supporting arguments'. *Pisteis* fall into two groups: *pisteis entekhnoi*, which the orator himself has to discover and develop; and *pisteis atekhnoi*, which require no such skill on his part. The former comprise a wide range of probability-arguments, and these are the real interest both of the orators and of the rhetoricians; but I shall say little about them. My concern here is with the *pisteis atekhnoi*. Aristotle (*Rhet.* 1, 1375a24–5) lists five of these: laws (including also decrees), witnesses, agreements or contracts (this appears to mean private documents in general), torture (the statements of slaves), and oaths.[21] It may come as a surprise that laws are considered as a form of 'evidence', rather than being the rules according to which the facts as attested are to be judged (thus Harrison 1971: 134–5); but laws are cited by the litigants rather than by the court, and they have persuasive not compelling force.[22] Indeed, Lykourgos can even cite foreign law, not for comparative purposes to elucidate the law of Athens, but in order to show what 'good law' is (Lyk. 1.129, cf. also Dem. XXIV.139–41).

How are we to make sense of Aristotle's list? I would suggest that it falls into two groups. One group consists of laws and witnesses and private documents: these carry a risk, but require no consent; and litigants make frequent use of

---

[21] *Rhet. pros Alex.* XIV–XVII, 1431b8–1432b4 has the makings of a similar list, which he describes as *epithetoi* ('supplementary') *pisteis* (1431b8): he includes witnesses, torture and oaths, adding also personal assertions by the speaker; but he omits the laws and the private documents.

[22] Soubie (1973: 182) speaks of 'proving the law' as a parallel to 'proving the facts'; but what you are doing is really using the law as a means of proof.

them. The risk for the witness has been explained already; private documents were normally attested,[23] and the witness to the document is similarly liable (as in Dem. XLV–XLVI, discussed below); in the case of a law the risk is the litigant's, because to cite a non-existent law is a capital crime (Dem. XXVI.24). The second group consists of torture and oaths: these can be used only with the consent of the opposing litigant; but if this consent has been received, the evidence once given carries no risk, and its validity cannot be impeached by legal process (Leisi 1907: 16–17 on the oath). This is why a woman can swear an evidentiary oath but cannot be a witness: to be a witness, she would need the capacity to be sued;[24] to swear an oath she needs merely the agreement of both parties, because the oath cannot give rise to a *dikē pseudomarturion*.

This distinction between risk-procedures and consent-procedures may also help to explain the vexed problem of torture. It is a commonplace in the orators that the statements of slaves under torture constitute the highest form of proof; and yet the process was apparently never used. Part of the difficulty here has been a failure clearly to analyse the problem. If you are certain that a man is either guilty or has guilty knowledge, then it is logically defensible (if cruel) to use torture to exact a confession or denunciation: he clearly has something to hide. But to torture a 'witness' is irrational: he is neither more nor less likely to tell the truth at last than at first,[25] a point which was already obvious to Antiphon (v.31–32), the first of the canonical Orators. Slaves and aliens in the former category were certainly tortured (a detailed list is given by Turasiewicz 1963), and this could be done on the initiative of the prosecutor without the need for the consent of the defendant, in this case the slave himself; this is hardly remarkable, and creates no problem. But to torture a slave in the second category required the consent of both parties. Now on forty-two occasions in the orators we find the challenge, either 'torture my slaves for evidence' or 'let me torture yours'. Forty times this challenge was

---

[23] Private documents were normally drawn up in the presence of witnesses (the only exception being the account-books of bankers, Bonner 1905: 39–40). Leisi (1907: 73) suggests that a man who agreed to witness the drawing-up of a will or a contract thereby took on the duty to witness to that document in court if need be. I doubt myself if this was a legal obligation, but it certainly seems to have been common practice. Even though Athenian law granted a certain privileged status to written documents in the later fourth century (in *dikai emporikai* (see n.12 above), for instance, a plaintiff who could produce a written contract could make use of a specially speeded-up procedure, for which MacDowell 1978: 233 gives details), nevertheless the courts seem to have remained deeply suspicious of the written without the support of the spoken word (cf. Dem. XXXVI.26–7). The effects of literacy, even at this period, did not run very deep (cf. n.15 above).

[24] Women can only be sued in those procedures where the penalty is death (Ant. I, *dikē phonou*) or enslavement (Dem. LIX, *graphē xenias*); because their legal capacity to dispose of property is extremely restricted, they cannot pay damages or a fine. This is presumably the point of Plato's suggested reform, that women and slaves should be allowed to witness if they can furnish sureties (*Laws* 937, cited above): the sureties are needed not because the woman may abscond, but to pay up if she is convicted.

[25] This distinction was first drawn by Headlam (1893: 1), and subsequently by Harrison (1971: 147–9), MacDowell (1978: 246) and Thür (1977). Soubie (1973: 239) however ignores the distinction and therefore fails to see that the second form of torture was never used.

flatly rejected; twice (Isoc. XVII.15–16, Dem. XXXVII.42) it was accepted but not carried through.[26]

The problem of torture may be distilled into two questions. In the first place, why could the statements of slaves only be admitted under torture and with the consent of both litigants? And secondly, why did the procedure excite so much noise and so little action?

MacDowell (1978: 245, cited above) offers a twofold explanation of the first question: torture is used to overcome the slave's fear of his master; and consent was needed because the slave was valuable property. But this is a rationalisation: it suggests that you are primarily interested in what the slave has to say; and this simply exacerbates the second problem: if MacDowell is right, why was torture never used? Soubie (1973: 226) is surely right to say that part of the reason for the use of torture is socio-political: torture is needed to emphasise to all concerned the status-distinction between slaves and citizens. There may also be the feeling that giving evidence ought to be a risky business: since a slave was in no danger of a *dikē pseudomarturion*, it was only right that he should suffer automatically. Ant. *Tetr.* II.d.7 complains that to accept without torture a denunciation of his killer by a mortally wounded slave is to allow him to speak *akindunos*, 'without risk'.

Why then was the challenge to torture never carried through? Headlam (1893) suggested a brilliantly economical answer, that this is simply a function of our sources. Torture, he argued, was a form of trial by ordeal: once the challenge was accepted, the slave's evidence would conclusively settle the whole dispute, and there would be no need for a trial; if no trial, no speech; and that, according to Headlam, is why we have no recorded instances of the challenge being carried through. Unfortunately, however, in several extant challenges hypothetical arrangements are made for recording the slave's statements and producing them in court. This point was immediately noticed by Thompson (1894); and Headlam's attempt to guard his flanks proved unsuccessful (Headlam 1894). All subsequent scholars have rejected Headlam's theory (e.g. Bonner 1905: 72; Lipsius 1915: 889 n.91; Harrison 1971: 148 n.1; Thür 1977: 205–7). Nobody however has produced a satisfactory alternative explanation, despite the attempt of Thiel (1966) to see the answer in terms of 'official' and 'unofficial' viewpoints; he cited for comparison public attitudes to the deterrent-effect of capital punishment in those contemporary countries which still retained it. The definitive account of the subject is that of

---

[26] MacDowell (1978: 246 and n.559) suggests three exceptions to this rule (Andok. 1.64, Lyk. 1.112, and *P.Oxy.* 2686). But in these cases there is no sign of a challenge, and there does not seem to be any need to gain the opponent's consent. Indeed, the context in all three cases is inquisitorial and not adversarial: the state is conducting an investigation on its own authority. These cases should presumably therefore be assimilated to the first group, in which the person tortured is believed to have guilty knowledge. Certainly they have no bearing on the question of the challenge to torture in the regular adversarial procedures. For the latter, Dem. XLVII.36 is surely conclusive: when a fight is about to begin, a man sends his slave into the street to summon citizens (i.e., as witnesses); this implies that he regards the slave himself as inadequate evidence for practical purposes.

Thür (1977),[27] which conclusively demonstrates that all the commonplaces in the orators about the high value of evidence obtained by torture are simply play-acting: to say that 'witnesses have often been convicted of perjury, but slaves under torture have never been shown to be lying' (Isaeus VIII.12, Dem. XXX.37) is a tautology, because there is no procedural opportunity whereby the statements of slaves could be tested (Thür 1977: 310); moreover, the challenge to torture is always drawn up in such a form as to guarantee rejection (for details, see Thür 1977: 233–61). But this is to answer the question 'how?' not 'why?'. To understand that, we need to compare torture with the other consent-procedure, the oath.

In an Athenian court, any litigant who wished could swear an oath himself or impose one on his witnesses; but this had no more than persuasive effect. If however you accepted the opponent's challenge to swear an oath, then this evidence had compelling force, because there was no procedural means of refuting the statement made on oath.[28] The parallel with the challenge to torture will be obvious. And like the challenge to torture, the challenge to swear an oath was always apparently rejected – with one intriguing exception. The politician Mantias was once sued by the brothers of his estranged wife Plangon to admit the paternity of her two sons (who were, according to Mantias, illegitimate). Mantias, we are told, agreed with Plangon to settle the case out of court: he would leave 30 *mna* on deposit in her name; he would then challenge her to swear to the truth of her claim; she would refuse the challenge and drop the case; and on refusing she would collect the money. The scheme backfired, because Plangon double-crossed Mantias and accepted the challenge. (Or at least, so we are told: the speaker in question is Mantias' son by a second marriage, and he is hardly impartial.) But Plangon's oath – this is the significant point – was, if not formally then in practice, decisive evidence: Mantias could no longer deny the facts alleged in the oath, because he had challenged her to swear it; he was therefore forced to admit paternity.[29]

---

[27] It is a striking and worrying fact that a book of this importance, which Finley (1980: 94 n.4) rightly described as 'replacing all previous accounts' of the subject, was still awaiting its first review in an English-speaking journal as late as *L'Année philologique* 57 (1986) – by which time it had already been reviewed in Italian by Biscardi in *SDHI* 45 (1979) 674–9, in French by Vélissaropoulos in *RD* 57 (1979) 85–6 and by Germain in *AC* 48 (1979) 731–2, and in German by Rupprecht in *ZSS* 97 (1980) 320–3 and by Hermann in *AAHG* 35 (1982) 75–8.

[28] If both sides challenged and swore, as almost happened in Dem. LV.27, presumably the effect was not decisive.

[29] We hear of very few examples of the challenge to the oath (references in Bonner 1905: 74–9 and Harrison 1971: 150–3); and it is notable that the only conclusive examples occurred before the arbitrator. Gernet (1955: 66 n.3, and 1955: 110–11, first published as Gernet 1937 and Gernet 1939 respectively) deduced from the case of Plangon in Dem. XXXIX–XL, and from Dem. LIX.60 where Phrastor refused a similar challenge and lost his case, that a challenge made at this juncture was legally binding on both arbitrator and litigants: if the party challenged swore the oath, he won the case automatically; if he refused, he lost it; either way, the arbitrator had no discretion. I wonder myself whether the rule may have been less formal than this: the language of Dem. LII.15 seems to me to suggest that the arbitrator may formally have had the discretion to ignore the result of the challenge, although he was certainly expected to deliver a verdict in

The reason in the consent-procedures why the challenge is always formulated so as to be rejected is that litigants are afraid of being stuck with whatever evidence comes up.

My final remarks concern the *dikē pseudomarturion*. The first point to be made about this procedure is that it is not strictly an action for 'perjury' (although for the purpose of shorthand it is sometimes convenient to use this term). Athenian witnesses are not normally on oath, except in special cases: witnesses in homicide trials, for instance, were obliged to join in the indictment, which itself took the form of an oath (the *diomosia*); and even in other cases witnesses under certain circumstances could swear an oath to strengthen the persuasive power of their testimony. The terminology throughout the orators, however, is consistent. Somebody who swears a false oath is described as *epiorkos* ('perjured'); this was an offence against the gods, but the offender could not be prosecuted. Somebody who gives false witness is described as *pseudomarturon* ('false witness'); the gods have no interest in the matter (indeed, the gods have no rôle in guaranteeing the truth of testimony), but the offender was liable to a *dikē pseudomarturion*. This observation may help to explain what is going on in the *exomosia* (cf. section II above). Harrison (1971: 144) seems to suggest that you are forcing the witness either to testify to a deposition prepared by yourself, or to deny knowledge on oath, in order that if he denies knowledge you can then sue him by *dikē pseudomarturion*; this view is tentatively accepted by Humphreys (1985c: 322). But this cannot be right, because if he swears the oath, he will not be a witness, and therefore he will not be liable to *dikē pseudomarturion*.[30] Instead, I suggest, you are forcing the potential witness to declare openly which side he is on. This is why the alternatives available to him are incomplete: it does not matter that he has no opportunity of replying, 'I do know the facts, but they are not as you allege' (cf. n.8 above); he has to support one party or the other.

If a convicted defendant brought a *dikē pseudomarturion*, this could under certain circumstances, it appears, annul the verdict against him.[31] Unfortunately the details are far from clear. The central problem concerns a fragment of Theophrastos' *Laws*, quoted by a scholiast on Plato, *Laws* 937: 'verdicts do not become *anadikos* (annulled) in every type of trial, but only in *xenias* (usurpation of citizen status) and *pseudomarturion* (false witness) and *kleron*

---

accordance with it. The latter of course would be the natural result if a litigant found himself procedurally unable to refute the contents of a statement made under oath after a challenge.
30 Aesch. 1.67 for instance attacks the recalcitrant Hegesandros as *epiorkos*, but gives no hint that he can be prosecuted.
31 It is possible that the mysterious *dikē kakotekhnion*, or private action for 'subornation of perjury', was used for this purpose: if you were successful (by *dikē pseudomarturion*) in convicting a witness of having given false or improper evidence, you could then proceed (by *dikē kakotekhnion*) to accuse your opponent of having suborned this evidence, and this second victory would enable you to re-open the original case. But this is only speculation, and the significance of *dikē kakotekhnion* is wholly obscure: Leisi (1907: 139–41) insists strongly that it was nothing more than a specialised action for damages.

(inheritances).' In the first place, we do not know whether Theophrastos is talking about Athens here; and secondly, even if he is, the sentence makes no sense.[32]

It is striking that false witness was dealt with by a *dikē* (a private suit) rather than by a public *graphē*.[33] Many scholars have tried to avoid the implications of this. Lipsius for instance (1912: 782) argued that instead of a *dikē pseudomarturion* you must have had the option of bringing a *graphē sukophantias* (public suit for malicious prosecution) but for this there is no evidence whatever. Bonner & Smith (1938: 262–3) claim that the *dikē pseudomarturion* was really a 'criminal' procedure; and Leisi (1907: 120–3) argues that the penalty must have included a fine payable to the state rather than simply compensation payable to the opponent.[34] It seems better to admit the obvious: *pseudomarturion* was an offence against the opposing litigant and not against the court; and it was a matter in which the state took no interest.

At first sight, the etymology of the term *pseudomarturion* would suggest a primary concern with what the witness had said. *Pseudes*, after all, means 'false'; and in the classic case of *dikē pseudomarturion*, in which Apollodoros prosecutes Stephanos for his evidence on behalf of Apollodoros' step-father Phormion (Dem. XLV–XLVI), the plaintiff certainly claims that Stephanos' testimony had been untrue. But it is clear even from this case that the word *pseudes* could be used to describe not only untrue but also illicit evidence: one, at least, of the grounds on which Apollodoros claims that the evidence had been *pseudes* was that it was inadmissible, because it was hearsay (Dem. XLVI.5–8 with Leisi 1907: 121). Moreover, Apollodoros' argument to prove that Stephanos' testimony had been untrue is as follows: Stephanos has testified to a fact which strictly speaking he cannot have known (that a document which he had not opened contained what it purported to). But Stephanos was not an important witness in Phormion's original case; and had

32 Clearly the verdict to be annulled is that of the original trial, for instance a *graphē xenias*. But the original trial could never have been a *dikē pseudomarturion*, which was available only as a secondary action. Moreover, *klēron* is the name not of a procedure (like the *dikē pseudomarturion* and the *graphē xenias*) but of a class of procedures ('those concerning inheritances'); Harrison (1968: 158 n.2) attempts to find an otherwise unattested *dikē klērou* lurking behind Isaeus VI.3 or XI.13, but the text in both passages is better translated as 'a/the *dikē* for an estate' (i.e., a *diadikasia*). The most recent and most comprehensive treatment of *anadikia* is that of Behrend (1975), but given the nature of our evidence the question is likely to remain contentious.

33 Apart from witnesses who appear in court, the other common use of witnesses in Athenian legal proceedings was as *klēteres* (summons-witnesses): it is notable that the action against a *klēter* was a public procedure (the *graphē pseudoklēteias*). Of course the explanation may be partly functional: as Harrison points out (1971: 198 n.5), a litigant who had been convicted in his absence as the result of a fraudulent summons might well have suffered *atimia* (loss of citizen rights), in which case his only option would have been to ask a friend to bring a *graphē* on his behalf. But this is hardly a complete explanation (by no means all absentee defendants suffered *atimia*); and the existence of a *graphē* against one form of witness certainly serves to point the contrast with the absence of a *graphē pseudomarturion*.

34 Leisi's argument is that the *dikē pseudomarturion* could be brought by the winner of the original trial, who had *ex hypothesi* suffered no damage; but this ignores the possibility of 'moral or intellectual damage'.

it occurred to him that Apollodoros would object, Phormion need not have called Stephanos to testify. It is hard to escape the conclusion that Stephanos was doing what witnesses regularly did; in other words, that nobody normally bothered too much if a witness testified to something that in strict logic he could not know. Finally, it is clear what has really annoyed Apollodoros: Apollodoros' original dispute with Phormion concerned family property; Stephanos is a marriage-relation of Apollodoros, and is therefore no direct relative of Phormion; and yet Stephanos has ratted and backed Phormion's side of the family. So even in the case where the concept of the witness as the means to truth is at its strongest, it is fighting a losing battle against the concept of the witness as a supporter.

Appendix: The frequency of witnesses.
Frequency in different orators

Orator	Speeches number	Length §§	Witnesses how often called		Frequency per 100 §§
Antiphon	3	178	8	→	4.5
Andokides	1	150	9	→	6.0
Lysias	29	983	49	→	5.0
Isocrates	5	270	9	→	3.3
Isaeus	12	536	69	→	12.9
Lykourgos	1	150	5	→	3.3
Hypereides	5	150	1	→	0.7
Deinarkhos	3	162	2	→	1.2
Aeschines	3	640	18	→	2.8
Demosthenes	41	3404	234	→	6.9
Demosthenes' speeches include:					
public	9	1705	19	→	1.1
semi-public[35]	3	225	36	→	16.0
private	29	1434	179	→	12.5
The total corpus of forensic oratory:					
	103	6626	404	→	6.1

Frequency of witnesses in different classes of speech

Procedure	Speeches	Length	Witnesses		Frequency
Public procedures:					
Against proposals	6	1267	5	→	0.4
4 *graphai paranomon* and 2 *graphai nomon mē epitedeion theinai*					
(but note that 85 laws/decrees are cited				→	6.7)
Impeachments	15	1166	39	→	3.3
6 *eisangeliai*, 5 *euthunai*, and 4 *apophaseis*					
Private procedures:					
Contracts	13	622	51	→	8.2
5 speeches about banks/loans, 5 about shipping, and 3 for damages					
Family property	25	1162	160	→	13.8
9 speeches about guardianship, 12 (exc. Isoc. XIX) about inheritance, and 4 others					

35 The abbreviation 'semi-public' is used to denote those three speeches which have been grouped with the private speeches in surviving manuscripts and modern editions, but which were written for public prosecutions: LIII (*apographē*), LVIII (*endeixis*) and LIX (*graphē xenias*).

3

Fowl play: a curious lawsuit in classical Athens (Antiphon XVI, frr. 57–9 Thalheim)[1]

PAUL CARTLEDGE

I

At a date towards the end of the fifth century B.C. Antiphon composed a forensic oration, of which a version was delivered before an Athenian People's Court, in indictment of, or defence against, one Erasistratos on a charge concerning peafowl.[2] This may have been just one episode in a long-running saga of interfamilial conflict (below, sections III and V). At all events, the ancient equivalent of a 'soap opera' was just what the officially appointed jurymen–judges and the informal *corona* of bystanders hoped to witness or participate in during a trial held in the Agora of Classical Athens.[3] Judging by the subject-matter of the lawsuit under scrutiny in the present essay, there is every reason to suppose that all hopes were well satisfied in this particular case.

However, Antiphon's *Against Erasistratos* should not be closely studied solely for its potential entertainment value. The deceptively simple question 'why did Antiphon file his peacock report?' masks a series of ever more deeply significant questions about Athenian politics, law, culture and society. By whom, why and how were the legal proceedings initiated, and on what charge precisely? Why was the case allowed, or forced, to come to trial rather than settled out of court? How and why were peafowl deemed to be fit matter for litigation? Why were they, or the suit, considered so important that the services of an Antiphon were found necessary or desirable? In what capacity exactly did Antiphon render those services? And so on.

---

[1] See Appendix for text and translation of the 'fragments' in Thalheim's Teubner edition (Leipzig 1914). The title as printed by Thalheim is taken from [Plut.] *Mor.* 833d (n.4, below); Harpokration fr. 61a agrees in including the definite article ('the' peafowl – omitted in the text of frr. 57 and 59), which has the merit of drawing attention to the singularity of the birds. On the title, and esp. on the significance of *pros*, see further section V below.

[2] On the date of the trial, nature of the suit and charge, and Antiphon's rôle, see section V; for a suggested identification of Erasistratos, section VI.

[3] 'Soap-opera' analogy: Humphreys 1983b: 7; cf. Freeman 1946: 28 (litigation appealed to the 'unfailing dramatic sense' of the Athenians). The *corona* of bystanders (*hoi periestekotes*): Bers 1985: 8. Location(s?) of courts: Camp 1986: 108–9.

Most of those or similar questions cannot, unfortunately, be answered unequivocally, let alone definitively. This is partly for sheer lack of the relevant factual information. In the first place, despite the fame achieved by the speech in antiquity, three 'fragments' are all that survive from it today; the longest supposedly verbatim quotation amounts to no more than two sentences of thirty-two words all told.[4] Moreover, we do not know for certain the identities of either prosecutor or defendant: that is, we do not know which Erasistratos was involved, whether he was prosecutor or defendant, or who his opponent was. We know neither the precise charge nor the type of action brought by the plaintiff. The catalogue of our factual ignorance embraces also the date of the trial and – not necessarily the same thing – the date at which Antiphon's speech was put into circulation in written form.[5]

Such ignorance is not blissful, especially as it is largely invincible. But it may also be positively salutary, if it compels concentration at least as much on the wider socio-political context and meaning of the case as on the biographical and legal minutiae. Besides, we do in fact know enough of the likely chief actors in the peafowl drama, VIPs to a man, and enough about Athenian politics, law, culture and society in the later fifth century to be able to make more than a little sense of the plot. Above all, though, the very idea of a major court-case revolving around peafowl counsels us to continue the quest for enlightenment, since, as the work of mediaevalists and early modernists has conclusively demonstrated, obscure, bizarre and seemingly inexplicable legal customs may yet be made intelligible in terms of a culture's *mentalité* or mind-set, and legal records can prove uniquely valuable sources of historical insight.[6] In short, the Antiphontic peafowl suit demands to be rescued from its present condition of near-oblivion for the light it can shed on the history of Classical Athens, not least on the *mentalité* of that to us irreducibly alien, and even by contemporary Greek standards highly exceptional, democratic polity.

II

Our discussion opens with politics, almost inevitably. For an Athenian People's Court (*dikasterion*) was not only a juridical and theatrical space, but also and essentially a politically defined arena. Like all ancient Greek states,

---

[4] See Appendix. Of the speech's ancient reputation [Plut.] *Mor.* 833d (= Vit. Ant. 20) writes: 'His most admired speeches are the *On Herodes, Against Erasistratos concerning the Peafowl, On the Impeachment*, and *Against* [pros] *Demosthenes the general in the matter of a writ alleging an unconstitutional proposal.*' Of these only the *Herodes* is extant: Freeman 1946; on the last-mentioned of the four see Sealey 1987: 161 n.47. On the *Vita* by [Plutarch] see text below and nn. 30–1.

[5] Antiphon or his client (on the lawyer–client relationship see text below and n.39) might well have wished to put copies into circulation immediately after the trial, especially if the client was acquitted (see section VI). But in the circumstances postulated for the trial (section V) more pressing tasks could have preoccupied Antiphon – as they did Cicero in the late 60s B.C. (in a letter of mid-60 B.C., *Att.* II.1.3, Cic. discusses with his 'publisher' the proposed circulation of texts of some speeches he had delivered in 63).

[6] Legal customs and ancient *mentalité*: Fustel de Coulanges 1864: 3; cf. on the *mentalité* concept, Stone 1987: ch. 8. Law and society in action in comparative perspective:

the Athenian democracy did not, and would not have wanted to, recognise the modern theoretical notion of the 'separation of powers' of government and public administration.[7] In the Athenian *demokratia* of the fifth century B.C., both in constitutional theory and in everyday political praxis the *demos* (People) exercised the *kratos* (sovereign power) in all three spheres of legislation, executive action and jurisdiction.[8] Even Aristotle, who was far from being a convinced democrat, saw no reason to indict the Athenian democracy on that ground. Indeed, struggling as usual in the *Politics* to render heuristically fertile the often hazy perceptions implied by popular linguistic usage, Aristotle concluded that the citizen (*polites*) of a Greek state was best defined as the relevantly qualified adult male who was entitled to participate both in *krisis* (decision-making, specifically judicial) and in *arkhē* (office-holding, including membership of a judicial body). Moreover, he conceded – realistically if also rather ruefully – that his refined definition applied most closely to the citizen of a democratic state (such as Athens), as opposed to the citizen of an oligarchy in which the active exercise of citizen-rights depended crucially on a citizen's wealth.[9]

Thus, the possession of citizenship in democratic Athens should in theory have implied the opportunity to take part in the administration of legal justice as well as to legislate and to execute political decisions. In practice, of all Greek democracies it was the Athenian that most fully measured up to Aristotle's ideal definition of the citizen as 'magistrate' (both in the ancient Roman sense of executive office-holder and in the contemporary sense of civil law-officer), not only in its day-to-day workings but also in its civic ideology.[10] One illustration of that ideology may suffice here. So attached was the good Athenian citizen to his juridical function in life that he might still cling on to his juror's identity-token (*pinakion*) in his grave, perhaps thereby hoping in due course to secure a place on the subterranean jury-panel drawn up by Rhadamanthys.[11] The institutional basis of that juristic civic ideology was laid down mainly in

Le Roy Ladurie 1975; Davis 1983; Davies & Fouracre 1986: esp. 233. However, on the tendency for exceptional people and behaviour to be overrepresented in surviving legal records of all kinds see Moore 1984: 89; and 'a rhetorical case should not be mistaken for a case-history' (Dover 1974: 13).

[7] For Montesquieu's decisive contribution to this theory see briefly Shackleton 1961: 298–301; on the relationship between theory and actual practice, however, see Maio 1983: 18 ('empty myth'); cf. Pannick 1987.

[8] Rhodes 1972: 147; Sinclair 1988: 82–3; see further chapter 1, section III and n.33, above.

[9] Definition: Arist. *Pol.* 1275a22–33, 1275b5–7; cf. Lévy 1980: 234–41, with Johnson 1984; and, for the contrast with oligarchic Sparta (which lacked a *popular* judiciary), Ste. Croix 1972: 349–50.

[10] See generally Sinclair 1988. Compare and contrast Waltman & Holland 1988: esp. 218–20 (Waltman on 'changing modes of political participation' in modern democracies).

[11] Kroll 1972: 9 ('Even today it is hard to think of a more appropriate symbol of an Athenian's nearly professional involvement in democratic government'); cf. Hansen 1983c: 234 and n.19.

the late 460s and the 450s by the reforms attributed to Ephialtes and Perikles.[12] A generation later, by which time Athenians born during the era of reform had reached the qualifying minimum age of thirty, the active exercise of the political rights of citizenship at Athens was intimately associated with serving for pay (*misthos*) from the public coffers on the annually recruited panel of 6,000 *dikastai* (judges as well as jurors) who staffed at need the various People's Courts.[13] So complete and familiar did the association of ideas become that in 423 Aristophanes (*Clouds* 206–8) could make one of his comic characters pretend not to recognise a map of Athens because he could see no *dikastai* depicted on it. Indeed, in the following year he went so far as to create an entire comedy, *Wasps*, the comprehensibility of which depended largely on the audience's having a quite close familiarity with not just the idea but also the procedures of the *dikasteria*. The importance of *Wasps* as evidence for the intimate implication of litigation with democratic politics can hardly be missed.[14] For present purposes, though, the play has a precise, biographical relevance as well.

III

At line 98 of *Wasps* a certain Demos is invoked as being *kalos* ('beautiful'), that is as the masculine, homoerotic equivalent of a maiden's being considered nubile.[15] Given the peculiarity of his name (below), there can be no doubt but that this Aristophanic Demos is identical with the 'Demos son of Pyrilampes' of Antiphon fr. 57. From that fragment we learn that it was Demos who was keeping or rearing or nurturing (*trephein*) the peafowl in litigious question, and it would therefore be most economical to assume that it was also he who was either plaintiff or defendant in the case and he who commissioned or otherwise solicited Antiphon's *Against Erasistratos*. But since the most economical hypotheses are not necessarily the correct hypotheses, I leave those issues open for the moment and pass on to review what we know about Demos apart from his involvement with peafowl, bearing in mind throughout this section the solemn warning that 'political prosopography is a type of study which requires a higher degree of caution than any other historical field'.[16]

---

[12] Evidence: Hill 1951: 350, Index II.3.3–5; cf. Rhodes 1970; 1972: 144–207; 1981: 309–19. Despite Sealey (1987: 67–8), *Ath. Pol.* 9.1 ('when the people are masters of the [judicial] vote, they are masters of the state') is anachronistic for Solon's day but appropriate to the post-Ephialtic situation.

[13] General accounts of the courts in English include Kennedy 1888: 351–77; Bonner 1927: 72–95; Jones 1956: 116–51; Carey & Reid 1985: 1–13; Garner 1987: ch. 1. Jury-pay: Markle 1985.

[14] MacDowell 1971; Horsley 1982; Storey 1987: 23.

[15] *kalos*-label: Dover 1978: 111–24 (citing *Wasps* 98 at p. 111). Alleged physical attractions of Demos (for the possibly fictitious Kallikles): Plat. *Gorg.* 481de, 513b.

[16] K. J. Dover in Gomme, Andrewes & Dover 1970: 288 (somewhat exaggerated, perhaps; for the achievements as well as the limitations of prosopography see Stone 1987: ch. 2).

Demos (literally 'People') was very oddly named – much more so, one might add, than the Athenian who in roughly the 470s/460s was given the comparably novel name Demokrates.[17] However, the thinking behind the choice of nomenclature was surely the same in both cases, namely the desire of their respective fathers to make a public statement of democratic political intent. If the *Wasps* reference to his *kalos* status could be used strictly as a chronological indicator, Demos should have been no more than about twenty in 422 and so born no earlier than about 442. But since Aristophanes elected to use his name at least partly for the sake of a double pun on *kemos* (the funnel of a judicial voting-urn) and *demos*, the chronological implication cannot be pressed. More likely, he was born rather earlier in the 440s, during the intense political competition between Perikles and Thoukydides son of Melesias which culminated in the ostracism of the latter in (probably) 443.[18] As there is some reason to suppose that his father Pyrilampes might have wished openly to dissociate himself from Thoukydides and to associate himself with the politics of Perikles on the questions of relations with Persia and the character of the Athenian Empire, a suitable explanation of Demos' remarkable name would be that Pyrilampes chose it as a means of proclaiming himself a good Periklean.[19]

However that may be, the habit of politically motivated nomenclature was without question deeply ingrained in the Athenian, as it was in other Greek, upper classes.[20] In the case of Demos, we have to deal with a social stratum very close to the summit of the Athenian 'top drawer'. Thus in the standard work on the Athenian propertied class of liturgy-payers and champion racehorse-owners (Davies 1971), he duly finds his place in the entry under Kritias, the extreme pro-Spartan oligarchic leader of 404–403, and more precisely in the section covering the family of Plato, as the accompanying stemma, incomplete and hypothetical though it is, is designed to illustrate (Fig. 1). For a sister of Pyrilampes, Demos' paternal aunt, became by way of her daughter Periktione, Demos' first cousin, the maternal grandmother of Plato. Periktione, moreover, after bearing Plato and his three siblings to

---

17 Birthdate and nomenclature of Demokrates: Hansen 1986; Sinclair 1988: 1 and n.1; cf. Hansen, *Was Athens a Democracy? Popular Rule, Liberty, and Equality in Ancient and Modern Political Thought* (Copenhagen 1989) 4 and n.11. On the coinage of the term *demokratia* contrast Sealey 1987: 98–102 with the preferable account in Ostwald 1986: 15 n.43.

18 Sources for ostracism: Hill 1951: 371 (esp. Index II.5.9–11); cf. Wade-Gery 1958: 240–3.

19 Anon. *Vit. Thuc.* 6 (late biography of Thuc. the historian) claims that Pyrilampes had once been defended by Thouk. against a charge brought by Perikles (that Pyr. had killed a boy in a love-affair); according to Plut. *Per.* 13.15, Pyr. was known as a *hetairos* of Perikles (see section IV, below). MacDowell (1971: 144) regards the former claim as 'improbable but not impossible', whereas Davies (1971: 330) takes it seriously enough to speculate that Pyr. 'had crossed over from the Thoukydidean to the Periklean camp in the 450s'. Such evidence should not perhaps be pressed.

20 See e.g. Herman 1987: 19–22 (naming habits among men united by ties of ritualised friendship, *xenia*).

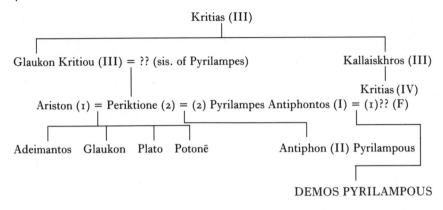

Fig. 1

Ariston, was later remarried to her own maternal uncle Pyrilampes, who thereby became Plato's stepfather as well as Demos' father, while Demos' cousin became simultaneously his stepmother.

This sort of complicated in-marriage, especially between uncle and niece, was thoroughly typical of the Athenian élite, being practised chiefly in order to prevent the dispersal of large ancestral estates and so preserve property-power.[21] It is regrettable, therefore, that we know so little about the patriline of Pyrilampes and not even the name of his first wife, the mother of Demos.[22] We do, however, know enough for Davies (1971: 329) to be able to state that Pyrilampes sprang from a 'rather shadowy family of considerable wealth'. For the passion for horse-racing exhibited by his father Antiphon could only have been indulged by a possessor of that degree of inherited or acquired wealth which led Davies (1971: xxv–xxvi) to make competitive horse-raising (*hippotrophia*) one of his criteria for including a family in his prosopography of the Athenian *propertied* class.

Pyrilampes, however, was no Lord Derby. In place of *hippotrophia* he engaged rather in *ornithotrophia* (bird-fancying). In itself there was nothing particularly remarkable about that. The Athenians at large kept an extraordinarily catholic range of native and exotic avifauna for ludic, gustatory, amatory and other purposes.[23] But what distinguished Pyrilampes uniquely

---

21 Source of stemma: Davies 1971: 329–30 (*Prosopographia Attica*, ed. J. Kirchner (hereafter *PA*) 8792). Uncle–niece marriage: Harrison 1968: 23; cf. Thompson 1972: 218 n.39 (Pyr. and Periktione). Property-power at Athens: Davies 1981: esp. 117–20; in the Greek world generally: Lane Fox 1985; cross-cultural comparison: Goody 1976: e.g. 15.

22 Ignorance of high-status Athenian women's names: Raepsaet 1973: 537; Schaps 1977.

23 Pollard 1948: 376 (Aristophanes' *Birds* as 'good evidence for the bird-mindedness of the Athenian populace in the fifth century B.C.' – but see also end of section v, below); Pollard 1977: esp. chs. IX (domestic), XI (food and sport), XV (pets); Koch-Harnack 1983: esp. 97–105 (cocks as love-gifts; add here, allegedly, Pyrilampes' peacocks – section IV).

was the fact that the birds he fancied were peafowl. His motives for doing so will be canvassed below (section IV). Here, the circumstances in which he came by his initial breeding pair(s) are our immediate concern.

On the basis of an Aristophanic passage linking peafowl with envoys from the Great King of Persia (*Acharnians* 63, produced in 425) it has been suggested that Pyrilampes could have received his first specimens through a channel open only to a very few privileged Athenians, namely as ambassadorial gifts from the Great King himself.[24] This is plausible enough in so far as it is stated in a Platonic dialogue named after another of Demos' cousins (*Charmides* 158a) that Pyrilampes had made many ambassadorial journeys to the King and others in Asia. Indeed, it is by no means unthinkable that it was as a member of the famous peace-making legation headed by Perikles' associate Kallias in about 450 that Pyrilampes was presented with his original peafowl.[25] Chronology, moreover, does not rule this hypothesis out of court. By the time Antiphon composed his *Against Erasistratos* the peafowl aviary founded by Pyrilampes had allegedly been open to the public for more than thirty years (fr. 57). That allegation is unlikely (for rhetorical reasons) to be very wide of the mark; and since Antiphon was dead by the end of 411, Pyrilampes' first peafowl should have reached Athens no later than 441 or 442.[26]

Enough has been said, it is hoped, to demonstrate that Demos was an Athenian of the very highest social and economic rank and to situate him within a focus of politics and diplomacy – the 'Persian Question' – that was central to Athenian public life throughout the fifth century and beyond. We shall return later (section V) to consider his possible rôle in the peafowl drama. Now it is time to transfer our attention to Erasistratos.

Since a humble and undistinguished Athenian is most unlikely to have become entangled with an adversary of Demos' or Antiphon's (below) stature and calibre, and since the name Erasistratos is attested very rarely indeed in Classical Athens, the choice in identifying our Erasistratos lies effectively between just two men: Erasistratos (I) and Erasistratos (III), who were grandfather and grandson respectively (Fig. 2).[27] Once again, if we are

---

[24] Hofstetter 1978: 159–60; Sommerstein 1980: 160. Compare and contrast the gifts received by his son Demos in the 390s (below, n.76) and by Timagoras in 367 (which helped secure his execution: Sealey 1987: 88 and n.78).

[25] The nature, timing, and very existence of a Peace (or Peaces) of Kallias are massively controversial, but see Hill 1951: 344, Index 1.6.15 (possible evidence), with Holladay 1986; Badian 1987; and for Pyr.'s possible participation, Kienast 1973: 597–8; Hofstetter 1978: 159–60.

[26] Given Athenian rhetorical conventions, the peafowl will not have been on display for *much* more than thirty years, and on the independent arguments for the date of the trial presented below (section V) the aviary would have been opened in about 445, *ex hypothesi* just a few years after Pyr. had brought back his original pair(s) from Susa. Pyr. lived at least until 424 (when he was wounded at Delion: Plut. *Mor.* 581d) but probably not long thereafter.

[27] After Davies 1971: 524 (*PA* 13921), 'proposed with more than the usual reserve'. Erasistratos (II) is ruled out of consideration by his age – too young to have been a principal in a trial that

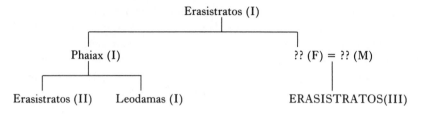

Fig. 2

looking in the right quarter, we have to do with a top-notch ambassadorial family of both economic and political distinction. Indeed, the comparability between the families of Demos and Erasistratos extends, *ex hypothesi*, to their continuity of high-profile political status during a period in excess of a century.[28] In light of the usual effects of partible inheritance and the tendency for inter- and in-marrying aristocratic families to fail to reproduce themselves either politically or physically for more than a couple of generations, such prominent continuity is quite remarkable.[29] It argues, besides brute physical fertility, political skill and economic adaptability of the highest order, especially in the radically unstable conditions of the fifth century B.C. at Athens. Not the least relevant of those conditions was the rise to effective political power of the Athenian *demos* through the *kratos* it wielded in the *dikasteria* (above, section II).

A closer identification of our Erasistratos may be postponed until the very end of this essay. Meanwhile, the attention is claimed by the only other known human actor in the peafowl play. Antiphon inevitably comes first in the *Lives of the Ten Orators* included in the corpus of Plutarch's writings, as he was the earliest in what by the second century A.D. was accounted the canon of 'Classical' Attic orators (*rhetores*) and speechwriters (*logographoi*).[30] In his brief life of Antiphon the unknown author does cite Caecilius, a respectable Sicilian Greek literary critic of the Augustan era who had tried to sift the genuine from the spurious in Antiphon's attributed corpus of some sixty works.[31] But that still did not save the author from comprehensively confusing our Antiphon (son of Sophilos of the deme Rhamnous) with two of his six known contemporary homonyms.[32]

occurred not later than 411/10 (date of Antiphon's death). As for Erasistratos son of Eraton (*PA* 5027), there is nothing apart from his name to connect him with this family.

28 The families of Kritias, Solon and Plato 'together yield a family line attested in Athens for just under three hundred years' (Davies 1971: 322), while the line of the Erasistratoi encompasses over one hundred years. Phaiax as ambassador: Kienast 1973: 597–8.

29 Compare e.g. Hopkins and G. P. Burton in Hopkins 1983: chs. 2–3.

30 [Plut.] *Mor.* 832b–834b; on the collection as a whole see Gomme 1945: 56 n.3 (a *Machwerk*); K. J. Dover in Gomme, Andrewes, & Dover 1970: 286n.1.

31 On Caecilius generally, M. Fuhrmann, *Kleine Pauly* I, 988–9; that he created or decisively shaped the Canon of Ten is doubted by Kennedy 1963: 125 and n. 1.

32 Blass 1887: 94n.; Ostwald 1986: 359–61 and n.88. See further text and n.62, below.

Such lamentable ignorance is partly attributable to the late development of the biographical genre in Greece, too late to provide reliable data even on famous fifth-century Athenians like Perikles.[33] But in Antiphon's case the general ignorance was aggravated by the singular character of his political and litigious activity. This he appears consistently to have preferred to conduct in the Athenian equivalent of smoke-filled back rooms, away from the normally mandatory glare of public exposure on the speaker's rostrum on the Pnyx or in a courtroom in the Agora.[34] It is therefore probably no accident that, despite his undoubted wealth, our Antiphon does not appear in Davies's prosopographical register. However, even though biographical reconstruction is problematic, the ancient claim that Antiphon was the first Athenian *logographos* to publish his speeches after the fact both is plausible in itself and offers an important clue to the chronology and significance of his intellectual and political trajectory.[35]

He was born probably after rather than before 480. Yet he is not reliably attested until 421, the likely date of the *Peisandros* in which the comic playwright Plato (fr. 103K) referred to him unflatteringly as 'greedy for money'; and none of his surviving writings can be dated much if at all before 420.[36] On the principle of Occam's razor, the timing of Antiphon's first public notice should indicate that it was in the 420s and not before that he inaugurated the practice of circulating commissioned forensic speeches in written form and thereby invented a peculiarly Athenian literary genre. For that innovation to be made successfully, several factors had to conspire: sufficient development of literacy and of the rhetorical art; sufficient demand at Athens for the kind of expertise embodied in published samples of the rhetorician's art; and sufficient appreciation of rhetorical skill on the part of those Athenians who were likely to judge the persuasiveness of speeches composed by professional logographers like Antiphon.

Persuasive speech of itself was no new desideratum in the fifth century, nor was it then desiderated only in Athens.[37] But in the 'city of words' it had become a desideratum of a uniquely intense and peculiarly Athenian kind, entailing nothing less than 'a change in attitude towards the use of words in

---

[33] Momigliano 1971; Cartledge 1987: 56.
[34] In the lapidary phrase of Blass (1887: 93), 'wie er im Dunkel bleiben wollte, so ist er es geblieben'; the translation of *logographos* as 'ghostwriter' (Kennedy 1963; Bateman 1966: 800) seems peculiarly apt in his case.
[35] Sources alleging Antiphon's priority are cited by Blass (1887: 95–6). For what follows in the text see esp. Blass 1887: 91–102; Dover 1950; A. Andrewes in Gomme, Andrewes & Dover 1981: 170–6, 198–201; Heitsch 1984: ch. 6; Ostwald 1986: 359–64. On his rhetorical technique, see n. 46.
[36] There may be an earlier attestation in *Wasps* 1301–2, where an Antiphon is associated with 'the high-living men about Phrynichus' (Ostwald 1986: 362; cf. Carter 1986: 65). Chronology of speeches: Dover 1950 (assigning the earliest datable speech in Ant.'s certainly genuine *oeuvre* to 422/1).
[37] Schofield 1986 (Homer); Buxton 1982: ch. 1.

this period'[38] and a privileging in the lawcourts of 'artificial proofs' (*pisteis entekhnoi*), that is rhetorical supporting arguments, over 'inartificial' (*atekhnoi*) ones such as exculpatory oaths and evidence given under torture (cf. chapter 2, section IV). Antiphon was probably not the first to compose speeches professionally for others to deliver, doubtless largely unaltered, in the Athenian lawcourts, let alone the first orator to write out the text of a speech before delivery.[39] But very probably he was indeed the first to publish commissioned speeches, making them available to the narrow circle of the lettered and leisured élite.

As such, his practice strongly parallels that of the so-called 'Sophists'. Since about 450 these mainly non-Athenian intellectuals had been selling privately what they claimed to be their unique technical expertise for practical political purposes to the select – often young and aristocratic – few, who both could afford and increasingly felt the need for their instruction.[40] In 423 Aristophanes testified obliquely to their success by viciously satirising Sophistic methods in the *Clouds*. But already in 427 the Sicilian Sophist Gorgias had reportedly dazzled a mixed public audience of mainly poorer Athenian citizens by the sheer rhetorical power of a set-piece oration (Plat. *Hipp. Ma.* 282b; Diod. XII.53.2–5 = 82A4D–K); and in that same year, if we may credit Thucydides (III.38, esp. 38.4–7), Kleon had taken to task pretty much the same Athenians for their readiness to be swayed by the deceitful cleverness of tongue-twisting intellectuals, meaning Sophists.[41] Those last two references happen to concern the Athenian Assembly, but the importance of rhetoric and the *kratos* of the *demos* were no smaller in the *dikasteria* than on the Pnyx, and the courts were probably staffed by much the same sort of citizens, if somewhat poorer on average, as those who regularly attended the Assembly (participation in which was not remunerated before 400 B.C.).[42]

By 427, then, our necessary conditions for the publication of forensic speeches had been satisfied. But are they also sufficient conditions? More precisely, was Antiphon motivated solely and merely by mercenary greed, as

---

[38] Goldhill 1986: ch. 3 (chapter-title), 202; cf. Lanza 1979: esp. ch. 2 ('Il discorso e il libro'); Buxton 1982: esp. 4, 11, 16, 24; and now Thomas 1989.

[39] Kennedy 1963: 3–14, 26–51; Lavency 1964; Bateman 1966; Dover 1968b: esp. 148–74 ('Client and Consultant').

[40] Pendrick (1987) dissents from the growing consensus – see now B. Cassin, *Gnomon* 60 (1988) 146 – that Antiphon of Rhamnous was identical with 'Antiphon the Sophist' (44 Diels-Kranz) and denies that the former taught rhetoric, but concedes the similarity between the professions of Sophist and logographer; cf. Plat. *Euthyd.* 305c, with Rankin 1983: 97 (Sophists as rhetoricians rather than philosophers; *contra* de Romilly 1988). Ostwald (1986: 363–4) cautiously favours the identification of these two Antiphons, as I do.

[41] Gorgias at Athens: Woodruff 1982: 37–8; Ostwald 1986: 243–4. Thuc. and Kleon: Macleod 1978: esp. 71; see also below, n.48.

[42] Sealey 1987: 86–7; Sinclair 1988: 123–35. The characterisation – or rather caricature – of Philokleon and his fellow-jurors in *Wasps* must on no account be taken literally. Assembly-pay: Markle 1985.

Plato Comicus perhaps scurrilously suggested, or did he entertain a hidden, political agenda as well? That is to say, was his publishing as well as writing of lawcourt speeches above all a way of conducting high (or low) politics by indirect, forensic means? It is always dangerous to assume consistency and principle of any politician, even a backroom one; and the dangers of anachronistic second sight are notorious. But in 411 Antiphon did emerge quite conspicuously as one of the moving spirits and leading theoreticians of the narrowly oligarchic counter-revolution (*metastasis*) of the Four Hundred: the speech he wrote – and, for once, necessarily delivered – in self-defence against a charge of high treason arising out of that coup adequately proves that.[43] Moreover, there is in what is preserved of that famous but unsuccessful speech a passage which, correctly read, seems to demonstrate the existence of that hidden agenda. The accusation that he had regularly composed speeches for others to deliver in court and had made material gain from the practice[44] – *that* he does not deny, in spite of the Athenian public's ambivalent attitude towards the trade of *logographia*.[45] What he does deny is that through his speechwriting (and, we may add, speech-publishing) he had aimed to bring about the coup of 411. He denies this, however, in a revealing way, indulging in his favourite argument from probability[46] while simultaneously giving it a brilliantly ironical and indeed sophistical twist: is it likely, he in effect asks, that *I* should have wished for an oligarchic régime, when under that oligarchy my speechwriting ability was politically unusable, whereas under the preceding democracy it had made me uniquely influential?

The pride of a master of his craft-skill (*tekhnē*) shines through this disingenuously rhetorical plea, and Thucydides (VIII.68.2) was no doubt justified in treating the speech as a whole as a masterpiece of oratory. But few Athenians sitting in judgement on Antiphon in 411/10 will have been swayed by that particular argument, and no more should we allow ourselves to be in the relative calm of our studies or libraries. In truth, behind the coup of 411 there lay a decade or more of patient preparation, in which the rôle of Antiphon, a major one, had been to lend or perhaps more often hire out his

---

43 Thucydides (VIII.68.1–2) both identifies Ant. as the coup's prime mover and praises the self-defence speech; cf. A. Andrewes in Gomme, Andrewes & Dover 1981: 198–201. The longest surviving fragment of what became known as the *Peri tes metastaseos*, on a papyrus now in Geneva, was first published by J. Nicole in 1907 but is best read in Thalheim; cf. W. S. Ferguson 'The condemnation of Antiphon' in *Mélanges G. Glotz*, 2 vols. (Paris 1932) 1: 349–66.

44 But Nicole's restoration – 'My accusers claim that . . . I took twenty per cent as my fee' – is both palaeographically incorrect (Gernet 1923: 165–6, citing the autopsy of V. Martin) and historically impossible (Lipsius 1915: 906 n.19). Maidment's '. . . and that The Four Hundred profited by this' (1941: 295) is no better.

45 Bonner 1927: 220–3; Lavency 1964; Dover 1968b: 155–9; 1974: 25–6; Carey & Reid 1985: vii, 13–18; Sinclair 1988: 186 and n.94.

46 For the 'rich variety of argumentative devices attested in Antiphon's extant works' (Lloyd 1979: 80 n.105) see Kennedy 1963: 125–33, 154–7, 203–4; Due 1980; Heitsch 1984; S. Usher in Edwards & Usher 1985: esp. 5–6. This particular ploy was not of course peculiar to Antiphon.

expertise as legal consultant and ghostwriter to 'front men' of variously oligarchic persuasion. In particular, his support will have been called upon by members of the upper-class sympotic groups known Homerically as *hetaireiai* ('comradely bands').

For such men were regularly – and not necessarily unjustly – selected as targets in the courts by opponents whom they then vehemently – and not necessarily justly – countercharged with being *sukophantai* (malicious or vexatious prosecutors) and *demagogoi* (mis-leaders of the People); and Thucydides (VIII.54.4) specifies the functional concentration of these 'sworn brotherhoods' (*xunomosiai*) at this period on lawsuits and elections to office.[47]

The *demos* at large was dimly aware of Antiphon's behind-the-scenes and subversive machinations, and the politically conscious democrats hated him for it. But in the short run at any rate, the *deinotes* (cleverness) of Antiphon triumphed over them.[48] Such was the subtle political operator who scripted the *Against Erasistratos*.

IV

Leaving Antiphon the ghostwriting *logographos* on one side, we pass from prosopography to peafowl, the final ingredient in our bird's nest soup. Just one page of the omnium gatherum entitled *Deipnosophistai* ('Banqueting Sophists'), which was compiled at Alexandria by Athenaeus around A.D. 200, preserves the largest collection of literary data on peafowl in Classical Greece: whence, for instance, Antiphon fr. 57 (from Athen. IX.397cd). Most of this page, however, is devoted to philological musings on the noteworthy fact that the Athenians both pronounced and spelled ταώς, their loan-word for 'peacock', with a rough breathing on the last syllable to represent the obsolete *digamma* symbol and sound (cf. Latin *pavo*). There could be no more graphic illustration of the peacock's irremediable foreignness, and more specifically its orientalism (the bird is a native of south India), to Athenian eyes and ears.[49] It was perhaps therefore mainly to avoid the stigma of barbarism that Antiphon in his speech avoided using the word altogether and substituted

---

[47] *hetaireiai/sunomosiai*: Calhoun 1913; A. Andrewes in Gomme, Andrewes & Dover 1981: 128–31; cf. Connor 1971: 25–9, 197 and n.83 (with rev. by J. K. Davies, *Gnomon* 47 [1975] 376–7). Connection of Ant.: Bonner 1927: 6; Jones 1956: 129, 172–3. Sykophancy: below, n.63. 'Demagogues': below, n.69.

[48] According to Thucydides (VIII.68.2), Ant. restricted his personal public appearances precisely because the masses (*plethos*) were suspicious of his reputation (*doxa*) for *deinotes*. The same concatenation of *deinotes, doxa,* and *plethos* at III.37.5 (speech of Kleon, 427) is surely not coincidental.

[49] P. Chantraine, *Dictionnaire étymologique de la langue grecque. Histoire des mots* IV (Paris 1980) *s.v.*; cf. Hehn 1911: 355–63 (kindly brought to my notice by Robert Sallares); Keller 1913: 148–54; Steier, *RE* XIX.2 (1938) 1414–21; Pollard 1977: 91–3. Further ornithological data in J. Bergmann, *The Peafowl of the World* (Hindhead 1980); cf. R. Dawkins, *The Blind Watchmaker* (Oxford 1986; Harmondsworth 1988) 199 (suggested evolutionary explanation of the peacock's tail).

a kind of plain man's Greek periphrasis, *poikiloi ornithes* ('spangled birds').

Specimens of peafowl may in fact have been first introduced to the Greek world on the eastern Aegean island of Samos as early as the eighth century B.C.[50] But they remained an extreme rarity, at least in Athens, down into the fourth century (Antiphanes *ap*. Athen. IX.397a); and the peafowl of Pyrilampes were almost certainly the first to be accorded resident alien status there.[51] Quite certainly, they were the only ones kept by an Athenian in a sort of aviary that was regularly opened to the general public, even if just on the first day of each lunar month. This prompts a question as to the motives of Pyrilampes and, since he continued the practice, of his son Demos.

Partly it was a matter of filthy lucre (*khrematismos*). So great were the rarity and consequent prestige-value of peafowl-fancying anywhere in Classical Greece at this time that, according to Antiphon (fr. 57), 'many people in their yearning (*pothos*) for a sight of the birds travelled from [as far afield as] Sparta and Thessaly and spared no effort to get hold of eggs' – perhaps by foul means as well as fair. It is possible that an entrance-fee was charged for admission to the aviary, but in any case the eggs will not have been given away *gratis* (except perhaps to personal *xenoi* and any other high-status individuals to whom Pyrilampes and Demos wished to pay or return a favour). Indeed, so lucrative and extensive was the 'business' side of the enterprise that a valuation of no less than 1,000 drachmas could be placed upon a – presumably breeding – pair (Antiphon fr. 58).[52] At that rate just twenty pairs would have placed Demos comfortably within the estimated tax-bracket for the compulsory liturgic payments to which only some 300–400 people at Athens were at any one time liable.[53]

This is an intriguing and unjustly neglected ramification of fifth-century Athenian economic diversification and development. But the significance of these peafowl was not confined to the economic sphere. From Plutarch (*Life of Perikles* 13.15) we learn that in contemporary comic drama Pyrilampes was

---

[50] Menodotos *FGH* 541F2; cf. Imhoof-Blumer & Keller 1889: pl. v.49; Shipley 1987: 18 and n.67.

[51] It would appear that the Greek *logopoioi* who told the cautionary tale of the Athenian aristocrat Hippokleides (Hdt. VI.130.1; dramatic date *c*.570) were unaware of its ultimate roots in the Indian story of the Dancing Peacock: Thomson 1935: 197–8. Aristophanes fr. 41 Kassel-Austin (from *Astrateutoi*, ?426) is perhaps the earliest Athenian reference to the keeping of peafowl.

[52] Admission-charge: Aelian *Hist. An.* v.21. Egg-production: Arist. *Hist. An.* VI.9, 564a25–31 (quoted *ap*. Athen. IX.397b) reports an annual clutch of a round dozen. Valuation: the alternative MS reading, '10,000 drachmas', is rightly rejected by Thalheim; S. Spyropoulos and E. Vanderpool, *Birds of the Athenian Agora* (Princeton 1985) 8 are therefore doubly wrong to report the valuation of a *single* bird as 10,000 drachmas. Pollard (1977: 91) gives the correct figure but palpably underestimates it as the equivalent of £1,000 at 1977 values.

[53] On the liturgic census (est. 3–4 talents minimum), see Davies 1981: chs. 2–3. The Athenian citizen body probably never fell below 20,000, so that the 400 or so fifth-century liturgy-payers (including some resident non-citizens) constituted at the very most just 2 per cent of this.

represented as dispatching peafowl as love-gifts to aid and abet the extra-marital *amours* of his comrade (*hetairos*) Perikles. Possibly Plutarch was right to dismiss the very idea as scurrilous slander, but it does at least show that some connection could be suggested to the public mind between Perikles, Pyrilampes, politics and peafowl. That connection, surely, was their common involvement in Persian *Ostpolitik* (above, section III). For the *ornithotrophia* of Pyrilampes (and Demos) is best explained as an exotic equivalent to the *hippotrophia* of Pyrilampes' father, that is to say, as a species of conspicuous consumption conceived as a political investment designed to secure a return of favour (*kharis*) from the Athenian *demos*.[54] It is true that exhibiting peafowl once a month was not on a par with, say, winning the four-horse chariot-race at the quadriennial Olympic Games (as Alkibiades most famously did). But regular public display of these exotic birds would constantly have reminded Athenians of Pyrilampes' successful diplomatic dealings with the Great King of Persia and thereby have helped to maintain his and Demos' elevated public status and high political profile.

V

The dramatic scene has now been set, the principal *dramatis personae* introduced, the salient exhibits rehearsed. It remains now to set them all in litigious motion in such a way as to account adequately, in terms of what we know of Athenian law, culture, society and politics in the late fifth century B.C., for the one scarcely dubitable fact in hand, namely that Antiphon wrote a speech *Against Erasistratos* which he later put into wider public circulation to eventual critical acclaim.

To begin with, it is reasonable to infer from the political and social eminence of the families most directly concerned that we are not dealing here with a one-off and purely personal dispute. Far more likely this was but a single episode in one of those long-running feuds involving 'year after year of provocation and retaliation' that were 'a conspicuous phenomenon of the upper-class society with which, in the main, extant Attic oratory is concerned'.[55] In fact, the Athenians collectively enjoyed or suffered a Hellas-wide reputation for litigiousness. However, their admittedly heavy commitment to the law-courts was due neither to some ingrained trait of character nor yet to administrative laxity but rather to the unusual degree of complexity and differentiation of Athenian society and its radically democratic political constitution.[56]

---

[54] On such politically motivated expenditure (*dapanē*) in general, see Davies 1981: esp. 97–105 (*hippotrophia*). But see also below, n.72.

[55] Dover 1974: 182; cf. Goldhill 1986: 83. Plato (*Laws* 679e) sarcastically damns lawsuits, together with *stasis* (civil strife/war), as 'techniques of warfare peculiar to city-life ... in which men concoct every possible device to damage and hurt each other by word and deed' (trans. Saunders 1970).

[56] Alleged litigiousness: Ar. *Clouds* 206–8, with Dover 1968a: *ad loc.*; Thuc. 1.77.1; naively interpreted by Jones 1956: 232 n.4; see rather Sinclair 1988: 210–11.

Thus the courts, as we have seen (section II), were a thoroughly politicised forum, the proper arena for certain types of political contest, in which business prosecuted also in the Assembly and elsewhere was naturally carried on.

It was almost inevitable therefore that public men such as Erasistratos (I or III) and Demos son of Pyrilampes should have pursued their emulous striving for 'honour' (*timē*), what Aristotle (*Eth. Nic.* 1095b19–31) characterised as 'virtually the goal of political life', in a People's Court. There men of this stamp conducted their personal and political *agon* ('contest', but also specifically 'lawsuit') before a jury deemed to stand for the *demos* of Athens, whose judgement as to both fact and law was final, and whose verdict served as a public measure of the relative *timē* of the opposing litigants.[57] Even if the developed fourth-century procedures of public arbitration designed to encourage and facilitate out-of-court settlements had been available, it is unlikely that either Erasistratos or Demos would have wished to avail themselves of them.[58]

The wonder, in brief, is not that Erasistratos, Demos and Antiphon became somehow mutually entangled in a lawsuit. The problem rather for us, as in a different sense it was for the original jury-panel, is to decide why a charge should have been brought concerning of all things peafowl. In order to resolve this, we must consider what type of suit was lodged, and by whom, and thus whether Antiphon's speech was written for delivery in person at the request of a relative or friend or on commission for delivery by a client (who might also be a personal friend or political ally), and whether it was a speech of prosecution or defence.

Taking the last point first, the obvious place to begin is with the title of the speech as transmitted by the ancient sources. Ancient titular classifications, which are known to have been recorded as early as the fourth century, are unfortunately notoriously unreliable; and in the case of the *Against Erasistratos* the title as preserved is anyway crucially incomplete, since neither the type of suit nor the charge is specified. However, the use of *pros* ('Against') in the title given by both the author of the Plutarchan *Lives of the Ten Orators* (*Mor.* 833d) and Aelian (*Hist. An.* v.21 = Ant. fr. 58) is likely to be correct, which helpfully narrows the range of formally possible procedures and charges. *Either* Antiphon's speech was written in prosecution of Erasistratos in a non-delictual private suit (*dikē*) involving some property of (or claimed by) the plaintiff.[59] *Or* it was written in defence of a litigant accused by Erasistratos,

---

[57] Striving for *timē*: Dover 1974: 227–30; Ste. Croix 1981: 80, 551 n.30. Litigation as measure of it: Dover 1974: 183; Osborne 1985b: 48–58.

[58] Arbitration, etc.: see generally Harrison 1971; briefly MacDowell 1978: ch. 4, esp. 57–61; Finley 1985: 102–3 ('openness' of the law and concern for equity implied by arbitration procedures).

[59] On the *dikē kata/dikē pros* distinction see Ruschenbusch 1969: esp. 392 (with some remarks on speech-titles at 389–90).

in a *graphē* or another kind of public suit, of having committed a crime somehow allegedly affecting the public weal.[60]

The former alternative, if indeed such a suit (*dikē pros*) actually existed, is hardly appropriate to a case centring on peafowl. The only way, therefore, to uphold the view that Erasistratos was the defendant in a private suit is to suppose, implausibly, that *pros* is an error for *kata* in the transmitted speech-title. That, in effect, is the line taken by, for example, the Loeb editor of Antiphon (Maidment 1941: 303–4). On this interpretation of the scenario Erasistratos was accused by Demos of the theft either of peafowl or of eggs. It is, I suppose, conceivable that Demos could and would have launched a private suit against a longstanding opponent on such a charge, the penalty for which in the case of property deemed to be worth more than 500 drachmas could be death or restitution of the property together with a fine payable to the plaintiff of double the claimed value of the stolen goods, and possibly five days and nights of public ridicule and physical discomfort in the stocks as well.[61] It is not so easy, however, to see why in those circumstances Demos should have gone to the lengths of commissioning a speech from Antiphon – unless Antiphon agreed to appear as a *sunegoros* (supporting advocate) because he was somehow related to Demos (whose paternal grandfather was also named Antiphon, though the name is not uncommon)[62] or agreed to do so for some other personal or political reason. But the last suggestion, at any rate, involving a public appearance in court, would seem to be ruled out by Antiphon's preferred behind-the-scenes mode of operation.

On the other hand, it is antecedently far more likely that a court case involving Demos and Antiphon would have been instigated by the lodging of a *graphē* (literally 'writ') or some other public action, in other words, that Erasistratos had brought such an action against Demos. For by so doing he could have claimed to be acting as a public-spirited citizen on behalf of the community at large rather than for the sake of any purely personal and private advantage or redress, although he would also have been careful to stress his personal enmity towards Demos so as to avoid the countercharge of sykophancy or malicious prosecution.[63] Fittingly, the penalties arising from a successful public action tended to be more severe than those resulting from a *dikē* suit, while the financial and political rewards for the prosecutor were

---

[60] In my view Gomme (1956: 634) was trebly mistaken in supposing that Ant. prosecuted Erasistratos (I) in his own behalf.

[61] On all matters regarding theft in Athenian law, see Cohen 1983, who denies, controversially, that there existed a *graphē* for theft but cogently stresses the likelihood that summary, self-help procedure would normally be preferred to litigation as a means of retaliation and redress.

[62] This possibility was suggested to me by David Harvey; cf. Humphreys 1986: 82–4 (patrikin as supporters in the courts); and Todd, this volume chapter 2 (witnesses generally as supporters). But apart from their (not uncommon) name and this trial, there is nothing to connect these two Antiphons.

[63] On sykophancy, see the papers by Osborne and Harvey in this volume (where this point is not at issue between them); on choice of procedures and their political implications, see Osborne 1985b.

commensurately greater. At the same time, however, the risks in bringing a public suit were also set higher in order to deter capricious prosecutions: a disastrous failure might lead to loss of full citizen rights on top of a heavy fine.[64]

On my view, therefore, which gives *pros* its natural meaning, much the more likely reconstructed scenario has Erasistratos prosecuting Demos in a high-status, high-risk public action. But on what charge? None of those for which we have specific evidence that the *graphē* procedure was available and used in Classical Athens fits easily or obviously a case involving peafowl.[65] But there did exist two further public procedures akin to the *graphē*, the character and function of which may be germane to Erasistratos' preoccupation with Demos and 'his' peafowl. For both *phasis* and *apographē* alleged the wrongful private possession or exploitation of public property and offered large financial incentives to a successful prosecutor.[66] The surviving 'fragments' of Antiphon's speech are compatible with this interpretation, which, moreover, yields a far more satisfactory explanation of Antiphon's rôle in the affair.

To judge from the wording and emphasis of the two longest supposedly verbatim quotations, Antiphon's client was explaining to the *dikastai* why what he consistently called the 'spangled birds' could not be given even more publicity and general accessibility than they already were. They could not be kept in the *polis* – a term which could mean either somewhere in the city-centre of Athens or specifically the sacred citadel of Athena, the *akropolis*[67] – because then they would fly away, unless their wings were clipped; but to do that would be to destroy the source of their beauty. That is a possible defence against a claim that the peafowl should have been exhibited in some public space, possibly the sacred Akropolis itself. The most straightforward basis for such a claim would have been the view that the birds were in some relevant sense public property, advanced on the grounds that it was in his capacity as ambassadorial servant of the Athenian *demos* that Pyrilampes had received his initial specimens. Athenian law, it should be added, did not recognise possession as something deserving protection in and of itself, let alone possession for a mere thirty or so years, and had only the haziest notions of ownership. Moreover, although the extremely high monetary valuation of a pair of peafowl could conceivably have been cited by Antiphon in order to discredit the mercenary motives of a prosecution by Erasistratos of Demos for wrongful possession of public property,[68] the alleged sum would quite certainly have been grist to the mill of Erasistratos were he trying to convince a

---

[64] Hansen 1976: 11–17; MacDowell 1978: 64–5, 74–5.

[65] Briefly, Osborne 1985b: 55–6.

[66] Harrison 1971: 211–17 (*apographē*), 218–21 (*phasis*); Osborne 1985b: 44–8 (commenting at 47 on the paucity of known cases of *phasis*).

[67] Thuc. 11.15.3; cf. Lonis 1983: 100–1 and nn. 44–5 (*polis* not replaced in inscriptions by *akropolis* until early c4), 107.

[68] For the successful prosecutor in a *phasis* the reward was one half of the proceeds.

jury of on the whole poorer citizens that Demos was making private super-profits at the expense of the Athenian *demos*.

Let us suppose, then, that Erasistratos brought a *phasis* or *apographē* against Demos concerning 'his' peafowl. Why, finally, did he think the game worth the candle? Did his confidence in his case stem wholly or in part from its intrinsic merits? From his own authority and skill as a litigant, or those of his witnesses and perhaps speechwriter? From such non-legal or extra-legal factors as the perceived relative status of himself and Demos, or the immediate political climate and circumstances? Or was it from some combination of all or some of these variables? An unimpeachable answer of course eludes us. But since the peafowl had been in the family of Demos and on regular public display during a period of more than thirty years already, it would not seem unreasonable to suggest that at least the timing of the prosecution was determined by the immediate political climate and circumstances.

In about 417 a particularly sharp bout of internecine strife among the leading political groups at Athens had resulted in the ostracism of the *demagogos* Hyperbolos.[69] Our Erasistratos was probably either uncle or nephew of the Phaiax who at least according to one account was centrally involved in that ostracism.[70] He would thus have been well situated and suitably motivated to take advantage of the witchhunt directed by *demagogoi* in 415 against suspected oligarchs, or against personal and political enemies who might plausibly be represented as closet oligarchs and even potential dictators.[71] Demos' ostentatious wealth and family connections (at any rate by his father's second marriage into the oligarchically minded family of Plato) made him peculiarly vulnerable to an allegation of this nature; indeed, the charge would derive no little support from the fact – if it is a fact – that Antiphon, by then surely actively oligarchic, was used as consultant defence lawyer and speechwriter. It may not be otiose to add that the very character and associations of the peacock might plausibly have been adduced in corroboration of Demos' alleged oligarchic or dictatorial tendencies.[72]

Equally conducive, I submit, to the timing of the putative prosecution were

---

[69] A. Andrewes in Gomme, Andrewes & Dover 1981: 258–64. On 'demagogues' generally (not a word used by Thuc.), see Finley 1962 ('a structural element in the system').

[70] [Andokides] IV; Plut. *Nik*. 11.10 (citing as authority Theophrastos fr. 139 Wehrli), *Alk*. 13; cf. A. Andrewes in Gomme, Andrewes & Dover 1981: 258–9.

[71] Thuc. VI.60.1, with Seager 1967; cf. K. J. Dover in Gomme, Andrewes & Dover 1970: 337 (by 415 'the Athenians regarded oligarchy and tyranny indifferently as the antithesis of democracy'); Tuplin 1985 (conceptions of tyranny).

[72] Of Demos' political inclinations at any time nothing is known for certain, but in 421 he was charged with stupidity in a comedy (Eupolis fr. 317 Kock), which is not incompatible with his being thought non- or even anti-democratic. Peacock's character: Arist. *Hist. An*. 488b24 (vanity its besetting vice); orientalism, see above, nn.24, 49. Democratic challenge to ostentatious flaunting of private wealth: Davies 1981: 115. (After giving a version of this paper in Oxford, I was told that in an Andalusian village in Republican Spain one man's ownership of peafowl was taken as an infallible sign of his anti-Republican sympathies and sufficient reason for a long jail-sentence.)

the boundlessly optimistic mood of the Athenian masses in or about 415, and the redirection of Athens' foreign policy and exponential increase of her military commitments which flowed therefrom. Not only did the Athenians then renew overt hostilities with Sparta in the Peloponnese by violating Sparta's own territory (Thuc. vi.105.2) and undertake concurrently what was virtually a second war in Sicily, but they also abandoned their longstanding *détente* with the Great King by supporting a highly placed Persian rebel in the Aegean theatre.[73] Under the new foreign policy dispensation Demos could be portrayed by Erasistratos as not simply anti-democratic but also pro-Persian. For Demos was quite probably a hereditary ritual friend (*patrikos xenos*) of Darius II, and it was an obvious and easy calumny to misrepresent that relationship as one of political collaboration and sympathy.[74]

Finally, whichever reconstruction of the trial's scenario is preferred, one further piece of evidence may support the dating of the trial to 415 or thereabouts. In early spring 414 the *Birds* of Aristophanes was produced at the City Dionysia festival. The play begins with its heroes seeking refuge from Athenian *dikasteria* (lines 38–41; cf. the coined word *apeliasta*, 'jurorphobics', at line 110); and although there is no peacock in the chorus of birds which gives the play its name, that is mainly because Aristophanes chooses not to treat the peacock as a bird at all but rather to distinguish generically between the two. Yet he does so in a seemingly gratuitous manner on two separate occasions (lines 102–3, 269), which suggests that in 415/14 peafowl were on his and his audience's mind. It is not therefore inconceivable that our peafowl case, surely a famous public event, actually inspired Aristophanes with the leading idea for his comedy.[75]

VI

As usual, the outcome of our trial is not known, but one thing at least is certain. Demos did not suffer irremediable harm at the hands – or rather voice – of Erasistratos, since he was alive, well and politically active as late as 390. Indeed, some years before then, when the Athenians' attitude towards Persia had necessarily become conciliatory, he had followed in his father's footsteps on the ambassadorial trail to the Great King (now Artaxerxes II) in

---

[73] Andok. iii.29, with A. Andrewes in Gomme, Andrewes & Dover 1981: 17–18, 369 (Athenian support of Amorges had probably begun by 414); cf. Badian 1987: 35 and n.62.

[74] Herman 1987: Appendix A includes a handful of such *xeniai* involving a Greek and a Persian Great King; cf. below, n.76 (Demos and Artaxerxes II). For comparable accusations of anti-Athenian activities in the 480s, see Herman 1987: 157 and fig. 15*a, b* (ostraka labelling respectively Kallixenos 'the traitor' and Aristeides 'the brother of Datis').

[75] Sommerstein (1987: 206) suggests that the *Against Erasistratos* 'may well have been delivered within a year or two before the production of *Birds*' but makes no other connection between them and, I feel, takes the playwright's playful taxonomy too seriously.

Asia.[76] So perhaps Antiphon's speech had helped to win the day for him in c.
415. That would at least be perfectly consistent with Antiphon's general
reputation for outstanding logographic skill and with the particular fact that
he subsequently made a written version of his speech available for different
audiences amongst whom it was rated one of his four most virtuoso productions. What, then, became of our Erasistratos? As a tailpiece I offer a
speculative and unoriginal, but none the less richly suggestive, identification.

A further judicious use of Occam's razor yields a perhaps better than even
chance that our Erasistratos should be identified with the Erasistratos who in
404–403 briefly lorded it over Athens as a member of the brutal, oligarchic
junta later justly ill-famed as the 'Thirty Tyrants'.[77] If the peafowl litigant and
the tyrant were indeed one and the same man, then our Erasistratos –
Erasistratos (III), grandson of Erasistratos (I) and nephew of Phaiax – would
join the ranks of the Athenian one-time *demagogoi* who are known to have
shed an extreme democratic persona and emerged in oligarchic plumage
during the unprecedentedly topsy-turvy decade between the exile of
Alkibiades in 415 and the installation of the Thirty.[78] As another politically
motivated litigant was to point out some years later, those who have suffered
punishment, loss or dishonour have an interest in oligarchic revolution (Lys.
xxv.8; cf. Dover 1968b: 49).

However, Erasistratos' oligarchic metamorphosis would not have been
achieved without a high degree of irony. For the junta of 404–403 was led by a
relative of his old foe Demos, namely Kritias, and one of the Thirty's
repressive measures was to ban the teaching of the art of rhetoric (Xen. *Mem.*
1.2.31; cf. Vickers 1988: 7 and n.11) – the very art by means of which .
Antiphon, despite his disingenuous disclaimer, had contributed so much
towards the first violent subversion of democracy in 411. On the other hand, if
our reconstructed scenario is on the right lines, it was also precisely through
Antiphon's deployment of that art that Erasistratos had suffered a grievous
diminution of *timē* in about 415. So perhaps his support for the Thirty's ban
was especially vociferous.[79]

Much will always remain unknown or uncertain in detail about Antiphon's
Against Erasistratos concerning (the) Peafowl. But if this essay has illuminated the peculiarly intimate and intense connection between politics and
litigation in democratic Athens, has rendered somewhat less outlandish the

---

[76] Lys. XIX.25 (at Babylon); cf. Hofstetter 1978: 48, no. 82; Wiesehöfer 1980: 21;
Vickers 1984; Strauss 1986: 194 and n.46; Herman 1987: 65–7.

[77] Xen. *Hell.* II.3.2, with Davies 1971: 523; but both Whitehead (1980: 210 [no. 5])
and Ostwald (1986: 233) remain unconvinced.

[78] Most relevantly and notoriously Phrynikhos and Peisandros: Lys. xxv.9, with
Dover 1968b: 50–1; A. Andrewes in Gomme, Andrewes & Dover 1981: 59, 116.
(Within more recent memory the careers of Mussolini and Oswald Mosley come to
mind.)

[79] Aristotle (*Rhet.* 1.11, 1370b30–71a8) expatiates on the pleasure to be derived from
revenge and competition and underlines the particular pleasure of a victory in the
courts; cf. Antiphon 'the Sophist' (but see above, n.40) 44 B 1.35–II.12 (enmity

very notion of a major political trial revolving around peafowl, and has done justice to the sorts of factors that have to be taken into account in any attempted explication of the nexus between peafowl, prosopography and pleading, it will have served its author's purpose.[80]

APPENDIX: ANTIPHON FRR. 57–9

ΠΡΟΣ ΕΡΑΣΙΣΤΡΑΤΟΝ ΠΕΡΙ ΤΩΝ ΤΑΩΝ

57. Ἀντιφῶντι δὲ τῷ ῥήτορι λόγος μὲν γέγραπται ἔχων ἐπίγραμμα περὶ ταῶν, καὶ ἐν αὐτῷ τῷ λόγῳ οὐδεμία μνεία τοῦ ὀνόματος γίνεται, ὄρνεις δὲ ποικίλους πολλάκις ἐν αὐτῷ ὀνομάζει, φάσκων τούτους τρέφειν Δῆμον τὸν Πυριλάμπους, καὶ πολλοὺς παραγίνεσθαι κατὰ πόθον τῆς τῶν ὀρνίθων θέας ἔκ τε Λακεδαίμονος καὶ Θετταλίας καί σπουδὴν ποιεῖσθαι τῶν ᾠῶν μεταλαβεῖν. περὶ δὲ τῆς ἰδέας αὐτῶν λέγων γράφει· εἴ τις ἐθέλοι καταβαλεῖν εἰς πόλιν τοὺς ὄρνιθας, οἰχήσονται ἀναπτόμενοι· ἐὰν δὲ τῶν πτερύγων ἀποτέμῃ, τὸ κάλλος ἀφαιρήσεται· τὰ πτερὰ γὰρ αὐτῶν τὸ κάλλος ἐστίν, ἀλλ᾽ οὐ τὸ σῶμα. ὅτι δὲ καὶ περισπούδαστος ἦν αὐτῶν ἡ θέα, ἐν τῷ αὐτῷ λόγῳ πάλιν φησίν· ἀλλὰ τὰς μὲν νουμηνίας ὁ βουλόμενος εἰσῄει· τὰς δ᾽ ἄλλας ἡμέρας εἴ τις ἔλθοι βουλόμενος θεάσασθαι, οὐκ ἔστιν ὅστις ἔτυχε. καὶ ταῦτα οὐκ ἐχθὲς οὐδὲ πρώην, ἀλλ᾽ ἔτη πλέον ἢ τριάκοντά ἐστιν.　　　　Ath. IX 397 CD.

58. ἐτιμῶντο δὲ τὸν ἄρρενα καὶ τὸν θῆλυν δραχμῶν χιλίων, ὡς ᾽Α. ἐν τῷ πρὸς ᾽Ερασίστρατον λόγῳ φησί.　　　　Aelianus H. A. V 21.

59. εὐοφθάλμως ἀντὶ τοῦ εὐπρεπῶς ᾽Α. ἐν τῷ περὶ ταώνων.　　　　Harp.

57. There is a speech by the orator Antiphon which has the title *Concerning Peafowl*. In the speech itself there is no mention of the word 'peacock', though he often refers to the 'spangled birds'. These he says were kept by Demos son of Pyrilampes, and many people in their yearning for a sight of the birds travelled from Sparta and Thessaly and spared no effort to get hold of eggs. Regarding their appearance he writes: 'If one were to bring the birds down and leave them in the *polis*, they would fly clean away. But if, to prevent that, one were to clip their wings, the source of their beauty would be removed. For it is in their wing-feathers, and not in their bodily form, that their beauty resides.' To show that the sight of them was indeed eagerly sought after, he says again in the same speech: 'On the first day of every month anyone who wishes is admitted. But on all other days absolutely no intending visitor is ever allowed in. And that has been the case, not just since yesterday or the day before, but for more than thirty years.'

58. They placed a valuation of 1,000 drachmas on a male–female pair, as Antiphon says in the speech *Against Erasistratos*.

59. 'Sightly' instead of 'becoming' (is used by) Antiphon in the *Concerning Peafowl*.

---

necessarily arises between a litigant and his adversary's witness — and so presumably his *logographos* too?).

[80] After its original presentation to the Cambridge Ancient History Seminar, versions of this essay were read in Bristol, Leeds and Oxford. To all those who offered comments in discussion, and especially to David Harvey, David Lewis, Paul Millett and Stephen Todd, who criticised the penultimate written draft, I am deeply indebted. But I, not they, am *hupeuthunos* for the final result.

4

Plato and the Athenian law of theft[1]

TREVOR SAUNDERS

'En cette matière, les *Lois* deviennent presque un modèle de confusion
inintelligible'.

(Gernet 1917a: n.49)

In the *Laws* of Plato, three elderly gentlemen go for a walk in the mountains of
Crete. One is effectively Plato himself, in thin disguise as an 'Athenian
Stranger'; the others are Kleinias, a Cretan, and Megillus, a Spartan. As they
walk, they fall to discussing plans for the foundation in the south of the island
of a 'practical' utopia, Magnesia, second-best to that of the *Republic* in being
governed not by the personal discretion of philosopher-kings but by the rule of
law. In furtherance of this project they formulate a new, radical penology; and
by drawing on and adapting the laws of Athens they equip their proposed state
with a model penal code in which that penology is meant to be embodied.
Certain parts of this code deal with theft. What does Plato make of this
extensive and important area of law? What are his reactions to Athenian
practice, and why and how does he modify it?

I   THE PLATONIC LAWS OF THEFT, NAKED

For the sake of clarity, I first set out the bare provisions of Plato's laws of theft,
without reference to historical Athenian law, and sharply shorn of their
contexts and the sometimes lengthy explanatory and exhortatory matter which
penetrates and surrounds them. In this naked form, they certainly seem to
justify Louis Gernet's despairing assessment.

---

[1] This essay is a slightly adapted version of one chapter of *Plato's Penal Code* (Clarendon Press,
forthcoming). I am grateful to the editors of *Nomos* for valuable suggestions regarding substance and presentation, and to the Institute for Advanced Study, Princeton, where in the
autumn term of 1986 I studied and wrote under ideal conditions. Unattributed references are to
the *Laws*. All translations are taken from Trevor J. Saunders, *Plato, The Laws: Translated
with an Introduction* (Penguin Classics, Harmondsworth 1970), © Trevor J. Saunders 1970,
and are reproduced (some with slight modifications) by permission of Penguin Books Ltd.

Passage A: Sacrilege[2] (854d1–855a2)

If a man is caught committing sacrilege, and he is a slave (*doulos*) or a foreigner (*xenos*), a brand of his misfortune shall be made on his face and hands, and he shall be whipped, the number of lashes to be decided by his judges. Then he shall be thrown out beyond the boundaries of the land, naked. . . . If a citizen (*polites*) is ever shown to be responsible for such a deed, . . . his penalty is to be death, . . . [and he will be] held in ignominy and banished from sight beyond the borders of the state.

Passage B: The comprehensive law (857a2–b3)

Again, a single law and legal penalty should apply to a thief (*kleptes*), no matter whether his theft is great or small: he must first pay twice the value of the stolen article, if he loses a suit of this kind and has sufficient surplus property over and above his farm with which to make the repayment; if he has not, he must be kept in prison until he pays up or persuades the man who has had him convicted [to let him off]. If a man is convicted of stealing (*klopē*) from public sources, he shall be freed from prison when he has either persuaded the state [to let him off] or paid back twice the amount involved.

Passage C: 'Diminished' theft (914b6–c3)

If . . . someone picks up an object of no great value and takes it home, and he is a slave, he should be soundly beaten by any passer-by who is not less than thirty years of age; if he is a free man (*eleutheros*), in addition to being thought ungentlemanly (*aneleutheros*, literally 'unfree') and lawless, he must pay the person who left the article ten times its value.

Passage D: Theft[3] from private sources (933e6–934a1)

When one man harms another by theft or violence and the damage is extensive, the payment he makes to the injured party should be large, but smaller if the damage is comparatively trivial. The cardinal rule should be that in every case the sum is to vary in proportion to the damage done, so that the loss is cured. And each offender is to pay an additional penalty appropriate to his crime, . . .

Passage E: Theft from public sources (941d4–942a4)

If anyone successfully prosecutes in court a foreigner or slave on a charge of theft of some piece of public property, a decision must be reached as to the fine or penalty he should pay . . . If a citizen . . . is convicted of plundering or attacking his fatherland,

---

[2] That 'sacrilege', *hierosulia*, is a species of theft, *klopē*, is shown below, pp. 69–70.
[3] The word *klepton*, 'stealing' (933e6), may have a wider reference than theft, and cover any kind of stealthy act, of which theft would be then a typical example. At any rate theft can hardly be excluded: note 'all' (*panton*) *klopaion*, 'acts of theft/stealth', 934c4.

whether he is caught red-handed (*ep' autophoroi*) or not, he must be punished by death
. . .

Passage F[4]: *Theft from public sources by officials (946 d2–e4)*

When they [the Scrutineers, *hoi euthunoi*] have sat in judgement, either privately and individually, or in association with colleagues, on those at the end of their term of office in the service of the state, they must make known, by posting written notice in the market-place, what penalty or fine in their opinion each official ought to pay. Any official who refuses to admit that he has been judged impartially should haul the Scrutineers before the Select Judges, and if he is deemed innocent of the accusations he should accuse the Scrutineers themselves, if he so wishes. But if he is convicted, and the Scrutineers had decided on death as his penalty, he must die (a penalty which in the nature of the case cannot be increased); but if his penalty is one that it is possible to double, then double he must pay.

II EXPULSION OF THE BOGUS LAW

The puzzles are obvious. After the straightforward law of sacrilege (A), we have the very different set of provisions in B, which are explicitly stated to apply whatever the amount of the theft, whether the source is public or private (or indeed sacred, as Kleinias notes, 857b5), without sociological distinction between offenders, or any regard to motive or circumstances. A further set of provisions applies in C to the removal of property of little value which is not in the immediate custody of its owner. D presents another law, restricted to theft from *private* persons.[5] E presents yet another, restricted to theft from *public* sources. Finally, F presumably embraces *inter alia* theft by officials, presumably of public money or property; but at first sight it differs from E in not making the death penalty mandatory for the citizen.

This is a dissipated and unhelpful mode of lawgiving. Plato is capable of better. For instance, in the lengthy sequence of important legislation which occupies approximately the last two-thirds of book IX there is evident striving for order and clarity.[6] Even in the less complicated sections of his legal code, in which the offences spill forth in only loosely systematic sequence and are often dismissed quite briefly, Plato usually rounds off his treatment of one before embarking on another. The fragmented nature of his law of theft is wholly exceptional. What accounts for it?

The key is the structure of the *Laws* and its penal code as a whole. By the end of book VIII some 40 offences have been dealt with; many, as the Athenian Stranger notes in the opening paragraph of book IX, concerned agricul-

---

[4] That this passage embraces theft is suggested below, pp. 78–9.
[5] 933e6 *allon*, 'another *person*'.
[6] The genera, (i) homicide, (ii) wounding, (iii) assault, and the species of (ii), come in descending order of seriousness; the species of (i) come in ascending order, followed by 4 brief appendices on special cases; (iii) is a complex but principled sequence of regulations, dealing with *all* varieties of assault.

tural affairs and were relatively trivial. In some cases the range of penalties was left open-ended; but the most swingeing penalties, notably death and exile, have not even been mentioned, let alone made mandatory. Now, however, more serious crimes are in prospect: 'sacrilege, and all the other similar crimes which are difficult or impossible to cure' (854a). The law of sacrilege (A and related material) follows accordingly; a description of procedure in capital cases ensues. Subversion and treason are then described; both naturally attract the death penalty. Finally, we are told that a 'single law' of procedure (865e5–857a1) should apply to all three offenders, temple-robber, traitor, and subverter of the laws of the state.

We now encounter passage B. Its opening words are obviously intended to link it closely to the laws of subversion, treason and sacrilege. In those cases, a 'single law' prescribed a single legal procedure *and mode of punishment*.[7] Similarly, a 'single law and legal penalty' is to apply 'again', this time to all thieves without distinction (857a3–4). The connection is slightly strained, in that the law of sacrilege, at least, did provide for variation of punishment, as between citizen and non-citizen; but the single law of theft permits no variation whatever, at any rate in the sense that all thieves without exception pay double.

Now this latter proposal is a very odd one, as Kleinias immediately complains:

How on earth can we be serious, sir, in saying that it makes no odds whether his theft is large or small, or whether it comes from sacred or secular sources? And what about all the other different circumstances of a robbery? Should not a legislator vary the penalties he inflicts, so that he can cope with the variety of thefts?

The Athenian Stranger smilingly agrees: for this example has shown that the business of laying down laws has not yet been 'properly worked out' (857c). The three interlocutors have not yet achieved their aim of becoming legislators, and some further explanation is needed of how to legislate for sacrilege, all theft, and all acts of injustice (859b). In short, there is a strong presumption that in formulating B they have in some way got the law of theft wrong.

The function of B now emerges quite clearly. It is merely to serve as a foil to the long and crucial penological excursus on which the Stranger immediately embarks, with the purpose of showing the proper way to prescribe penalties.[8] The course of this excursus is serpentine, and bedevilled by textual cruces; but its central conclusion is certain enough, namely that punishment should never be inflicted vindictively or retributively, but always for the purpose of the 'cure' of the criminal. Certainly, an injured party is always entitled to exact recompense from the offender; but that is not a *penal* measure. Effective 'cure'

[7] 856e5–6; but *dikon* may mean not 'punishments' but 'trials'.
[8] 859c–864c. See my summary in Saunders (1970: 367–9), which is based on my detailed analysis (1968). The most valuable of recent discussions is by Schöpsdau (1984).

demands accurate diagnosis of the criminal's 'unjust' psychic state; and his penalty, which is distinct from the recompense he has to pay, must be carefully calculated to fit his state of mind, in order that it may be 'cured'. Hence the elaborate differentiations of punishments found throughout Plato's penal code.[9] It follows that Plato would never tolerate a law of theft without a single such differentiation. The law of theft in passage B is therefore bogus. It is a piece of coat-trailing,[10] destined to be corrected and superseded. When, after the laws of homicide, wounding and assault in book IX, and the lengthy theodicy that occupies the whole of book X, we come at last to the genuine laws of theft in books XI and XII, their defective predecessor has been entirely forgotten.

When the 'normal business' of legislation is resumed at the start of book XI, passage C occurs within two pages; it is prompted by a discussion of the unauthorised removal of buried treasure. Twenty pages later comes passage D; it is part of a *generalised* description of the various ways in which one person may harm another, a description apparently stimulated by a set of laws relating to certain highly *specific* ways of inflicting injuries, i.e. by drugs etc. Passage E appears after a further eight pages; the mention of Hermes, a god who delights in theft, brings that topic into Plato's mind. Passage F then occurs after only a further six pages, in connection with the duties of Scrutineers. In all these cases Plato proceeds by a loose association of ideas: he allows one topic to trigger another. Seen in this light, his untidy mode of presenting his law of theft has a certain rationale, or at least an intelligible genesis.

It is, however, necessary to spend a little longer in the company of passage B. For David Cohen, in two recent publications,[11] takes it very seriously indeed. He believes it to be the definitive statement of certain parts of Plato's law of theft, and to embody its central principle, 'one law, one penalty'; other passages are to be interpreted in harmony with it. This attempt to iron out the explicit and implicit discrepancies between B and every other passage seems to me unconvincing.[12]

(1) Cohen does not explain certain suspicious, or at least striking, discrepancies between B and the law of Athens on the one hand, so far as we know it, and between B and the laws of Magnesia on the other:

    (i)   Indefinite imprisonment until payment of a fine – usually but not always when the state is itself the aggrieved party – is certainly known in Athens; but it is not known in the law of theft.[13] But this of course is an *argumentum ex*

---

[9] How Plato supposed the pain of a punishment could *cure*, brute deterrence apart, is too large an issue to discuss here.

[10] This is not a new suggestion: cf. e.g. Vering 1926: 181 n.90 ('Anknüpfungspunkt'), and Knoch 1960: 11 ('Kunstgriff').

[11] Cohen 1982, and 1983: esp. 116–30. He is the first to have attempted a systematic study of Plato's law of theft in its relation to Athenian law, a most welcome venture.

[12] Not least because he ignores D (and F) entirely. 'It is not until 941 [E] that the promised consideration of theft [859b] finally comes' (121).

[13] Harrison 1971: 242–4; Rhodes 1972: 151; MacDowell 1978: 166–7, 257.

silentio; and even if the provision did not apply in that law, Plato may be making an innovation.

(ii)   Formal 'letting off' (*aidesis*, not that the word occurs in в) by a victorious litigant, of an imprisoned person unable to pay a fine, seems similarly unattested. It is, however, not wholly unlikely in practical terms,[14] and Plato may again wish to innovate, by building it into his law.

(iii) The general arrangements for the execution of judgement in Magnesia, in disputes between private persons, make no provision whatever for imprisonment (958a–c), nor indeed, as we have seen, does any other passage relating specifically to theft.

(iv)   However, those regulations regarding inability to pay a fine which occur only just before passage в (but which may refer only to cases in which the state is the aggrieved party) do indeed specify 'long imprisonment open to public view, and various humiliations' (855a–c). This suggests something like the stocks; but it is surely implausible to suppose that such exposed confinement, though long, would last indefinitely, at the pleasure of the victorious prosecutor – who is not even mentioned, let alone given licence to 'let off'.

(2) In в, the private prosecutor and the state are obviously both injured parties. In a Platonic state, it is wholly unlikely that the penalty would not be more severe for injuring the state than for injuring a private person (see 884ff).

(3) Cohen takes the word which in в I translate 'from public sources', *demosiai*, as referring merely to 'theft of private property from public places'. But the passage clearly implies that the public is the *injured party*; the location is not at issue.[15] Moreover, if that is all *demosiai* means, there would be no separate provision here, in a law which is obviously intended to be comprehensive (as Kleinias noted), for theft from public sources, an omission which in a Platonic state is inherently unlikely. The vagueness of 'in a public way' is all Plato needs for the purpose of what is a non-law anyway.

(4) Most crucially, Cohen (1983: 118) supposes that Plato subscribes to 'one overriding principle: one law and one penalty for theft, regardless of amount or circumstances'. But that would be quite alien to the elaborate attention Plato frequently pays to such considerations, as determinants of penalty, elsewhere in the code. Indeed, he would abominate the principle;[16] for as a tool of reform it is blunt. Plato is anxious to fit penalty/cure to the precise mental state, character and circumstance of each individual criminal.[17]

---

[14] In spite of the implications of Dem. xxiv.125, 135; cf. Barkan 1936: 339–40, Partsch 1909: 78 n.2. *Aidesis* is of course known in homicide law.

[15] MacDowell (1984: 231) rightly argues that the contrast between 'persuades the man who has had him convicted' and 'has . . . persuaded the state' clinches the matter. Cohen (1983: 120–1) sees no conflict between в (allegedly wholly about private property) and е (public property).

[16] *Pace* also Schöpsdau (1984: 109). Note how 859bc recognises 'every [variety of] theft', *pases klopes*: it is a complex thing, and like assault (*to tes aikias pan genos*, 879b, 'assault of every type'), requires a *range* of penalties.

[17] 933e–934c; cf. the concern for precision of diagnosis and prescription at (e.g.) 866d ff. and 878e (cf. *Phaedrus* 270a–272b). We may reasonably assume that the more elaborate of such passages are models for the laws without such analyses: the Magnesian jurors are to act in the spirit of the former (cf. 718b and 876de).

That penalties should vary freely, often at the discretion of the judges, is essential. B is therefore flatly inconsistent with Plato's radical and reformative penology, in particular with its fundamental distinction between recompense and 'cure'.

Perhaps that is why Cohen does not notice the possible significance in B of the word 'first' [the thief must pay double]. Conceivably, the double is merely recompense; 'second' would come punishment/cure. But as Plato has not yet drawn the distinction between recompense and cure, and B is to be abandoned anyway, he simply drops the point.[18] To be sure, a gap in a law does not rule it out as a law; but the oddity of a 'first' without a 'second' needs to be accounted for.

So I again conclude that, as a serious statement of Platonic law, passage B is fundamentally vitiated both by its context and by its content. Contrary to his usual practice, and uniquely among the six passages,[19] Plato provides no explanation or justification – because none is available. On the contrary, he indicates that B is quite unsatisfactory.[20] It is therefore pointless to attempt to reconcile the other passages with it.

We now turn to passages A and C–F. Close examination of them in their context demonstrates that the consideration which controls their form and content, and their differences from Athenian law, is Plato's new penology. We shall, however, be handicapped by the fact that although the corpus of the Athenian orators is huge and constitutes the main source of our knowledge of Greek law, no surviving speech deals with theft; we have only incidental references. Further, the laws of theft seem not to have been enacted as a single unified corpus, but at different dates and piecemeal, without regard for overall consistency. At any rate, they exhibit considerable variety and intricacy.

III   THE PLATONIC LAWS OF THEFT, CLOTHED

Passage A: Sacrilege (853b1–855a4)

Like the Athenian orators, Plato does not define sacrilege, but it seems to me certain that he means at least broadly what they meant; if his understanding of it had been substantially different, he would have explained just how. In spite of Cohen's useful review of the evidence,[21] I am not persuaded that Lipsius

---

[18] Note that even if B does confine itself to recompense, serious contradictions with A and C–F remain: notably, recompense in D seems only single recompense, not double, and in A and E an offender can hardly be executed *and* 'kept in prison till he pays' (B). (England (1921), on 857a5, says that 'first' 'marks off the case of the man who can pay from that of the man who cannot'. Perhaps; but 'first' suggests a sequence, not an alternative.)

[19] Except F, where strong disapproval of misdemeanour by officials, and the appropriateness of a possible death sentence, are simply taken for granted.

[20] Cf. the 'bare' law of marriage, which is, however, unsatisfactory not so much in itself as because it lacks explanation: 720e–723d, with 772de, 774a, 785b.

[21] 1983: 93–100; cf. 128. Pollux VIII. 40 indicates the charge was a *graphē* (a 'public' suit, which could be brought by anyone, as distinct from a *dikē*, which was open to the injured party only).

(1905–15: 442–3) was far wrong in taking the word to mean 'theft of sacred objects from sacred places'. By 'sacred objects' I mean *valuable* sacred objects (statues, arms, money, implements etc. of precious metal or other material),[22] not the trivial things like wood and water mentioned in the inscriptions Cohen marshalls (1983: 99, cf. (1) on 102). As he says,[23] 'The "standard case" of *hierosulia* as theft of sacred property from temples is clear, for this is the type of case described in what Athenian evidence there is.' I have little doubt that theft of such objects from anywhere would indeed constitute sacrilege;[24] but normally it is in temples that they are found. Given the orators' lack of interest in the precise definition of offences, this is about as far as we can go; and Plato makes the same assumption as they do, namely that one just does know what *hierosulia* is.[25]

The Athenian Stranger introduces (853b–854a) the law of sacrilege by explaining that slaves and foreigners are likely to be the most frequent offenders. The reasons are psychological, and are expressed partly in medical terms: not having had the education enjoyed by citizens, they will be open to the 'disease' of wishing to commit this and similar crimes, which are 'hard or impossible to cure'. The penalties now follow; they incorporate briefly their psychological/penological justifications:[26]

(a) *A slave or a foreigner* should have a brand of his 'misfortune' (*sumphora*, i.e. his criminality) put on face and hands, be whipped as much as his judges decide, and be thrown naked out of Magnesia. For perhaps by paying that penalty he will become 'better', 'having been made restrained' (*sophron*). No *dikē* imposed by law aims at evil, but usually makes the punished person 'either better or less wicked'.

(b) *A citizen* who does 'such a thing'[27] must be regarded as incurable, suffer death ('least of evils'), and by being thrust out of sight beyond the borders of the state in ignominy serve as an example to others. The justification advanced for inferring incurability is that in spite of his education and

---

[22] E.g. the robes mentioned in Dem. xxv, hypothesis 1–2.

[23] 1983: 115; cf. the sources on 96, esp. Dem. LVII. 64.

[24] Cf. Cohen 1983: 97–100, esp. Xen. *Hellenica* 1.7.22.

[25] He speaks at 853d5–6 of a law *hieron peri suleseon*, which probably means 'pillaging of temples', but could mean simply 'pillaging of sacred objects'; at 854a7–b1 *hieron* probably has the latter sense. To judge from 955e–956b, the objects to be found in Magnesian temples will not be valuable; they will be cherished and protected precisely because they are holy. In historical states, of course, they needed protection not only for that reason but because of their sheer monetary value.

[26] 854d1–855a. 885b1 casually reveals that the law covers sacrilege 'by force and by stealth'.

[27] Glossed immediately (854e) as 'having committed one of the great and unspeakable acts of injustice in regard to gods or parents or state'. Cohen (1983: 128) rightly notes that thieves of public property also commit plunder (*sulan*) against their fatherland (942a). He could have added 931a, where we learn that parents are 'shrines', and 869b, where the killer in anger of a parent is liable to swingeing penalties of *hierosulia*, because he has 'plundered' (*sulesas*) the soul from his begetter; likewise the voluntary killer of a parent at 873a 'deprives' the body of a parent of its soul. The gloss in question seems then to embrace not only *hierosulia* as such but theft from public sources and part of the law of homicide, not to speak of subversion and treason (856b–857a).

nurture he has not refrained from the greatest evils. In short, the determinant of penalty is psychological assessment of curability.

The address to the person tempted to commit sacrilege runs in full:

My dear fellow, this thing that at present drives you to sacrilege is neither human nor divine. It is a sort of goad (*oistros*), innate as a result of acts of injustice of long ago that remained unpurified (*akatharton*) by men;[28] it travels around working destruction (*aliteriodes*), and you should make every effort to take precautions against it. Now, take note what these precautions are. When any of these thoughts enters your head, seek the rites that free a man from pollution (*apodiopompeseis*), seek the shrines of the gods who avert evil (*theoi apotropaioi*), and supplicate them; seek the company of men who have a reputation in your community for being virtuous. Listen to them as they say that every man should honour what is fine and just – try to bring yourself to say it too. But run away from the company of the wicked, with never a backward glance. If by doing this you find that your disease abates somewhat, well and good; if not, then you should look upon death as the preferable alternative, and rid yourself of life.[29]

A considerable commentary could be written on this remarkable passage; here I try merely to extract its significance for the penalties Plato prescribes.

It is fundamental that at some time *injustice* has been committed, for which the injured party, whoever he is, has not received recompense in the form of purification. We are surely in the realm of homicide, or at least of some equally serious offence;[30] the injured party is probably a murdered person whose killer has not given satisfaction to him or his relatives in the form of purification, or perhaps exile or death. His resentful desire for reciprocal justice[31] in the only form available to him has as its tool the 'itch', *oistros*, to commit sacrilege; it is a tool that may be wielded either by himself or by a surrogate, perhaps the Furies (cf. Euripides, *IT* 1456). Neither dead men nor surrogates are *men*; but they are not gods either. They belong to some sinister intermediate world, where, having lost track of the original offenders, they – or rather the itch – still wander round blindly trying to inflict reciprocal suffering on somebody, no matter whom.[32] That suffering is not just the itch itself: it is the *punishment* for the offences which the itch prompts the person to commit. This theme is an old one.[33]

The crudely vindictive reciprocal justice which the *oistros*-wielders seek to

---

28 *Oistros*: 'itch', 'strong yearning'; cf. 782e, *Timaeus* 91b, *Phaedrus* 240d, 251d.
29 854b1–c5. On the technical terms, see Parker 1983, esp. 109 (*aliterios*), 28–9, 373 (*apodiopompesis*), 220 (*apotropaios*).
30 E.g. assaults on parents (880e ff.; note *aliteriodes*, 881e4); cf. *katharasthai* and *apodiopompesasthai* of the property of major criminals (877e).
31 The fury of the dead man is important in Plato's homicide law: 865d–866b.
32 Plato is obviously aware of the kind of 'subculture' of debased religion represented for example by the *katadesmoi* ('binding spells') placed in tombs, whose operation depended on the assumption that a dead man's anger could be diverted to targets chosen by cursers: see *Republic* 364c, and *Defixionum Tabellae* ('curse tablets') in general. Much as he deprecates such practices (933a–e), he is prepared to exploit for his own ends the beliefs which inspire them.
33 Herodotus II.139; Dem. XXIV.121; Dover 1968a: 272, on *Clouds* 1458–61.

enforce is of course grossly *un*just, in the sense that the person assailed by the urge to commit sacrilege has done nothing to deserve it.[34] The temptation comes to him involuntarily, like a disease; and a disease is precisely what the *oistros* is; for Plato seeks in this passage to marry religion and medical penology.[35] Religion and medicine had a noticeable overlap of vocabulary and concepts, notably 'purification' (Parker 1983: ch.7, esp. 213–21). Plato exploits the overlap for his own purposes. If the *oistros* to commit sacrilege is a mental disease, it may be cured by mental regimen:[36] not only must the tempted person resort in pious faith to purificatory and prophylactic rites of religion, but he must associate with good men and say what they say, that everyone must honour what is fine and good. In other words, by echoing the moral doctrines of good men a tempted person can diminish his moral disease; for we all tend to believe what we ourselves say.[37] Social, religious, and mental regimen should be resorted to curatively and prospectively, in the hope that it may prevent the offence. In effect the cure for the *oistros* is simply a particular application of that regimen which is submission to the educational and religious influences which bear on the Magnesian at every turn. Plato blends religion, psychology and medicine: the *oistros* of religious thought = the *epithumia* of psychology = the *nosos* of medicine; for, as we know from the *Timaeus*, mental diseases are, like physical diseases, physical configurations of a physical soul, and are curable, as they are, by the appropriate type of regimen.

A man who finds nevertheless that he still has the urge to commit sacrilege had better die; for it is better to die sinless than to suffer the pains of sin after death (959bc). Does that mean he should commit suicide? If so, he will be justified by the second and/or third of the criteria given in the law about suicides: obedience to a legal decision of the state, and the compulsion of some excruciating and unavoidable disaster (*tukhē*: 873c6). For sacrilege *is* a misfortune (*sumphora*), which is branded on the face and hands of the slave or foreigner who commits it – a misfortune in the sense that wickedness ineluctably entails suffering; hence one never really wants to be wicked, and if one does so want, it must be 'involuntarily', in the Socratic sense.[38]

After all this, it is easy to see why Plato regards a citizen who commits sacrilege as incurable. The penalty is the same as in Attic law: death without

---

[34] It is worth reminding ourselves that Plato distances himself from this injustice: it belongs neither to the world of men (where there is potentiality for good) nor to the world of gods (who do no evil); cf. 933a. The *oistros* is a wayward 'surd' in the scheme of things; but we have to take account of it, just as we must the 'wandering cause' of the *Timaeus* (48a), to which England (1921), on 854b, compares the 'wandering' *oistros*.

[35] The medical content occurs at 853d8, 854a3, c4, e4.

[36] In medicine, Plato is a partisan of regimen, as against drugs (*Timaeus* 89a–d, cf. *Republic* 405d–408b).

[37] In committees, this is called 'falling for your own propaganda'. (England (1921), on 854c2, splendidly misses the point: 'a curious recipe for inducing belief'.)

[38] Cf. 881e4, the *aliteriodes tukhē* catchable from the assaulter of a parent, and Parker 1983: 218–9, 268. *Oistros* leads to misery: *Republic* 577b ff., esp. e; cf. 573b1 and *Laws* 734a ff.

burial in the state;[39] but while Attic law also confiscated the offender's property, the peculiar conditions of land-tenure in Magnesia forbade it, as Plato goes on to explain immediately.[40] When he describes the penalties for slaves and foreigners he explicitly (and incredibly) envisages that they may serve to make 'better'. Such persons have not been exposed to the Magnesian education, and cannot be said to have betrayed it; there remains some hope that the pain and shock of punishment will induce self-control.[41] We cannot say exactly what the 'writing of the misfortune on face and hands' means; presumably it is some sort of tattooing (Jones 1987: 146–9, esp. nn.39, 47, 58). Expulsion naked beyond the confines of the country might be enough to kill. But even if the man survives, and is cured, Magnesia itself, apparently, will not benefit, since he will no longer be resident in it. At any rate, a metic (an alien registered as resident in Athens) would have suffered the same penalty as a citizen (Lysias v), and so too presumably would an itinerant alien (and perhaps a slave – we simply do not know).[42] So formally the foreigner in Magnesia is punished less severely, though more elaborately, than the foreigner in Athens; and this innovation is a direct consequence of Plato's penology.

Passage c: 'Diminished' theft (914b1–e2)

When in passage E Plato deals with theft from public sources, he describes the thief of a small piece of public property as simply 'the thief', but the thief of a substantial piece as 'the remover of what he has not deposited' (941c5–d1). He thus brings theft of public property under the general prohibition of 'removing what one has not deposited' (844e), which is in turn connected with the celebrated maxim, 'don't move what is not to be moved' (684e, 842e). On the same grounds, just before passage c, the simple removal, as distinct from outright theft, of lost or abandoned property is similarly forbidden (913a–914a). Such property is under divine protection, and the case of any man removing valuable treasure-trove must be referred to Delphi (with a hint that some awful divine punishment awaits him). Plato then, in passage c, applies

---

[39] Diodorus Siculus xvi.25; Xen. *Hellenica* 1.7.22, *Memorabilia* 1. 2.62, Lyk. *Leocrates* 65, Cohen 1983: 101 n.22, cf. Parker 1983: 170 ff. Hansen (1976: 45–6) argues that *hierosuloi* were liable to *apagogē*: cf. pp. 75–7 below on 'aggravated' theft, Lipsius 1905–15: 443 n.88 and Cohen 1983: 102–3.

[40] 855a ff: except in certain extreme cases (856c–e), Magnesia's *kleroi* are inalienable from the owner's family.

[41] At 854a3, 'hard to cure' may refer to the actions of foreigners and slaves, but 'impossible to cure' to those of citizens (cf. 854e4). In theft of public property too we see the same pattern: slaves and foreigners are punished less severely than citizens (passage E), though precisely how is not specified; but it is certainly, and interestingly, implied that the punishment even of non-citizens is cure: 941d4–942a1.

[42] There is no need to assume uniformity of practice. Unless an itinerant was a citizen of a state with which Athens had a judicial agreement, he could find himself in the same position as a slave: liable to summary punishment without trial. At any rate, the penalties of itinerants and slaves would hardly be *less* than that of the citizen and metic.

'the same rule' to every object, great or small, that has been 'left' or 'lost': if a slave removes it and takes it home,[43] and it is *small*, he must be whipped by any passer-by over thirty years of age; if a free man does so, he must be accounted 'ungentlemanly and no sharer in law', and he must pay the person who left the object ten times its value. (The restriction 'small' seems to apply to both thefts, though the Greek is not quite clear.) Plato then describes the procedure under which ownership may be settled in case of dispute (914c3–e2).

One is perhaps left to assume that removal of a *valuable* object would be dealt with by some further regulation, but none is given; or perhaps Plato believes he has already dealt with the point in the provisions about treasure; most probably, he would deal with it under regular theft (passage D). For the apparent restriction to 'small' makes good practical sense. On the whole, one does not 'lose' a large object of some value, like a wagon or a plough, except by outright theft – which is provided for under the relevant law of theft from private sources (D); and even if one 'loses' something automobile, such as a pig, one does not abandon ownership, but searches. But if one inadvertently loses something trivial, or deliberately leaves it somewhere for some reason, intending to collect it later, its status will not always be clear to the finder: is it just 'left', or actually abandoned? To appropriate it, on the blithe assumption[44] that the owner has effectively relinquished ownership, is neither theft nor not-theft:[45] it betokens some minor psychic injustice, which may be cured by a beating for a slave, and for a free man by social disgrace and repayment on a scale which in point of the multiple is large (ten times), but, since *ex hypothesi* the object is of small value, will not amount to much.[46]

Plato's discussion of 'lost property' is surprisingly lengthy, and this may be some indication that he felt he was supplying a gap in Attic law, in which, as Cohen[47] has pointed out, the concepts of 'appropriating' and 'stealing' tend to merge, the word 'lose' being used ambiguously. Plato succeeds in effect in inventing a formal category of 'diminished' theft; and his ruling consideration is that to find and appropriate a small thing is less 'unjust' than to find and appropriate a large one such as treasure (where the assumption of abandoned ownership is implausible), and less unjust than regular theft by force or fraud. Again, psychological considerations seem to have led to innovation and reform.

---

[43] As Cohen notes (1983: 126), taking home may be 'an objective requirement for liability'. The remover can argue he is not stealing but 'removing for safe keeping', *vel sim.*; but the plea is less plausible if the article is (in use?) in his home.

[44] One can always find a reason: cf. 913b1–3.

[45] As Cohen rightly notes (1983: 124), the words for 'theft' do not occur in this section. It is the concept of 'not removing what one has not deposited' that provides the link with theft.

[46] Cohen (1983: 125), however, regards the penalty as 'severe', and suggests (126) a connection with the (debatable) ten-fold fine for private theft (see p. 75 n.50 below).

[47] 1983: 64–8, 126 on Dem. XXIV.105, Lys. XXIX.11, Arist. *Problems* 952b21, Hesiod *WD* 348.

Passage D: Theft from private sources (933e6–934c6)

Whenever one man commits theft or violence against another, he must pay compensation up to the point at which the harm is cured. A further penalty should be suffered or paid; it is to be calculated in the light of a number of elaborately detailed psychological considerations, e.g. overpersuasion of youth, pleasure, pain, envy, anger. This penalty is not for the sake of the past crime, but to encourage 'abatement' of the offender's 'misfortune' (*sumphora*, i.e. his criminality; cf. p. 70).

It is quite clear that the passage legislates for theft from private sources, that the injured party is to receive simple (but full) recompense, and that any extra payment is curative.[48] No upper or lower limit is prescribed: apparently the scale of this 'extra' is to vary open-endedly in direct proportion to the seriousness of the psychic state. Here then is what we need in a law of theft: recompense and cure, firmly distinguished.

At the end of the passage Plato indicates that the legislator must sketch, for the guidance of judges, the types of penalties that ought to be imposed on the various categories of theft and violence. This apparent promise to relate specific penalties to specific crimes is never fulfilled, at least in the systematic form suggested. At any rate, Plato obviously envisaged a law of theft which is more finely graded than that of passage B.

What was the law of Athens on private theft? Certainly a *dikē klopēs* existed;[49] the penalty varied according to whether the stolen article was recovered by the owner or not. If it was, the offender paid the injured party twice the value in addition; if not, he paid the article's value, *plus* that value multiplied either by two or by ten.[50] The court also had discretion to order five days and nights in the stocks in addition to the payment, by way of inflicting social disgrace.[51] In certain circumstances[52] it was permissible to resort to

---

[48] It is not stated to whom the 'extra' is paid, whether to the injured party or to the state; but *mekhriper*, 933e9, suggests *not* to the injured party, who receives payment 'right up to' (but not beyond?) full compensation. Nor is an indication given of the legal procedure: one assumes a simple *dikē klopēs*, private suit for theft.

[49] Dem. xxiv.114, Cohen 1983: 62–8. On the possible existence of a *graphē klopēs* from *private* sources, see Dem. xxii.26–7, Cohen 1983: 44–9, MacDowell 1984: 229–30, Harrison 1968: 207 n.1.

[50] The text of Dem. xxiv.105 says 'ten'; but 'two' (cf. 114) would make the position of the injured party the same in both cases, and Heraldus' emendation to that effect has been almost universally adopted. However, 'ten' should not be too firmly ruled out: see Cohen (1983: 62–4).

[51] Dem. xxiv. 105, 114. The origin of the provision is discussed by Rhodes (1981: 161). On the location of the stocks, see Barkan (1936: 338–9).

[52] Day-time theft of more than 50 dr., theft of equipment of a value higher than 10 dr. from harbours or gymnasia, theft of minor articles from certain public places: Dem. xxiii.60, xxiv. 113–14, Isoc. xv.90, Aesch. i. 91, *A.P.* 52. 1, MacDowell 1978: 148–9, Hansen 1976: 36–53. Cf. also Dem. xxii.26, *ephegesis*, leading the Eleven to the thief. The special provision relating to the use of force suggests that the kind of theft normally dealt with by a *dikē klopēs* was carried out by stealth alone; cf. Cohen 1983: 90. Red-handedness may have been the defining characteristic of theft in which self-help followed by the death penalty was possible: Cohen 1983: 58–61, but cf. MacDowell 1984: 230–1. Caravan 1984, however, argues that summary execution was distinctly unusual.

various degrees of self-help. (a) One could arrest (*apagogē*) the thief and take him to the board of officials called 'The Eleven', who kept him in prison till the trial; the penalty on conviction was death. (b) Thieves who were caught red-handed (*ep' autophoroi*) and confessed guilt were summarily executed by the Eleven. (c) In the case of theft at night, or when force was used on the person of the owner, the latter could kill the thief with impunity.

This mixed picture is presumably the result of an historical process.[53] I assume, but cannot prove, that the extreme specificity of the provisions for those cases which may be called collectively 'aggravated' theft (a–c above) indicates that this part of the law is a relic of unrestricted self-help: because these particular thefts were 'so serious' or 'so easy' (MacDowell 1978: 148), or because they were connected social problems, or for all these reasons, the law still permitted, or had at some point reintroduced, self-help – but self-help restricted to theft *at night, over certain sums, from certain places*. In the absence of a confession, there had to be trial; and the infliction of the penalty had to be in the hands of officials, not of the arrester (except for theft at night, and when force was used). Thefts not meeting these criteria would presumably have had to be dealt with by a normal *dikē klopēs*, which I take to have been introduced either before or simultaneously with those restrictions.[54]

Now if that reconstruction is right, and if one may argue from Plato's silence on the topic of 'aggravated' theft,[55] he has achieved a radical simplification of Athenian law. He has pushed it even further in the direction in which it had already gone naturally, of relying on public trials rather than on self-help. He has swept away most of the Athenian apparatus of self-help against private theft,[56] and with it the possibility of the death penalty for the theft of quite trivial things and in special circumstances. He probably limits the injured party's recompense to simple damages, and certainly abandons the single inflexible penalty awarded in the *dikē klopēs*, a fine calculated in terms of a fixed multiple of the value of the theft.[57] Crucially, he substitutes *open-ended*

---

[53] Cf. Ruschenbusch 1984, Cohen 1983: 75, Gernet 1959b: esp. 394–5, 399; cf. in general Latte (1968: 286–94).

[54] Dem. xxiv.113–14, for what it is worth, attributes most of the regulations for aggravated theft to Solon.

[55] One slight indication that we can so argue is that Plato says 'red-handedness' is irrelevant to theft from public sources (passage E), and we may probably assume *a fortiori* that it is irrelevant to private theft also. If so, then given its importance in Athenian aggravated theft, aggravated theft too may be taken to have been dropped as a separate category.

[56] Cf. Cohen 1983: 120–1. There are two exceptions: the night-time thief and the *lopodutes*, 'snatcher of clothes' (see Cohen 1983: 79–83) may be killed (874bc). Yet even here there is the same tendency to be parsimonious in the scope allowed to self-help: the thief has to be *breaking into the house*, and the *lopodutes* may be killed *only in self-defence*. Cohen (1983: 72–83) has a discussion of the relation of these provisions to Attic law.

[57] In Athens, suits were either *timetoi*, 'needing an estimate', or *atimetoi*, 'not needing an estimate'. In the former, the prosecutor and defendant each made an estimate (*timesis*) of the penalty to be awarded in case of conviction, and the court had to adopt one or the other. In the latter, the penalty was fixed by law. Where Plato does not specify penalties in his code, he takes *timesis* for granted, but is strikingly insistent on the discretion to be allowed to the *jurors* to fix

penalties, not necessarily related to the value of the theft, but adjusted to psychic states and calculated to promote each criminal's self-control.[58] The discretionary period of five days and nights in the stocks also disappears; but it could no doubt be used if the court decided it would constitute an effective cure. In short, the crude two-fold distinction of Attic law between 'simple' and 'aggravated' theft, and the crude alternatives – stocks apart – of a fine or death,[59] are largely replaced by a single category of theft from private sources, and by a single sliding scale of penalties based on motives and psychic states.

Passage E: Theft from public sources (941b2–942a3) and
Passage F: Theft from public sources by officials (946d2–e4)

A brief prelude to E decries crimes of violence and theft, and the belief that since the gods commit them they must be legitimate. Plato then argues as follows:

(i)   The pilferer and the greater thief deserve 'the same' *dikē*, penalty/justice.
(ii)   *For* the former has stolen with 'the same' love/lust, *eros*, but with less power, *dunamis*; whereas the latter commits injustice, or is unjust, *adikei*, to the full.
(iii) *Therefore* the law demands a lesser penalty for one thief than for another because the one would probably, *isos*, still be curable, the other not.
(iv)   The law does *not* so demand because of the amount of the theft.
(v)   A slave or foreigner is probably curable, and the penalty must be assessed open-endedly; a citizen is incurable, and must therefore die.

To say the least, the train of thought is curious. How can the penalties be 'the same', when as we learn in (v), they are to be different?[60] In interpreting this passage it is essential to realise that, contrary to what the reader of (i)–(iv) is tempted to think, the pair of thieves in (iii) is *not* the pair in (i) and (ii), the pilferer and the greater thief, but the pair in (v), the citizen and the non-citizen.[61] The argument hinges on 'therefore' at the start of (iii). The

penalties, presumably without being limited to accepting one of the two estimates (876a–e, and cf. Gernet 1951b: CXLII–CXLIV). The Athenian *dikē klopēs* seems to have been an 'estimated' suit (Dem. XXIV.114): the estimate (presumably of the disputed object's value) adopted by the court was the basis of the assessment of the multiple. If Plato permitted *timesis* in trials for private theft (914bc and 954b2 may suggest it), he limits its employment to the assessment of *recompense*, and entrusts the assessment of *penalty* to the informed judgement of the jurors. To that extent, he shifts from an adversarial to an inquisitorial system. Most of A, all of C, and part of E, are on the face of it *atimetoi*; cf. however 876d7–e3.

58 *Sophronistuos heneka*, 934a1, cf. *sophron* in A(a), p. 70.
59 In Athens, death of the offender presumably robbed the injured party of any 'extra' recompense: the death was his only 'satisfaction'. Plato *guarantees* him his (simple) recompense: note *para panta*, 933e8, 'above all'.
60 I find Cohen's attempt (1983: 121–2) to answer this obvious difficulty, in effect to reconcile E with B, hard to follow. For how can one inflict (on the principles of B) the 'same' penalty, 'regardless of amount and circumstances', and at the same time sharply vary penalties (death etc., in E) 'according to internal moral states'?
61 I am indebted to Professor P. J. Rhodes and Dr J. G. F. Powell for this suggestion.

pilferer has the same lust as the greater thief, but contingently enjoyed less power or opportunity to indulge it (ii). So he too is 'fully' unjust, and incurable; hence he deserves the same penalty as the other (i). *Therefore* variations in penalty will not depend on the comparative amounts of the thefts, but on some other consideration, namely whether the thief is curable; on this criterion, the non-citizen *is* probably curable, the citizen is not. The doctrine is harsh: any theft, however tiny, from the resources of his own state by a citizen betokens ineducability and therefore incurability: he is plundering and violating the fatherland.[62] The basis of differentiation of punishment is therefore sociological, as in sacrilege.

No mention of recompense is made, nor of the legal procedure to be used; possibly there would be a *graphē klopes*, under the provisions of 767bc. Nor is the point of the stipulation, 'whether caught red-handed or not', made clear.[63]

What, in Athens, is the counterpart of this law? At first sight, it is the *graphē klopes demosion khrematon*, the public suit for theft of public money (or objects?); this charge could be brought at their 'audit' or 'scrutiny', *euthuna*, against officials about to demit office; the penalty was a fine of ten times the amount stolen.[64] Yet Plato, in passage F, has his own special procedures for the conduct of audits: the Scrutineers are to judge the conduct (presumably including financial conduct) of officials at the end of their term of office, and can apparently impose any penalty including death.[65] Obviously E is not in conflict with these provisions, and could indeed provide the justification for imposing the death penalty in F on officials judged at scrutiny to have stolen public property;[66] yet its scope seems far wider, covering *all* theft of *all* public property (*demosion*, 941d5, cf. c5) in general, and embrac-

---

[62] 942a1–4. Cf. Arist. *Rhet.* I, 1374b28: the thief of three consecrated half-obols would stick at nothing.

[63] See Cohen 1983: 123–4. I suspect that if E is a Platonic innovation (see below), he wished to make clear that just as (by implication, see pp. 75–7 above) in D, the time and circumstances of the offender's *detection* do not affect assessment of his mental state.

[64] Cohen 1983: 49–51, *Ath. Pol.* 48. 4–5, 54. 2, Dem. XXIV.112, 127, cf. Aesch. III.22–3, Andok. I. 74 (who adds *atimia*, a disqualification from some citizen rights). MacDowell (1984: 229–30) believes the *graphē* could be brought other than at the audit. Another *graphē* (if indeed it existed) concerned theft of sacred property, *hieron khrematon*, for which also the penalty may have been ten times the sum at issue: Ant. II. α. 6, Dem. XIX. 293, XXIV. 111, Cohen 1983: 100–2. It was also possible to prosecute, at any time, by means of an 'impeachment' or 'denunciation', *eisangelia*, before the *boulē* or *ekklesia* (e.g. Hansen 1975, case 143); in this event either the death penalty or a fine could be imposed. See in general Hansen (1975) and Rhodes (1979); the details are complex and controversial. On variations in penalties, see Cohen (1983: 51 n.56); I have followed Hansen 1975: 33–6. (As Piérart (1973: 450) points out, Plato has scrapped *eisangelia*: no doubt he mistrusted such democratic procedures, and thought his select body of Scrutineers more suitable for the important and specialised job of examining officials: cf. Hyp. IV.1–3, Morrow 1960: 219–29, esp. 227–9.)

[65] Evidently on their own authority, unlike in Athens, where cases were referred to courts; cf. n.64, on *eisangelia*.

[66] Especially as the immediately preceding lines, 941a1–b1, concern misdemeanours by officials (on embassies etc.).

ing, among the potential thieves, the categories of foreigners and slaves, to whom scrutinies are irrelevant, since they could not hold public office.

E seems then simply to deal with theft of public property by a private person, whether citizen, foreigner or slave. Cohen (1983: 49 n.46) reports that 'no text describes theft of public property by a private citizen [in Athens]'. If the lacuna is not simply a lacuna in our sources but an indication of a gap in Athenian law,[67] then Plato, anxious as always to provide fully against offences against the communal interest, supplies the need. So F includes theft of public property by officials;[68] E deals with theft of public property by private persons; D[69] caters for theft of private property by private persons.

IV LEGISLATION AND PENOLOGY

What emerges from these lengthy complexities? In sum, that Plato has both abridged and expanded Athenian law, partly in order to rationalise and simplify, but chiefly under the guidance of a penology based on the psychology of the criminal. Once the law in B has been ruled out as unsatisfactory, he can be seen to meet its deficiencies by providing a graduated set of penalties for a variety of thefts exhibiting psychic 'injustice', on an ascending scale:

C.   *Mild* 'injustice' is catered for in a new formal category: quasi-theft, which is simply the picking up of some trivial thing which the thief fondly hopes has been abandoned.
  Penalties: *Slave*:   a whipping.
        Freeman: reputation   for   ungentlemanliness   and   tenfold repayment to depositor.
  It is sufficient to rely on social pressure and a slap at the offender's pocket.
D.   *Normal* 'injustice', shown in theft by private persons from private sources, is of variable intensity: the offender may be young and overpersuaded by the folly of someone else, or be a victim of his own foolish emotions and desires.
  Penalties: Stated without sociological distinctions: suffering or fines graded open-endedly in direct ratio to the seriousness of the vice and its presumed curability. Psychic disorder thus becomes the single determinant of the severity or mildness of the penalty (but *not* of the amount of the recompense). Practically the entire self-help procedure against theft of Athenian law is thrown overboard, and with it most of the differentiations of punishments depending on considerations of the hour and location of the theft, and the value of the stolen object.
E.   *Serious* 'injustice' is displayed in theft from public sources. It is however not calculated by reference to the value of the theft. The determinants of psychic

---

67 Obviously such offences had to be catered for somehow, perhaps by a *dikē* (or *graphē*?) *klopes*, or by a *graphē klopes demosion khrematon*, independently of any *euthuna* (audit, scrutiny).
68 Cohen's remark (1983: 122) about E (public property), that 'no distinction is made . . . between theft by officials and theft by private citizens', though true, hardly matters, in view of F.
69 Not (*pace* Cohen 1983: 118 and 129) B, which should *not* be 'read together' with E (public property) as he suggests (121–2), in disregard of D (private property).

state and hence of penalty are status-distinctions: slaves and foreigners who steal from public sources are 'probably' curable, but citizens are not.

Penalties: *Slave and foreigner*: suffering or fine calculated open-endedly,
        as in D.
 Citizen: death.

The law seems to cover all theft from public sources by all persons whatever. No separate provision is made for financial malfeasances of officials, but the law of E would justify or demand the death penalty at audit (see F). So whereas Attic law permitted death or fines, probably according to procedure, Plato seems to permit, to judge from E, only the former. *Eisangelia* is suppressed.

A. *Very serious* 'injustice' is exhibited in sacrilege; it is traced to an overpoweringly strong desire, which comes from some supernatural but not divine source. Elaborate advice based on religion, psychology and medicine is given prophylactically.

 Penalties: *Slave and foreigner*: branding and expulsion naked.
 Citizen: death, expulsion from state.

In A, C, and E the penalties are differentiated by socio-political groups; in C foreigners are bracketed with citizens as free, and are therefore not to suffer the degradation of a whipping, but with slaves in A and E, in which the citizen is isolated as a particularly heinous offender against the gods and the state that nurtured him. There is a general tendency for incurability to be more readily assumed, and for penalties therefore to increase, in proportion to the grandeur of the interest offended: individuals (C and D), state (E and F), gods (A).[70]

Although the Attic penal code was certainly capable of distinguishing formally between voluntary and involuntary acts (e.g. in homicide), the law of theft, so far as we know, was framed without reference to intent; that is to say, it assumed that everyone knows roughly and intuitively what theft objectively is, and left the subjective elements, intentions and excuses, to be argued out in the speeches delivered at the trial.[71] In this respect it must have been typical of a great many offences; and indeed the lack of any reference to intent in any Athenian law of theft is natural enough: one can easily kill without wishing to, but if theft means something like 'stealthy removal of another's property', then it is difficult (though not impossible) to claim that one did *that* involuntarily. However that may be, Plato does for theft what in principle he does for his

---

[70] Cf. 884a–885a. The open-endedness of some penalties, however, imports some uncertainty about what their application would have been in practice. Compare the tinge of hesitation in E (*schedon*, 'pretty well' incurable, 942a3) with the confident inference in A (854e4).

[71] See Cohen (1983: 86–91). If, as he suggests (90), *Ath. Pol.* 51.1 implies that thieves hauled by *apagōgē* before the Eleven were killed if they merely admitted the objective act, even if they advanced apologies and excuses ('I genuinely but mistakenly thought the object was mine', *vel sim.*), then in *apagōgē* 'objective liability' applied, and one would either have to deny the deed itself to get a trial (so would it not usually be denied?), or at least supply a *prima facie* title to the object one is alleged to have stolen. (Objective liability would be appropriate to a procedure that obviously developed from self-help.) If that was indeed the practice, then Plato's apparent abolition of *apagōgē* for theft becomes the more significant: he is opposed to strict liability, precisely because it ignores calculation of states of mind.

penal code as a whole: he provides an outline of the considerations jurymen should bear in mind when reaching verdicts and sentencing.[72] The discretion of Athenian jurymen to formulate their own criteria would have been far greater. Not that Plato is interested in excuses or aggravations as such, as a means of arriving at reciprocal justice; his sole concern, recompense apart, is to establish curability or incurability, and if the former applies, to estimate that punishment which will be the most effective cure. For efficient treatment of a disease demands its efficient diagnosis. Here as elsewhere his attention to mental states is in advance of Attic law: he builds them into his code.

Cohen (1983: 119) rightly states Plato's position, that 'the legislator's evaluation of an act must not be based upon external circumstances, but rather the moral state of the actor'. But he is quite wrong in supposing that this approach 'justifies the principle of uniform penalties', or 'one law, one penalty'. As my summary of Plato's law of theft shows, Plato applies, if anything, a more complicated, or rather a more flexible, range of penalties for theft than Attic law. His law is 'one' only in the sense that it provides for penalties in accordance with a single criterion: the relative intensity of the 'injustice' in the offender's soul.

Cohen (1983: 119–20) also detects 'competing motivation', in that Plato's 'philosophical theory' conflicts with his 'larger political concerns'. He claims 'clear inconsistency' between his penology and the provisions that 'two similarly situated offenders may meet with vastly different fates depending simply upon the fortuity of external circumstances; how much property they have, whether or not someone else is willing to lend them the money, whether or not they are let off by the injured party, etc.' It is helpful here to remember Plato's firm distinction between backward-looking recompense and forward-looking curative penalty. If x is prepared to supply money to y to enable y to pay recompense, that is not a penal matter. Only if y cannot pay a fine intended as a penalty would his bailing-out be inconsistent with Plato's penology, and then only if the bailing-out were a gift and not a loan.[73]

Plato legislates for theft in a decidedly broken manner, for which the artistic structure of the *Laws* may in part be to blame. Naked, his scattered provisions are a puzzling and incongruous collection. Garbed in his penology, and after the expulsion of the rogue law of B, they are an impressive array, with a clear and consistent rationale. I find no sign that they were conceived and written by someone whose mental powers were failing. Plato the statesman and legislator is firmly in control, and knows exactly what he is doing. He takes Athenian law as basic; he excises, he supplements, he re-shapes; and he

---

[72] See especially 934bc (the continuation of D). Note too the brief assessment of an intention/state of mind at 874b8: the night-time entrant to a house is acting 'for purposes of (*epi*) theft'. The receiver of stolen goods must *know* them to have been stolen if he is to be punished as the thief is (955b; cf. Cohen 1983: 84–6).
[73] On bailing-out, see 855b. Unqualified letting-off is found only in B.

splices it to a reforming 'medical' penology. It is perhaps a tribute to the quality of the historical model that a philosopher of Plato's persuasion can see fit to retain many of its contours. Indeed, his procedure in the case of theft is fundamentally the same as in the other parts of his legal code.

5a

Vexatious litigation in classical Athens: sykophancy and the sykophant

ROBIN OSBORNE

I   WHAT WAS A SYKOPHANT?

General histories of classical Greece ignore the sykophant: sykophants do not get into the indexes of Bury's *History of Greece* (even as revised by Meiggs, ed. 4, 1975), Hammond's *History of Greece* (ed. 3, 1986), Davies' *Democracy and Classical Greece* (1978), Hornblower's *The Greek World* (1983) or *The Oxford History of the Classical World* (1986). Even in books specifically about classical Athens they make but a fleeting appearance: Jones' *Athenian Democracy* (1957) has two references, Connor's *New Politicians* (1971) one, Ostwald's monumental *From Popular Sovereignty to the Sovereignty of Law* (1986) devotes only two paragraphs expressly to them in more than 500 pages, and Sinclair's *Democracy and Participation* (1988) has one paragraph and half-a-dozen passing references. The implication would seem to be that none of these scholars regards the sykophant as a significant actor on the stage of Greek history, or even of Athenian democracy.

Works on the Athenian legal system, on the other hand, give sykophants a prominent, or even a very prominent place. Bonner and Smith devoted a whole 35-page chapter to them (1938: 39–74), and there is a five-page discussion in MacDowell's *Law in Classical Athens* (1978: 62–6), quite apart from the monograph on them by Lofberg (1917). More important than the length of these discussions, however, is the interpretative tendency lying behind them; for these writers, sykophancy was a 'curse' (Bonner & Smith 1938: 69), a 'disease' (Lofberg 1917: 23) and, more importantly, a profession (Lofberg 1917: 24). The generally accepted position is neatly summed up by Rhodes (1981: 444–5) when he defines the sykophant in the following way: '*sukophantes* ... is applied frequently by Aristophanes and later Athenian writers to the men who took advantage of the laws allowing prosecution by *ho boulomenos* on "public" charges ... to make a profession

83

of prosecuting, in order to obtain the rewards offered to successful prosecutors or payments from the victims or their enemies . . .'.[1]

In this paper I shall raise objections to both the general and the specialist treatments of the sykophant. Against the general tradition I will argue that sykophancy was vitally important to the nature and running of Athenian democracy; and against the specialist tradition I will maintain that there were no sykophants, in the sense that there was no class of people who could be called professional prosecutors motivated purely by pecuniary considerations.

Central to this enquiry is the problem of defining the sykophant. The term *sukophantes* is widely used in a great variety of contexts, but it is always a term of abuse, with no straightforward polite equivalent. Classical authors invariably employ the term in an argumentative context. The historian's problem is how to tell whether this sykophant invoked by comic writers and forensic orators is anything more than a straw man, whose features it is expedient to attribute to real opponents. Just as a portrait painter's image of an individual may give no emphasis at all to those physical features which cartoonists delight in emphasising to excess, so the historian who simply reproduces a tendentious caricature is failing to exercise properly critical historical judgement. It is not difficult to write a history of the use of the word *sukophantes*; the problem is how to tell anything from that history about the working of the Athenian legal system and Athenian society.

The great Victorian expert on the orators and the Athenian courts, Charles Rann Kennedy, described the sykophant as 'a happy compound of the common barrator, informer, pettifogger, busybody, rogue, liar and slanderer' whose methods included 'calumny and conspiracy, false accusation, malicious prosecution, threats of legal proceedings to extort money, and generally all abuse of legal process for mischievous or fraudulent purposes'.[2] As a description of the figure evoked by the orators this is fine, but more recent scholars, while quoting Kennedy with approval, have attempted to reduce this composite description to a 'core' meaning. Yet how are primary uses of *'sukophantes'* to be distinguished from secondary? Arbitrarily to isolate certain senses of the term as primary can only lead to circularity of argument.[3]

---

[1] Compare Bonner & Smith 1938:42 'It was only when men made a profession of prosecution for financial gain that public opinion was hostile. Such persons were known as "sykophants"...'; and also Sinclair 1988: 73. More bluntly, Harvey (1985: 78 n.7) writes: 'The sykophant was a professional blackmailer, informer and prosecutor.' Contrast Fisher 1976b: 36–7, who, in the best short treatment of sykophants, writes: 'A special term, *sukophantes*, was applied to anyone involved in prosecutions of which one strongly disapproved.'

[2] In Smith 1848 s.v. *'Sucophantes'* and in Kennedy 1894:345. In English writing of the sixteenth century 'sycophant' was used both in its classical sense of 'informer' and in its modern sense of 'flatterer'; thereafter the sense of 'informer' is rare except in writing about classical Athens. The sense of 'flatterer' is already found in Latin New Comedy (and compare the association of informer and flatterer in Menander fr.223 Kock). For the narrow divide between informing and flattering in a ruler's court compare Hall, *Chron. Hen. IV* 2b: 'He ... was very glad (as tell tales and scicophantes bee ...) to declare to the king what he had heard.'

[3] There is something close to a *petitio principii* both in Lofberg's statement (1917: ix) that 'It was natural that ... the term [sycophant] came to be used for all scoundrels. However such

The definitions of the sykophant given by the orators themselves are persuasive definitions aimed at furthering the speaker's argument, and they cannot serve as a secure starting point for an historical enquiry into what a sykophant was.[4] I want to start not from the texts in which sykophant is defined, but from those where the meaning of sykophant is assumed, and in particular from metaphorical uses of the term sykophant. Communication itself is endangered if an author or speaker is radically redefining the terms he employs in his metaphors, and there is therefore some justification for believing that in the metaphorical use of a term an irreducible core of significance is uncovered. That the same features are in question in all the metaphorical references to sykophantic behaviour further strengthens this belief.

Plato, in *Republic* I, has Thrasymakhos expostulate, 'You are a sykophant, in these arguments, Socrates', after Socrates pushes the logic of Thrasymakhos' statements harder than Thrasymakhos wishes, to bring out implications which Thrasymakhos is unwilling to espouse. In the ensuing discussion Thrasymakhos retreats to a position with which he defies Socrates to quibble (*sukophantein*), and Socrates protests that he would no more try to play the sykophant with Thrasymakhos than he would try to shave a lion.[5]

Aristotle makes a similar point in a more general context in the *Topics*, where he writes, 'Similarly too if he has made a statement, when the subject which is being defined bears several senses, without distinguishing them; for then it is uncertain of which sense he has given the definition, and it is possible to make a sykophantic allegation on the ground that the description does not fit everything of which he has given the definition'; and again, 'It is possible to make a sykophantic allegation against one who has spoken metaphorically, representing him as having used the word in its literal sense.'[6]

The metaphorical use of 'sykophant' is not confined to philosophers: Demosthenes, a frequent user of the word, comments, 'But it might be claimed that I'm being sykophantic on this point', after a detailed quibble about the exact wording of a law and its implications.[7] All those metaphorical uses focus upon

extension in the use of the term has no part in this study', and, especially in view of the use of 'sykophant' in the Demosthenic private orations, discussed below, in the claim of Bonner & Smith (1938: 72) that 'In the nature of the case sycophants could rarely avail themselves of *dikai*.'

[4] See e.g. Lys. xxv.3, [Demosthenes] LVII.34, Aesch. II.145 (discussed below), Lyk.I.31.

[5] Plat. *Rep.* 1,340d1: συκοφάντης γὰρ εἶ, ἔφη, ὦ Σώκρατες, ἐν τοῖς λόγοις. 341a5: εἶεν, ἦν δ'ἐγώ, ὦ Θρασύμαχε· δοκῶ σοι συκοφαντεῖν; πάνυ μὲν οὖν, ἔφη. οἴει γάρ με ἐξ ἐπιβουλῆς ἐν τοῖς λόγοις κακουργοῦντά σε ἐρέσθαι ὡς ἠρόμην; 341b9: τὸν τῷ ἀκριβεστάτῳ, ἔφη, λόγῳ ἄρχοντα ὄντα. πρὸς ταῦτα κακούργει καὶ συκοφάντει, εἴ τι δύνασαι. 341c2: οἴει γὰρ ἄν με, εἶπον, οὕτω μανῆναι, ὥστε ξυρεῖν ἐπιχειρεῖν λέοντα καὶ συκοφαντεῖν Θρασύμαχον;

[6] Arist. *Topics* 139b24–7: ὁμοίως δὲ καὶ εἰ τοῦ ὁριζόμενου πλεοναχῶς λεγομένου μὴ διελὼν εἶπεν· ἄδηλον γὰρ ὁποτέρου τὸν ὅρον ἀποδέδωκεν, ἐνδέχεταί τε συκοφαντεῖν ὡς οὐκ ἐφαρμόττοντος τοῦ λόγου ἐπὶ πάντα ὧν τὸν ὁρισμὸν ἀποδέδωκεν. 139b34–6 πᾶν γὰρ ἀσαφὲς τὸ κατὰ μεταφορὰν λεγόμενον. ἐνδέχεται δὲ καὶ τὸν μεταφορὰν εἰπόντα συκοφαντεῖν ὡς κυρίως εἰρηκότα· οὐ γὰρ ἐφαρμόσει ὁ λεχθεὶς ὅρος.

[7] Dem. xxiii.61: ἀλλὰ νὴ Δία συκοφαντοῦμεν τὸ πρᾶγμα. Compare Menander fr. 635 Kock: 'The laws are exceeding fine; but the man who observes the laws too scrupulously appears to be

captiousness, quibbling which pulls apart the arguments of others in an overprecise and literalistic way. The connotations are by no means totally negative. Demosthenes anticipates criticism in order to disarm it, but he is clearly not afraid that the possibility that his argument will be seen as sykophantic itself destroys his point. Plato acknowledges that Socrates' methods might be held to be sykophantic, but this is presumably not meant to make the reader ridicule Socratic dialectic or disregard Socrates' particular arguments here. The sykophantic allegations referred to by Aristotle draw attention to features which he does think it important to avoid since they are sources of obscurity and confusion. Clever speech clearly was enough to raise the flag 'sykophant', but that flag did not render the clever point made ineffectual.

If we can trust the ancient lexica, 'being sykophantic' was also used metaphorically in a rather different way which also focuses on the 'niggling' aspect of sykophantic activities. The *Etymologicum Magnum* and the Souda both claim that 'Plato and Menander' used the verb *sukophantein* in the sense of to tease or stimulate sexually.[8] If this is true, Plato and Menander were in part playing on the verbal and metaphorical connection between figs and female genitals, but they may also have been alluding to procedures characteristic of those labelled sykophants.

Skill in speaking, ignored by modern definitions of the sykophant, is central not only to this metaphorical use of the term but also to Isocrates' definition in the speech *Against Euthynos*. 'Those who are clever at speaking but poor', Isocrates claims, 'are particularly keen to bring sykophantic allegations, and their favoured victims are those who are incapable as orators but able to pay out cash.'[9] This definition is very much in the interests of the rich man who fears that he will lose the argument, and it seems to have become standard to allege sykophancy in any case where a poor man was involved as plaintiff.[10] Nevertheless, this claim that the sykophant is a blackmailer who brings a prosecution solely for the reward, either in or out of court, has been emphasised in modern scholarly treatments of the sykophant.

a sykophant' (καλοὶ οἱ νόμοι σφόδρ' εἰσίν· ὁ δ' ὁρῶν τοὺς νόμους / λίαν ἀκριβῶς συκοφάντης φαίνεται).

8 *Etymologicum Magnum* 733.47 and Souda s.v. συκοφαντεῖν both claim that 'Plato' and Menander use the verb in the sense of κνίζειν ἐρωτικῶς. Kock assumes that the Plato in question is not the philosopher but Plato the comic poet (Plato Comicus frg. 255) and conjectures that Plato and Menander may have used not συκοφαντεῖν but συκάζειν, citing Hesychius s.v. συκάζει. Adler (*Suidae Lexicon*, Leipzig 1935) s.v. συκοφαντεῖν suggests a reference to Plato *Rep.* 340d (above n.5) is intended, but to my mind nothing is added to that passage by substituting κνίζει ἐρωτικῶς for συκοφαντεῖ.

9 Isoc. xxi.5 μάλιστα συκοφαντεῖν ἐπιχειροῦσιν οἱ λέγειν μὲν δεινοί, ἔχοντες δὲ μηδέν, τοὺς ἀδυνάτους μὲν εἰπεῖν, ἱκανοὺς δὲ χρήματα τελεῖν.

10 Compare Menander *Georgoi* fr.1 Sandbach (fr.93 Kock): 'The poor man is easy to despise, Gorgias, even if what he says is just. People say the only reason he speaks up is to get something, and the man whose clothes are threadbare is called a sykophant even if in fact he is the one who has been wronged' (εὐκαταφρόνητόν ἐστι, Γοργία, πένης, / κἂν πάνυ λέγηι δίκαια· τούτου γὰρ λέγειν / ἕνεκα μόνου νομίζεθ' οὗτος, τοῦ λαβεῖν / καὶ συκοφάντης εὐθὺς ὁ τὸ τριβώνιον / ἔχων καλεῖται, κἂν ἀδικούμενος τύχηι).

In various procedures in Attic law the successful prosecutor was financially rewarded (Osborne 1985b: 44–8). For an assessment of sykophancy the most important of these procedures is that known as *phasis* (denunciation). Connecting sykophants with *phasis* is encouraged not only by the possible etymological connection between *phasis* and the '-phant' of 'sykophant', but also by the frequent linking of sykophants and *phasis* in one of the earliest sources to mention sykophants, Aristophanes.[11] When Dikaiopolis in Aristophanes' *Akharnians* sets up his own private *agora* (market), he announces 'Let no sykophant come here, nor any man from Phasis',[12] and later in the play a sykophant does make an appearance, to denounce the Megarian for illegal trading (a true allegation).[13] In the *Birds* Aristophanes again makes fun of the irritation caused by sykophants, and although no particular legal action is specified the putative defendants are once more non-Athenians.[14] *Phasis* may also be in question at the opening of Lysias' speech *Against the Corn-sellers*, where the speaker claims that the Council, however much it regards the corn-sellers as guilty, also regards those who accuse them as sykophants.[15]

It is difficult to assess the significance of these general statements connecting sykophants with *phasis*. We know little about actual cases of *phasis* and have no way of testing the insinuations of Aristophanes against the evidence of prosecutions brought under this procedure. Aristophanes certainly implies that those who bring *phaseis* are a nuisance, but he does not imply that their *phaseis* are groundless; the prosecutors may observe the letter rather than the spirit of the law, but there is apparent legal justification for their actions. The opening of Lysias xxii implies that Athenians were inclined to unjustified suspicion of those who accused the corn-sellers (by *phasis*?), rather than that those who brought *phaseis* were unjustified.[16]

Orators and comic writers frequently imply that sykophants made money

11 The etymological impenetrability of the word and its sudden appearance in the late fifth century might suggest that there was some original *cause célèbre* (a *phasis* involving figs?) which earned vexatious litigants this sobriquet.

12 Ar. *Akh.* 725–6: ἐνταῦθα μήτε συκοφάντης εἰσίτω / μήτ' ἄλλος ὅστις Φασιανός ἐστ' ἀνήρ. Φασιανός means 'from the area around the River Phasis' and was normally used in the phrase 'Phasian bird' to refer to pheasants.

13 *Akh.* 819 'I am jolly well going to denounce these little pigs as enemy goods, and you too' (τὰ χοιρίδια τοίνυν ἐγὼ φανῶ ταδὶ / πολέμια καὶ σέ), and compare 908 'Here comes Nikarkhos to make a show' (καὶ μὴν ὁδὶ Νίκαρχος ἔρχεται φανῶν). Aristophanes also puns on *phasis* occasionally when sykophants are not clearly in question, see *Knights* 1256, *Birds* 68.

14 *Birds* 1410–69. Note that Aristophanes could joke that the sykophant was a product unique to Athens, *Akh.* 904.

15 Lys. xxii.1 'Gentlemen dikasts, many have come up to me in amazement that I was proposing to accuse the corn-sellers in the Council, pointing out that you regard those who bring charges concerning them as sykophants, even if you think they are in the wrong. So I will first explain what has compelled me to accuse them' (πολλοί μοι προσεληλύθασιν, ὦ ἄνδρες δικασταί, θαυμάζοντες ὅτι ἐγὼ τῶν σιτοπωλῶν ἐν τῇ βουλῇ κατηγόρουν, καὶ λέγοντες ὅτι ὑμεῖς, εἰ ὡς μάλιστα αὐτοὺς ἀδικεῖν ἡγεῖσθε, οὐδὲν ἧττον καὶ τοὺς περὶ τούτων ποιουμένους λόγους συκοφαντεῖν νομίζετε. ὅθεν οὖν ἠνάγκασμαι κατηγορεῖν αὐτῶν, περὶ τούτων πρῶτον εἰπεῖν βούλομαι).

16 Compare [Dem.] LIII.1 where the speaker presupposes that the dikasts might think that someone who brought an *apographe* was litigating vexatiously.

out of their prosecutions.[17] Occasionally the sykophant is clearly alleged to have brought his prosecution merely in order to reach an out-of-court settlement for a sum of money. Photios and the Souda quote a single line from Aristophanes' lost play the *Daitales* in which 'being a sykophant' is associated with 'threatening, demanding money, and fleecing'.[18] Similarly, when in Aristophanes' *Wealth* (850–959) the sykophant appears as one of those done out of his livelihood when the god Wealth regains his sight, I take it that the sykophant is impoverished not, or not only, because he is himself one of the wicked no longer allowed to prosper, but because there is no longer scope for accusing men who are rich in the hope that their guilty consciences will make them pay their accuser off; for now that Wealth has his sight back only the good are rich.

The clearest specific cases of alleged sykophantic blackmail in the fifth century concern Nikias and Kriton. Our 'information' on the payment of a large sum of money by Nikias to a potential prosecutor comes solely from a passage of a comedy by Telekleides quoted by Plutarch, and arguably it tells us more about Nikias' comic *persona* than about anything else.[19] Kriton's employment of a counter-sykophant to protect himself against vexatious litigation is the subject of a more trustworthy account in Xenophon's *Memorabilia* and it will be necessary to examine it in detail later.

Allusions to, and some specific allegations of, sykophantic blackmail occur in fourth-century orators, but the percentage of references to sykophancy which turn on blackmail is small. Sykophancy figures prominently as an evil in Isocrates,[20] but the closest he comes to making a blackmail allegation is in the speech *Against Kallimakhos*. The centre of the defence is the allegation that Kallimakhos' prosecution contravenes the Amnesty Law of Arkhinos (403 B.C.), but the speaker also claims both that he was not guilty of the crime alleged, and that Kallimakhos is going against an earlier agreement to settle out-of-court for a sum of money.

The background to the case is as follows: the speaker had been with the *arkhon basileus* Patrokles when Patrokles seized some money from Kalli-

---

[17] Cf. the vague references to sykophancy providing a livelihood in Aristophanes, *Birds* 1432, 1452.

[18] Ar. fr. 219 K–A: ἔσειον, ἤτουν χρήματ᾽, ἠπείλουν, ἐσυκοφαντοῦν quoted by Photios and the Souda s.v. σεῖσαι.

[19] Plutarch, *Life of Nikias* 4.5 (Telekleides fr.41 Kock): 'So Kharikles paid up 100 dr. to stop him revealing that he was the first child his mother had bought. Nikeratos' son Nikias gave 400 dr., but I am his friend and so it is only decent that I should keep mum, even though I know well why he gave it.'

(Χαρικλέης μὲν οὖν ἔδωκε μνᾶν, ἵν᾽ αὐτὸν μὴ λέγῃ,
ὡς ἔφυ τῇ μητρὶ παίδων πρῶτος ἐκ βαλαντίου.
τέσσαρας δὲ μνᾶς ἔδωκε Νικίας Νικηράτου·
ὧν δ᾽ ἕκατι τοῦτ᾽ ἔδωκε καίπερ εὖ εἰδὼς ἐγὼ
οὐκ ἐρῶ, φίλος γὰρ ἀνήρ, σωφρονεῖν δέ μοι δοκεῖ.)

We do not, of course, have to imagine anything more than scandal-mongering to be invoked by this passage.

[20] As well as XXI.5 see XV.164, XVIII.64, XXI.8, 13.

makhos on the grounds that it was public property. After the restoration of democracy Kallimakhos brought a case against Patrokles and settled out-of-court for 1,000 dr. Subsequently Kallimakhos brought an allegation against one Lysimakhos (presumably in the same connection) and settled with him for 200 dr. The prosecution of the speaker followed. The speaker claims to have a witness to an agreement with Kallimakhos that Kallimakhos would drop the prosecution for a payment of 200 dr., and claims that even this agreement was only made because Kallimakhos had so publicised his case that those who heard him had strongly advised the speaker to settle out-of-court. When Kallimakhos continued to press his charges the speaker put in a special plea (*diamarturia*) that the prior agreement made the prosecution illegal. By failing to challenge this plea with a charge of false witness Kallimakhos effectively conceded its validity; nevertheless he then proceeded with exactly the same charge again, as it appears, and in the case from which we have his speech tried an injunction (*paragraphē*) on the grounds that the prosecution breached the Amnesty.

There is a very great deal in this affair which Isocrates' speech does not reveal. If one takes a view sympathetic to the speaker and, with Norlin in the Loeb Classical Library, translates 'to act as a sykophant' as 'blackmail', and 'some of those acquainted with this man' as 'his friends', then a classic case of sykophantic blackmail is produced. But if one takes a view sympathetic to Kallimakhos, noting that he was the injured party (the essence of his story is never denied) and had not reneged on his out-of-court settlements with Patrokles and Lysimakhos, whereas the speaker had taken refuge in the Amnesty, then it is not at all clear that the simple version of the story of the original out-of-court settlement can be swallowed whole, still less that the insinuations about the way in which that settlement was brought about can be accepted at face value.[21]

Allegations of blackmail (as opposed to simply making money by prosecuting)[22] are no more frequent in Demosthenes and Aeschines, and all the cases where blackmail is clearly in question concern men who brought charges against full-time politicians. Although the speech *Against Aristogeiton* is full of insinuation and allusions it brings little detailed evidence in support of its interpretations of Aristogeiton's behaviour. It cannot be denied that Aristogeiton frequently threatened to bring prosecutions, but it is another matter to decide whether he did so *simply* in order to get paid off. The best that Demosthenes can manage in the way of blackmail allegations is vague, 'he took

---

[21] At Isocrates XVIII. 51–2 Kallimakhos is accused of having witnessed falsely to a serving girl's being dead only to have the girl produced alive. The speech states that he was one of a very large number of witnesses to this 'fact', and this might suggest that the case was not quite as Isocrates represents it.

[22] Cf. e.g. Dem. XIX.222.

something', 'he engaged in every improper behaviour imaginable, attacking allotted magistracies, begging and exacting payments'.[23] The case of Theokrines is more complex. Mikon, against whom he brought a *phasis* which he dropped after Mikon had paid him 200 dr., was not a politician. But although we do not know as much as we would like to about Mikon, he certainly came from a respectable family which was involved in public life at least to the extent that his brother was priest of Dionysos and honoured by the Paraloi, probably for service as financial officer of the state trireme the *Paralos*.[24] The other prosecutions brought by Theokrines mentioned in Demosthenes LVIII are a, necessarily political, *graphē paranomon* against the father of Epikhares, in which Theokrines secured a conviction after the defendant refused to settle out-of-court for 10 talents, and a subsequent and related case against a Polyeuktos (possibly the politician Polyeuktos of Sphettos), settled out-of-court for 300 dr. As these latter prosecutions were political, so it is also possible that there were political overtones to the prosecution of Mikon. Theokrines' success in securing a conviction with a huge fine of 10 talents should not be lightly dismissed.

The burden of the argument so far has been that neither the metaphorical use of the term sykophant nor the specific allegations made against individual 'sykophants' support those modern scholars who identify the sykophant by his pecuniary motivation. It is to be noted that orators make claims that prosecutors are employing bribery and blackmail without associating sykophancy with this charge. There are sometimes good reasons for this: the claim that other prosecutors have been paid off may be part of a strategy designed to indicate that the current prosecutor is not alone in thinking that the defendant deserves to be brought to court.[25] But this explanation will not apply in all cases. There seems, for example, no good reason why the general allegations of blackmail and bribery made in the speech in defence of Polystratos (Lys. xx.7, 15) should not employ the word sykophant, which occurs elsewhere in the speech (§ 12) without reference to money passing. Similarly Theomnestos alleges that Stephanos was hired to prosecute Apollodoros and did it for the money without calling him a sykophant ([Dem.]LIX.10), although Apollodoros himself is happy to bandy that charge against Stephanos later in the case (LIX. 39,43,44,68).[26]

23 Dem. xxv.47 λαβὼν ὁτιδήποτε, xxv.50 τὰς δὲ κληρωτὰς ἀρχὰς σπαράττων, αἰτῶν, εἰσπράττων ἀργύριον, τί κακὸν οὐ παρέχων.
24 Priest *IG* ii² 410.16–17, honoured by Paraloi *IG* ii² 1254.2,6–7. See Davies 1971: 57–8.
25 Lys. xxix. 1–2 'I had expected more people to get themselves involved in this contest, dikasts. For a large number threatened and asserted that they would accuse Philokrates. None of those makes an appearance now, and I take that to be a sign that my accusation is true: for if Philokrates did not have a large amount of Ergokles' money he would not have been so capable of paying off his accusers.' (ὁ μὲν ἀγὼν οὗτος, ὦ ἄνδρες δικασταί, ἐρημότερος γεγένηται ἢ ἐγὼ προσεδόκων. πολλοὶ γὰρ ἦσαν οἱ ἀπειλοῦντες καὶ οἱ φάσκοντες Φιλοκράτους κατηγορήσειν· ὧν οὐδεὶς νυνὶ φαίνεται. ὃ κἀμοὶ δοκεῖ οὐδενὸς ἔλαττον εἶναι τεκμήριον τῆς ἀπογραφῆς, ὅτι ἀληθὴς οὖσα τυγχάνει· εἰ γὰρ μὴ πολλὰ τῶν Ἐργοκλέους εἶχε χρημάτων, οὐκ ἂν οὕτως οἷός τ' ἦν ἀπαλλάξαι τοὺς κατηγόρους.)
26 Cf. [Dem.] LVII.60 for a blackmail charge which does not use 'sykophant'.

But if labelling someone a sykophant did not imply that he was a person who brought charges for money, what did it imply? In attempting to answer this question we are in a much stronger position for the fourth century, with its wealth of forensic uses of the term, than for the fifth century, when most of our evidence for sykophants comes from comedy – and indeed it is not impossible that the use of the term changed slightly from fifth to fourth century (see below n. 54). Here I shall proceed by looking in some detail at a tendentious definition given by Aeschines and by examining the uses of the allegation in the Demosthenic corpus.

In the *False Embassy* speech, Aeschines rounds at one point on the prosecution claim that, just as he, Aeschines, had urged that Timarkhos be condemned on the evidence of *phemē* (rumour), so Aeschines too stands condemned by his own bad reputation. In his reply Aeschines attempts to separate his own argument in the case of Timarkhos from that which is being used against himself.[27] He claims that *phemē* and *sukophantia* are two very different things: *phemē* is when the majority of citizens, of their own accord and with no ulterior motive, pass on an allegation; *sukophantia*, which is what his opponents are now engaged in, is when one man makes a slanderous accusation in the Assembly or Council. Two features of this argument should be noted: first, that Aeschines can suggest that *phemē* and *sukophantia* are so close together that they need to be carefully distinguished (cynically one might say that *phemē* is what I use and *sukophantia* what my opponent uses); second, that the motive and possible financial considerations of the *sukophantes* are not invoked at all. Not only does the allegation of sykophancy evidently not require insinuations of monetary greed as a motive, but Aeschines actually forgoes the opportunity to make such a suggestion. This is consistent with the company which sykophancy keeps in the Timarkhos speech: there it is associated with coarse behaviour, cockiness, luxuriousness, cowardliness, shamelessness, and not knowing to blush at what is base.[28] None of these is a quality an Athenian would be proud to have attributed to himself, but none of them involves criminal behaviour.

Aeschines' use of 'sykophant' is consistent with usage in the Demosthenic corpus. 'Claims that the speaker's opponent is a sykophant are commonplace' (Carey and Reid 1985: 169) but they occur with far greater frequency in some speeches than others, and in particular the frequency differs between 'private' and 'public' cases and between speeches for the prosecution and for the

---

[27] Aesch. II.145: εὖ ἴστε, ὦ Ἀθηναῖοι, ὅτι πλεῖστον διαφέρει φήμη καὶ συκοφαντία. φήμη μὲν γὰρ οὐ κοινωνεῖ διαβολῇ, διαβολὴ δὲ ἀδελφόν ἐστι καὶ συκοφαντία. διορῶ δ᾽αὐτῶν ἑκάτερον σαφῶς. φήμη μέν ἐστιν, ὅταν τὸ πλῆθος τῶν πολιτῶν αὐτόματον ἐκ μηδεμίας προφάσεως λέγῃ τινὰ ὡς γεγενημένην πρᾶξιν· συκοφαντία δ᾽ἐστίν, ὅταν πρὸς τοὺς πολλοὺς εἰς ἀνὴρ αἰτίαν ἐμβαλὼν ἔν τε ταῖς ἐκκλησίαις ἁπάσαις πρός τε τὴν βουλὴν διαβάλλῃ τινά. καὶ τῇ μὲν φήμῃ δημοσίᾳ θύομεν ὡς θεῷ, τῶν δὲ συκοφαντῶν ὡς κακούργων δημοσίᾳ προβολὰς ποιούμεθα, μὴ οὖν σύναγε εἰς ταὐτὸν τὰ κάλλιστα τοῖς αἰσχίστοις.

[28] Aesch.I.105: ἀλλὰ τούτῳ ἀντὶ τῶν πατρῴων περίεστι βδελυρία, συκοφαντία, θράσος, τρυφή, δειλία, ἀναίδεια, τὸ μὴ ἐπίστασθαι ἐρυθριᾶν ἐπὶ τοῖς αἰσχροῖς.

defence (for the raw data see the list of testimonia concluding Harvey's reply below).

Fourteen of the thirty-two 'private orations' do not use words of the sykophant root at all. Where we have the speech of the prosecution in a *dikē*, no allegation of sykophancy on the opponent's (that is, the defendant's) part is made. Accordingly there are no uses of 'sykophant' words in Demosthenes XXVII, XXVIII, XLVI, XLVII, XLIX, L, LIV, or LVI (and only one trivial instance in the *antidosis* speech [Dem.] XLII). In [Demosthenes] LIII, the speech of the man responsible for bringing the *apographē* (denunciation) from which the particular dispute at issue in this speech arises, the speaker is at pains to point out in the first sentence that he is *not* being a sykophant. Two of the five prosecution speeches which do use the word are not in fact *dikai* (LVIII is an *endeixis*, LIX a *graphē*), and all five belong to sequences of legal actions: XLV is a prosecution for False Witness, that is, effectively, an appeal, and hence a speech by the original defendant; XXXIX and XL are two of a long series of speeches in a complex of cases apparently begun by the man who is the defendant here. The use of sykophant in these speeches is thus consistent with the pattern in actual defence speeches: five of the seven defendant's speeches (XLI, LI, LII, LV, LVII) use 'sykophant' words; only the two inheritance speeches fail to employ the charge (XLIII and XLIV). Similarly all but one of the injunction (*paragraphē*) speeches use 'sykophant'; these are all speeches to establish that the case is inadmissible, and hence speeches by the original defendant against the original prosecutor. The exceptional speech which does not use 'sykophant' is a reply to an injunction, and hence a speech by the original prosecutor (XXXV).

The pattern in the orations delivered in connection with 'public' cases is very different. As is illustrated by the Theokrines and Neaira cases mentioned above, prosecutors in these cases are quite prepared to allege sykophancy. Demosthenes himself uses sykophant more or less liberally in his prosecutions of Meidias, Leptines, Aristocrates and Aristogeiton; only Androtion and Timocrates escape. Nor did those who prosecuted Demosthenes himself let him escape untarred.[29]

A clear picture of the use of the charge 'sykophant' emerges from the Demosthenic corpus. Prosecutors in private cases avoided the 'sykophant' words altogether: unless they were engaged in a prolonged struggle with the defendant in which they themselves had been prosecuted, they had little cause to allege that the defendant was a sykophant, and they may have tried to avoid putting it into the dikasts' heads that they might themselves be being sykophantic. Defendants in such cases, on the other hand, almost invariably alleged that the prosecution was sykophantic, and they did so both in bringing injunctions and in making their main defence. By contrast, in *graphai* and other cases where the prosecutor was not himself the injured party but was

---

[29] See Aesch. II.5,39,99, III.176; Dein. I.6. Compare Dem. XIX.98,222.

claiming to act for the public good, the allegation of sykophancy was thrown around by both prosecution and defence alike.[30] It should by now be clear that even Rhodes' rather cautious statement of the traditional view of the sykophant is seriously misleading. 'Sykophant' was applied to men who took advantage of the laws allowing volunteer prosecution in order to obtain rewards or payments, but it was by no means applied exclusively to them. It was applied to *any* prosecutor, and it implied not that the prosecutor was acting for corrupt motives, unless that was additionally specified, but rather that the prosecutor did not have a good case, that his case depended on improbable assumptions, empty assertions or over-meticulous quibbling. 'Sykophant' was a term with some abusive content, liable to be strung together with other terms of abuse, but to allege that someone was a sykophant was not to press a very serious charge. Demosthenes does note the fact that Aristogeiton had been convicted of sykophancy, but he does so in a virtual parenthesis, and Apollodoros leaves the allegation that Kallippos has acted as a sykophant to the penultimate word of the speech against him.[31]

To say that 'sykophant' was a relatively mild term of abuse is still not to tell the whole story. It was also an *ad hoc* allegation. A prosecutor showed himself a sykophant by bringing a particular prosecution, not by adopting any particular kind of prosecution as a profession. All the orators use parts of the verb 'to act as a sykophant' and the abstract noun 'sykophancy' much more frequently than they use the noun 'sykophant', and only Isocrates, in his epideictic not his forensic speeches, talks of sykophants in the plural with any frequency.[32] Isocrates xv. 288 talks of the 'genus of sykophants', but there is no trace of the profession of sykophant in the orators,[33] and the very cases most frequently alleged in the modern scholarship as professional sykophancy

---

[30] For the effective distinction between *graphai* and *dikai* see Osborne 1985b.

[31] Dem. xxv.19, [Dem.] LII.33. Cf. Diphilos fr. 31.12–17 K–A, from his *Emporos*: 'He is a man who cannot live without causing trouble. Do you know what I mean? He needs must either spend his nights on petty burglaries or housebreaking or helping those who do such things, or acting as a sykophant in the agora, or bearing false witness. We are getting rid of all such scum.' (οὐκ ἐνδέχεται γὰρ ζῆν ἄνευ κακοῦ τινος / τοῦτον· συνιείς; ἀλλ' ἀναγκαίως ἔχει / ἢ λωποδυτεῖν τὰς νύκτας ἢ τοιχωρυχεῖν, / ἢ τῶν ποιούντων ταῦτα κοινωνεῖν τισιν, / ἢ συκοφαντεῖν κατ' ἀγοράν, ἢ μαρτυρεῖν / ψευδῆ. τὸ τοιοῦτον ἐκκαθαίρομεν γένος.)

[32] Thus Lysias has 17 uses of some part of the verb *sukophantein*, three of the abstract noun *sukophantia*, one use of *sukophantes* in the singular, and six uses of *sukophantai* in the plural. Isocrates has 26 uses of some part of the verb, 8 uses of the abstract noun, 4 uses of *sukophantes* in the singular and 14 of *sukophantai* in the plural (all the *sukophantai* come in the epideictic orations VIII or XV). Aeschines has seven uses of the verb, 5 of the abstract nouns, 8 of *sukophantes* in the singular, and 3 of *sukophantai* in the plural. The Demosthenic corpus has 100 uses of some part of the verb, 21 of the abstract nouns, 19 of *sukophantes* in the singular, and 8 of *sukophantai* in the plural.

[33] On 'the sykophant bureau' (ἐργαστήριον συκοφαντῶν) of [Dem.] xxxix.2, xl.9 see the cautious treatment of Bonner & Smith 1938: 54 and n. 3 (contrast Carey & Reid 1985: 168). This phrase seems to have misled Calhoun 1913: 44–5 also: the facts of the case demand nothing more than that Boiotos received help and advice from a group of friends, whether formally describable as *hetairoi* or not. It is in the speaker's interest to put this advice in a bad light.

vanish on close examination.[34] Thus Isocrates alludes to the *graphai* and *dikai* Kallimakhos brought, but the fact is that we can only be sure of his involvement as prosecutor in a single complex of cases in which he himself was, or could successfully represent himself as being, the injured party. Theokrines made three prosecutions that we know of, two of them directly related to the same affair, and the third possibly involving part of the same family. Aristogeiton was certainly a loud-mouthed politician, who specialised in allegations rather than prosecutions, but Quintilian acquired from somewhere a high opinion of him as an orator, and we may be over-influenced by the fact that all that survives to us are three speeches made against him.[35]

II   THE IMPORTANCE OF SYKOPHANCY

The sykophant thus disappears before our eyes, but the phenomenon of sykophancy, of vexatious litigation, remains. When a man stands up in court and calls his opponent a sykophant he is not claiming that he is bringing the prosecution to make money, but he *is* claiming that the man is a pest, causing him and the court unnecessary trouble. That the Athenians felt the need for a special term for the *vexatious* litigant implies that some Athenians at least believed that there was an amount of litigation which caused more trouble than it was worth. At least as early as Isocrates, the existence of three different ways of prosecuting the vexatious litigant at Athens was taken as evidence for the scale of the problem;[36] but it also bears witness to the difficulty of drawing the line between proper and improper, or vexatious, prosecutions. One aspect of this problem is the difficulty of preventing sykophantic use of measures against sykophants,[37] but a second, and more significant, lies in the intimate

---

[34] Lofberg 1917 tendentiously groups the information on four very well known prosecutors dubbed 'sykophants' by their opponents (whose words, alone, we have) in a chapter he entitles 'Typical Athenian sycophants'!

[35] Quintilian, *Inst. Or.* XII.10.22: 'I pass over several orators – Lykourgos, Aristogeiton and Isaeus and Antiphon who were earlier than them. These might be described as men of the same family but with different individual characters' (transeo plurimos, Lycurgum, Aristogitona et his priores Isaeum, Antiphonta: quos ut homines inter se genere similes, differentis dixeris specie).

[36] Isoc. XV.313–14, MacDowell 1978:66, Bonner & Smith 1938: 63–71. For ways of proceeding against sykophants see [Arist.] *Ath. Pol.* 43.5, 59.3 and cf. 35.2–3. It is completely unclear what you had to do to get convicted of sykophancy. Certainly it is not necessarily the case that either frequency of (unsuccessful) litigation or the receipt of/demand for money were in question.

[37] [Arist.] *Ath. Pol.* 43.5 puts a limit on the number of sykophants who can be arraigned on any one occasion: 'In the sixth prytany, in addition to the stated business they also hold a vote about whether or not to have an ostracism, and they hear Athenian and metic sykophant allegations (with a limit of three of each) and any accusations that someone has not done what he promised the people he would' (ἐπὶ τῆς ἕκτης πρυτανείας πρὸς τοῖς εἰρημένοις καὶ περὶ τῆς ὀστρακοφορίας ἐπιχειροτονίαν διδόασιν εἰ δοκεῖ ποιεῖν ἢ μή, καὶ συκοφαντῶν προβολὰς τῶν Ἀθηναίων καὶ τῶν μετοίκων μέχρι τριῶν ἑκατέρων, κἄν τις ὑποσχόμενός τι μὴ ποιήσῃ τῷ δήμῳ). If the *Ath. Pol.* were written in the best literary Greek, it would be imperative to translate this to mean 'hear accusations about informers, whether Athenians or metics (with a limit of three of each)'; but since it is not, it is possible that the

connection between litigation and the proper functioning of Athenian democracy.

A strong link between sykophancy and democracy has been noted by earlier scholars, but they differ on how to evaluate that link. Ehrenberg, in his only mention of sykophants in *From Solon to Socrates* (1973: 215–16), writes:

When more and more political decisions were going to be made in the courts, the way was prepared for the rule of the masses, in both ecclesia and courts. This means at the same time that the frontier zone between legislation and jurisdiction grew narrow and vague, a fact which led to an increasing part being played by the professional informers, the sykophants. In the long run it destroyed the very basis of the polis as a state founded on law.

On the other hand, Finley, in 'Athenian Demagogues' (1974: 23), wrote:

If Athens largely escaped the extreme forms of *stasis* so common elsewhere, she could not escape its lesser manifestations. Athenian politics had an all-or-nothing quality. The objective on each side was not merely to defeat the opposition but to crush it, to behead it by destroying its leaders. And often enough this game was played within the sides, as a number of men manoeuvred for leadership. The chief technique was the political trial, and the chief instrumentalities were the dining-clubs and the sycophants. These too, I would argue, were structurally a part of the system, not an accidental or avoidable excrescence.

Although both Finley and Ehrenberg invoke sykophancy, they both focus on a very narrow area of sykophantic activity, and are more concerned with the world of Aristogeiton than with sykophantic allegations brought against private individuals in the dikasteries.[38] But just as consideration of only part of the evidence for sykophantic activity leads to a partial and misleading definition of the term sykophant, so it leads to an inadequate assessment of the importance of sykophancy within Athenian society.

Ehrenberg and Finley treat attacks on political figures as central to the political importance of sykophancy, but others have stressed the significance of sykophantic attacks on the rich. Humphreys (1983b: 30) writes: 'the genitives do not all refer to the same persons, and hence the limitation might be that three Athenians and three metics could bring charges against sykophants in this way annually.

[38] Hansen 1974: 54 claims that 'the introduction of the *graphē paranomon* created another type of sykophant: the citizen who would undertake to act for money as a proposer and let his name be inscribed on other citizens' proposals', but the evidence he cites in support of this is inadequate. Isocrates VIII.129–30 is concerned with those who sit as dikasts or attend the Assembly and get paid for doing so, not with '*rhetores* [full-time politicians] and demagogues who make their living acting in the assembly and before the courts'. Apollodoros ([Dem.] LIX.43) alleges that Stephanos is not a full-time politician (*rhetor*) but a sykophant, and that he hangs around the Speaker's Platform (*bema*), brings *graphai* and *phaseis* for pay, and puts his name on others' proposals, but this does not mean that the latter activity is what justifies calling him 'sykophant'. Timokrates and Ktesiphon are not called sykophants in the passages referring to their political activity (Dem. XXIV.3,14,66,200,201,203; Aesch. III.243), and the allusion to Aristogeiton's conviction for *graphē paranomon* is not connected with the subsequent mention of his sykophantic attacks on private individuals (Dem. XXV.40–1). Hansen's extended meaning of 'sykophant' would be conceivable only if acting for money were the primary meaning of 'being a sykophant'.

typical victim of the sycophant was thought to be the rich quietist or ally rather than an active member of the political élite'. Carter (1986: 129) develops this position in saying, 'Sycophants preyed especially, perhaps exclusively, on the rich . . .', but he fails to see the importance of this for democracy because he never examines his conviction that the sykophant was primarily interested in hush-money. Thus, concerning Lysias VII, he writes (107–8): 'The prosecutor clearly depended on the defendant's fear and dislike of lawsuits or any kind of public business; such a man would be prepared to pay a sycophant to desist. The fact that on this occasion the sycophant was mistaken in his victim does not alter what is, on the evidence of Lysias' speeches, a rule.'

That the victim of a sykophantic prosecution is wealthy does not entail that the prosecutor brings his case in order to extract some of that wealth. The wealthy man acquires a whole variety of abilities and powers by virtue of his wealth. Grote saw the relevance of this and began his account of the working of the dikasteries at Athens with the observation that 'To make rich and powerful criminals effectively amenable to justice has indeed been found so difficult everywhere, until a recent period of history, that we should be surprised if it were otherwise in Greece.'[39]

To be wealthy in classical Athens was to have privileged access to political and social power. There can be no doubt at all that politics throughout the classical period was dominated by the wealthy, and that it was so dominated at every stage and every level, even in offices that were in theory equally open to all (Davies 1981; Osborne 1985a: 66–9). But to be wealthy was also to incur obligations, some enforceable, like the obligation to perform liturgies, others more a matter of social expectations and the maintenance of standing and status in the *polis* as a whole, the deme, and in other divisions of the *demos*. The rôle of sykophantic prosecution within democracy must be seen against this background of varied obligations, duties and opportunities.

The classic case of a rich Athenian troubled by sykophantic allegations is that of Kriton. In the *Memorabilia* Xenophon relates how Kriton complained to Socrates that a man could not 'devote himself to his own affairs'.[40] Certain men, he alleged, brought cases (*dikai* is the word used) against him because they knew that he would rather pay than have trouble. Socrates recommends that Kriton procure a human guard-dog to ward off those trying to wrong him.[41] They find Arkhedemos, a man 'very good at speaking and acting', but

---

[39] Grote, *History of Greece* ch.46 'Changes at Athens under Perikles' (the quotation comes from p.124 of vol.iv of the London edition of 1862).
[40] Xen. *Mem.* ii.9.1 τὰ ἑαυτοῦ πράττειν.
[41] Note the association of democratic/demagogic politicians with dogs already in Aristophanes: Taillardat 1965: 403–5 (sec. 695: 'Le chien de Démos'). Xen. *Mem.* ii.7.13–14 has a fable on the need to have a guard-dog. Cf. also Theophrastus, *Characters* 29.5: 'He is favourable to the man who speaks in the Assembly or is on trial in the *dikasterion*. He is fond of saying to the assembled body that "one must not judge the man but the facts of the case". He says that he is the people's watch-dog, for he guards them against those who would do them harm' (καὶ εὔνους δὲ εἶναι τῷ ἐν ἐκκλησίᾳ λέγοντι ἢ ἐπὶ δικαστηρίῳ κρινομένῳ· καὶ πρὸς τοὺς

poor (and thus a man who has just the qualities Isocrates attributes to sykophants!). Kriton cultivates Arkhedemos by providing him with produce from his own estates and by inviting him to sacrifices and so on, and in return when men make sykophantic allegations against Kriton Arkhedemos investigates them, finds out where they themselves have contravened the law and who their enemies are, and threatens to prosecute them unless they refrain from prosecuting Kriton.

Modern discussions of this anecdote have tended to regard Kriton as the lamb-like victim described by Aristophanes in the *Knights*,[42] but he can be seen in a rather different perspective. Kriton is unashamedly, and complacently, self-centred. He wants to opt out and live in his own little world. He will do anything for a quiet life, and will not involve himself with the society of which he is part. He has no scruples about using his wealth, presumably inherited, to buy himself into a particular way of life in which he does not have to worry about the laws of the city. Kriton's attitude emerges very clearly from the dialogue which Plato named after him: there Socrates expresses his reservations about fleeing prison by imagining what the Laws (personified) might say to him, but Kriton can only think in terms of the possibility that Socrates might fear that, if he fled, sykophants would attack him and oblige him to spend all his money to get rid of them. Kriton reassures Socrates that sykophants are cheap (Plato, *Crito* 44e–45a). Kriton is proposing to use his wealth in order to evade the laws of the city; when Grote wrote that in Athens 'the rich and great men were not only insubordinate to the magistrates but made a parade of showing that they cared nothing about them', he might have been thinking of Kriton.

Kriton's employment of Arkhedemos merits further examination. Somewhat coyly presented by Xenophon in the *Memorabilia* passage, Arkhedemos is almost certainly the blear-eyed Arkhedemos of comedy, singled out for his depravity by Aristophanes and said by Eupolis to be of foreign extraction. Lysias accuses him of public fraud and makes associating with him a source of abuse against the younger Alkibiades.[43] In the *Hellenika* (1.7.2) Xenophon himself presents Arkhedemos as the champion of the people, looking after the *diobelia* and responsible for setting on foot the prosecution of the generals after Arginoussai with an allegation of peculation against the general Erasinides. Arkhedemos' reputation for having corrupted the people by largesse went before him into the fourth century (Aeschines II.76, 139; cf. Plutarch

καθημένους δὲ εἰπεῖν δεινὸς ὡς "οὐ δεῖ τὸν ἄνδρα, ἀλλὰ τὸ πρᾶγμα κρίνεσθαι". καὶ φῆσαι αὐτὸν κύνα εἶναι τοῦ δήμου· φυλάττειν γὰρ αὐτὸν πρὸς τοὺς ἀδικοῦντας).

42 Ar. *Knights* 264–5 (Chorus addressing Kleon): 'You look about for some citizen who has the mind of a sheep, is rich, not depraved and is scared stiff of public business' (καὶ σκοπεῖς γε τῶν πολιτῶν ὅστις ἐστὶν ἀμνοκῶν, / πλούσιος καὶ μὴ πονηρὸς καὶ τρέμων τὰ πράγματα). Contrast the use of the sheep image in Philippides fr. 29 Kock: 'The roughest of sykophants will go away softer than a lamb if you give him a couple of hundred drachmas' (ὁ τραχύτατος δὲ συκοφάντης μνᾶς δύο / λάβων ἄπεισιν ἀρνίου μαλακώτερος).

43 Blear-eyed: Ar. *Frogs* 558, cf. Eupolis fr. 9 κ-α; depravity: Ar. *Frogs* 425; foreign birth: Eupolis fr. 80 κ-α, Lys. xiv.25.

Mor. 575d). The man behind whom Kriton shelters was thus a man extremely active in politics. He used his skill at speaking to check the excessive power of rich men in a way not unlike that in which others tried to use their oratorical skill to make Kriton do his civic duty. Kriton diverted to his own use the powers that were otherwise deployed in the service of the whole city. He did so by applying to the individual Arkhedemos the sort of patronage which politicians of the Kimonian mould had bestowed on whole communities. Kriton managed to protect himself, to secure his position as an island beyond the reach of the city and its laws, only by perverting both traditional and 'new' methods of gaining political influence and support to his own personal use.[44]

We know of no parallel for Kriton's use of Arkhedemos, and we may suspect that the story of Kriton and Arkhedemos may have been improved in the telling. But the rôle of sykophantic prosecutions in making life difficult for wealthy men who refused to participate in the democratic working of society is clear from other cases – one thinks of Diognetos who fled Athens to get free of sykophantic slanders, or of Iskhomakhos who felt compelled to practise oratory in order to meet a prosecution.[45] It becomes a forensic *topos* (e.g. Lys. XXV.16) for a rich man to say that he has performed liturgies and public services in order to store up credit against the time that he might have to face the dikasts. Kriton was not the only rich man who thought money could buy off justice: men offered money both to prosecutors and to witnesses (cf. the denial at Lys. VII.21). Kriton's attitude is precisely that shared by all who preferred to reach out-of-court settlements, by fair means or foul.

Modern scholars have often assumed that when out-of-court settlements were reached this was because the prosecutor had brought the charge in the expectation, or at least the hope, of settling out-of-court. But some thought needs to be devoted to those who pay up. By definition the person who can pay for an out-of-court settlement can also afford the best legal aid and advice in defending himself. Despite this he chooses to duck the charge. While we cannot judge the justice of such cases, we would clearly be grossly over-simplifying if we assumed that the prosecution invariably had a weak case.

A man who prosecuted by *dikē* was claiming that he himself was the injured party, and as such he had at least some right to accept out-of-court payment in settlement of his grievance. Those who threatened *graphai* or other public actions and who dropped prosecutions for payment were in a rather different position, but they should not be condemned as blackmailers without further question. Such prosecutors were often exploiting men who both shrank from involvement in government and ignored, to a greater or lesser degree, the laws of the city, and they were compelling them either to re-enter the public stage

---

[44] See further Millett 1989: 16–19, and more generally on traditional and 'new' politics, Connor 1971, who discusses Arkhedemos at 35 n.1, and the review by J. K. Davies, *Gnomon* 47 (1975) 377.

[45] Lys. XVIII.9, Xen. *Oikonomikos* XI.21–5. Contrast the common view that the Sophists owed their existence to the demand from the rich for oratorical training in order that they could maintain their political influence in democracy.

and risk having to surrender some of their resources to the city, or to refuse to enter and have some of their wealth privately taken from them (cf. Isocrates xv. 318). Even the vexatious litigant who withdrew his action for a payment can be seen to be pressurising non-participants into an awareness of the contradiction of trying to maintain such a position in the democratic *polis*.[46]

Sykophantic allegations were an important democratic mechanism of social regulation; by them the rich were prevented from using their wealth in an anti-social way, and were also prevented from withdrawing their means from public service. The sykophant accomplished at an informal level what the *antidosis* also aimed to achieve, the transfer of wealth in accordance with public activities (Gabrielsen 1987). Victims and opponents represented vexatious litigants as politically over-active and endeavoured polemically to assert the positive value of political inactivity,[47] but for all Athenians the threat of sykophantic allegations was a constant reminder of the rule-bound nature of residence in a community, and of the impossibility of being a good Athenian simply by avoiding making enemies. The orators commonly associate democracy with the rule of law: that rule depended as much upon bad prosecutions as upon good ones.[48]

This positive view of the sykophant has been in part anticipated by two previous workers in the field: Moses Finley and Solon (or at least the Solon of tradition). Finley's conviction that 'conflict is not only inevitable, it is a virtue in democratic politics, for it is conflict combined with consent, and not consent alone, which preserves democracy from eroding into oligarchy' (1974: 23) underlies my own view of sykophants as it does Finley's view of demagogues; but Finley seems to see sykophants solely, or at least primarily, as directly political actors, important in redressing power in and between political groups. I too want to stress that sykophants had a structural part to play in democracy, but in addition to emphasise the rôle of sykophancy outside the narrow area of debates in the Assembly and indictments for unconstitutional proposals.

'Solon' made the sykophant central to his political thought. He said that the

46 One might compare Ar. fr. 102 κ–α, quoted by Plutarch, *Life of Nikias* 8, from the *Georgoi*, although, as David Harvey has pointed out to me, the parallel is not an exact one. In modern Britain the closest equivalent to the sykophant is perhaps provided by the scandal-raking of the tabloid newspapers.

47 Ar. *Peace* 191, Lys. xiii.76, Isoc. xv.230, cf. [Dem.] xxxix.34. The *topos* that the speaker is legally naive and *apragmon* must be seen as the converse of the charge of sykophancy: *contra* Carter 1986, it cannot be read off out of context as implying a positive value to inactivity in fourth-century Athens.

48 Lyk. i.3–6 is an eloquent defence of political and litigious activity, in which Lykourgos makes a point of denying personal factors (contrast Lys. xiii.1, xiv.1–2, Dem. xxiv.7–8, [Dem.] liii.1). Compare the not entirely unsympathetic treatment of the sykophant in Aristophanes' *Wealth* (cf. n. 54, below). On the creation of the identification of democracy and the rule of law see now Ostwald 1986. Plutarch, *Life of Timoleon* 37.1 remarks that 'Since it is necessary, so it seems, not only for every lark to have a crest, as Simonides said, but also for every democracy to have a sykophant, two of the demagogues even attacked Timoleon' (ἐπεὶ δὲ χρῆν ὡς ἔοικεν οὐ μόνον πᾶσι κορυδαλλοῖς λόφον ἐγγίνεσθαι, κατὰ Σιμωνίδην, ἀλλὰ καὶ πάσῃ δημοκρατίᾳ συκοφάντην, ἐπεχείρησαν καὶ Τιμολέοντι δύο τῶν δημαγωγῶν).

best city to live in was the one in which those who are not wronged attack and punish wrong-doers as much as the wronged do (Plut. *Solon* 18.5). The orators, by contrast, frequently take the fact that the prosecutor was not himself wronged as a sign that the prosecution is sykophantic.[49] Sykophantic attacks on rich non-participants are very much in the spirit of the 'Law of Stasis' ascribed to Solon by which those who do not take an active part in politics lose their political rights. In Plutarch's *Life of Solon* (5) Anakharsis likens Solon's laws to spiders' webs, saying that they would trap the weak but be broken by the rich and capable; but 'Solon' claims that he has made breaking the law unprofitable for all. Sykophants came to play a major part in bringing 'Solon's' ideal world to pass.

'Solon's' ideal world and the democracy founded on conflict were no more to all Athenians' taste than they are to all English people's taste. The importance of conflict to democracy is brought out very clearly, however, by what the Thirty Tyrants felt they had to do about sykophants and about 'Solon'. As part of their move to set up the 'ancestral constitution', the Thirty repealed not only the laws of Ephialtes and Arkhestratos about the Areopagites, but also those of Solon's laws which were subject to disputed interpretation and which therefore gave considerable scope to the dikasts to exercise power.[50] They publicly proclaimed that their motive for so doing was to abolish a route and method for reasoning by which sykophantic attacks were made; and they also, as their very first act, rounded up and had executed 'those who lived from sykophancy and were burdensome to the *kaloi kagathoi*'.[51] This was a

---

[49] See note 48 and also Xen. *Mem.* II.9.1, Dem. XXIX.41, XXXVI.53, XXXIX.25.

[50] [Arist.] *Ath. Pol.* 35.2: 'So at first they were moderate towards the citizens and made a claim to be administering the ancestral constitution: they removed the laws of Ephialtes and Arkhestratos about the Areopagites from the Areopagus, and abolished those laws of Solon that were of disputed interpretation and ended the sovereign power that lay with the dikasts, on the grounds that they were correcting the constitution and making it beyond dispute. For example, they made a man able to give his property to anyone he wanted without qualification, removing the additional difficulties that he could not do so if he were mad, senile, or under the influence of a woman so as to deny scope for an attack by sycophants' (τὸ μὲν οὖν πρῶτον μέτριοι τοῖς πολίταις ἦσαν καὶ προσεποιοῦντο διοικεῖν τὴν πάτριον πολιτείαν, καὶ τούς τ᾿ Ἐφιάλτου καὶ Ἀρχεστράτου νόμους τοὺς περὶ τῶν Ἀρεοπαγιτῶν καθεῖλον ἐξ Ἀρείου πάγου καὶ τῶν Σόλωνος θεσμῶν ὅσοι διαμφισβητήσεις εἶχον, καὶ τὸ κῦρος ὃ ἦν ἐν τοῖς δικασταῖς κατέλυσαν, ὡς ἐπανορθοῦντες καὶ ποιοῦντες ἀναμφισβήτητον τὴν πολιτείαν, οἷον περὶ τοῦ δοῦναι τὰ ἑαυτοῦ ᾧ ἂν ἐθέλῃ κύριον ποιήσαντες καθάπαξ τὰς δὲ προσούσας δυσκολίας, ἐὰν μὴ μανιῶν ἢ γηρῶν ἢ γυναικὶ πιθόμενος, ἀφεῖλον ὅπως μὴ ᾖ τοῖς συκοφάνταις ἔφοδος). Fourth-century theorists take up this argument, and frequently discuss the need for laws to be clear and unambiguous in order to limit the powers of the *dikasterion*: see [Arist.] *Ath. Pol.* 9.2, Arist. *Rhet.* 1354a26–31, 1354b4–22, Plat. *Politicus* 294a10–295a7, Plut. *Life of Solon* 18.4, and cf. Arist. *Pol.* 1273b41–1274a21.

[51] Xen. *Hell.* II.3.12: 'First of all they arrested those whom all knew to live from sykophancy in the democracy and who were burdensome to the *kaloi kagathoi* and condemned them to death. The "Council" was happy to condemn them, and none of those who knew that they themselves were not such people were worried.' (ἔπειτα πρῶτον μὲν οὓς πάντες ᾔδεσαν ἐν τῇ δημοκρατίᾳ ἀπὸ συκοφαντίας ζῶντας καὶ τοῖς καλοῖς κἀγαθοῖς βαρεῖς ὄντας, συλλαμβάνοντες ὑπῆγον θανάτου· καὶ ἡ βουλὴ ἡδέως αὐτῶν κατεψηφίζετο οἵ τε ἄλλοι ὅσοι συνῄδεσαν ἑαυτοῖς μὴ ὄντες τοιοῦτοι οὐδὲν ἤχθοντο.) Cf. [Arist.] *Ath. Pol.* 35.3 (quoted in n.53), Diod. XIV.4.2.

politically astute move: it cost nothing, for no one courted the abusive title 'sykophant'; and it attracted wider support from those who had been persuaded that sykophantic attacks had been responsible for causing allies to revolt and thus the war to be lost.[52]

Xenophon and [Aristotle] say that the attack on sykophants was initially popular with the 'Council', the *polis* and those 'confident that they themselves were not [sykophants]'.[53] But in a situation where all prosecutors were liable to be called sykophants there was bound to be a problem of limits: where was the line to be drawn between proper and improper litigants? As the attacks inevitably extended to personal enemies and to men held to be *kaloi kagathoi* the action lost its popularity: the charge of sykophancy was bound to be no more susceptible to close definition than Solon's ambiguous laws.[54] Despite the façade of legal reform, all that had occurred was that the power of the courts had been transferred from the hands of dikasts advised by (vexatious) litigants into the hands of a small group of men who were a law unto themselves. Ironically, but not inappropriately, Lysias (XII.5) calls the Thirty themselves sykophants.

Scholars from Aristotle on have been inclined to ridicule the tradition that Solon made his laws deliberately open to a range of interpretations, and have preferred to see the 'open texture' of Solon's laws as a chance product of the passage of time.[55] Some caution is required, however, before jumping to that conclusion. One of the most notable things about all Greek laws from the very beginning is the way in which they focus on procedure and do not concentrate either on defining criminal activity or on establishing fixed penalties for fixed crimes (Gagarin 1986). The focus on procedure gives law a focus on the control of relations between persons within the community. It is clear from his own poems that the Solon of history was very much concerned with the regulation of relations between citizens within the *polis*. If it is accepted that conflict has a vital rôle to play in the defence of democracy, then we should also contemplate the possibility that the connection of the Thirty with the 'clarification' of the law was not purely accidental, and that the democratic

---

52 See Lys. xxv.19 (the defence of an 'oligarch'). For sykophancy and the allies in general see [Xen.] *Ath. Pol.* 1.14 and Ar. *Birds* 1422.

53 Xen. *Hell.* II.3.12 (quoted in n.51), [Arist.] *Ath. Pol.* 35.3: 'At the beginning, then, they did these things and slew the sykophants and those who curried favour with the people contrary to its best interests and were mischievous and good for nothing. The city was pleased that this happened, thinking that they were doing this in order to do what was best.' (κατ' ἀρχὰς μὲν οὖν ταῦτ' ἐποίουν καὶ τοὺς συκοφάντας καὶ τοὺς τῷ δήμῳ πρὸς χάριν ὁμιλοῦντας παρὰ τὸ βέλτιστον καὶ κακοπράγμονας ὄντας καὶ πονηροὺς ἀνῄρουν, ἐφ' οἷς ἔχαιρον ἡ πόλις γιγνομένοις, ἡγούμενοι τοῦ βελτίστου χάριν ποιεῖν αὐτούς.)

54 Xen. *Hell.* II.3.38, [Arist.] *Ath. Pol.* 35.3. It is possible that it was this use of the label sykophant as an excuse for attacking all and sundry by the Thirty that led to its debasement into a term of almost meaningless abuse, at least for a period in the fourth century. In defence of my treatment of fifth- and fourth-century evidence together in this paper I would note that, although less bitterly treated, the sykophant of Aristophanes' *Wealth* (388 B.C.) is clearly closely related to the sykophants of the plays of the 420s and 410s.

55 For Aristotle see *Pol.* 1274a11–21, [*Ath. Pol.*] 9.2. For modern scholars see Rhodes 1981: 162. The question is further discussed in Osborne 1985b: 40–4.

overtones of Solon's legal legacy might be part of history and not just a part of tradition.[56]

[56] An earlier version of this paper was read to seminars in Manchester and Oxford, as well as to the Law and Society seminar in Cambridge. For advice, encouragement and criticism I am much indebted to the three editors, Colin Austin, David Harvey, David Lewis, Robert Parker, Anton Powell, Christopher Tuplin and David Whitehead.

5b

The sykophant and sykophancy: vexatious redefinition?[1]

DAVID HARVEY

μισεῖ τὸν συκοφάντην ἅπας.

Aristotle, *Rhetoric* II. 1382a7

Robin Osborne's contribution to this volume is scholarly, provocative and quite unsykophantic, on any definition. We are in agreement on many issues; above all, that *ho boulomenos* was indeed a vital element in the Athenian democracy. As the author of the *Athenaion Politeia* said (IX.1), the right of *ho boulomenos* to take action on behalf of an injured person was amongst those reforms of Solon from which the common man gained most (*demotikotata*); and no one would dispute that '*some* such prosecutors prosecuted those whom they believed to be guilty, and for public-spirited motives' (Adkins 1976: 309).

There is, however, much to be said in favour of the traditional view of the sykophant as one who abused the rights of *ho boulomenos*. I shall begin by discussing our sources; then I shall review Osborne's arguments in more or less the order that he deploys them.

I   SOURCES AND PROBLEMS

Several major difficulties obstruct our enquiries. First, all our witnesses are members of the upper class – a familiar phenomenon, for it was only the rich who had the leisure necessary for writing. But in the case of sykophancy, this

[1] I am indebted to numerous friends and colleagues for their help. My family assisted with proofreading; Margaret McKie provided accommodation in Oxford; Dr Robin Osborne sent me successive drafts of his paper with admirable speed. I am grateful for criticism and other kinds of help from Drs Paul Cartledge, Geoffrey de Ste. Croix, Su Braund, Paul Millett and Professor D. M. MacDowell.

The standard discussions of sykophants are cited by Osborne in his first note: Lofberg 1917, Bonner & Smith 1930–8: 39–74, and MacDowell 1978: 62–6, 225–6, 232. Adkins 1976: 307–11, 316–19 arrived independently at conclusions very close to those of Osborne. Other treatments include: Lipsius 1905–15: 448–51; Bonner 1927: 59–71; Calhoun 1944: 42–4; Ehrenberg 1951: 343–7 (a very black picture); Crawley 1970; Cohen 1973: 83–92; Harrison 1971: 60–2,

is an even greater obstacle to our understanding than usual, since it was precisely the rich who were attacked by sykophants.[2] This is bound to result in a seriously unbalanced picture, and may indeed be thought to undermine my argument at some points.

Furthermore, our evidence comes overwhelmingly from the Orators, and some passages in Aristophanes: notoriously unreliable and slippery material (Dover 1974: ch.i, esp. 8–14, 18–33; cf. Ostwald 1986: 209). When a client of Lysias (XIII.67 [65]) blithely assures the jury that there is no need to go into detail about 'the vast number of sykophantic cases that Agoratos has brought', we may suspect that Lysias is inventing most of them, though there is no reason to doubt his statement that Agoratos was publicly convicted on a charge of *sukophantia* (see section II below). The word *sukophantes* and its cognates are not used by Herodotus or Thucydides. It is not surprising that they are absent from Herodotus, as sykophancy hardly impinges on his world. But why not in Thucydides? True, he tells us less about internal politics at Athens than we would like to know; but it is surely surprising that he does not use the 'sykophant-words' in his description of the aftermath of the Herms and Mysteries affair, a passage that contains a number of words associated with sykophants elsewhere.[3] Nor, apparently, do the words appear on inscriptions. Perhaps it was too undignified and abusive a word for official documents, and for Thucydides' taste. Xenophon admits it, but he is less of a literary purist.[4]

Thirdly, we very rarely have a pair of prosecution and defence speeches. So, when a litigant calls his opponent a sykophant and describes his activities in the worst possible light, we never hear his adversary's version.

Fourthly, it would help if we had speeches arising from cases against sykophants (section II below). But we do not. Lysias wrote a speech against the philosopher Aeschines, according to Diogenes Laertios (II.63), which is probably the source of his fr.1 (Gernet & Bizos 1955–9, II: 247–8 = Athenaios XIII.611e). 'I think it would be difficult', says the speaker, 'to find a more sykophantish (*sukophantodesteran*) case than this ... I would never have imagined that a pupil of Socrates, who goes around delivering so many sermons about justice and virtue, would behave in the same way as any

---

219–21; Fisher 1976b: 35–7 (lucid and impartial); Carter 1986: 83–4, 105–6, 111–16, 128; Ostwald 1986: 80–2, 209–11, 223, 480. Gerst 1963: 47–88, 126–35 is known to me only from *Kleine Pauly* s.v. *Sykophantes*. References to Osborne without a date are to his contribution to this volume.

[2] Ste.Croix 1972: 363 n.10; Adkins 1976: 308, 316, 318; cf. Ostwald 1986: 210–11, 480. Xenophon (*Hell*. II.3.12) significantly says that sykophants were a pain in the neck (*bareis*) to the *kaloikagathoi* (misleadingly paraphrased by Lofberg 1917: 25 as 'to anyone but the extreme democrat'; similarly Bonner 1927: 66). On *kaloikagathoi* see Ste. Croix 1972: 371–6; Dover 1974: 41–5.

[3] E.g. *ho boulomenos* (VI.27.2); *diabolē* (29.2, 3; 61.6); *poneroi anthropoi, poneria* (53.2; see n.20 below); also *aitiasthai* and its compounds (28.2, 53.2, 60.4); *boan* (28.2); *kategorein* (60.4); *menuein* and cognates (27.2 *bis*, 28.1, 29.1, 53.1, 53.2 *bis*, 60.2, 60.4 *bis*, 61.2, 4). And according to Plutarch (*Alkib*. XIX.7), this was an episode in which sykophants were very active.

[4] See Treu s.v. *Xenophon: Wortschatz* in *RE* IXA.2 (1967): 1898–1901, with bibliog. at 1901; Higgins 1977: 2–4.

common criminal (*ponerotatoi kai adikotatoi*).' Entertaining stuff, but it tells us nothing about sykophancy.

Fifthly, we do not know about the origin of the curious word *sukophantes*. Etymology would not explain everything (a silly bugger is no longer a simple Bulgarian heretic), but it ought to be enlightening. The ancient notion that a *suko-phantes* is a man who reveals (*phainei*) a fig (*sukon*) always raises a smile, no doubt because the obvious way to reveal a fig is by removing a fig leaf. Ancient etymologies are unconvincing and mutually contradictory: they speak of an otherwise unattested ban on the export of figs,⁵ or illegal fig-picking, or even the payment of fines and taxes in figs, wine and olives – in which case why not oinophants or elaiophants? Modern efforts are no happier.⁶

There is one final obstacle to our enterprise: the howling gap between the first appearance of the sykophant, and the first appearance of the sykophant-words in surviving literature. Aristophanes' *Knights* alludes to a fig-joke in Kratinos in a context referring to bribery: the *Knights* was produced in 424 B.C., so Kratinos' joke is earlier than that. The word itself is first attested in Aristophanes' *Acharnians* of 425, or in the Old Oligarch, whichever was written first.⁷ Osborne does not seriously intend us to regard the sykophant as the creation of Solon (pp. 99–100), but the notion of *ho boulomenos* was (*Ath. Pol.* IX.1); so we have some 170 years of silence.⁸

There are five texts which might be thought to fill the lacuna,⁹ but they are all insecure or problematic. This lack of early material is particularly

⁵ This story would be more plausible if our sources did not consign it to the mists of antiquity (Plut. *Solon* XXIV.2; schol. Ar. *Plut.* 854); some (schol. Plato, *Rep.* 340d; *Souda* S1330, *Etym. Magn.* 733.41) even connect it with the discovery of the fig.

⁶ See Daremberg-Saglio IV.2: 1574 n.1; Lofberg 1917: vii–viii; *RE* IVA.1 (1931): 1028–30; Boisacq 1950: 924; Frisk 1960–72: 818–19; Chantraine 1968: 1069, none of whom has much better to offer. The variety of explanations to be found in Plutarch and the lexica implies that no unequivocal information was available to them, which suggests that the word was a fairly early coinage. *Sukophantes* looks like a comic compound (Marr 1983: 53); but, if so, how did it become a technical legal term? It cannot be a corruption of *sukhnophantes*, 'one who frequently brings *phaseis*', for linguistic reasons kindly explained to me by Dr G. C. Horrocks. The connection with figs is not confined to the comic poets and late lexica. When Aristotle retired to Khalkis lest the Athenians should 'sin twice against philosophy', he alluded to the perpetual supply of sykophants at Athens by punning on Homer's *sukon d'epi sukoi* – 'fig on fig' (fr. 667 Rose; *Odyssey* VII.121).

⁷ The 'Old Oligarch' ([Xen.] *Ath.Pol.*) has been dated as early as 443 B.C. and as late as 405. Ste. Croix 1972: 307–10 reviews earlier discussions and inclines towards 424. Against an early date, Marr 1983: 45–7.

⁸ Marr 1983: 53 ingeniously connects the earliest sykophants with those who laid information about men who imported contraband goods in defiance of the Megarian decree(s); cf. Bonner & Smith 1938: 44–5; Ste. Croix 1972: 383–6. If, however, the wisps of evidence for an earlier date (n.9 below) are accepted, the argument *e silentio* vanishes.

⁹ Epikharmos, *P.Oxy.* XXV.2429 fr.7 with Lobel *ad loc.*; Krateros *FGrH* 324 F12 (= Plut. *Arist.* XXVI.2); Plut. *Kimon* X.9; *Per.* XXXVII.4; Diod. XII.39.2–3. Carter 1986: 105 is inclined to accept Plut. *Arist.*, but note Plutarch's own doubts about the tradition. Plutarch uses the sykophant-words 86 times; Dr R. W. Sharples generously supplied me with a print-out of the relevant passages at short notice. In the Testimonia I have cited only those that refer to classical Greece. At *Alkib.* XIII.5, however, Plutarch says that the *demos* 'employed' (*ekhreto*) a sykophant when they wanted to attack distinguished citizens; one wonders whether he understood what went on.

lamentable, since it prevents us from grasping the original nature of the crime of *sukophantia*.

II   THE CRIME OF *SUKOPHANTIA*[10]

For sykophancy was a crime; and that is fatal to Osborne's thesis. If a plaintiff failed to secure one fifth of the jury's votes, he was liable to a fine, and in some cases partial loss of citizen rights: he was probably not permitted to bring any similar cases in the future.[11] It is at this stage, it seems, that the acquitted man could retaliate (but only if he wished: Lipsius 1908: 450–1). Various procedures were open to him (see Bonner & Smith 1938: 63–6, 70–1; MacDowell 1978: 65): *graphē*,[12] *probolē*[13] and *phasis*,[14] and at certain periods also *eisangelia*,[15] *endeixis* and *apagogē*.[16] It is because a convicted sykophant was a criminal that Peisetairos advises the sykophant in Aristophanes' *Birds* to turn to a lawful profession (*ergon nomimon*, 1448–50, with punning reply).

There ought surely to have been *some* legal definition of sykophancy, even if it lacked the precision that a modern lawyer might desire. Our texts make such a bewildering number of remarks about what a sykophant is that it is difficult to find it.[17] Lipsius (1905–15: 449) offers the most probable definition,

[10] The whole of this section rests on advice from Dr de Ste. Croix, who is however not responsible for the way in which it has been used.

[11] Lipsius 1905–15: 449; Bonner & Smith 1938: 56–7; MacDowell 1978: 64. Harrison 1971: 83 dissents. See esp. Theophrastos *Nomoi* (Szegedy-Maszak 1981: fr.v.4 = Schol. Dem. XXII.3 with Pollux VIII.53); for an example of *atimia* imposed on the man because 'he tried to sykophant', Hyp. *Euxen*. 34.

[12] Lys. XIII.67 (65), Isoc. XV.314; Navarre in Daremberg-Saglio IV.2, 1575–6; Lipsius 1905–15: 448–51; Latte in *RE* IVA.1 (1931): 1031–2; Harrison 1971: 62–3; unconvincingly denied by Crawley 1970.

[13] *Ath.Pol.* XLIII.5; Isoc. XV.314; Lipsius 1905–15: 213–14, 448–9; Bonner & Smith 1938: 67–70; Harrison 1971: 61–2. I agree with Osborne (n.37) and Rhodes 1981: 527 that it is puzzling that *Ath.Pol.* seems to say that a maximum of three *probolai* could be brought annually against citizen sykophants, and a maximum of three against metics. Puzzling for two reasons: (*a*) A sykophant needed to be able to prosecute. Could a metic bring a *graphē*? The modern consensus is *yes* – Harrison 1971: 193–6, esp. 194 n.2; MacDowell 1978: 76, 78, 222–4; Whitehead 1977: 94–6; Rhodes 1981: 527, 655; but only in exceptional cases. If so, it is surprising that citizen and metic maxima are identical. (*b*) Since the number of citizens greatly exceeded the number of metics, this would imply, not that metics were *as* active as citizens in sykophancy, but that they were *more* active – even odder since their numbers dropped in the fourth century when the *Ath.Pol.* was written (Whitehead 1977: 97–8, 159–60).
    Sommerstein 1983: 218 had already suggested that the *Ath.Pol.* 'may have erred through careless compression of its legal source'. Thus Osborne's translation (n.37) whereby the metics become the victims, not the accusers, is very attractive. For non-Athenian victims at Athens, see Plut. *Kim*. x.9 (a Persian); Eupolis *PCG* fr.99.81–105 (an Epidaurian). Lofberg 1917: 90 n.20 is unsatisfactory on this point.

[14] *Phasis*: Lipsius 1905–15: 313–14, 448; Bonner & Smith 1938: 41; MacDowell 1978: 62–3; Osborne p.87. The arguments of those such as Harrison (1971: 218–19), who deny that *phasis* was used against sykophants, are refuted by Cohen 1973: 89–92.

[15] *Eisangelia*: Isoc. XV.314; Lipsius 1905–15: 201, 449.

[16] *Endeixis* and *apagogē*: Dem. LVIII.10–13; MacDowell 1978: 65.

[17] On the difficulty of finding a clear definition, Bonner 1927: 63–4; Bonner & Smith 1938: 42–3; Crawley 1970: 84–93; Harrison 1971: 60–2; Osborne n.36. MacDowell 1978: 65–6 believes there may have been no legal definition, but lists what may have counted as relevant evidence.

Gewinnsucht oder Leichtsinn: in other words (I take it), when the case came to court, the prosecutor could provide no proper evidence, witnesses or proofs, so that it became clear that he had either hoped that his victim would pay him not to go to law, or that he was bringing the case solely in order to obtain the prosecutor's share of the fine (see p. 112 below). A clear example of this sense appears in Hyperides, who says that one Teisis had brought a case in the hope of gaining three-quarters of Euthykrates' property – 45 talents, a huge sum – but he had been punished 'because he had tried to sykophant' his victims (*Euxen.* 34).[18]

Sykophancy, then, was a crime. That alone makes it impossible for Osborne to rehabilitate the sykophant in the way that Finley (1974) rehabilitated the demagogue.

III A DIRTY WORD

But whatever their original legal meaning, the sykophant-words came to be used in a very wide range of senses. Definition is never a simple process (Robinson 1954), and the sykophant-words are not simple concepts. In the first place, they are value-words, and secondly, even if they originally had a 'core' meaning, by the time they surfaced in literature they had certainly lost it (Osborne p. 84).

By calling the sykophant-words 'value words' I mean, of course, that they are pejorative words indicating that the person who is using them disapproves of what he is referring to. But like many value-words, they carry a descriptive content as well (Hare 1952: esp. 111–26). So to call a man a sykophant is not simply a way of being rude, it conveys a certain amount of information.

No one in real life would say 'I'm a *sukophantes*', just as no one nowadays would state on his passport that his occupation was Jerry Builder or Confidence Trickster. When the man in Aristophanes' *Birds* does so (1432), that in itself is a joke. The sykophant in the *Plutus*, it should be noted, says *boulomai* (908) – in other words, he is claiming to be a *boulomenos*. In this respect, *sukophantes* is unlike, say, *sophistes*, or *demagogos*, which started life respectably.[19] And this is another reason why it is impossible to rehabilitate the sykophant.

Sukophantes is not only a dirty word, but is frequently found in the company of other words of ill repute. The sykophant is unfeeling (Dem. XVIII.289), unjust ([Arist.] *Virt. et Vit.* 1251b2–3; Dem. XVIII.112, XLI.23, LI.16, LII.33; Diod. XX.10.3; Isoc. XVIII.14, 55, XXI.5; Lys. XXI.17, XXV.26, frs. 1.2, 43; Xen. *Hell.* II.3.22 *bis*; *Mem.* IV.4.11; P. Mich.Zen. 57.3), shameful (Aesch. II.145; Ar. *Ekkles.* 560; Dem. XIX.222, XXV.9 *bis*; Lys. fr. 1.1), impure (Dem. XXV.63), unrestrained (Plut. *Pelop.* XXV.5), lacking in

---

[18] See Bonner & Smith 1938: 49–50; it is not a *graphē sukophantias*.

[19] A *sophistes* was originally a wise man, later a 'sophistical' arguer; *demagogos* means literally 'leader of the people', but soon acquired its modern pejorative sense.

self-control (Isoc. xv.224), an impostor ([Arist.] *Virt. et Vit.* 1251b2–3), unsociable (Dem. xxv.52; Isoc. xv.300), shameless (Aesch. 1.105; Dem. xxv.41, xxxvii.3), brazen (Dem. xxv.9, 35, lv.28; Plut. *Alkib.* xiii.5), unmanly (Aesch. iii.231), rootless (Dem. xxv.52), unholy (Aesch. ii.5), foolish (Plut. *Alkib.* xiii.5), impious (Dem. xxv.52, 53, 63), licentious (Aesch. 1.32; Arist. *Polit.* 1304b21), implacable (Dem. xxv.52), ungracious (Dem. xxv.35), oppressive (Xen. *Hell.* ii.3.12), a maligner (Dem. xviii.189, 242, 317, xxv.83), disgusting (Aesch. 1.105; Dem. xxxvi.58), harmful (Isoc. xv.316), defamatory (Dem. xviii.95, 256, xxv.52, xxxix.34), a shouter (Dem. xxv.47, 49, lix.43; Plut. *Phok.* xii.3), coward (Aesch. 1.105), slanderer (see p. 113 below), vexatious (Dem. xviii.189), ill-willed (Dem. xxv.82, Isoc. xv.288), a persecutor (Dem. xxxvi.52; lv.35), deceiver (Dem. lviii.40; Isaeus xi.4; Lys. 14 [cf. Dem. xxv.41]), plotter and perjurer (*Etym. Magn.* 733.54; Dem. xxxvii.3, xxxix.34, xl.43, lv.33, lvii.57; Hyp. *Athen.* 26; Isoc. xv.230, xvii.46, xviii.51 [cf. p. 113 below]; Dem. xxv.35), bold (Aesch. 1.105; Dem. xxv.97; Isoc. xv.316), malicious ([Arist.] *Virt. et Vit.* 1251b2–3; Menand. *Theoph.* fr.1; Plut. *Pelop.* xxv.5), wicked (Aesch. 1.105; Ar. *Acharn.* 829, 909, 936, *Birds* 1413, *Plutus* 879; Dem. xxv.46, 48, 52, 82; Diod. xii.12.2; Isoc. xv.313, 317; Plut. *Mor.* 998b; cf. Isoc. xv.164), an evil meddler (*Ath. Pol.* xxxv.3; Isoc. xv.224, 225, 300; Hesykhios s.v. *sukophantes*), mischievous (Aesch. ii.145; Dem. xl.43; Plato *Rep.* 341ab), accursed (Dem. xviii.212), a flatterer (Ar. fr.539; Menand. *Theoph.* fr.1; Theopomp. F 281), screamer (Dem. xxv.9,47), stirrer-up (Ar. *Peace* 654), chatterbox (Ar. *Acharn.* 933, *Peace* 653, Her. Krit. 1.4; cf. Hesykhios s.v. *sukophantes*), abusive (Aesch. iii.215; Dem. xviii.138, xxv.41, lvii.34, lviii.40), a man who treats people outrageously (Isoc. xii.142, xv.318), filthy (Dem. xviii.289, xxv.41), bloodstained (Dem. xxv.84), misanthropic (Dem. xviii.112; Isoc. xv.315), wretched (Alexis fr.182; Ar. *Acharn.* 517), a villain (Ar. *Birds* 1463, *Ekkles.* 437, *Peace* 652; Schol. *Plut.* 31; [Arist.] *Virt et Vit.* 1251b2–3; Eupolis *PCG* 99.85; Lys. iii.44), lawless (Dem. xxv.19), a busybody (Aesch. iii.172; [Arist.] *Virt. et Vit.* 1251b2–3; Her. Krit. 1.4), cruel (Dem. xxv.45, 83, 84, 96; Isoc. xv.300; Schol. Ar. *Plut.* 854), grasping (Dem. lv.1; Plut. *Sol.* v.4), meddlesome (Ar. *Plut.* 913; Isoc. xv.230, 237; Menand. *Perikeir.* 374; Plut. *Mor.* 523a; Schol. Dem. xviii.95), a besmircher (Plut. *Alkib.* xiii.5), causer of confusion (Ar. *Peace* 654 with schol.; Dem. xxv.50; Diod. xi.37.5, xv.40.1; Isoc. xviii.43), bold (Ar. *Ekkles.* 560; Dem. xxv.9; Isaeus xi.13; Isoc. xv.317, xviii.22), rough (Philippides fr.29), hubristic (Aesch. ii.181; [Arist.] *Rhet. ad Alex.* 1424b13; Dem. xxv.49–50, liii.1; Diod. xii.12.2), unhealthy (Ar. *Acharn.* 956; Dem. lviii.12), treacherous (Her. Krit. 1.4), worthless (Isoc. xv.317), envious (Dem. xviii.121, xxv.52, xxxix.34; Diod. xii.32.2, 3, xx.10.3; Isoc. xv.163; Krateros F12 [= Plut. *Arist.* xxvi.2]), a lover of blame (Dem. xviii.242), of quarrels (Isoc. xv.315, 317; *Souda* s1330), of fault-finding (*Etym. Magn.* 733.55), of litigation ([Arist.] *Rhet. ad Alex.* 1444a31), of rivalry (Lyk. 1.5), of meddling (Lyk. 1.3), an intimidator (Aesch. 11.181, 183; Arist. *Pol.* 1304b22; Dem. xxiii.15, 180, xxv.52, xxxix.2; Diod. xx.10.4; Isoc. xxi.8; [Plato] *Alkib.* 11.142a), difficult (Dem. xviii.256; Isoc. xv.300, 313), false (Aesch. 11.5, 170, 183; Dem. xxi. 124, xxv.9, 50; Diod. 1.77.4; Lys. xix.51; *Etym. Magn.* 733.39–40; Hesykh. s.v. *sukophantes*; *Souda* s1330) and cruel (Dem. xviii.212, 275, xxv.63, 83, 84; Isoc. xv.315).

Above all, the sykophant is *poneros*, plain bad, a word associated with him at least fifty times.[20] So closely, indeed, that according to Plutarch (*Phok.* x.3), when the notorious Aristogeiton[21] registered for military service hobbling along on a stick, and with his legs in bandages, Phokion said: 'Enter him as a *poneros*' – a pun on 'unfit for military service' and the traditional epithet of the sykophant. Moreover, Theopompos (*FGrH* 115 F110) assures us that Philip of Macedon founded a city in Thrace which he populated with sykophants and other evil types, to the number of some two thousand: its name was Poneropolis – Crooksville, or High Wyckedombe (Lofberg 1917: 94 n.41 rightly characterises this 'information' as preposterous and Aristophanic). Indeed, sykophants are associated with various types of rogues: with thieves, burglars, cut-purses, muggers, temple-robbers, kidnappers and pirates (Plato *Rep.* 575b; Ar. *Ekkles.* 438, *Plut.* 30–1, 869, 909, 935, fr.539; Diphilos fr.32; Theopomp. F281; Hyp. *Lyk.* 2). And they are also compared with a small menagerie: with beasts in general (Dem. xxv.8), and specifically with monkey (Dem. xviii.242), wolf (Xen. *Mem.* ii.9.2, 7; Dem. xxv.40; Menand. *Monost.* 440 = 603), fox (Andok. 1.99; Dem. xviii.242), dog (Dem. xxv.40 with Osborne n. 41), snake (Dem. xxv.52, 96, cf. Plautus, *Poen.* 1032), scorpion (Eupolis fr.231; Dem. xxv.52) and poisonous spider (Dem. xxv.96).

Now of course I am not saying that this abusive language was always justified; but if we clear away all this muck, then we are not simply re-assessing the sykophant's rôle: we are destroying an essential part of the way in which he was perceived by his contemporaries. The muck is, as it were, part of the picture. Clean it away, and you have not restored the picture to its original condition: you have ruined it.

IV   FAMILY RESEMBLANCES·

Besides being pejorative, the sykophant-words are not simple concepts. They carry an agglomeration of senses, of which any one may be prominent, or any

---

[20] Aesch. 11.99; Ant. v.80; Ar. *Plut.* 31, 862, 869, 920, 939, 957; *Ath.Pol.* xxxv.3; [Arist.] *Rhet. ad Alex.* 1444a32; Dem. xviii.242, xxi.122, xxv.9, 39, 46, 49 *bis*, 50, 53, 82, 97 *bis*, xli.23, lv.1, lvii.32, lviii.27, 38, 40; Schol. Dem. xviii.95; Diod. xii.12.2; Isoc. xv.164, 224, 241, 242, 314, 316, xvii.56, xviii.51, 55; Lys. vii.1, xxv.24, fr.1.2; Menand. *Perikeir.* 377 (restored); Plut. *Nik.* iv.5, *Phok.* x.3; Theopomp. *FGrH* 115 F110 *ter*; Xen. *Mem.* ii.9.6.

'Plain bad' is an over-simplification, since *poneros* also carried snobbish class overtones. It was used contemptuously by the upper classes of their social inferiors: Neil 1901: 206–8 (oddly mistaken on Orators); Ste.Croix 1972: 358–9, 373–5; Dover 1974: 52–3, 64–5.

[21] Aristogeiton gets a uniformly bad press: Dem. xxv, xxvi, Dein. ii, Plut. *Phok.* x.3, x.9 with *Mor.* 188b.

one may be dropped, in any particular context. Not every item in the bundle is present every time the words are used. Wittgenstein's notion of family resemblances (1958: sections 66–7) may be helpful in this context.[22]

It is because sykophancy is a word of this type that it is impossible to find a neat, short definition. Attempts at such definitions can be found in the ancient lexica: the *Souda* (s1330) defines *sukophantein* as 'to accuse someone falsely'; Hesykhios says that the *sukophantes* is 'a false accuser, an evil meddler'; *sukophantai* are *hoi epereazontes*, people who threaten abusively; *sukophantia* is *katalalia*, slanderous talk. The scholiast on Dem. xviii.95 explains: '*sukophantes* is used not only of the liar, but also the man who is a busybody (*polupragmon*) with regard to things that do not concern him, and who says bad things (*ponera*).' All these are inadequate. The lexica also tell us that *sukophantein* means 'to tickle erotically', but that is clearly a mistake – the definition, I mean, not the pastime.[23] Modern attempts at a snappy definition also fail:[24] e.g., 'one who brings a false accusation, usually for filthy lucre' (Rouse 1898–9, vii: 398): but the accusations of the sykophant were not always false (p. 112 below).

I have therefore adopted a different approach. I have gone through the testimonia (some five hundred) and picked out those that seem most useful in clarifying the concept – for example, where the author is generalising, or associating an idea very closely with that of sykophancy. I am aware that this method may be subjective and imprecise, but when my conclusions are compared with Osborne's, the results may be of some interest.

V   MONEY-GRUBBING

Half a dozen major characteristics of the sykophant emerge from this exercise. The first is *monetary motivation*. Since Osborne denies this, I will adduce the evidence: the job of the sykophant is to bring a charge against the innocent – that is what brings him most profit (Lys. xxv.3). Another speaker says that he paid one Kallimakhos a sum of money not to bring a certain matter to court (Isoc. xviii.9–10). Then he goes on: 'but so that he should not be able to sykophant me again . . . ' – in other words, the cash settlement is referred to as sykophancy. (As there is no precise English equivalent, I translate the Greek verb *sukophantein* as 'to sykophant a person'. It takes the accusative – what else?) Isocrates says that those who have nothing[25] go in for sykophancy

---

[22] Wittgenstein's views on this are widely scattered; see e.g. Kenny 1975: 153, 163, 224; Brand 1979: 77–9, 113, 126, 130–1.

[23] Other snappy misdefinitions in schol. Plato *Rep.* 340d; *Souda* s1332; *Etym.Magn.* 733.39, 54. Erotic tickle: *Souda* s1329, *Etym.Magn.* 733.47–9; Osborne p.86 with n.8.

[24] E.g. Navarre in Daremberg-Saglio iv.2, 1574: 'délation, escroquerie et chantage'. The best modern definitions are therefore complex: e.g. Sommerstein 1980: 181–2. Some scholars (e.g. Bonner 1927: 48, 50; Hansen 1987: 59–60) speak of different 'types' or 'kinds' of sykophants: I am not sure that such reification is justified.

[25] Adkins rightly points out that, although our sources give the impression that sykophants were usually poor men (cf. Osborne p.86), this was not in fact so. However, I doubt that most of

(XXI.5): i.e. to make money. He adds that people who want to sykophant act against men whom they see to be rich (XXI.8). Demosthenes associates sykophanting with begging for and exacting money (XXIV.41), and describes the notorious Aristogeiton as looking for someone to intimidate and exact money from (XXV.52). He also says that the sykophant prosecutes by *graphē* and by *phasis* for cash (LIX.43, dismissed on inadequate grounds by Osborne, n.38).

Cumulatively, these testimonia suggest that making money was perceived as an important characteristic of the sykophant,[26] though not a necessary one. How did he do it? 'Occasionally', Osborne writes, 'the sykophant is clearly alleged to have brought his prosecution merely in order to reach an out-of-court settlement for a sum of money' (p. 88). 'Occasionally' is an understatement: I find thirty-four clear examples of the practice.[27] There are also five references to 'demanding (*aitein*) money', without further explanation;[28] the phrase 'he will bring them to a state of fear and extract money from them' in Demosthenes XXV.52 seems to be the key here. 'Demanding' or 'extracting money' means demanding hush-money: the sykophant promises his victim that if he gives him some cash, he will not take him to court – blackmail, in fact.[29]

In Osborne's view (p. 89), the Demosthenic speech against Aristogeiton (XXV) 'brings little detailed evidence' in support of its insinuations, and its allegations are 'vague'. Yet in section 47 the jury is reminded of how Aristogeiton sold the *eisangelia* against Hegemon; how he gave up the *graphai* against Demades; how in the case of Agathon the olive-merchant he shouted and screeched and went *iou iou* ('hullo hullo hullo'), saying at meetings of the assembly that he should be tortured; then he pocketed a certain sum and kept quiet when he was acquitted; he threatened Demokles with an *eisangelia* – and then what did he do? The last phrase is marvellously vague (perhaps a call for audience participation: cf. Bers 1985), but all the rest is precise and detailed enough – though whether it is true is another matter.

them were 'from the city rather than rural Attica' (316–17), despite Ar. *Peace* 191, Lys. XX.12. Athenian society was more complex than that. Many who lived in the city had farms in the countryside (e.g. Lys. I.11), and many who came from rural demes might live in the city (Osborne 1985a *passim*, esp. 1–22, 47–50, 64–70, 183–9; Hansen 1987: 64 with n.413).

26 In Aristophanes' *Plutus* (924–5) the sykophant exclaims that he would not change his occupation 'for Wealth itself, and all the silphium of Battos' – or as we would say, 'for all the tea in China'. This does not indicate that Aristophanes 'is constrained to admit that mercenary motives are not the most important' (Adkins 1976: 317).

27 Andok. I.101, 105; Ant. v.79–80; Ar. *Knights* 439; fr. 219; Dem. XXV.47, 50, 52; XXXVIII.20; LVII.60 *bis*; LVIII.6 *bis*, 8–13, 26, 28–9, 32 *bis*, 34–5, 42, 43; Hyp. *Lyk.* 2; Isoc. XV.174; XVIII.7, 9–10; XXI.13–14; Lys. VII.20–1, 39; XX.7; XXV.25; Philippides com. fr. 29; Teleklides com. fr. 41; Xen. *Mem.* II.9.1.

28 Dem. XXV.50 (Osborne p.90 with n.23), XXXIX.222, XXV.41, LVIII.64; Lys. XXV.3. I use the term 'hush money' for payments to a sykophant (a) not to bring a case at all, and (b) to drop a case on which he had embarked (Bonner 1927: 66; Bonner & Smith 1938: 54, 58–63).

29 Andok. I.99; Dem. XII.19; XXXIX.25; LII.33; LV.6; LVIII.62; LIX.39; Isaeus XI.31; Isoc. XVII.46; XXI.5, 19; XVII.46; Lys. XXI.17; XXIV.2; XXVI.24; Menander, *Georg.* fr.1; Plato *Crito* 44e; Xen. *Hell.* II.3.22; *Oik.* II.21; *Symp.* IV.30.

I would argue, therefore, that Osborne has understated the frequency with which sykophants are associated with blackmail. But I agree that there are many passages where sykophants are said to have 'taken money' where it is difficult or impossible to see just what they are being accused of. Sykophants could make money in at least three ways. One was by extracting hush-money (n.27). Plutarch reveals one means by which a sykophant might get hold of a guilty secret: by reading a deceased person's correspondence (*Eumenes* XVI.4). Some have wondered whether there was much point in making such an agreement: the sykophant could always pass your secret on to someone else, and *he* could prosecute you. But since people did pay up, the sykophant must have promised not to reveal your secret to a third party (Bonner 1927: 67–8; Bonner & Smith 1938: 54). Secondly, there are those cases where the prosecutor was entitled to a fine (p. 107 above).[30] MacDowell (1978: 62; cf. Sinclair 1988: 73) says that these must have been the kinds of case for which volunteers came forward most readily. He is surely right, though surprisingly our sources rarely allege that a sykophant was motivated by a desire to grab his share of the fine (only Hyp. *Euxen*. 34; Dem. LVIII.13, 64). However, when a sykophant alludes vaguely to a sykophant's monetary motives (n.28), no doubt he often has this in mind.[31] Thirdly, the sykophant could make money by *prosecuting people for a fee* (Dem. XXI.103, LI.16, LIX.43; Aesch. I.20; Bonner & Smith 1938: 55), presumably because he was an abler speaker than the man who hired him (Dem. XXI.103).

A number of statements about money are ambiguous and could refer to any of these three methods (e.g. Lys. XXV.25; Dem. LVII.60). Sometimes, no doubt, the speakers deliberately used vague phrases, because they had no evidence to back up their smears.[32]

VI   OTHER CHARACTERISTICS OF THE SYKOPHANT

Let us turn now to the other characteristics of the sykophant. Sykophancy is frequently said to be a matter of bringing *false charges*. There were occasions (Osborne p. 87) when allegations made by sykophants were in fact true. Never mind: that was not how he was usually perceived: passages in the Orators make it clear that his accusations were normally thought of as a pack of lies; and this image is perpetuated by Diodorus and the lexicographers.[33]

Thirdly, *sophistical quibbling*, to which Osborne gives pride of place. In the

---

[30] See e.g. Bonner & Smith 1938: 40–1; Ostwald 1986: 209, 223; contra, Osborne 1985b: 44–8.

[31] Plato approved of this practice, and introduced it into his 'ideal' state (*Laws* 745a, 928bc): the prosecutor gets half the fine.

[32] Osborne's case is not greatly strengthened by passages concerning blackmail where the sykophant words are *not* used (p.90).

[33] False charges: Aesch. II.5, 39, 183; Dem. XVIII.95 with Schol., 121; XXV.3; LVIII.30–1; Diod. I.77, 92; *Etym.Magn.* 733.39; Hesykhios s.v. *sukophantes*; *Souda* S1330, 1332; Schol. Dem. XVIII.95. Cf. Plut. *Alex.* LXXIV.5. Adkins 1976: 208 puts it well: the word 'gives a general impression of decrying accusers for making false allegations, but seems also to be available to decry any behaviour which the writer regards as scoundrelly in a legal context'.

first book of Plato's *Republic*, Thrasymakhos says that Socrates is sykophanting him not only because he believes he is indulging in logical quibbles, but
also because he is *attacking* him. 'Do you think I'm *deliberately* maltreating
you?' asks Socrates (341a7) – just as in the Aristotelian *Problems* (952a3–4) the
sykophant always does wrong *ek pronoias*, deliberately, with malice afore-
thought. The passages in Aristotle's *Topics* cited by Osborne (n.6) also refer to
fraudulent quibbles, arguments that cheat by exploiting ambiguities, or by
confusing metaphorical expressions with literal ones (see also *Soph. El.*
174b8–12; *Topics* 157a26–33; cf. *Rhet.* 1402a14). Here the meaning of
quibbling or sophistry merges with that of fallacy, falsity and making a charge
against one's opponent. In other words, the *quibbling* notion overlaps with the
falsehood notion, and bits of the *attacking* notion that we will examine next.
We find the same association of ideas in non-philosophical texts: when
Epameinondas was put on trial over a technicality, Plutarch calls the charge a
sukophantema (*Pelop.* xxv.4).[34]

Fourthly, then, *slanderous attack*. Osborne (p. 91) lays some stress on
Aeschines' contrast between *phemē*, gossip, and *sukophantia* (11.145) though I
find it forced and awkward ('pedantisch und nicht glücklich', Wankel 1976:
899; cf. Crawley 1970: 86): all they have in common is that they involve
allegations. As we might expect, Aristotle is more sensible about the close
relationship between hatred (*ekhthra, misos*), slanderous attack (*diabolē*) and
sykophancy (*Rhet.* 1382a1–7). But we may agree with Aeschines (11.145) that
diabolē is the sister of *sukophantia*: reckless abuse is characteristic of the
sykophant, in the assembly and in the courts (Dem. xxv.41). This is
Hesykhios' *katalalia* (p. 110 above). It is also what lies behind Aeschines'
surprising statement (111.231) that Homer calls Thersites a coward and a
sykophant. A glance at *Iliad* 11.211–77 will make it clear that what Aeschines
has in mind is Thersites' aggressive abuse: he was immoderate in speech, he
was always quarrelling with those who had more conventional hair-styles, he
shrieks and he shouts: Odysseus tells him off for his offensive abuse, and
wallops him. Everyone says that this is the best thing Odysseus has ever done:
'that'll teach him (Thersites) to upbraid kings with his insulting words'.

Fifthly, the sykophant *frequently takes people to court*. This is rarely stated
explicitly (Dem. xxxvi.53–4, xxxviii.3; Dein. 11.12), but the references to
sykophancy as a full-time occupation or as a 'trade' (section vii below) are sufficient to indicate its importance. The modern word for it is 'vitilitigation'.[35]

Finally, the sykophant characteristically *acts after the event and rakes up
old charges*. The true adviser, according to Demosthenes, makes decisions in
advance, whereas the sykophant snipes at them later (xviii.189, 239); he
attacks decisions already taken (*Prooim.* 35.2). So too in private affairs:

---

[34] Quibbling: Arist. *Eud. Eth.* 1221b5–7; *Poet.* 1456a4–7. Non-philosophical examples: Lyk.
Leok. 31; Dem. xxv.18.

[35] For an example, see the *London Evening Standard*, 5 March 1987 (I am indebted to Dr Paul
Cartledge for the parallel). It is surprising that the *Souda* (s1324) speaks of a female sykophant
(*sukophantis*): perhaps an insult aimed at some women in comedy.

'Nikomakhos, you should have brought forward witnesses at the time' (Lys. VII.20; cf. Dem. LVII.49); or, 'but that was twenty years ago' (Dem. XXXVI.26–7, 53). If men do not contest charges immediately, but later, they are regarded as sykophants and *poneroi* (Dem. XLI.23).

My family characteristics, then, are monetary motivation, false charges, sophistic quibbling, abusive attacks, the raking up of the past, and the frequency with which the sykophant resorts to litigation. It goes without saying that he must also be a *fluent speaker* (Osborne p. 86). Homer says that the protosykophant Thersites 'knew many words'; according to Isocrates, everyone knows that sykophants are clever speakers, and this is how Kriton's side-kick Arkhedemos is described.[36] For if the sykophant's victim called his bluff by going to court, the sykophant would incur heavy penalties if he failed to obtain the requisite number of votes (p. 106 above).

What would the sykophant have to say for himself in reply? The answer will be found in Aristophanes' *Plutus* 900 and 907–8 – but it is important to note the incredulous and sceptical reactions of Dikaios;[37] in Demosthenes LVIII.63–4, where his argument is rejected; at Lycurgus 1.3–6; in the panegyric in Plato's *Laws* 730d; and of course in Osborne's paper.[38]

VII   WERE THERE PROFESSIONAL SYKOPHANTS?

Osborne asserts (p. 93) that 'there is no trace of the profession of the sykophant in the Orators'. I would dispute this. Isocrates says that Lysimakhos has chosen to live from sykophancy (xv.164). Demosthenes alleges that Theokrines and his friends make a living from sykophancy. Aristogeiton, he says elsewhere (xxv.82), likes to see everyone involved in lawsuits and malicious prosecutions: that's his substitute for farming, and for business: for (sections 51–2) he is not involved in any craft, farming or business himself, but spends all his time on sykophantic pursuits. According to Hyperides (*Lykophron* 2), Ariston went around threatening everyone with lawsuits, and if they did not pay him, he would bring them to trial: but if they *were* prepared to pay him, he would let them go, and he would give the cash to Theomnestos. With this cash, Theomnestos was able to buy slaves whose activities provided him with food, and he paid Ariston one obol a day for each slave, which in turn enabled Ariston to be an *athanatos sukophantes*, a non-stop sykophant – a fascinating and unusually detailed picture of one way the 'trade' worked. These statements may be untrue, but they had to be plausible to a large jury. They surely constitute more than a 'trace' of sykophancy as a profession in the

---

[36] *Iliad* 11.213; Isoc. xxi.5 (*deinoi legein*; cf. Plut. *Pelop.* xxv.5); Xen. *Mem.* 11.9.4 (*panu hikanon legein*); Plato *Rep.* 575b; cf. Osborne p.96.

[37] Adkins 1976: 308–10, 316–17 draws attention to these; Osborne (n.48) does not.

[38] Osborne (n.48) cites Plut. *Timoleon* XXVII.1: 'as every lark must have a crest, so every democracy, it seems, must have a sykophant'. But Plutarch means that it is a *necessary* attribute, not an attractive one (cf. *Mor.* 91e, 809c).

Orators (see also Xen. *Hell.* ii.3.12, cited by Osborne, p. 100; cf. Andok. 1.99).

All this strongly suggests that Aristophanes' jokes must have had some basis in reality. In the *Birds*, Peisetairos congratulates the sykophant on his *tekhnē* (trade) and asks him whether this is the job[39] he works at. 'Yes,' he replies, 'you see, I've never learned to dig.' Peisetairos points out that there are other respectable professions from which a man may earn his living (1422–35). Then the sykophant protests (and this *must* be a joke: Ehrenberg 1951: 344 takes it seriously) that sykophanting is the *bios* that he has inherited from his grandfather – his way of life and, presumably, his means of livelihood – and he cannot disgrace his family name. In *Plutus* (906–8; cf. 931) the sykophant tells Karion that he is not a farmer, he is not an *emporos* (trader), and he has not learnt a craft.[40] He is a voluntary prosecutor; he speaks as though that is an activity comparable with farming or trading (cf. *Ekkles.* 562–3).

Could people really make a living from sykophancy? Or are the Orators exaggerating, Aristophanes fantasising, and Xenophon merely revealing his upper-class bias? Kriton says that sykophants were 'cheap' (Plato, *Crito* 45a); Demosthenes (xxv.50, lviii.63) and Isocrates (xviii.10, 14) agree. There are a number of passages that state exactly how much money a sykophant took, though no jury could check the accuracy of such information, and the comic 'evidence' should not be taken too seriously. The smallest sum is one mina, and the commonest two, but we also hear of larger sums such as ten minas, thirty minas and even three talents.[41] What was 'cheap' for a man like Kriton or Isocrates was not cheap for the ordinary Athenian: if we accept Markle's calculations (1985: 293–7), two minas was four-fifths of the annual income of an unskilled labourer in the late fifth century.

If the alleged figures are not entirely phoney – and they too had to be plausible – then three or four deals a year should have brought in a comfortable sum. But what we are told about Stephanos (Dem. lix.39, 68) reveals another possibility. At first, according to his prosecutor, Stephanos had no income apart from what he could earn as a sykophant (contrast here

[39] Sykophancy is called an *ergon* here (*Birds* 1430; cf. 1450; Lys. xxv.3), an *ergasia* at Dem. xx.152, and the verb *ergazomai* is used here, *Birds* 1430 and at Dem. xxv.83. The place where people *ergazontai* at an *ergon* is an *ergasterion*, and this is surely the explanation of the *ergasteria sukophanton* of Dem. xxxix.2 and xl.9. On this I agree with Osborne n.33, as against e.g. Calhoun 1913: 23–5, 44–6, 79–81; cf. Bonner & Smith 1938: 54. 'Gangs' (Bonner 1927: 68) is a better word than 'clubs'. For a group of sykophants allegedly sharing out profits, see Dem. lviii.40. Whether sykophancy was a *tekhnē* is a different matter. Pro: Peisetairos in Ar. *Birds*, and Isoc. xv.314; contra, the sykophant at *Plutus* 905, Dem. xxv.51.

[40] Demosthenes must have been familiar with this passage: not only do xxv.51 and 82 echo lines 903–5, but xxiii.190 also recalls the sykophant's claim to be *khrestos* and *philopolis* (line 900). The image of the sykophant as a scorpion (xxv.52) comes from Eupolis fr.231. These are remarkable instances of the kinship between Greek oratory and comedy (Dover 1974: 23–33).

[41] The following sums are specified: 1 mina: Telekleides fr.41, Dem. lviii.34; 2 minas: Dem. lviii.32, Isoc. xviii.7, 10, Philippides fr.29; 4 minas: Telekleides fr.41; 10 minas: Isoc. xviii.7; 30 minas: Isoc. xxi.14, Lys. xxvi.24 (30 minas each from an unspecified number of prisoners); 100 gold staters: Eupolis fr. 99.86–7 *CGF*; 1 talent: Ar. *Knights* 439; [Plut.] *Mor.* 842a; 3 talents: Dem. xxxviii.20.

Hansen 1987: 59–60 with Osborne n.38), but then he bought the glamorous Neaira, and her immoral earnings helped to maintain his household. In other words, Stephanos had a second, if not a third, source of income – he also lent money at interest (Dem. XLV.69–70). Such a situation may well have been more common than our sources suggest: men who are alleged to 'live off sykophancy' might often have been making money in some other ways, from a farm, for example, or a slave workshop: sykophancy was only their most *conspicuous* activity.

VIII   THE EFFECTS OF SYKOPHANCY

Finally, the effects of vitilitigation. Kriton, you remember, a rich *apragmon*, employed the shady[42] Arkhedemos to deal with sykophants (Xen. *Mem.* II.9; Osborne pp. 96–7). But that was not the only possible strategy. Xenophon offers us two other vignettes. Kharmides in the *Symposium* (IV.30) was always afraid of burglars and sykophants when he was rich; so he *etherapeue* the syko-phants – he cultivated them, or buttered them up – presumably with gifts, monetary or otherwise. Iskhomakhos in the *Oikonomikos* (XI.21–5; briefly, Osborne p. 98) had naively hoped that his prosperity would make him a *kalos-kagathos*, but found that it in fact exposed him to attacks by sykophants. So he took up oratory, and practised it at home; he would even get members of his household to prosecute him, and speak in his own defence, and vice versa. The point of the exercise was that, if he were ever hauled to court by a sykophant, he would be capable of putting up a good defence (cf. Isoc. XXI.5).

These two anecdotes show that we should not take Kriton's adoption of a hit-man as a *typical* strategy.[43] Indeed, since Xenophon tells Kriton's story in some detail, it is presumably unusual; and within the same circle, there were other methods of dealing with sykophants.

Osborne's final and, in my view, least convincing argument, is that, broadly speaking, sykophancy was (to use the terminology favoured by Sellar and Yeatman) a 'Good Thing'.[44] Otherwise a rich man like Kriton, says Osborne, could evade (p. 97) or ignore (p. 98) the laws of the city: 'the threat of sykophantic allegations was a constant reminder of the rule-bound nature of residence in a community' (p. 99). If we say that sykophancy might deter the rich from *breaking* the laws, rather than evading them, then to that extent Adkins, Osborne, Solon and I are in agreement.

But Osborne also maintains that sykophancy 'made life difficult for wealthy men who refused to participate in the democratic workings of society' (p. 98); such prosecutors 'were compelling those rich men who shrank from

---

[42] 'Shady': I agree with Osborne (pp.97–8; cf. Carter 1986: 111–13), as against e.g. Calhoun 1944: 43, who calls Arkhedemos 'poor but honest' and, apparently without irony, 'this worthy gentleman'. Calhoun memorably describes Kriton's strategy as 'fighting the devil with fire'.

[43] 'Unique' (Carter 1986: 112) rather than 'common' (Calhoun 1944: 43).

[44] Two of the most distinguished historians produced by Oriel, the college of which the Regius Professors of History at Oxford are members.

involvement in government to re-enter the public stage' or else to forfeit some of their wealth (p. 98). These are the 'rich *apragmones*' of Adkins (1976: 317, 319) and Carter (1986: 99–130). Here we part company, for I can find little, if any, evidence for this. In particular, the fragment from Aristophanes' *Farmers* (fr.100) is not even an inexact parallel (Osborne n.46) to 'pressurizing non-participants into an awareness of the contradiction of trying to maintain such a position in the democratic *polis*' (p. 99). Plutarch cites the lines in the context of Nikias' withdrawal from the command of the Athenian troops at Pylos (*Nik.* viii). 'I want to farm,' says one character (A). 'Who's stopping you?' asks another (B). 'You (plural),' replies A: 'so I give one thousand drachmas if you'll let me off the *arkhai*.' 'OK,' says B: 'that makes two thousand together with Nikias' drachmas.' What does 'If you'll release me from the *arkhai*' mean?[45] Character A cannot have been chosen by lot or elected to office against his will, since candidates were not drawn from the entire citizen body, but only from those who had put their names forward.[46] Like Nikias, he must already have been elected or allotted to some *specific* magistracy, and he is asking to be relieved of it, just as Nikias had been relieved of the command at Pylos. Part of the joke would seem to be that Nikias is represented as having bribed his way out of the generalship, whereas we know from Thucydides (iv.28) that he withdrew from it in the Assembly. B, who is addressed in the plural, is presumably the leader of the chorus, one of the Farmers.

There is in fact plenty of evidence that vitilitigation did *not* lead to participation in democratic *politics*. Osborne's own example is Diognetos in Lysias xviii.9, the brother of Nikias,[47] who was so slandered by sykophants that he withdrew into exile – not the most obvious way of re-entering public life. Elsewhere, Lysias (xxv.26) speaks of the Athenians after 411 condemning men to exile and disenfranchising them, as a result of the activities of three sykophants (Ant. v.78; Aesch. ii.124). Aeschines also refers to men 'syko-

---

[45] Carter 1986: 83 writes: 'The sykophant claims to be able to mislay or lose (the farmer's) name when the lists are drawn up.' But the fragment hardly permits such precise interpretation; moreover, the lists have apparently been drawn up already.

[46] The evidence for this, which is vital for an understanding of the workings of the Athenian democracy, is almost invisible. Headlam 1891: 53–4 argued that candidature for the *boulē* was compulsory (but was refuted by MacGregor in the second edition of his book [196–7]) whereas candidature for minor office was voluntary, though the state might if necessary compel men to serve (94–5: no evidence). Hignett 1952: 227 believed that candidature for office may have been voluntary in most instances, but that compulsion was perhaps necessary to fill the chief financial posts. Sinclair 1988: 109–11, 195 also believes in volunteers, with a little pressure in the case of the *boulē*. The fact that jurymen were chosen from those who put their names forward – and pay was offered to attract them to do so (Markle 1985) – suggests that the same was true of minor magistracies.

[47] Nikias was exceptionally wealthy by Athenian standards (Davies 1971: 403–5), and, since he was also timid, an ideal target for sykophants: Plut. *Nik.* ii.5–6, viii.2–4 (chronologically confused), xxii.2; *Comp. Nik. & Crass.* i.2. Since xxii.2 accords with Thuc. vii.48.4, it looks as if Nikias' 'comic persona' (Osborne p.88) has some basis in reality. For sykophantic attacks on his brother, see the next paragraph.

phanted out of the state' (*politeia*; III.226), and there are other examples.[48]
Aristogeiton, says Demosthenes (xxv.83), always demanded the death
penalty in the courts, and he was not the only one (cf. e.g. Lys. xxv.26). The
death penalty will have created a dead Athenian, who will hardly have taken a
very lively part in political affairs; whereas the *threat* of the death penalty is
likely to have driven a man into exile rather than into politics. At a local level,
one Antiphilos contrived to expel ten demesmen of Halimous from their deme
(Dem. LVII.60): again, not an obvious method of forcing them into politics.
Another speaker complains that his opponents 'are driving me right out of my
deme with their sykophanting' (Dem. LV.35).

Furthermore, far from benefitting and vitalising the democracy, sykophancy is said to have had precisely the opposite effect. Sykophants are
accused of having turned the rich against the *demos*, of making them
oligarchs, and of causing *stasis* and the overthrow of democracy. Sykophantic
activity, say Lysias (xxvII.26) and Demosthenes (xxv.50, cf. 52), leads to
stasis.[49] Isocrates, admittedly not the most unbiased of writers, claims that
sykophants reproached the most respectable citizens with being oligarchs and
Lakonizers (xv.318; cf. Lys. xxv.27). Aristotle, a more reliable source, tells
us that revolutions in democracies are caused by demagogues who make men
of property band together, sometimes because they sykophant them (*Politics*
1304b20–24, 1305a3–7).

Conversely, there are examples of men who *were* politically active,[50] but
found their actions curbed or frustrated by sykophants. The politicians most
frequently affected were the *strategoi*, the generals (cf. Sinclair 1988:
146–52). There are several instances in Plutarch (*Nik.* xxII.2, cf. II.4–5,
IV.2–4; *Alkib.* xxxIV.7; *Phok.* xII.3). Demosthenes (xxIII.15) speaks of
intimidation of *strategoi* by sykophants, which reduced them to inactivity.
Aristogeiton, we are told, harassed the *strategoi* for money, and when they
refused to give him any, he said they were not fit to be lavatory-inspectors, let
alone generals; and he extended his activities to the magistrates chosen by lot
(Dem. xxv.49–50). Plato's timarchic man (*Rep.* 553b) devotes his life and his
money to the city, or holds a *strategia* or some other great magistracy – and
then is taken to court and ruined by some sykophant (cf. [Plato] *Alkib.*
II.142a; Diod. xx.10.3–4). Thus sykophants frequently drove rich men *out*

---

[48] E.g. Andok. 1.105; Plato *Rep.* 533b, [Plato] *Alkib.* II.142a; Diod. xv.40.1. The Old Oligarch
(1.14) also speaks of men from the Athenian empire being driven into exile by Athenian
sykophants. Lofberg 1917: 23–4 cites Ar. *Knights* 259–63, which need not allude to an exile.
Plut. *Mor.* 803f refers to Plutarch's own time.

[49] For sykophants in the Athenian empire see Old Oligarch 1.14, Ar. *Birds* 1422 with MacDowell
1978: 225–6, Lys. xxv.19, Isoc. xv.318 (a malicious conflation of sykophants and demagogues); Ostwald 1986: 210–11, Osborne p.101. Sykophants in 4th-century Ainos: Dem.
LVIII.37–8. According to Diodorus, sykophants also caused *stasis* in Syracuse (xI.87.5) and
the Peloponnese (xv.40.1).

[50] By 'politically active', I do not mean 'merely casting one's vote in the assembly or serving on the
boulē' (Adkins 1976: 319); I refer to *hoi politeuomenoi*: Finley 1962; Perlman 1963; Hansen
1983a, 1983b; Sinclair 1988: 34–48, 136–45, 212–15.

of, rather than into, politics; and their attacks on active politicians hindered their conduct and deterred others from involving themselves in public life.

IX EPILOGUE: THE CROWN OF TAMARISK

Osborne treats us to a story about Solon, Anakharsis and the spider's web (Plut. *Solon* v.4–5; p. 100). But the context shows that Plutarch's 'laws of Solon' are the measures that he took to prevent tyranny, and had nothing to do with the introduction of the voluntary prosecutor. A better story, which encapsulates the traditional view of the sykophant, can be found in Diodoros (xii.12.2). The lawgiver at Thourioi decreed that those convicted of sykophancy should walk around wearing a garland of tamarisk, so that it should be obvious that they had been awarded the first prize for wickedness. Some men found themselves unable to cope with this disgrace and committed suicide. Subsequently all the sykophants were sent into exile; and so the state was relieved of a great evil, and enjoyed a *makarios bios* – or, as we should say, everyone lived happily ever after.[51]

TESTIMONIA

Square brackets indicate a passage which refers to sykophancy but does not use the sykophant words.

AESCHINES I. 1, 3, 20, 32, 105, 107; II. 5, 39, 66, [93], 99, 124, 145, 170, 177, 181, 183; III. 64, 172, 216, 226, 231, 256.

ANDOKIDES I. 86, 93, 99–101, 104–5, [121].

ANTIPHON [*Tetral.* I.2.13]; v.78–80; vi.43.

ARISTOPHANES *Acharnians* 515–22, 559, 725–6, 818–28, 840, 904–58; *Birds* [68(?)], 285, 1410–69, 1479, [1694–9]; *Ekkles.* 436–9, 452, 562–3; *Knights* [258–65], [300], 437–44, [529], [1256]; *Peace* 191, 652–4; *Plutus* 30–1, 850–958, 970–1; *Wasps* 145–6, 897, [1037–42], 1094–6.
  Fragments (the first figure refers to Kock *CAP*, the figure in brackets to Kassel-Austin *PCG*): 40 (–) (*Amphiaraos*); 100, 108 (=102, 110) (*Georgoi*); 219 (=228) (*Daitales*); 439 (=454) (*Pelargoi*); 539 (=552) (*Telmesseis*).
  Scholia on *Birds* 38, *Plutus* 31, 854; Hypoth. to *Birds* III (OCT) 1–2. Cf. *Vita Aristophanis* 27–31 (*PCG* III.2, p.2).

---

[51] I hope to discuss this passage elsewhere. Diodoros, by a chronological miracle, attributes the laws of Thourioi, founded in 443 B.C., to the sixth-century Kharondas. The law-giver is generally believed to have been Protagoras: see Harvey 1966: 589 n.10; Muir 1982 – though Aristotle does not, as Muir 20 with n.24 implies, refer to the odder enactments.

ARISTOTLE *Eth.Eud.* II. 1221b5–7; *Poet.* 1456a3–7; *Pol.* II. 1268b22–5; [v. 1304b20–31, 1305a2–7]; *Probl.* 952a2–6; *Rhet.* II. 1382a1–7, 1402a14–6; *Soph.El.*. 174b8–12; *Top.* VI. 139b23–140a2, VIII. 157a26–33; [fr. 667 Rose].

[ARISTOTLE] *Ath.Pol.* [IX.1], XXXV.2–3, XLIII.5, LIX.3; *Rhet.ad Alex.* 1424a26–32; 1424b11–4, 1444a30–5; *Virt.et Vit.* 1251b2–3.

COMIC FRAGMENTS (figures refer to Kock, unless otherwise indicated)
Old comedy Epicharmos 84 *CGFP* = P. Oxy. 2429 fr.7; Eupolis 231 (*PCG* 245), *PCG* 99.78 (*Demoi*); *PCG* 259 (*Prospaltioi*); Kratinos 69–70 (*PCG* 70) (*Eumenides*); Plato 14 (*Amphiaraos*), 255 (*Fab. inc.*); Telekleides 41; Adesp. 7.
Middle and new comedy Alexis 182 (*Poietai*); Diphilos 32 (*PCG* 31) (*Emporos*); [Euboulos 74 (*PCG* 74)]; Menander (ed.Sandbach) *Epitrepontes* 218, *Georgos* fr.1, *Perikeir.* 373–8, *Samia* 578, *Theophor.* fr.1, *Fab.inc.* Körte 545, 919; *Gnomai monostichoi* 440–603; Philippides 29; Adesp. 251.
Uncertain date Adesp. 905, 1186.

DEINARKHOS I. 6; II. 2.

DEMOSTHENES V. 6; VII. 21; IX. 56; XII. 9, 19; XVIII. 95, 112–13, 118, 121, 138, 189, 192, 212, 232–5, 239, 242, 249, 256, 266, 275, 289, 317; XIX. 98, 222; XX. 62, 152; XXI. 103, 116–18, 122, 124; XXIII. 15, 61, 67, 180, 190; XXIV. 3, 7–8, 14, 66, 200–1, 203; XXV. 8–9, 18–19, 35–7, 39–41, 45–52, 63, 82–4, 96–7; XXIX. 22, 25, 30, 41, 55; XXXII. 26–8; XXXIII. 2, 16, 37; XXXIV. 40; XXXVI. 3, 12, 14, 21, 24, 26–7, 52–4, 58, 60; XXVII. 2–3, 8, 13, 17–18, 24, 35, 39–41, 45, 49, 52–3; XXXVIII. 3, 16, 20; XXXIX. 2, 25–6, 34; XL. 3, 9, 43; XLI. 23; XLII. 13; XLV. 47; LI. 16; LII. 33; LIII. 1; LV. 1–2, 6, 9, 21–3, 26–9, 33, 35; LVII. 32, 34, 44, 49, 57, 60; LVIII. 2, 6, 8–13, 23, 26–9, 32–7, 40, 42–3, 62–5; LIX. 39, 43–4, 68; *Prooim.* XXXV. 2; *Epist.* II. 9.

DIODOROS I. 77.4, 92.5; IV. 8.5; XI. 87.5; XII. 12.2, 24.2–3, 39.2–3; XV. 40.1; XX. 10.3–4.

DIOGENES LAERTIOS II. 63.

HERAKLEIDES KRITIKOS I. 4 (Pfister).

HYPEREIDES *Athenog.* 25–6; *Demosth.* 3; *Euxenipp.* 33–4; *Lykophr.* 2.

ISAEUS I. 42, 50; XI. 4, 13, 31.

ISOCRATES VIII. 123, 129–30, 133; XII. 9, 13, 142; XV. 8, 21, 23, 88, 96, 163–4, 174–5, 224–5, 230, 237, 241–2, 288, 300, 308–9, 312–20; XVI. 1–2, 42, 46; XVII. 42, 46, 56; XVIII. 2–3, 7, 10, 14, 22–4, 37, 43, 51–2, 55, 64; XXI. 5, 8, 10–11, 13–14, 19.

KRATEROS *FGrH* 342 F 12 (= Plut. *Arist.* 26.1–4).

LYKOURGOS I. 3–6, 13, 31.

LYSIAS I. 44; III. 44; IV. 14; VI. 31; VII. 1, 20–1, 38–9; XII. 5; XIII. 67, 76; XVIII. 9; XIX. 9, 51; XX. [7], 12; XXI. 17; XXII. 1; XXIV. 2; XXV. 3, 19, 24–7; XXVI. 24; XXVIII. 5–6. Frr. I. 1–2, 43 Thalheim = 38.1–2, 22 Gernet–Bizos.

PLATO *Crito* 44e–45c; *Rep.* I. 340d–341c; VIII. 553b; IX. 575b. Cf. *Laws* V. 730d, 745a; XI. 928bc.

[PLATO] *Alk.* II. 142a.

PLUTARCH (see n.9 above) *Alexander* 74.5; *Alkibiades* 13.5, 19.7, 34.7; *Aristeides* 26.2; *Demosthenes* 14.4; *Eumenes* 16.1–4; *Kimon* 10.9; *Nikias* 2.5–6, 4.2–5.2, [8.4], 22.2; *Comp. Nikias & Crassus* 1. 2–3 with *Mor.* 541ef, 842ab; *Pelopidas* 25.1–7; *Perikles* 37.4; *Phokion* 10.3, 10.9 with *Mor.* 188b, 12.3, 16.2, 29.4, 32.3; *Solon* [18.6–7], 24.2; *Timoleon* 37.1–3; *Moralia* 187ab, 523ab, 959d, 998ab.

THEOPHRASTOS *Char.* XXIII. 4; XXVI. 5.

THEOPOMPOS *FGrH* 115 F 110, 281, 327.

XENOPHON *Hell.* II. 3.12, 22, 38; *Mem.* II. 9; IV. 4.11; *Oik.* XI. 21; *Symp.* IV.30.

[XENOPHON] *Ath. Pol.* ('Old Oligarch') I. 14.

PAPYRI P.Cairo Zen. 212 (254 B.C.); 628 (3rd c. B.C.), 1–5; P.Mich.Zen. 57 (248 B.C.) 1–5; Wilcken *UPZ* I. 112 (203/2 B.C.) 3–8; 113 (156 B.C.), 8–18; P.Tebt. 42 (118 B.C.), 22–7; 789 (*c.* 140 B.C.), 20–4.

LEXICA, SCHOLIA, etc. (mostly etymologies) Schol. Ar. *Plutus* 31, 854; Schol. Dem. XVIII. 95; Schol. Plato *Rep.* 340d; *Etymol. Magn.* 733.39–57 s.vv. συκοφαντία, συκοφάνται; Festus 393 Lindsay; Hesykhios s.vv. συκοφάντης, συκοφάνται, συκοφαντία; Istros *FGrH* 334 F12; Philomnestos *FGrH* 527 F1; Plut. *Solon* 24.2, *Mor.* 523ab; *Souda* E2830–2, S1324, 1329–33.

6a

The law of hubris *in Athens*[1]

NICK FISHER

I

This paper examines the operation of the law of *hubris* in classical Athens; the paper by Oswyn Murray in this volume considers the law in the archaic period, and comparable laws elsewhere. While my views on the traditional problems of this law, its date and the interpretation of the term *hubris*, will become clear, I am centrally concerned with the basic paradox posed by the law's operation in democratic Athens: this paradox is that, whereas the law appears to occupy a high profile in Athenians' consciousness of their legal system as a whole, and plays a large part in their defences of its rôle in the preservation of democracy and stability, there is little evidence (though not as little as sometimes stated) that the law was actually much used in the courts. As we shall see, there are a number of good reasons why in many, or most, cases where an action for *hubris* might lie, litigants might choose to exercise that wide choice which the system offered,[2] and bring an action other than that of *hubris*. Thus a paradox, and a question: did the law of *hubris* serve a useful purpose in the Classical democracy?

We possess the text of the law as it stood in the fourth century; the initial phrase, which is all that it offers by way of explanation of the offence, runs: 'If anyone commits *hubris* against another, whether child or woman or man, whether free or slave, or if he does anything outrageous (*paranomon*) against any of these, let any one who wishes (*ho boulomenos*), of those Athenians who are entitled, bring an indictment (*graphē*) before the judges (*thesmothetai*)' (Dem. xxi.47).

I hold, but do not argue here, that the law, and probably at least this initial phrase of the text, was an integral part of Solon's innovative introduction of

[1] I am grateful to all the participants at the Cambridge seminar when this chapter and Oswyn Murray's were first read, to the editors, Paul Cartledge, Paul Millett, and Stephen Todd, for very helpful suggestions on the draft, and above all to Oswyn Murray for much stimulating discussion, many generous ideas, and some friendly disagreement.
[2] Cf. esp. Osborne 1985b, *passim*.

the volunteer prosecutor and the popular law court, in order to restrain the excesses of the rich, and to instil a greater sense of justice and community values in the city (cf. Murray's paper).[3] Other cases, such as adultery and theft, where a public interest seems to have been perceived in addition to the wrong to the individual, support the view that the introduction of the *graphē* system, and the prosecution by 'any one who wishes' (*ho boulomenos*), cannot be explained solely in terms of the need to protect defenceless victims.[4]

A useful starting point is provided by the ancient traditions which offer explanations of Solon's introduction of the *graphē* procedure for offences against individuals. For the Aristotelian *Constitution of the Athenians* the purpose was to 'enable *ho boulomenos* to seek justice/revenge (*timorein*) on behalf of those wronged' (*Ath.Pol.* IX.1), said to be one of the three elements in his political reforms that most favoured the people (*demotikotata*); which does not explain the reason for the public concern in such cases of wrong-doing. But the fuller version in Plutarch is more suggestive:

If a man has been struck or treated with force or suffered damage, it was permitted to anyone who was able and who wished to bring a *graphē* and prosecute the offender, since the lawgiver correctly aimed at accustoming the citizens to feel and sympathise with one another as if they were parts of one body. When asked which seemed to him to be the best managed of the cities, he said it was that city in which those who had not been wronged were no less ready to prosecute and punish the wrong-doers than those who had been wronged (*Solon* 18).[5]

Now there is a distinct possibility that such traditions have some basis in a belief in the Solonian origin of the law of *hubris* and in readings of Solon's poems – where we do find some sentiments which are not very dissimilar in spirit from these;[6] but for my purposes here it is more important to see that these statements accord perfectly with the justifications of the law of *hubris* and its importance in the judicial system that we find in the fourth century. The basic notion in Plutarch is that some offences against the individual must be corrected in the public interest; and Plutarch seems to have particularly in mind violent offences against the person, and hence above all the *graphē hubreos*. This fundamental point is spelt out explicitly and repeatedly in the many lawcourt speeches which, starting from the point that the criminal's offences would have laid him open to such a charge, dilate on the public nature of the law of *hubris*.

---

[3] For further arguments for a Solonian date, against the fifth-century date argued for by Ruschenbusch 1965, and Gagarin (1979: 234), cf. Humphreys (1983a: 238–9), and Fisher (forthcoming: ch.2). MacDowell (1976: 26–7) argues for a sixth-century date, without committing himself to Solon. On the meaning of *paranomon* (transgression of any social/moral norms, not of any specific statute), cf. Ostwald (1986: 111–29).

[4] Cf. Humphreys (1983a: 239), and Fisher (forthcoming: ch.2), against e.g. Ruschenbusch (1968: 47–53), Harrison (1971: 76–8).

[5] On these passages, cf. Osborne (1985b: 40–4). Also relevant is the alleged Solonian law forbidding neutrality in time of *stasis*, and Plutarch's comments on it (*Solon* 20.1); see Manville (1980: 217–19).

[6] Cf. Vlastos (1946: 69–70).

Many of these passages will be discussed later. First it will be advisable to give a brief account of the way *hubris* is interpreted in our forensic texts, of the types of acts which are envisaged as in principle leading to actions of *hubris*, and the evidence for actual cases. Let us start with the latter. Despite some statements to the contrary,[7] there is, as Osborne's catalogue shows (1985b: 56, cf. also 50), one *hubris* charge which certainly came to court, one which was started but then dropped, and there are also a number of possible cases.

The certain case concerns the allegedly villainous Diokles of Phlya. Isaeus, attacking him for his depredations against his relatives' properties, mentions that at one stage he shut his brother-in-law up in a house, perhaps in an attempt to kill him, and achieved his *atimia* – dishonourable deprivation of citizenship; and concludes that 'though he has been indicted on a *graphē hubreos*, he has not yet paid the legal penalty' (VIII.41, cf. also VIII.44, on a prosecution impending against him). The existence, known to lexicographers and similar late sources, of another of Isaeus' speeches, *Against Diokles on hubris*, suggests that he was subsequently brought to court on a *graphē hubreos*, in which the locking up and deprivation of citizen status – i.e. the infliction of the most severe dishonour on a citizen, thereby rendered unable to bring a case himself – was probably the central feature.[8]

The other case is the admittedly unusual one of Apollodoros' objections to his father's allegedly forged will, depriving him of the bank and imposing the marriage of his mother to Phormion; the purpose was clearly to move the issue towards one court or another, and at that time private suits, *dikai*, were temporarily unavailable ([Dem.] XLV.3–5). But the notional basis of the case must have been the insult to himself of such a settlement of the property and marriage to an ex-slave (however ludicrous that could be made to seem in view of the fact that he was himself the son of an ex-slave). This, which has not always been seen by modern scholars, is made virtually explicit by Demosthenes in the speech he wrote on Phormion's behalf (Dem. XXXVI.30).[9]

The more doubtful cases are, first, the possibility of a political trial in the aftermath of the 411 revolution, the prosecution by Sophocles (probably the tragedian) of Peisandros, for so outraging Euktemon that he forced him to commit suicide (Arist. *Rhet.* I, 1374b35–75a2);[10] then there are a number of cases of violent assault at festivals, referred to in the *Meidias* as parallels to Meidias' attack, which may have been *graphai* or may have used the *probolē* procedure for offences at festivals (on which cf. below);[11] there is the

---

7 MacDowell (1976: 29) is technically correct, but perhaps over-cautious: 'I do not know of any quite certain case in which a person was formally found guilty of *hubris* in an Athenian law-court'. The Diokles case was certainly brought, and may well have produced a conviction. Cf. also below p. 134.

8 Cf. Isaeus VIII.40–46 (and Wyse 1904: 621–2), frs. 5–6 (Thalheim), Baiter-Sauppe (1850: 230–1), and Davies (1971: 313–14).

9 Neither Gagarin (1979: 230 n.4), nor Dover (1974: 54 n.16) quite brings this out, while over-emphasising the abnormality of the case. It is to be noted that here too citizen status is at issue; cf. Murray, below p. 140.

10 Cf. Jameson (1971: 555–7).   11 Cf. Dem. XXI.36–40, 71–6, 175–81.

Lysianic case against Teisis, alleging a horrifically brutal revenge whipping, which may possibly be a *hubris* charge, but, like many another, may be rather a *dikē aikeias* (a 'private' action for 'battery', for which the defining criterion was striking first);[12] and, finally, there are a few even more obscure cases where many charges are possible, and, of course, a great many threats, in comedy as well as in oratory, to bring a *graphē hubreos* which ended in a different, or in no, charge being brought.[13]

II

If one asks, then, what is the basic criterion in these fairly disparate acts that would enable a charge of *hubris* to be considered, there is one clear answer, which, it seems to me, fits exactly what the sources consistently say (above all Dem. xxi *Meidias*, Isoc. xx *Lokhites*, Dem. liv *Konon* and a number of passages in Aristotle's *Rhetoric*). It is surprising that, despite this unanimity on the part of the sources, very different views have often been taken by modern scholars. The view I hold is that the essence of *hubris* is the deliberate attack on the *timē* (honour) of another. That is, it is constituted by intentional, often gratuitous action, frequently but by no means always violent, and specifically designed to inflict shame and public humiliation. This, as can readily be seen, does account for all the actual or threatened legal cases, and can indeed explain the uses of *hubris* in Solon's poems about the crisis facing the *polis* and his legal, economic and political reforms; and it is spelt out, as clearly as one could wish, in Aristotle's definition in *Rhet.* ii, and in Dem. xxi.71–6. This view of the law of *hubris* has been taken by the majority of scholars in the field, from Cope and Lipsius to Harrison and MacDowell;[14] as I shall argue more fully elsewhere, it does also explain the uses of the concept of *hubris* in the whole range of Greek literature, in Homer and tragedy, as well as in Demosthenes.

But those who have not accepted this interpretation of forensic *hubris* have had their reasons, and their explicit or hidden assumptions, and they merit a little examination. The most recent article on the law, by Gagarin, restating the position of Hitzig, looks briefly at some of the passages bearing on the interpretation of legal *hubris*, finds them 'conflicting', misses, or perhaps

---

[12] Lys. fr. xvii (Gernet/Bizos). Most (e.g. Gernet, *Budé* ed. ii: 241) go for a *dikē aikeias*; but against the phrase *ho pheugon ten diken* one can set the fact that the speaker of the case is a friend of the victim.

[13] E.g. [Dem.] liii.16, Dein. 1.23, Ar. *Wasps* 1417–49, *Clouds* 1297–1302, *Birds* 1035–57, *Wealth* 886–936.

[14] Lipsius (1905–15: 420–9); Cope (1877) i: 239–40; Thalheim in *RE* s.v. *Hubreos Graphē*; Morrow (1939: 38–41); Harrison (1968: 168, 172); MacDowell (1976; 1978: 129–32); Fisher 1976a; Dover (1978: 34–9); Cantarella (1983: 85–96); Cole (1984: 99). MacDowell's interpretation of *hubris* focuses more on the state of mind of the man committing *hubris*, 'having energy or power and misusing it', mine rather more on the intention specifically to insult and the effects of dishonour achieved; my emphasis makes it easier to see why *hubris* was such a serious social and moral offence, and the subject of a legal action that could carry the death penalty.

denies, the clear concentration on the presence of the intention seriously to insult and on its effects in shame, and puts in its place as the criterion distinguishing *hubris* from 'lesser' assaults the notion of 'serious and unprovoked assault'.[15] One explicit argument is that to prove in court the presence of a 'hybristic state of mind', the intention to insult, was too difficult; underlying this seems to be an assumption that ideas such as 'dishonouring' and 'infliction of shame' are too vague and subjective to be used as the agreed criterion in a legal charge, and that the degree of force or violence deliberately applied is a more satisfactory, more objective and more patent criterion. What is wrong with this account is, first, that while it does, as we shall see, identify a problem, the answer offered fits neither those texts which give extended discussions of the nature of culpable *hubris*, nor the range of acts which, according to the sources, led or might have led to a *graphē hubreos* (and Gagarin's accusations of 'conflicting evidence of the orators' are captious, and disappear on close examination); and second, that it under-rates the central importance of the concepts of status, of honour and shame, in discussions of the aims and effects of social actions inside Greek communities. The use of the terms *atimia, epitimoi*, etc., to indicate citizen rights is merely one of the more striking examples, which is directly relevant to the one secure case of a *graphē hubreos* (that of Diokles), and may have been to many others.

Another, more popular, line has been to take the element of public interest or concern as the determining criterion. This line has been followed, in various forms, by Partsch, Latte, and Wolff,[16] but the fullest exposition, and indeed in many ways the most interesting treatment so far of the *graphē hubreos*, was that of Gernet in his 1917 Paris thesis, who makes his assumptions helpfully explicit. He raises, more than any other critic, the right questions; but, at a time when he was himself so heavily influenced by the sociological theories of Durkheim and Mauss, and by the work of Glotz (1904), he came up, I think, with the wrong answers, through over-emphasis on the collective and the religious in place of outraged individual honour.[17]

Gernet accepted that many texts in the fourth century do focus on the intention to insult as the commonest distinguishing mark; but, he argued, they do not all do so consistently or coherently, and their accounts do not inspire confidence. A different account was necessary, in his view, to explain the underlying rationale, the collective 'représentations', that apparently

---

[15] Gagarin 1979; cf. Hitzig 1907. Gagarin is also probably influenced by the desire to find a specific set of acts at which the *graphē hubreos* was targeted, in the belief that a legal system should permit only one procedure for each offence; I agree fully with Osborne 1985b that the Athenian system made a virtue of 'open texture', of allowing a choice of procedures to suit a variety of social and political needs.

[16] Partsch 1920, followed by Latte (1968: 283), Wolff in *Lexikon der Alten Welt* (Zürich & Stuttgart, 1965) s.v. *Hubreos Graphē*.

[17] Gernet (1917b: esp. 183–97). On the place of this work in Gernet's development, cf. also Humphreys (1978: 77–87), R. Di Donato, in Gernet (1983: 403–5), and briefly, in the context of the *hubris* law, Garner (1987: 34–6).

enabled the legislator to frame such a law, even though later advocates and philosophers could no longer fully recover it.

Gernet's accusations of inconsistency and incoherence should be resisted; like Gagarin's (who takes much from Gernet) many of them amount in fact to the observation that a passage gives, in accordance with its forensic or theoretical argument, a partial, not a complete, account of what makes an act *hubris*. This is not surprising, since, on my view, the concept is certainly complex, involving as it does in its full form types of behaviour, a type of intention, and the corresponding effects or results. Thus, for example, where a passage says that 'striking free men' can be accepted as a definition of *hubris*, this does not prove that it could be considered the only addition necessary, nor that the author (Aristotle, *Rhet.* II, 1402a1–3) was contradicting what he said elsewhere or that he was unable to distinguish *hubris* from *aikeia*. Nor does it follow from the disjunctive account offered at *Rhet.* I, 1374a13–5 – striking someone is *hubris* only if he does it for a reason, such as dishonouring him, or pleasing himself – that the concept is hopelessly confused, or that Aristotle contradicts himself: in some cases the effect of the dishonouring, in others the gratuitous nature of the agent delighting in his infliction of pain and shame, may be uppermost, and contribute most to making it actionable *hubris*. But the 'pleasure' involved in striking is surely the pleasure of treating others with contempt, or the pleasure of sadism; and hence insulting intentions, or at least contemptuous indifference to the honour of others, are in fact present in both halves of the disjunction.[18] Again, many of Gernet's accusations of incoherence directed at different places in the *Meidias* speech concern the accompanying circumstances – drink, anger, past hatreds, the presence of other people and so on – that can make acts seem, in their felt contexts, more or less hybristic. Here, in fact (XXI.36–41, 72–4, and 175–81), Demosthenes' analyses are interesting; they merit a moment's consideration, and to be placed in a broader context.

There are in Demosthenes two very full, and different, descriptions of illegal hybristic acts, which share the claim to be classic cases of *hubris*; of these, one fits the category of upper-class, sympotic, *hubris*, the other rather the category of sober, deliberate, gratuitous assault on an enemy. Which would be thought to be the more 'classic', or the more dreadful and anti-democratic, might vary – and in a forensic case would naturally depend on one's forensic need. In the speech against Konon (LIV), Demosthenes emphasises not only that Konon, his son and his friends were grossly drunk on the evening they laid into his client, but also that they were regular *sumpotai* (drinking-companions) of long standing, much given while drinking to violent and indiscriminate assaults, to obscene mock-initiation rites, and thus to committing *hubris* against poorer, less 'gentlemanly' (*kaloi kagathoi*) citizens than themselves. Drunken *hubris*, that is, would seem a natural and normal

---

[18] There are also confused discussions of this passage in Gagarin (1979: 231) and Cole (1984: 99 n.13, slightly misstating my view).

type, characteristic of the upper class, and hence was especially what the law was designed to stop.[19]

On the other hand, Meidias assaulted Demosthenes when sober, which Demosthenes argues made it less excusable; for he offers a variety of contrasting cases where drink, anger and other passions, and social settings offered mitigations (thus confirming, to some extent, the prevalence of such forms of drunken, contemptuous violence), and yet, he claims, such cases were rightly judged harshly in many instances by the Athenians. Clearly it is plausible, and the natural course for Demosthenes in this case, to say that behaviour like Meidias' premeditated and blatantly public acts of *hubris*, culminating in his assault at the Dionysia, was the worst of all types, if not necessarily the most typical.

Despite Gernet's accusations of sophistry and contradiction against these argumentations, if we put together the various types of acts and contexts described throughout speech xxi, we see careful distinctions being drawn. The worst case is the Meidias-type. After it come cases of hybristic assaults where drink played a part, which can themselves be further subdivided: into cases (like Ktesikles', 180) where it was felt the drink was merely a mask for the deep-rooted desire to assault and humiliate his enemy, unprovoked; cases where drink helped to induce those naturally and habitually inclined to assault to do so insultingly (Konon, or the Euaion case, 71–6); and even cases where drink – or drink allied to love or other passion – can induce an assault that carries no serious intention to insult, and no *hubris* (cf. the case of Polyzelos, 36–41). Thus, summing up, some drunken violence can be described as scarcely hybristic at all; other instances may reveal a spontaneous intention seriously to insult; other cases are more deeply hybristic, because a pre-existing desire to attack an enemy finds expression, or a habitual delight in insulting social inferiors is gratified; but on this view cases of sober, premeditated and contemptuous assaults constitute the worst *hubris* of all.[20]

III

However, with a scholar of Gernet's standing, and this 'methodologically remarkable book' (Humphreys 1978: 85), one should also pay attention to his alternative view, and to his assumptions, even after his criticisms of the 'représentation' of *hubris* so well founded in our texts have been rebutted. He states explicitly that it would be surprising if the hallmark of *hubris* were a

[19] On the speech, cf. now Carey & Reid 1985; on *sumposia* and their dangers in classical Athens, Murray (1983: 268–71, and forthcoming, 1990), Fisher 1988.

[20] Gernet also saw the alleged extension of the law to cover *hubris* against slaves as a sign of incoherence; cf. however Murray, below, and further, slightly different, arguments in Fisher (forthcoming: ch. 2). Whatever the reasons for the inclusion of slaves in the law in Solon's time, in the classical period it was taken as an indication that slaves had some minimal *timē* that entitled them to protection against the grossest maltreatment (in effect, no doubt, from others than their masters), while [Dem.] liii.16 confirms that tying up and beating an intruder might be taken to be *hubris* if he was free, and not if he were slave.

'preoccupation with dishonouring': 'But if the society was relatively uninterested, in general, in offences suffered by an individual, how could one hold
that it would be especially revolted by an element in the outrage that is even
more subjective?' And of Dem. xxi.72–6, he writes: 'Nothing makes it easier
to understand, despite what he is saying, the antithesis between the individual
and subjective notion and the objective and social notion of the injury – and
that the first could not be a basis of the second.' Gernet's aim seems to be to
look back beyond the 'rationalising and incoherent rationales' of the fourth
century to the earlier 'représentations' which, according to him, still leave
their traces in Demosthenes' and others' intuitions; even so, it seems a
remarkable generalisation, only explicable in terms of the views he held at that
time about archaic Greek society, that offences against the honour of
individuals could not arouse much concern in such a society and its laws. That
view seems much less plausible now. The supposed dominance of the *genē* and
other kinship organisations in archaic Greece would appear to have been
greatly exaggerated;[21] and many works have laid proper emphasis on the
concepts of honour and shame in the treatment of Greek values in texts and
institutions from the *Iliad* onwards, aided by much comparative material from
other Mediterranean societies.[22] It now seems clear that we should not speak
of the subordination of the interests and feelings of the individual citizen to
those of the wider kindred or the growing city, but rather of the close
interrelationship, and interdependence, of individual, close family (*oikos*,
ankhisteia) and city; an important aspect of this interdependence is that
attacks on the honour of the citizen bring, in addition, shame on his close
relatives and friends, and lesser shame on more distant kin and friends; and
successful attacks of a particular type (say drunken or calculating assaults by
rich on poor), if uncontrolled by the collective action of the city, may affect in
turn many another, or as Solon put it, 'thus the public evil [produced by too
many acts of *hubris* etc. leading to *stasis*] comes home to each individual, and
the courtyard doors can no longer keep it out' (fr. 4.26–7 West).

Gernet, like others, sees problems for the 'intention to dishonour' view in
Demosthenes' observations on the difficulty in making clear to an audience the
real horror of the dishonour and indignity of some acts of *hubris* (xxi.72).
Gernet seems to see in this passage only the inexpressible, instantaneous
intuition of the man who feels himself outraged, which cannot be made
apparent in its full horror to anyone other than the victim, and therefore could
not be the basis of serious legal actions. But that is not Demosthenes' point; he
is arguing that what is at the time quite clearly grossly insulting behaviour, as
is made clear through language, gesture, look, and type of blow – and is
perfectly clear also to all the witnesses – is harder to recreate fully for the
benefit of a jury at a much later date. Demosthenes, like others, finds no

[21] Bourriot 1976, Roussel 1976; on the way offences committed by and on individuals may have
been handled in Athens even before Solon, cf. Humphreys (1983a: 231–7).
[22] E.g. Finley 1978, Redfield 1975, Adkins 1972, Strauss (1986: 31–6), Davis (1977: 89–101).

difficulty in supposing that the infliction of dishonour, especially in public, is a deep personal blow, which will arouse the alarm, sympathy and fear of neutral by-standers, and encourage them to give assistance (*boethein*) as helpers, or as witnesses, out of self-interest as well as pity. Indeed, Gernet's preferred solution, that originally, and still in the 'instincts' of fourth-century orators, the essence of indictable *hubris* was the attack directly on the collective interests of the community and its religious principles, lacks textual support in any source from the sixth to the fourth centuries.[23]

None the less, a strong public interest does of course exist in repressing acts of *hubris*; and the speeches make it very clear what is meant by asserting that they constitute a danger to society. All the speeches that discuss the danger of *hubris* are in essential agreement. What we have of Isocrates' speech *Against Lokhites* starts from the view, directly contrary to Gernet's, of the supreme importance of offences against the person (*soma*): 'you know that one's person is the thing closest to home (*oikeiotaton*) for all humans, and that it is to protect it that we have established the laws, that we fight for our freedom, that we care passionately for our democracy, and do every thing else that we do in our lives' (xx.1). The speaker points out the public nature of suits involving assault, and especially of the *graphē hubreos*; and then argues against the obvious point that the injuries sustained were not serious:

if no *hubris* had been present in addition to what was done, I certainly would not have appeared before you. But as it is, I have come to obtain justice from him, not for the sake of the general damage arising from the blows, but for the sake of the *aikeia* and the *atimia*, for the sake of which it is especially appropriate for free men to become angry and to attain the greatest revenge (5).

He develops at length the arguments that small offences can lead to major, disastrous political consequences, that acts of *hubris* can affect all one's affairs, can destroy households, and ruin cities; and, not surprisingly in a speech of the 390s, he associates Lokhites, as a rich young *hubristes*, with the hybristic outrages of the oligarchs of 411 and 404.[24] At the same time, if less explicitly, the speaker of Lysias 1 starts with the bland, if unprovable, assertion that only in the case of adultery do the laws of all Greek states give equal opportunities to rich and poor victims alike to take revenge: 'so it is that all men regard this *hubris* to be the most frightful' (i.e. all cases of *hubris* are very serious, but that committed against the sexual honour of the householder and his house is the most grave).[25] The much later speech against Konon concentrates equally on exciting the jury's pity and anger at the physical and emotional sufferings of the victim and on encouraging the jury to believe that it is in their own

[23] Cf. also Garner (1987: 32–5).

[24] Cf. Strauss (1986: 26–7, 56–9), on the use of such class-based arguments after the Peloponnesian War, while noting, with a reference to Dover (1974: 110–11), that such arguments are found at other periods as well.

[25] On the *hubris* involved in adultery, and evidence for penalties in other Greek states, Cole 1984, and Cohen (1984: 151–2). See further Cohen's essay in this volume.

interests to check the anti-social careers, the random, drunken thuggery, of Konon and his wealthy co-symposiasts.[26] Aeschines' speech *Against Timarkhos* elaborates the view that all forms of *hubris* were incompatible with citizenship in a democracy.[27]

The most important text on *hubris* in the whole of Greek literature, the *Meidias*, is the one which explores the public nature of the offence best, as it also poses most sharply the problem of the effectiveness of the law. From the countless passages that could be cited, I may here mention, first, the sequence early on (42–6) where the public interest in various suits is discussed, and the climax is reached with the *graphē hubreos*; the conclusion is that all acts involving force (*bia*) were public offences, directed against those not involved as well as the victims, and in particular that the *graphē hubreos* offers the chance of a public prosecution to *ho boulomenos*, but reserves financial penalties only to the city, because the man who has committed *hubris* has wronged the city as well as the victim, and the victim should be content merely with the satisfaction of revenge.[28] Second, the sequence of arguments from 130 onwards, where the long catalogue of Meidias' crimes of violence, insult, intimidation, his legal chicanery and his gangs of witnesses are said all to provide good cause for fear

to each one of the rest of you, trying to live as best you can on your own individual resources. And it is for this reason that you band yourselves together, so that where each of you may be inferior to someone else in friends, or in possessions or in anything else, you may by banding together be stronger than each of such people, and put an end to his *hubris* (140).

A comparison with the most notorious *hubristes* of all then compliments the success of earlier Athenians in exiling Alkibiades because of his multiple acts of *hubris*, despite his many substantial inherited and personal attributes and qualities, and urges that Meidias, who has the vice with none of the virtues, be given the same treatment. Overall, finally, the successful career of a wealthy *hubristes* like Meidias is said to threaten the security of all citizens, and their confidence in the laws and the democracy; hence it could end in the establishment of an oligarchy, and the collapse of any protection for ordinary citizens, under a régime which would regard any expression of freedom by any one of 'the many' as in itself an act of *hubris* (208–12). Thus Meidias is presented as a major public enemy, because of his acts of *hubris* against his

---

[26] Cf. Carey & Reid (1985: 74–7) on Dem. LIV.1.

[27] On these arguments, cf. Dover (1978: 34–9).

[28] This passage is referred to by Garner (1987: 34), in his discussion of Gernet's views on the *graphē*; but he dismisses Demosthenes' arguments as an 'obviously biased attempt . . . to gain the sympathy of the audience . . . merely using one of the two most common antitheses in both forensic and deliberative oratory – (harm both) private/individual and public/common'. Garner misses the central point that connects the Demosthenes passage with the others, the emphasis on the way in which the assault on the individual may genuinely be felt to threaten the common interest.

fellow-citizens, and Demosthenes presents himself, with unusual directness, as a representative of the people in bringing him to its justice.

If the sense of *hubris* and the substantially political purpose of the *graphē hubreos* are now clear, we may ask how far it succeeded in maintaining the streets and houses of Athens relatively free from hybristic violence and insults, and restraining the expressions of contemptuous hostility and exploitation of members of the *demos* that many wealthy and powerful Athenians may have wished to indulge in. Although it is widely held that the *graphē hubreos* was rarely used in the courts, it is difficult to assess this claim with any precision. The catalogue of known *graphai* and *dikai* in Osborne (1985b: 55–58) mentions two cases of *hubris*, as against, for example, two of 'being an alien', *xenia*, four of 'battery', *aikeia*, and three each of 'slander', *kakegoria* and of deliberate wounding, *trauma ek pronoias*. Osborne cautiously excludes the many cases cited by speech-title only; on the assumption that these are probably not all incorrect, it is at least worth mentioning the five further cases of *graphai hubreos* thus attested,[29] in addition to the possibilities discussed above. None the less, a number of reasons can be given why litigants who claimed to wish to punish a case of *hubris* preferred in practice to adopt a different remedy.

Many actual victims of *hubris* may have wished to gain a financial reward besides revenge, as well as to avoid the financial penalties that could result from a grossly unsuccessful *graphē*, or from a withdrawal of the charge before trial; equally important, as emphasised by Osborne, may be the awareness of the *graphē* as a major, public, trial of strength where the shame of failure was the greater. Further, if prosecution were being considered by someone other than the victim, the risk of allegations of sykophancy might well have been a deterrent, granted that Athenian attitudes to the motives of those who brought prosecutions in the courts were shot through with contradictions and suspicion.[30] Finally, the need to demonstrate, before a jury some time later, and with persuasive witnesses often available to both sides, that patent, serious, insult had been inflicted may have persuaded some to seek a different charge. (The difficulty of *proving* the state of mind of the accused, emphasised by MacDowell (1976: 28–9), seems to me of less significance, since in most cases the intent to insult would not be open to serious doubt.) It may not be

---

[29] Ant. fr. xviii (Baiter–Sauppe) 'Case of *hubris* against the free boy' (the word *hubris* is a plausible supplement in the text of Harpokration that refers to this case); Lys. fr. lxviii (B–S) 'Case of *hubris* against Kallias' and fr. cxiv (B–S) 'Case of *hubris* against Sostratos'; and Dein. 'Prosecution for *hubris* against Proxenos' and 'Defence of Epikhares against Philotades' on the same charge, included in the list of 'genuine private speeches' (*sic*, cf. Dover 1968b: 11–12) in Dion.Hal. *Dein.* 12. In fact two cases of 'deliberate wounding' provide two of our best cases of drunken fighting over disputed 'sex-objects' – a 'Plataian' boy, and a *hetaira* (Lys. iii and iv); to bring such a case, heard, like homicide cases, by the Areiopagos, it seems one needed to show a wound inflicted with a weapon; the relative frequency of this action cannot be determined either.

[30] Cf. Dover (1974: 187–90), Fisher (1976b: 35–9), Osborne (1985b: 50–3), and the essays by Osborne and Harvey in this volume.

coincidence that the one case that certainly did reach a court, and may have attained a conviction, that brought against Diokles, involved the indubitable form of 'dishonour' constituted by legal *atimia*.

IV

Evidence of a change in the law – the introduction of the *probolē* procedure – may suggest that some of the difficulties of the *hubris* law were recognised. According to Demosthenes (XXI.147), 'this law' – presumably the law enabling the *probolē* procedure to be used for gross offences against individuals committed at major public festivals (when drink might be flowing, and where the humiliations inflicted were especially public) – did not exist in the late fifth century, when Alkibiades punched his fellow-*khoregos* Taureas.[31] It might, then, be suggested that at some point, for example at the restoration of the democracy in 403, it was decided to increase the attractiveness of bringing such cases to court and the likelihood of convictions being achieved, by encouraging the victims, or any others who were willing, to win the initial advantage of a swift, preliminary vote in the assembly, many of whose members would be likely to have witnessed the event, and whose memories would be fresh. As was the usual rule in the democracy, the final decision was left to a court.[32] Such an addition to the laws suggests that some concern had been felt that the laws dealing with such outrages needed strengthening, perhaps in the interests of preventing disruption of the festivals as well as of dealing with particularly insulting crimes.

But that the law of *hubris* may have needed this reinforcement, and that many litigants, for fully understandable reasons, often chose a lesser charge, does not mean that the law of *hubris* was a failure. The *probolē* was intended to help it to work more effectively in certain important cases, not to replace it generally; and the continued existence and recognised importance of the *graphē* gave a legitimacy and a solidity to the rhetoric with which litigants pleading a wide variety of cases were able to enhance the illegal humiliations they had allegedly been subjected to. In other words, *hubris* was not only a term of very strong moral weight for use in condemning such insults (with, it may be, some religious overtones on occasions);[33] but since it was the title of the most serious crime in the area of offences against the person, the argument that great *hubris* had been committed, and a *graphē hubreos* could have been brought, seems likely to have increased the average jury's sense of anger and

---

31 Cf. MacDowell (1978: 194–7).

32 On this principle in the democracy, and the issues it raises, cf. above all the work of Hansen (e.g. 1983a: 139–40, 155–60); while the ideological significance, and indeed the precise formulation, of the relationship between assembly and lawcourts remain alike controversial, the very wide (and final) powers of the courts are not in dispute.

33 The religious aspects of Meidias' offence at the festival are not exploited as insistently as might have been expected (cf. 51–5, 97–8, 126–7), nor is *hubris* used explicitly of the offence against the gods. Cf. also Dover 1974: 251, and on the (greatly exaggerated) 'religious' overtones of *hubris*, cf. Fisher (1978 and forthcoming, 1990).

outrage, and, in itself, to have increased its readiness to convict and apply serious penalties for hybristic behaviour, whatever the charge. This tactic seems admirably exemplified in the speeches against Konon and Lokhites (and perhaps also the Lysias fragment against Teisis). If so, awareness of these possibilities may also have played some part in deterring some potential offenders from such behaviour.[34]

But, of course, hybristic behaviour was scarcely eradicated; drunken fights over *hetairai* (call-girls) or boys, general fights at *sumposia* or in the streets, drunken assaults on enemies or passers-by, deliberate, sometimes vicious, sometimes homicidal, attacks on enemies, all seem to occupy a not inconsiderable part of the 'conspicuous' behaviour of the wealthy and politically active classes that most of our sources concern; and often, not surprisingly, and for a variety of reasons, conviction of such offenders, and execution of judgements, were difficult to achieve (and in many cases, of course, the outcome of a trial is not known to us).[35] Do we, though, have any reason to suppose that any *hubristai* were actually damaged by any accusations relying on, or rhetorically making use of, the *graphē hubreos*?

Diokles the villain of Isaeus VIII may well have been incommoded, or even punished, by one or more of the charges brought against him, including the *graphē hubreos*.[36] Other interesting cases, where some progress may possibly be made, would seem to be those of Meidias and some of the comparable cases Demosthenes mentions in his speech. It might be foolish to believe all that he says of successful prosecutions of men for *hubris* against slaves (49), of cases where people avoided laying hands on those they might have been thought to have had grounds for so insulting because they were deterred by the existence of the laws and the spirit of the democracy (62–5), of other cases of *probolē* for wrongdoing at the festival, where cases involving little or no *hubris* were taken seriously, and one taken to involve considerable *hubris* brought death (175–81); and one must note other cases where he seems to complain that the courts are more lenient to rich offenders than to poor (36–41, 182–3; cf. also [Andok.] IV. 21–3). But there may well be some evidence here that prosecutions for hybristic behaviour, or the fear of them, did occasionally produce significant results.

The *cause célèbre* of Alkibiades at least, mentioned by Demosthenes (143–50) as by many other sources, provides solid evidence that a politician of the highest birth, wealth (at least at first), and natural qualities of charismatic leadership, generalship, rhetorical powers and charm, was destroyed, above

---

[34] Cf. also Dover (1974: 54), on the use of *hubris* to evoke an emotional response by finding hybristic elements in a variety of offences; many examples are given in Fisher (forthcoming: ch.3). Some evidence that the possibility of a *graphē hubreos* was thought to be a serious deterrent might be found in the relevant passages of Aristophanes (n. 13 above), especially in the extreme reaction of the sober Bdelykleon to the threat of the action: 'Hubris? For the gods' sake, don't please bring that summons', and an offer to settle on any terms (Ar. *Wasps* 1419–20, and cf. Powell 1988: 316–17).

[35] Cf. Fisher (1976b: 37–45), Osborne (1985b: 50), Calhoun 1917.

[36] Davies (1971: 313–14).

all, by his incurable *hubris*, or, more fully, by his contradictory impulses to win honour and power from his city and simultaneously to treat its citizens and their religious and moral values with contempt, and where convenient with violence.[37] Cases of *hubris* seem to have been notable in the late fifth century ([Xen.], *Ath.Pol.* III.5, and cf. perhaps the case of Sophocles and Peisandros); even if Alkibiades evaded conviction on such a charge, the damage done to his career (and to Athens) by the accumulation of plausible accusations is patent, and thereafter set an example for other such politicians operating in the restored democracy.[38]

The case of Meidias himself, however, seems in itself the strongest evidence of the unfettered opportunities for wealthy, unscrupulous men with good connections to get away with repeated acts of *hubris* in fourth-century Athens; it was so presented by Finley (1981: 85–6), as part of the obviously correct argument that achievement of the ideal of equality before the law was, and is, extraordinarily difficult for democracies to achieve in practice, and that even Athens, among ancient societies, lacked the technical machinery, and the consistent hardness of will, to deal with such an obstinate villain. Finley's strictures on modern scholars for dismissing this speech 'as an unfinished draft of an undelivered speech' are, at least in some cases, unfair; that view of the speech seems clearly well-founded, in the light both of the internal state of the text, and of the allegations in Aeschines (III.52) and elsewhere that Demosthenes 'sold the case' to Meidias for 30 *mnai*; and, as some scholars have recognised, this makes the apparent sequence of events no less interesting, and at first sight no less depressing, than the alternative, less plausible, view that the speech was delivered, and that Demosthenes, at some point in the trial, accepted a mere financial penalty and stopped proceedings. That is, on the view I accept, Demosthenes, after years of maltreatment at the hands of Meidias and his brother and the final insult at the Dionysia, won a vote in the assembly on the *probolē* charge; he had anyway prepared, over a period of years, a massive invective against Meidias, to be delivered in court (and, no doubt, some of this found its way into the assembly speech at the *probolē* hearing at least); but, before the case came into court, he agreed to drop the case for 30 *mnai*, and even so still allowed his arguments to go into 'circulation' in Athens: hence it has come down to us.[39] So, it would seem, Meidias got away with it again.

Precisely why Demosthenes settled out of court cannot be known; the relative importance of the fear of Meidias and his friends, doubts about the possibility of a conviction, hope for a *rapprochement* to strengthen his position

---

[37] On Alkibiades' contempt for democratic values, cf. Seager 1967, Murray 1990a.

[38] Cf. Thuc. VI.15, and the continuing debate on his *hubris* in relation to his son in the early fourth century, in Lys. XIV and Isoc. XVI; cf. also Strauss (1986: ch.4).

[39] Cf. e.g. the restatement by Dover (1968b: 172–4), against Erbse 1956. The compromise might have occurred when Demosthenes was co-operating with Euboulos before the peace embassies, and the circulation encouraged when disputes on the peace broke out. Cf. Cawkwell (1963: 49).

in the foreign policy debates, or desire for a quick cash settlement, cannot begin to be unravelled. One may note, on the one hand, that Meidias survived, to be *pulagoras*, sacred delegate to the Delphic Amphiktiony, in 340, and to leave his sons liturgical estates;[40] but also, on the other, that Meidias' reputation must have suffered somewhat by the vote in the assembly, so that he preferred to pay than face another trial and possible penalty, and that Demosthenes probably reckoned that renewed exposure, to the reading public, of his crimes would do Meidias more harm than the reminder of the settlement thereby risked would further harm himself. On the personal level Demosthenes achieved at least a minor victory; and Meidias' capacity to insult and damage other citizens might have suffered something of a blow, even if he was far from ruined. The Athenian Establishment, like many another, for all its bitter internal vituperation, could sometimes seem to outsiders a closed circle of friends (e.g. [Dem.] LVIII); but what may seem like an illicit and hypocritical closing of ranks and collusion in criminality might at least on some occasions be, or be intended to be, a settlement that constituted some sort of a diminution of status and of wealth, and perhaps of the opportunity to commit further crimes, on the part of the man who paid up.

Control of the wealthy and determined was bound to be difficult; and the contradictory attitudes to the rich on the part of the *demos* included some vicarious admiration for their 'goings-on', which only comedy could afford them an opportunity to fantasise themselves enjoying.[41] None the less, among the mechanisms, both legal and social, for persuading or compelling the rich and powerful to spend some of their wealth on the community and not on their pleasures,[42] and to treat fellow-citizens with decency and not with contempt, the law of *hubris* surely played a major rôle; its existence gave the opportunity to litigants to sharpen and intensify their accusations of disgraceful, oligarchic and contemptuous insolence, whatever the actual charge, and thereby to reinforce the cohesive, egalitarian, ideology of the democracy. The law of *hubris* no doubt did not work as well as it should have, or as Solon may have intended it to;[43] but there is good reason to suppose that, even if not used all that frequently, it played a considerable part in making the daily lives of many

---

[40] Cf. Davies (1971: 386–7), Finley (1981: 86).

[41] On comedy and fantasies of hybristic behaviour, cf. Dover (1972: 31–41). Some of the ambivalence of Athenian attitudes to the luxury and *hubris* of top people seems to have been picked up, in typically exaggerated fashion, by Theopompos (*FGH* 115F213 = Athen. XII.532c-d), where Chares' goings-on while on campaign with flutes, *hetairai* and *hubris* are said to have been tolerated by the *demos* who liked such things themselves.

[42] On the complex patterns of 'liturgical' bargaining between the rich and the *demos* (e.g. Dem. XXI.151–167), cf. Davies (1971: xvii–xxiv), Fisher (1976b: 25–30), Whitehead 1983, Sinclair (1988: 61–5, 188–90).

[43] Cf. Solon's supposed 'debate' with the wandering Scythian Anacharsis on whether his laws would be strong enough to catch the toughest offenders, or whether, like spiders' webs, they would only catch the weak (Plut. *Solon* 5). In my view, both the *graphē hubreos* and the volunteer prosecutor were integral parts of Solon's legislative package designed to restrict the anti-social activities of the 'powerful and rich'. Cf. also the essay by Osborne in this volume.

Athenians less fearful and less oppressed than they would otherwise have been.[44]

[44] The law of offences against the person in use in Ptolemaic Alexandria (cf. Partsch 1920) included – in addition to a variety of fairly precise provisions against assaults, threats with an offensive weapon, violence committed when drunk, at night, in a temple, and so on – a law against *hubris* 'of a type not covered in the written code', with penalties fixed at double the damages assessed; this was a 'private' *dikē*, not a public action, with lesser penalties. The differences between this law and the Athenian may well be the result of conscious reflection; one may in fact suspect that the Alexandrian legislators disliked the extremely democratic feel of the Athenian law, or thought that a less intimidating law might actually produce more prosecutions and convictions: or even both.

6b

The Solonian law of hubris

OSWYN MURRAY

In the preceding chapter, N.R.E. Fisher has discussed the way in which the law of *hubris* was perceived in Classical Athens, and the extent to which it functioned as an active part of the legal system; I wish to consider its purpose in the Archaic period, and to try to reconstruct the intentions of the lawgiver by setting the Athenian law on *hubris* in the wider context of archaic lawgiving and archaic society. Many of the reasons why I reject the arguments of Gernet and others against the attribution of the law to the early sixth century will become clear in the course of the argument; but I should perhaps begin by saying that I accept the conclusions reached by Fisher (above pp. 134–8); and I therefore think it more important to place the law in its archaic context than to argue in detail against an alternative interpretation.

I begin by drawing out two points already made by Fisher:

In the Classical period, *hubris* in its legal sense is seen as a cornerstone of the democratic legal system, even though the evidence suggests that few cases were actually brought to court. This emphasis on the importance of the crime clearly goes back to the origins of the law, since its prosecution lies in the public arena as a *graphē* not a *dikē*. On the other hand, the offence itself concerns the intentional inflicting of *atimia* (dishonour) *on an individual*: that is of course the central paradox noted by Gernet and others. The question of the lawgiver's intent is closely bound up with this curious combination of public interest and private wrong.

Secondly, I note the characteristic profile of the offender in cases of *hubris*. Aristotle says, 'it is the young and the rich who are especially *hubristai* (those who commit *hubris*), because they think that thereby they show their superiority' (*Rhet.* II, 1378b28–9); and this assertion is well supported in the evidence. Not only is Meidias the archetypal *plousios* (rich man), but the whole of Demosthenes XXI is built around the typical relationship between wealth and hybristic behaviour. As for the young, again the speech against Konon (Dem. LIV) sets out to argue from an accepted connection of hybristic

139

behaviour with the *sumposia* (drinking parties) of the young as *epheboi* (adolescent males) to the question of its limits, and the disgracefulness of a mature man of over fifty continuing in such behaviour; the anticipated response of the defence is based on the naturalness of young men engaging in such drunken escapades (esp. LIV.22).[1]

In addition to the arguments put forward by Fisher, there seems to me one important difficulty in the view that such a law could have been passed in the age of the Classical democracy. The law seems to be primarily concerned, not with particular types of action and the damage resulting from them but with the intention behind them, an intention to cause shame (*aiskhunē*) and the consequent loss of honour (*timē*).[2] It is not easy to see how such concepts relate to the interests of Athenian law of the Classical period. It is true that the idea of *atimia* in particular is important in the law of the fifth and fourth centuries, but as a legal concept that is already well-defined.[3] It was connected with the increasing emphasis on the definition of the legal status of citizenship, and it referred to the loss of certain citizen rights as a penalty for various offences, especially for being a public debtor;[4] more seriously, a man could be described as *atimos* if he were completely deprived of citizenship, or were in danger of having his claim to citizenship rejected in the courts. In other words, in a legal context, *atimia* refers to the legal status of an individual as citizen, rather than to his social standing or his honour in a more general sense: '*atimia* was the penalty *par excellence* which an Athenian might incur in his capacity of a citizen, but not for offences he had committed as a private individual' (Hansen 1976: 74). The idea of a law on *hubris* concerning the *timē* of an individual in any sense other than that of his citizen rights seems contrary to the conceptions prevalent in Athenian legislation of the Classical period: such a law would have had to envisage a situation involving the treatment of free men as if they were slaves, or citizens as if they were foreigners, or slaves (who are specifically mentioned as within the scope of the law) as if they were – what? By the Classical period the law has disregarded (or is in process of disregarding) the formal distinctions between grades of citizens introduced by Solon:[5] the *geras* (honour) which each of the Solonian *telē* (census-classes) possessed in unequal portions has been reduced to a single privilege of citizenship, in which all Athenians are equal. Further, any offence which is

---

[1] In general the behaviour of young aristocrats at *sumposia* is often regarded as 'hybristic', though it might fall outside the sphere of *hubris* in the legal sense: the Mysteries for instance were portrayed in *sumposia* in a spirit of *hubris* (*eph' hubrei*: Thuc. VI.28.1); see Murray (1990a).

[2] This is most clearly brought out in Arist. *Rhet.* I, 1374a13–15; II, 1378b23–6; Isaeus VIII.41; Dem. XXI.72.

[3] For this legal usage, I select from the many passages cited in Welskopf (1985.1: 277–85): Lys. XXV.11, 27; Dem. XX.156; XXI.32–3, 87, 91–2, 113; XXII.34; XXIII.62; XXIV.46, 50, 201; XXVI.11; LVIII.45; Plato, *Laws* X.890c; Lyc. *In Leocr.* 41; Hyp. fr. 27, 29 Jensen; compare, of the Spartans, Thuc. V.34.2. The fundamental discussion of legal *atimia* is Hansen (1976: ch. III).

[4] On the categories of *atimoi* see Andok. I.73–9.

[5] For the practice of disregarding a Solonian *telos*, see *Ath. Pol.* 7.4.

committed against a citizen in order to dishonour him is capable of being brought under the scope of another law such as *aikeia* (assault). This seems to me the fundamental reason why so few cases of *hubris* are actually known from the Classical period: damage to the *timē* of a citizen of the Athenian democracy can only be achieved by due legal process, or by physical acts already within the scope of other laws.

The two certain court cases of *hubris* about which we have reasonable evidence seem to confirm this analysis, for both can be construed as attacks, not on some aristocratic conception of the honour of an individual, but on the actual citizen status of the wronged individual. In Isaeus VIII.41, Diokles of Phlya has inflicted *atimia* on his victim by actually walling him up, that is (presumably) by depriving him of his citizen status and treating him as a slave. In the case brought by Apollodoros, the claim is that a forged will has involved the speaker's mother in marriage with an ex-slave, Phormion:[6] the fact that the argument is so patently ridiculous in the case of a family itself of slave extraction merely reinforces the impression that only threats to the citizen status of an individual appeared now to qualify as formal *atimia*. The same difficulty in defining the loss of *timē* involved may be seen in the attempts of Demosthenes to suggest that office-holders have some sort of special protection under the law of *hubris*, a claim that is clearly not supported by the examples he adduces (Dem. XXI.36–41).

In contrast, the concepts of *hubris* and *timē* were fundamental to the social and political life of Archaic Athens. Solon's poems identify clearly the cause of the social unrest in the *hubris* and *koros* (insolence) of the wealthy.[7] These are appropriate objects for the attention of the lawgiver: it is the task of *eunomiē* (good government) to put an end to *koros* and to weaken *hubris*. On the other hand honour is related to social status: *geras* (cf. above) and *timē* are not to be apportioned equally:

I gave to the *demos* as much *geras* as is fitting, neither taking away from their *timē* nor giving them too much; while to those who had power and were blessed with wealth, for these I took care that they should suffer nothing unseemly. (fr. 5.1–4 West)

In this fragment it is remarkable that even the *demos* has *timē*; but Solon clearly recognises that different social classes possess it to different degrees. In the Solonian constitution *timē* was for the first time legally defined, in the rights to office allocated to different groups on the basis of a property qualification: each class (*telos*) had its appropriate *geras*. Moreover, it was possible to change one's *telos*, at least upwards, as the dedication quoted by *Ath. Pol.* 7 demonstrates.[8] It is therefore clear that the concept of *geras* or *timē*, graded according to social status, existed in Solonian Athens, and that Solon legislated in the interest of such distinctions, though we may be

---

6 Dem. XLV.3–5; XXXVI.30; see Fisher above p. 125.
7 They are paired in fr.4.8–9, 34 West and fr.6.3; cf. fr.4c.2; 13.11, 16.
8 The date of this dedication is uncertain, but it is perhaps most likely to be after the Persian Wars; for other problems concerning it, see Rhodes (1981: 143–4).

uncertain how far Solon's new legal definitions corresponded to older, less formal categories. Moreover, if it were possible to rise in *timē* according to the Solonian code, it must also have been possible to conceive of losing *timē*. To say that the *timē* in question is a legal status, not a social quality, would be to offer too rigid a distinction between the world of the lawcode and the Archaic society, whose preconceptions it serves to mirror and protect: in the shame culture of early Greece, honour and the possibility of dishonour are closely related to social and political status with their attendant rights and duties. A lawgiver might well wish to legislate to protect the individual from loss of *timē*. *Hubris* in Solon's poetry, as in the later legal texts, designates behaviour intended to have an effect on the social fabric, by depriving those of whatever class of their due *timē*. But what is the context in which such *hubris* is likely to occur?

Solon connects the *hubris* of the wealthy with their feasting: 'they know not how to restrain their *koros* (cf. above) or to order their present *euphrosunai* in the quiet of the feast' (fr. 4.9–10 West). In Archaic poetry *euphrosunē* is a word designating the delights of the *sumposion*; Solon combines this with images drawn from Homeric feasting, and Odysseus' description of his own palace (*Odyssey* XVII.264–71): the doors of the court are not able to keep out 'the public ill', 'but it jumps over the high barrier and pursues a man, even if he flees into the depths of the inner chamber' (fr. 4.26–9). The imagery mixes traditional Homeric language with the concerns of an aristocracy whose distinguishing mark lies in the forms of commensality characteristic of the Archaic world.[9] The threat of disorder arises in two directions: the failure to 'restrain their *koros* or to order their present *euphrosunai* in the quiet of the feast' seems to imply, not merely disorder in the context of the *sumposion*, but an extension of this disorder outwards into the community. The response will be an invasion of the inner space of the aristocracy by the public ills.

The *sumposion* itself is a rule-bound area; one of its most striking characteristics is the eagerness of participants both to isolate themselves from the larger world of the *polis*, and to create an alternative set of *nomoi*.[10] On the other hand, drunken violence is a recognised characteristic of its proceedings: in the words of the fourth-century comic poet Eubulus, the first three *kraters* (mixing bowls) belong to the well-ordered *sumposion*; 'the fourth *krater* is ours no longer, but belongs to *hubris*', and from then on various types of disorder are the rule.[11]

In fact, in both the Archaic and the democratic periods there is little sign of cities attempting directly to regulate activities within the *sumposion*. Such

---

[9] On this subject see further Murray 1983 and the essays in Murray (1990).
[10] See especially Pellizer (1990).
[11] Eubulus fr.83 Kassel–Austin = 94 Kock, in Athenaeus II.36b–c; see Murray (1983: 258).

associations are included among those whose rules are granted legal status in the Solonian code:

> If a deme or *phratores* or † *orgeones* or *gennetai* † or *sussitoi* or *homotaphoi* or *thiasotai* (various types of association) or pirates or traders make arrangements among themselves, these shall be binding, unless forbidden by the public writings. (*Digest* XLVII.22.4)

Although the Greek text is corrupt and difficult to restore, the presence of types of association connected with the *sumposion* is certain; the Digest quotation is taken from Gaius, who quotes this passage in relation to the Twelve Tables, and specifically refers to privileges granted there to '*sodales* who belong to the same *collegium*, which the Greeks call a *hetaireia*'. There are however traces of legislation concerned with sympotic activity in one area, the question of who might or might not drink wine. The matter is discussed in Athenaeus x.429a–b. In a number of cities citizen women were forbidden by custom or law to drink wine; Massalia, Miletus and Rome are mentioned; in Rome freeborn males were not permitted to drink wine before the age of thirty, and a little later Athenaeus (x.440b) cites Plato's *Laws* II.666a, which envisages a similar prohibition before the age of 18.[12] These laws and customs essentially concern restrictions placed on full membership of the *sumposion*, excluding citizen women and those considered as minors. A law of Zaleukos allegedly went further, in prescribing that wine must be mixed with water, on pain of death, unless it were being used for medical reasons.[13]

Apart from these areas it seems clear that the internal *euphrosunē* (cf. above) of the *sumposion* was no direct concern of the city.[14] This fact contrasts with the willingness of the Archaic city to legislate in other areas of aristocratic display. Sumptuary legislation in the archaic period seems indeed often to have had a social rather than a moral purpose, in seeking to limit those rituals of conspicuous consumption which served to distinguish the aristocracy from the community, and which were intended to display their wealth and power. In one such area C. Ampolo has recently made a comprehensive survey of Archaic Greek laws concerning public display at funerals in relation to the laws of the Twelve Tables (Ampolo 1984a). From this it is clear that there is a widespread tendency to limit such aristocratic activity at funerals. From his list I select two examples. The first is the famous case of Athens: the 'laws of

---

[12] See Tecuşan (1990).
[13] The prohibition on *servilis unctura* and *circumpotatio* in the Twelve Tables (Cic. *de leg.* II.24.60) may also be relevant here; the latter at least (if it means drinking rounds) was not allowed at Sparta, in contrast to Athens, according to Kritias fr.6 West. But the Roman law may refer to funerary banquets, if Ampolo (1984a: 88 n.48) is right to connect *circumpotatio* with the Greek *perideipnon*. On Roman customs see further the works cited in Murray (1985: 48 n.34).
[14] In fourth-century Athens, presumably in accordance with a *nomos*, the ten *astunomoi* regulated the hiring of musicians at a fixed price (*Ath.Pol.* 50.2): it is likely, however, that this refers to public festivals rather than private occasions.

Solon' regulated displays at the funeral in detail, in relation to the numbers and activities of female mourners, funeral banquets, the procession, the tomb, sacrifice, clothing, offerings and the presence of strangers.[15] The second case is that of Mytilene, where Pittakos limited participation in the funeral.[16] Such sumptuary laws may serve a variety of social purposes: in Rome for instance they seem to have had the general aim of limiting aristocratic display in the interests of maintaining a cohesive group mentality and so protecting the privileges of the aristocracy.[17] But in Greece Ampolo is surely right to connect such laws with the development of the *polis*, and the desire to limit public displays of power and wealth by the aristocracy.[18]

It is in this context that a Solonian law of *hubris* fits best. One of the disadvantages of the *sumposion* as a social ritual was that, while it created internal forms of bonding important to the maintenance of aristocratic control, this process was invisible to the external world. Consequently the *komos*, the drunken revel through the streets which terminated the *sumposion*, was an essential element in the sympotic life-style, and a necessary corollary as a public display of aristocratic self-definition; and, as the public aspect of the *sumposion*, the *komos* was more likely to provoke legislation by the city. Archaic Mytilene in the age of Alkaios and his companions is once again the obvious parallel: Pittakos imposed double fines for violence committed when drunk (Arist., *Pol.* II, 1274b18–20). I have argued elsewhere that this is to be connected with the alleged activity of the Penthilidai, who roamed the streets beating passers-by with clubs; for that is surely the characteristic activity of a band of drinking companions intent on displaying their power over the people through the *komos*.[19] Such activity in turn provides a historical background to the deliberately 'hybristic' pattern of behaviour which Demosthenes attributes to Meidias.

Hubris, conceived of as drunken violence committed in relation to the *sumposion*, in the Archaic period is not mere drunken assault; it is part of a pattern of behaviour intended to assert the supremacy of an aristocracy over its rivals; it involves the deliberate dishonouring of those who are not members of the group in order to reduce their *timē* in the community. It was such considerations which made Solon regard *hubris* as a threat to the structure of a community based on carefully regulated grades of *timē*, and which therefore caused him to define it as a public crime to be granted special status under the procedure of the *graphē*.

One small indication seems to me to support this characterisation of the law

---

[15]   The passages are cited in Ruschenbusch (1966: fr. 72): Demetrius of Phaleron distinguished a law of Solon about funerals and mourning, and a later law concerning the tomb itself, perhaps correctly.

[16]   This is mentioned in the same famous passage cited in Ruschenbusch: Cicero, *de leg.* II.26.66.

[17]   See Bonamente 1980, Clemente 1981, Miles 1987.

[18]   Ampolo 1984a; see also more generally Ampolo 1984b and Cozzoli 1980.

[19]   *Pol.* v, 1311b23; see Murray (1983: 268).

of *hubris*. To fourth-century commentators it was already a major problem that *hubris* could be committed against slaves as well as free persons: Demosthenes makes great play with this in the Meidias speech (xxi.47–50),[20] and regards it somewhat implausibly as a demonstration of the *philanthropia* (humanitarianism) of the Athenians. On any account it is odd that the *graphē* procedure should even hypothetically be available to protect the *timē* of a slave, even if we may perhaps doubt the claim of Demosthenes that many have in fact been executed for this offence! But in the context of the aristocratic world, and especially the *sumposion*, the protection of slaves takes on a different significance. In the *sumposion* the slave, both male and female, plays an essential rôle as servant, as companion and as entertainer: the wine-pourer, the flute-girl, the dancer, are all, despite their servile status, accepted in the group; *hetairai* in particular are a necessary accompaniment, and a personal possession. Physical violence against such people was common enough, as Aristophanes' *Wasps* or the speech against Neaira show (*Wasps* 1341–87; Dem. LIX.33). In this context to dishonour a slave may in fact be to dishonour the master, and at least it is likely to lead to wider consequences: we know of one serious act of *hubris* as a result, when someone struck an *arkhon thesmothetes* who was trying to abduct (or rescue) a flute-girl – but, says Demosthenes, he had an excuse, for he was both drunk and in love (xxi.36, 38). It is in such a context that slaves too may possess *timē*, in relation to that of their masters.

Solon's concern for the position of slaves in the law of *hubris* relates to a more general interest in the proper use of slaves in the context of the aristocratic life-style. It is likely enough that the possession of slaves was largely confined to the aristocracy in this period; but the specific laws against a slave stripping naked and anointing himself in the *palaistra* (wrestling-school), or becoming the *erastes* (lover) of or pursuing a free boy, show a more precise concern with relationships within the world of aristocratic *truphē* (luxury) (Ruschenbusch 1966: fr. 74).

The world of *hubris* is one where the spheres of public and private are not clearly separate, in which the public order of the *polis* was threatened by forms of violence which a later generation might come to regard as belonging to the private sphere of the aristocratic *sumposion*. The concern of the legislator was only partially with the individual honour of the victim of *hubris*, far more with the dangers to the community which were posed by a whole nexus of behaviour on the part of both victim and aggressor. It is thus that we can perhaps dispel the worries of Gernet and others about the existence of such concern with the rights of the individual in an age of collective representations.[21]

[20] See also Aesch. 1.17; the subject is clearly a rhetorical *topos*.
[21] Many thanks to the participants in the Cambridge seminar at which this chapter was first presented in March 1987, for their comments and suggestions; and especially to my fellow speaker Nick Fisher for much help both earlier and later.

7

The social context of adultery at Athens

DAVID COHEN

Before examining the norms, values, and social practices that define the social context of adultery at Athens a few remarks about the *legal* regulation of adultery are appropriate. In my opinion, fundamental misunderstanding prevails in the scholarly literature on the Athenian law of adultery. The traditional view holds that *moicheia* at Athens was not defined in terms of the marital relation, but included illegitimate intercourse with any female member of the family – mother, sister, daughter, etc. This view, which would make Athens unique among early Western and Near Eastern legal systems, rests upon blatant misinterpretations of certain crucial passages and a confusion as to the distinction between prohibitory norms and excusing conditions. Space does not permit a full presentation of the evidence here, so I will simply assert that in classical Athens the law defined *moicheia* as adultery, that is, as a sexual violation of the marital relation. Athenian law thus defined adultery in the same way as biblical, Assyrian, Babylonian, and classical Roman law, and, like those legal systems, permitted the husband to subject the adulterer taken in the act to certain summary procedures. In Athenian law this means that the adulterer (*moichos*) was classified as a *kakourgos*, a category of offenders subject to the procedure of *apagoge* or summary arrest and, possibly, summary execution.

Understanding *moicheia* in this legal context permits a hypothetical reconstruction of the statute on adultery:

If someone takes an adulterer let him do with him whatever he pleases or take him to the Eleven. If he admits his guilt death is the penalty, but if he denies it let him be brought into court . . . When he has caught the adulterer, it shall not be lawful for the one who has caught him to continue living with his wife, and if he does so he shall lose his civic rights; and it shall not be lawful for the woman who is taken in adultery to attend public sacrifices; and if she does attend them, let her suffer whatever may be inflicted upon her, except death, with legal impunity.[1]

[1] A detailed analysis of the evidence for this reconstruction of the law of adultery may be found in Cohen 1984. I should emphasise again the hypothetical nature of my proposed text; the general sense is quite likely accurate, but the particular wording may have been rather different.

What scholars of Greek law often forget is that reconstructing what penalties the statutes provided is, in itself, not particularly interesting. The bare statutes tell us relatively little about the law as applied, interpreted, violated, and avoided in the social system of which the law is but one part. In other words, one must move from the legal positivist interpretation of the criminal law as a set of prohibitory rules that impose order upon society to an understanding of legal norms as but a part of the complex structure of social practices through which a social order is maintained and reproduced. Building, then, upon this narrowly legal exposition, I turn now to the broader social and ideological context of which the law and practice of adultery form a part.

The modern Anglo-American reader, accustomed to the decreasing legal and social significance of adultery, may wonder why this particular sexual delict should provide the focus for investigation. First of all, one should note that, although in modern western society it is rape which has become the pre-eminent or paradigmatic sexual crime, in Athens this was apparently not the case. Apart from exceptional circumstances such as tyranny or the sacking of a city in wartime, we hear relatively little about the rape of free Athenian women, and the nature of the statutory provisions is somewhat obscure. Structural factors arising from the social organisation of modern Mediterranean societies may account for the relative infrequency of rape in such societies, structural factors which also hold good for classical Athens.[2] For present purposes, however, it suffices to note that, whereas modern law focuses upon coercive, non-consensual sexual transactions, making rape the pre-eminent sexual delict, Athenian law accords this place of honour to adultery, which is clearly the paradigmatic sexual offence in the Athenian orators, tragedy, and Old Comedy.[3] Further, this preoccupation with adultery also characterises modern Mediterranean societies, and the following analysis will discuss why this should be the case, and will relate the context of adultery to more general problems concerning women, the family, and sexuality.

In sketching this social context, the seemingly banal questions of how and why furnish a convenient starting point. If, as much contemporary scholarship holds, women were strictly confined to their houses, watched by their husbands, and accompanied in their every movement by relatives or slaves, how did they form adulterous relationships and then consummate them? Further, why did men and women run the considerable risks that adultery entailed? After all, as Lysias' oration, On the Murder of Eratosthenes, makes clear, some husbands, at least, were not loath to exercise the summary procedures provided by the law, and other passages attest to the ill-treatment

[2] Statistics on rape in contemporary western European societies suggest that this pattern may still hold, for Italy and Greece have far lower rates of (recorded) rape than do, for example, Britain and West Germany.

[3] Rape of young, unmarried women at festivals plays a prominent rôle in the plots of several comedies of Menander, but it is often not clear whether the sexual transaction really was based upon force or is simply referred to as such in order to help preserve the reputation of the girl.

which adulterers were likely to suffer if apprehended. Indeed, the question of motivation arises with particular force for men, since, according to many scholars, the only significant romantic attachments for men were homosexual, and sexual gratification, in this slave society, was ubiquitous and cheap. Indeed, if Andromache's description of her life in Euripides' *Trojan Women* is taken as typical, one wonders why and how adultery happened at all, let alone achieved its pre-eminence in the pantheon of sexual misconduct:

I made good reputation my aim; I was fairly successful; but now I have lost what I gained. As Hector's wife I studied and practised the perfection of womanly modesty. First, if a woman does not stay in her own house, this very fact brings ill-fame upon her, whether she is at fault or not; I therefore gave up my longing to go out, and stayed at home; and I refused to admit into my house the amusing gossip of other women ... Before my husband I kept a quiet tongue and modest eye; I knew in what matters I should rule, and where I should yield to his authority.[4]

Such statements are all too often regarded by scholars as representative, yet they contrast markedly with the many assertions of the sexual intemperance of women and the frequency of adultery one finds in the sources. As a character in Euripides' *Stheneboea*, mouthing a commonplace, puts it, 'Many a man, proud of his wealth and birth, has been disgraced by his wanton wife.' What accounts for the antithetical descriptions of the married woman and her rôle which one finds throughout the classical sources? An examination of this ambivalence about the characterisation of women may serve as a first step towards understanding adultery and the context in which it occurred.

Conflicting characterisations of women in the ancient sources have caused considerable confusion, which scholars have dealt with in two ways. The more primitive method denies the force of the antinomy, explaining it away in some fashion. Thus, Flacelière (1965: 55) accepts the Andromachean typology at face value:

Whereas married women seldom crossed the thresholds of their own front door, adolescent girls were lucky if they were allowed as far as the inner courtyard since they had to stay where they could not be seen – well away even from the male members of the family.

He admits, though, that Aristophanes presents a very different picture of Athenian women, but concludes (1965: 69) that this must represent a change towards greater freedom in the late fifth century – a rather desperate expedient, since we have almost no evidence *before* the second half of the century. More recently, Gould (1980) and Humphreys acknowledge the contradiction, but Humphreys rather unsatisfactorily contents herself with commenting that, 'This contradictoriness must be to some extent a product of the nature of our sources, which are heavily dominated by cultural themes in which women are seen through a grid designed to fit men.'[5] Gould, more

---

[4] Eur. *Tro*. 643–56, trans. Vellacott 1975: 89–90.
[5] Humphreys 1983b: 49; *contra* Henderson 1975: 206.

sensibly, tries to relate the contradiction to profound cultural conflicts concerning women and their sexuality, conflicts expressed with particular force in myth. These conflicts arise out of a central cultural ambiguity about women and sexuality, based upon a dynamic of dependence and hatred, desire and fear, which, it will be argued below, is typical of Mediterranean societies. A satisfactory explanation, however, must go beyond the realm of myth, important as that may be, and attempt to explain these contradictions in terms of what Giddens (1984: ch. 1) calls the 'structural properties' of social systems. Looking at similar difficulties that have arisen in describing the social rôle of women in the contemporary Mediterranean world may prove helpful in addressing this task.

Anthropologists, predominantly male, had long formulated a view of Mediterranean women as secluded, powerless, and isolated from the life of their society. A later generation of researchers, however, challenged this widely accepted thesis. Clark, for example, in her social anthropological study of a modern Greek village, acutely formulates the contrast between these different interpretations of the rôle of women in traditional Mediterranean societies:

When we began our field study at Methana it was soon evident that characterisations of Greek women in some of the ethnographic accounts did not fit the women we were encountering. While we had read about powerless, submissive females who considered themselves morally inferior to men, we found physically and socially strong women who had a great deal to say about what took place in the village. The social and economic affairs of several households were actually dominated by older women, including the house of village officials.[6]

Clark's explanation of this contradiction focuses on the way in which the gender and marital status of the researcher largely determine the information to which he or she has access.[7] A significant body of recent research has confirmed these findings, revealing how conceptualisations of the rôle of women vary according to the perspective of the informant and the rhetorical nature of the context in which the view is expressed. Both perspectives exist within this social context, and both reflect the values and norms of the society. What is misguided is to try to identify one as 'correct', on the assumption that such norms and values must form a coherent 'system', free of ambiguity, ambivalence, or conflict. A further source of difficulty in anthropological assessments of women in Mediterranean societies arises from the related problem of failing to differentiate first-hand observation from informants' accounts, based as they often are upon the conscious and unconscious manipulation of norms and cultural ideals so as to convey a particular point of view. In assessing the status of women, as well as related questions like seclusion, classical scholars have perhaps often fallen prey to the same trap,

[6] Clark 1983. See also the pioneering article of E. Friedl, 'The position of women: appearance and reality', *Anthropological Quarterly* 40 (1967) 97–108 (repr. in Dubisch 1986: 42–52).
[7] For the most recent studies on this question, see Whitehead & Conaway 1986.

failing to distinguish between ideology and (sometimes conflicting) normative ideals on the one hand, and social practices on the other.[8] Too often normative ideals are taken as objective structures which determine behaviour, rather than as what Bourdieu calls 'official representations of practices', which are manipulated according to the strategic exigencies of particular practical contexts.[9] Seeing the way such norms operate as an element of social practices illuminates the otherwise perplexing contradictions.

The two Athenian authors who were most acutely aware of the problems of women in their society, Aristophanes and Euripides, were also fully cognisant of such contradictions. That is, the contradiction between conflicting normative idealisations of woman: desire and fear, dependence and hatred, Medea and Andromache, and the further conflict between those positive and negative ideals on the one hand, and the life of the society on the other. Euripides in *Medea, Trojan Women, Bacchae, Hippolytus*, and other plays deliberately embodies in drama these conflicting positions. In *Melanippe*, a play noted in antiquity for its collection of antithetical characterisations of women, one character thus exclaims, 'The worst plague is the hated race of women.' 'Except for my mother I hate the whole female sex.'[10] On the other hand, in the same play a woman asserts that,

Women manage homes and preserve the goods which are brought from abroad. Houses where there is no wife are neither orderly nor prosperous. And in religion – I take this to be important – we women play a large part ... How then can it be just that the female sex should be abused? Shall not men cease their foolish reproaches, cease to blame all women alike if they meet one who is bad?[11]

The way in which Euripides repeatedly plays upon the conflicts inherent in these views, stereotypes and ideals should have indicated to classical scholars that great caution is required in evaluating the portrayal of women in Athenian sources. He depicts a society whose values reflect profound ambivalence about women and their sexuality, and his conscious dramatic manipulation of ideologically determined stances shows the way in which neither Andromache's speech, nor nominally non-fictional accounts like that in Xenophon's *Oeconomicus*, can be taken at face value as reflecting 'how it really was'.[12] If Euripides used this conflict as the fuel of tragedy, Aristophanes no less brilliantly placed the same antitheses and ambiguities at the centre of some of his most serious comic creations. In *Lysistrata, Ecclesiazusae*, and *Thesmophoriazusae* much of the sexual humour derives from the way in which he exploits the contradictions between the cultural ideal and real life, between

---

[8] The most penetrating analysis of the manipulation of such categories is Bourdieu 1977: 36–43, 58–71, a classic study.
[9] Bourdieu 1977: ch. 2. [10] Eur. frr. 496, 500, trans. Vellacott 1975: 97.
[11] Translation by Vellacott 1975: 97. These views as preserved are expressed in isolated excerpts, but they can nevertheless serve to exemplify Euripides' employment of antithetical views of women in his plays. Familiar instances abound: e.g. *Medea, Hippolytus*, and *Hecuba*.
[12] To translate loosely Leopold von Ranke's 'wie es eigentlich gewesen', on which see the critique by Finley 1985: 47–66.

woman as men think she should be, woman as men fear she is, and the mothers, maidens, wives and widows of everyday existence.

If the conflicting portrayals of women in the sources all reflect something about the norms and values of classical Athens, how is one to relate these products of ideology to the social practices which they inform? It was suggested above that in order to illuminate the motives and conduct associated with adultery one would have to broaden the enquiry to include the sexual rôle of woman. Now, using comparative evidence, the scope of the discussion must be further expanded to cover the broader normative context encompassing female sexuality, that is, the related antinomies of honour and shame, public and private, and the social and sexual rôles associated with them.

One may begin by briefly sketching some of the central features of the system of honour and shame as it applies to sexuality in modern Mediter- ranean societies.[13] The crucial point here is that the honour of men is, in large part, defined through the chastity of the women to whom they are related. Female honour largely involves sexual purity and the behaviour which social norms deem necessary to maintain it in the eyes of the watchful community. Male honour receives the active rôle of defending that purity. A man's honour is therefore involved with the sexual purity of his mother, sisters, wife and daughters – of him chastity is not required. The vigilance of men is necessitated therefore by the free play which social norms give to the expression of masculinity through the seduction of the women of others, and also by the view of female sexuality which posits that women need to be protected from themselves as well. As Pitt-Rivers puts it,

The frailty of women is the inevitable correlate of this conceptualization, and the notion is not, perhaps, displeasing to the male who may see in it an encouragement of sexual conquest. Thus, an honourable woman, born with the proper sentiment of shame, strives to avoid the human contacts which might expose her to dishonour; she cannot expect to succeed in this ambition unsupported by male authority. This fact gives justification to the usage which makes the deceived husband, not the adulterer, the object of ridicule and opprobrium . . .[14]

Associated with these beliefs is the fear and hatred of unbridled female sexuality, which only the force of social convention and male vigilance can restrain. Since the expression of this sexuality in illicit ways may bring humiliation and dishonour to a family and lineage, women are dangerous and are often seen as the sexual embodiment of the daemonic. The violence with

---

[13] The general interpretation of honour and shame in Mediterranean societies follows that proposed in such classic studies as Pitt-Rivers 1977; cf. Peristiany 1966, which includes Bourdieu's classic essay 'The sentiment of honour in Kabyle society'; and Davis 1977. Of course, the kind of overgeneralisation for which Davis has been criticised is a danger in this area: see Herzfeld 1980. But Herzfeld, on the other hand, is now generally regarded as going too far in his campaign for ethnographic particularism: see, for the most recent conspectus of opinion on honour and shame, Gilmore, D., ed., *Honor and Shame and the Unity of the Mediterranean* (Washington, D.C. 1987), a special issue of *American Anthropologist*.

[14] Pitt-Rivers 1977: 23.

which transgressions are punished expresses this implicit hostility, for, as it is usually put, the dishonour can only be washed away with the blood of the transgressors. Thus, Bourdieu notes the proverbial saying in Kabylia that 'Shame is the maiden', and women are often called the 'cows of Satan' or 'the devil's snares'.[15]

This nexus of honour and sexuality characterises Athenian society as well. As one of the passages from Euripides quoted above puts it, 'Many a man, proud of his wealth and birth, has been disgraced by his wanton wife.' This is not simply a literary formula, for in the Attic orators it is not uncommon to attack an opponent by referring to the unchastity of his women. Further, numerous orations reveal the way men feel dishonoured when their women are compromised. For example, the cuckolded husband in Lysias' *On the Murder of Eratosthenes* claims that the adulterer he killed disgraced his children and humiliated him by entering his house and seducing his wife. Indeed, the code of honour and shame is enshrined in the law of homicide, which allows a man to kill anyone found having intercourse with his wife, mother, sister, daughter or legal concubine – precisely those relationships which Pitt-Rivers listed in the passage quoted above. In such a law rape, seduction, and adultery are all implicitly included. From the standpoint of honour such legalistic definitions are unimportant, for any act of intercourse with a woman whose sexual purity must be protected can be avenged with blood.[16] The Athenian code thus embodies the principles expressed in the customary law of the Bedouins, and which still persist in many Mediterranean communities alongside the national legal codes which now prohibit such vengeance. Whether among the Bedouin, the Sarakatsani, or in classical Athens, the need for such rules is apparent, for they define the circumstances under which such killings must be accepted by the family of the victim so that blood feud may be avoided.[17]

Space does not permit a full discussion of the way in which the sexual purity enjoined by the code of honour and shame is defined, embodied, and protected. The discussion will instead focus on one important facet of the social rôles connected with honour and shame, namely the sexual aspect of the dichotomy of public and private spheres, expressed spatially in the related dichotomy of inside and outside. It may be helpful to begin by contrasting ancient and modern views, and then move to consideration of some confusions in classical scholarship which comparative evidence can help to dispel.

In traditional Mediterranean societies the general identification of the public sphere with men and the private sphere with women is familiar and requires little elaboration.[18] Men are associated with commerce and politics, the marketplace, café, fields, and so on, the women with the home. The man's rôle requires him to be outside; as Xenophon puts it, men who stay at home

---

15 Bourdieu 1977: 44–52.   16 See Cohen 1984: 151.
17 For Bedouin law, see Chelhod 1971: 104–23; for traditional Albanian unwritten law, Hasluck 1954: 212–13. The Sarakatsani will be discussed below.
18 See, e.g., Bourdieu's definitive treatment of the connection between spatial relations and honour, in Peristiany 1966: 208–33.

during the day are considered womanish (*Oec.* 7.2; 7.30). The woman's rôle, on the other hand, requires her to stay indoors. As Bourdieu puts it:

The opposition between the inside and the outside . . . is concretely expressed in the clear-cut distinction between the feminine area, the house and its garden, and the masculine area, the place of assembly, the mosque, the café, etc. In the Kabyle village the two areas are distinctly separate . . .[19]

The house is the domain of secrecy, of intimate life. Honour requires that its sanctity be protected, and the mere fact that strangers gain entrance to it, avoiding the vigilance of male members of the family, itself calls the chastity of the women into question. Any violation of the house is an attack on the honour of its men and the chastity of its women, even if the intruder be only a thief. The separation of women from men and the man's public sphere within this protected domain is the chief means by which sexual purity is both guarded and demonstrated to the community.[20]

As is generally recognised, these dichotomies – public/private, inside/outside – also characterise society in classical Athens. Xenophon and [Aristotle], for example, expound at length on how by their very natures men are suited for the outside, women for the inside.[21] Apart from Andromache's eloquent testimony to the connection of honour and seclusion, husbands in Aristophanes typically grow angry on discovering that their wives have been out, and their immediate suspicion is of sexual transgression (e.g., *Thesm.* 414, 519, 783). In *Ecclesiazusae* a wife, reproached by her husband when she returns from assisting a friend in childbirth, asks him, 'Do you think I've been to see my lover (*moichos*)?' (520 and cf. 1008).[22]

Not only ought women to remain within, but they must also guard themselves from contact with any men who pass by or call for their husbands. Thus, in Theophrastus (*Char.* 28.3), insulting a woman by saying she addresses those who pass by on the street, or that she answers the door herself, or that she talks with men, are all roughly equivalent to saying 'This house is

---

[19] Bourdieu in Peristiany 1966: 221. Bourdieu 1977: 41–71, 159–97 examines the fluidity of operation of such categories within the complex pattern of social and political strategies, rhetoric, and action. See also M. Herzfeld, 'Within and without: the category of the "Female" in the ethnography of modern Greece', in Dubisch 1986: 215–33. On men who are ridiculed for staying around the house, see Maher 1974: 112; and, for a comparative perspective, Gregor 1985: 23.

[20] See Campbell 1964: 185, 203, 268–74, 301–20; Du Boulay 1974: 121–200; Handman 1983: 71–175.

[21] Xen. *Oec.* 7.17–40; [Arist.] *Oec.* 1.3–4.

[22] Handman 1983: 164–6 notes that in Pouri (Greece) the men always suspect their women of lying; but how else are they to visit a neighbour for a chat except by saying, truly or falsely, that they have to borrow something? Most of the pleasurable activities for women are covered by lies – a necessity which becomes a sort of reflex. What ensues is a complicated game of sexual politics whereby women preserve a sphere for themselves through the ruse and the lie, which the men know and accept but, through their suspicion and questioning, attempt to limit and control. Handman notes that lying in circumstances where there is no apparent benefit from doing so seems to be, for many women, a way of leading a life of their own.

simply a brothel', or 'They couple like dogs in the street.'[23] Lysias, in a rhetorical variation of the familar *topos*, emphasises the honour of women who had led such orderly lives that 'they are ashamed to be seen even by their kinsmen' (III.6). Again, such normative judgements of women's conduct seem typical of many Mediterranean communities. To name but one of many such examples, Davis, in his study of the modern Italian village of Pisticci, reports that, 'Several men told me that I was the first man not their kinsman to cross their thresholds.'[24] This statement is, of course, no more true than Lysias' rhetorical exaggeration of 'proper' feminine modesty.

Some scholars, however, have taken statements like those of Lysias as veracious descriptions of actual conduct, using them to support their portrayal of the isolated and secluded Athenian woman. How, then, can one distinguish ideology and social practice in such passages? The problem with the ancient evidence is that it is like a jigsaw puzzle where most of the pieces are missing and the picture on the cover of the box has inconveniently been lost. Evidence from social anthropology, in my opinion, can provide different possible 'pictures' in the form of models of social systems. The model which can provide the most plausible explanation of the evidence we do have can therefore help to reconstruct the social practices which produced it. As a first step towards such a reconstruction, I have very briefly sketched such a model above, and, with further elaboration, I believe it can provide the basis for a critique of certain important misconceptions concerning the public/private dichotomy and the rôle and status of women.

To begin with, there is a marked tendency to take the public/private dichotomy as an absolute ontological category and hence to confuse separation and seclusion. That is, it does not follow that because, generally speaking, the man's sphere is public/outside, and woman's is private/inside, women live their lives in total isolation from all but their slaves and their family. Separation of spheres of activity does not imply physical sequestration, and, consequently utter subjection, as does seclusion. While it is undeniable that women did not operate in the public and political spheres in the way that men did, it does not necessarily follow that they did not have public, social, and economic spheres of their own, nor that these categories were not fluid and manipulable as opposed to rigid and eternally fixed. Scholars too often assume this to be the case, however, misled by the well-known, ideologically determined texts like Andromache's speech or Xenophon's picture of the ideal wife, and do not attempt to test critically the validity of these models. Thus Flacelière (1965:55) assumed that women never left the house and adolescent girls never even reached the courtyard. Or, more recently, Tyrrell uncritically accepts Xenophon's idealised description arguing that 'The outer door of the

---

[23] Compare a female informant's account in Williams 1967: 76–7: 'A good girl walks in the street and doesn't speak to anyone ... The bad one, she tries to talk to everybody even if a man doesn't greet her.'

[24] Davis 1973.

house is the boundary for the free woman. Segregated from women of other households, with only female relatives by marriage and slaves for company [one wonders how the relatives got there!], women tended to the domestic chores of running the house for their husbands.'[25] Walcot also speaks of the seclusion of women, but he is sensible enough to note that 'we have no way of being certain how far social reality corresponded to the social ideal of female seclusion'.[26]

I, however, would argue that we do have a way of making such distinctions, for social anthropological studies of modern Mediterranean societies show that the patterns of male–female rôle divisions in classical Athens are typical products of forms of social organisation prevalent in traditional Mediterranean communities. Because of the tendency to view Greek society as somehow isolated from the rest of western civilisation scholars like Eva Keuls[27] tend to view such patterns as unique, bizarre, or even pathological, when in fact they are quite normal aspects of certain kinds of social systems. It is within such an intellectual framework that the significance of adultery in Athenian society becomes clear, for it is the larger structure which makes the sexual purity of the wife of paramount importance for the reputation and standing of a family.

In taking separation to imply seclusion, the prevailing view tends to ignore a considerable body of evidence which indicates that Athenian women partici-pated in a wide range of activities which regularly took them out of their houses. These included working in the fields (Ar. *Peace* 535, Dem. LVII.45), selling produce in the market (Dem. LVII.30–1, 34; Ar. *Acharnians* 478, *Wasps* 497, 1380–5, *Lysistrata* 445, *Thesmophoriazusae* 405, 440), acting as a nurse or midwife (Dem. LVII.35, 45; Plato, *Theaetetus* 149) and many other such occupations. There is no need to list all the passages on the various economic activities of women, for they were collected as long ago as 1922 (Herfst 1922). Such a pattern, of course, is just what one would expect in a poor region like the Mediterranean, where most families could not dispense with the labour of women and children. Aristotle makes this point with considerable force in the *Politics*, when he says that in a democracy it is impossible to prevent the women of the poor from going out to work (1300a7, 1323a5–7). Athenian law, moreover, made it a delict to rebuke any citizen, male *or female* with selling in the marketplace (Dem. LVII.30–1). Married and unmarried women often worked outside their homes because economic survival required it. As will appear, however, whether in classical Athens or the modern Mediterranean, there may be a wide discrepancy between economic realities and ideological statements about what sorts of things women *ought* to do. As social anthropologists from Malinowski on have recognised, however, informants often offer such normative ideals as matter-

---

[25] Tyrrell 1984: 45; cf. R. Padel, 'Women: model for possession by Greek daemons', in Cameron & Kuhrt 1983: 8: 'confined to the innermost part of the mudbrick domestic house with only limited exit even from the private home.'

[26] Walcot 1984; cf. Humphreys 1983b: 16; Gould 1980.   [27] E.g. Keuls 1985.

of-fact descriptions of how things actually are. In Malinowski's case, his investigation of incest among the Trobrianders taught him that failure to appreciate this rhetorical fact could result in a massive misconstrual of the patterns of social behaviour.[28]

In Athens, women's activities which took them out of the house were not exclusively economic. They might include going to their favourite soothsayer (Theoph. *Char.* 11.9–10; 16.12), participating in a sacrifice (Ar. *Acharnians* 253), or in religious festivals. Indeed, married women alone arranged for major festivals like the Thesmophoria (Isaeus VIII.19–20; III.80; VI.49), and historians have failed to explore the social implications of the fact that Athenian women's networks were organised enough to carry out the full range of activities associated with such an undertaking (including election of officials, rehearsals, supplies and finances, etc.). Further, as is the rule in many Mediterranean communities, apart from the wealthy, women were also responsible for bringing water from the well and washing clothes in the fountain (Ar. *Lysistrata* 327–31; Eur. *Electra* 109–11, *Hippolytus* 130).[29] They visited husbands or relatives in prison (Andok. 1.48; Lys. XIII.39–41; Plato, *Phaedo* 60a), participated in funeral processions (Dem. XLIII.63; Lys. 1.8), went to the public baths, appeared before arbitrators (Dem. XL.11), attended the public funeral orations (Thuc. II.45.2) and were brought by their fathers, husbands, or sons into court to arouse the sympathy of the judges (Aesch. II.148, 152; Plato, *Apology* 34c–35b; Dem. XIX.310; XXI.99, 186; XXV.84; LIV.35; Ar. *Wasps* 568–9, *Plutus* 380). They participated in wedding feasts where the bridesmaids danced and male guests might talk with the bride (Hyp. *Lycophron* 34; Isaeus VIII.18; Ar. *Acharnians* 1056, 1067–8; Eur. *I.T.* 1140). Husbands expected their wives to go out, and those wealthy enough gave them slaves to accompany them, as Theophrastus' satire of the parsimonious husband reveals (*Char.* 22. 10, 13).

The passages just enumerated indicate that, although women did not participate in exclusively male activities like war and politics, they were not confined in their houses in 'oriental seclusion' (as some scholars rather romantically think of it, having little idea that, in fact, 'oriental seclusion' also includes activities like carrying water, visiting friends and neighbours, and so on),[30] never seeing anyone outside their immediate family. Indeed, one of the most important activities of women included visiting or helping friends and relatives. As men had their circle of friends, there is considerable evidence to indicate that, as in modern Mediterranean societies which also separate the male and female spheres, Athenian women formed intimate friendships, particularly with neighbours, and visited one another frequently – whether to

---

28 Malinowski 1929: 503–72 vividly portrays how fortunate he was that an accident brought this distinction home to him before he had published his account of the sexual life of the Trobrianders.

29 See also Keuls 1985: 233.

30 See Fernea 1969 on women in Iraq; and for a description of the actual lives of women in societies usually associated with notions of 'oriental seclusion', see Altorki 1986.

borrow food, utensils, or a dress, or simply to chat (Theoph. *Char.* 10.13; Ar. *Ecclesiazusae* 460, *Lysistrata* 300; Dem. LV. 23–4; LIII.4; LVIII.40; Lys. XXXII.10; Eur. *Electra* 1130). In Athenian drama, the commonplace condemnations of women's excessive gossiping and visiting imply that such activities are all too common (see, e.g., *Andromache* 950).

This intimacy of neighbours, attested in a variety of sources, constitutes one of the contexts in which adulterous relationships could arise. In Demosthenes LIII, for example, a man describes his intimate friendship with a neighbour and reports that when he went away on public or private business he left his house and financial affairs completely in the hands of his friend. Clearly this close friend (*panu oikeios*: 4) had access to the house and must have been well acquainted with his friend's wife. Such occurrences were no doubt a common phenomenon that gave rise to the sentiment reported by Aristotle that it is particularly easy to have an adulterous relation with the wife of a friend or neighbour (*N.E.* 1136a5; *M.M.* 1188b17). What made it particularly easy was that close friends had access to the house and were already acquainted with their friend's wife. Thus, Electra comments in Euripides' play that, 'When an adulterer corrupts his neighbour's wife . . . [he] is forced to marry her . . .' In a similar vein, Demosthenes notes that the law permits a man to kill even his friends if they commit *hubris* against or seduce the women of his family (XXIII.53–6).[31] The association of adultery with neighbours is common enough in the ancient world, as the Commandment not to covet thy neighbour's wife makes clear. Adultery served as a focus of obsessive sexual fears in the ancient and modern Mediterranean precisely because women regularly engaged in activities which brought them into some sort of contact with other men. In a face-to-face society, as anthropological studies reveal, this contact is most intimate, and most unavoidable, in the neighbourhood.[32]

One possible objection to this interpretation is that certainly some Athenian families could afford enough slaves so that the women *could* stay at home. Athenian and comparative evidence, however, suggests that they may well have none the less pursued relationships with other women in social and public religious networks extending beyond their families. Whether in ancient Rome, or in the Thesmophoria at Athens, or in the Church organisations of the Andalusian communities studied by Pitt-Rivers, it is women of the upper strata who figure most prominently in women's rôles in religious life. Moreover, what Maher, in her excellent study, *Women and Property in Morocco*, terms 'ostentatious seclusion', primarily occurs among a few *nouveaux-riches* and other middle class families where the husband is anxious to demonstrate that he has enough money literally to isolate his wife. Even there, however, this normally only occurs in large cities when a woman has married a man who lives far from the village where she grew up, and hence finds herself isolated from the supportive network which sustains most

---

[31] *Hubris* has a strong sexual connotation here: see Cohen 1987: 7–9.
[32] See Freeman 1970; Handman 1983: 105–25; Du Boulay 1974: 169–229.

women.[33] Likewise, in his classic study of Portuguese rural society Cutileiro notes that, 'The wife should remain secluded at home. This is only possible among the wealthy, however. Wealthy wives are much more restricted to their houses, and the layout of these houses makes their seclusion even greater.' Though Cutileiro does not seem particularly aware that he is citing normative precepts rather than social descriptions, his further comments reveal that these arrangements do not imply real seclusion, for he adds that such women devote their time to 'needlework, churchgoing, charity work, visiting, and last, but not least, sheer idleness'.[34] Not having to work outside the home, or, better yet, work at all, is a great mark of economic status.

As classical scholars have typically assumed that separation necessarily implies seclusion, so earlier ethnographic accounts often built upon similar premises.[35] Recent studies of Spanish, Portuguese, Italian, Greek, Turkish, Iraqi, Lebanese, and Moroccan societies have shown, however, that such assumptions may be wildly inaccurate.[36] The paper by Clark on gender-bias quoted above represents an attempt to show some of the reasons for such confusion. To take but one further example, one might refer to the article by Lloyd and Fallers on sex-rôles and the public/private dichotomy in Edremit, Turkey. In this paper, while confirming that the 'world of women ... in Edremit is the private world of the house and the courtyard', they document the wide range of women's activities and relationships and the autonomy of the women's sphere. They employ these observations as the basis for a re-evaluation of the thesis for isolation advanced by Forster in his study of Italian towns:

What he (Forster) meant to suggest was that men's monopoly of the town's public space made it possible for them to interact ... unencumbered by the contingencies of their individual ties with women. It must follow from this, he apparently reasoned, that the women were pining away, each in her own home, awaiting the return of their

---

33 Maher 1974: 2–3, 61, 117, 150–1; cf. Williams 1967: 67, 83. Maher's treatment also reveals the importance of distinguishing seclusion from separation. Seclusion, in those few cases where it does literally occur, tends to reduce the woman to a state of utter subjection. Separation, on the other hand, even in societies like those of rural Iraq or Saudi Arabia in which it is very strictly enforced, allows women to sustain themselves in extensive supportive social networks: Fernea 1969; Altorki 1986.
34 Cutileiro 1971: 107.
35 Many such ethnographic accounts are based exclusively on what male informants told the male anthropologist about women whom he had no opportunity to observe or talk with: see e.g. M. Berger, *The Arab World Today* (New York 1962) 119–22; E. Marx, *Bedouin of the Negev* (New York 1967) 103–7. Earlier anthropologists, because complicated networks of women's relations were not accessible to them (owing to the very fact of separation), often assumed that such networks did not exist and that separation meant virtual isolation. Most classical scholars seem to persist in this view, but see Walcot 1984: 38: 'men and women in the Greek world led separate and distinct lives'.
36 Portugal: Cutileiro 1971. Spain: Pitt-Rivers 1971; Freeman 1970. Italy: Maraspini 1968; Davis 1973. Greece: Campbell 1964; Du Boulay 1974; E. Friedl in Dubisch 1986: 42–52; Handman 1983; R. Kennedy, 'Women's friendships on Crete: a psychological perspective', in Dubisch 1986: 121–38. Turkey: Lloyd & Fallers 1976; Stirling 1966. Lebanon: Williams 1967; Fuller 1961. Iraq: Fernea 1969. Morocco: Maher 1974; Bourdieu 1977; Pehrson 1971.

lord and master . . . Now this, as we have shown, is not the case in Edremit. If relations among males are relatively unencumbered by their relations with females, it is also the case that females' relations with each other are similarly, if in lesser degree (since male authority and possession of public space do inhibit women's movements), free of male interference. Our point is not the familiar one that women, submissive in public, manage to influence their fate by domestic scheming, manipulation and henpecking. Our point is rather that women in Edremit have an institutional structure and sense of solidarity of their own, parallel to those of men which give them a substantial field for self-assertion and a psychological independence of men . . .[37]

These conclusions represent a widespread pattern found in most traditional Mediterranean societies. In such communities the sexual politics of space and labour are far more complex than the thesis of seclusion and isolation would allow. As Bourdieu (in Peristiany 1966: 222) says of Kabyle society,

The fountain is to the women what the *thajmaath* (assembly) is to the men. It is there that they exchange news and carry on their gossip . . . It is commonly assumed that in North African society the woman is shut up in the house. In fact this is completely untrue because the peasant woman always works out of doors. Moreover, it should be remembered that the house being the domain of women the men are to some degree excluded from it . . . Men who remain too much in the house during the daytime are suspect . . .

This latter point is no less true in classical Athens (Xen. *Oec.* 7.2, 30), and, as a woman of the Marri Belouch says, 'What do the men know about the household affairs? They are away from home a lot . . . What do they know about what their women do?'[38] Indeed, part of men's fear of adultery arises from their ignorance about what their wives do. The suspicious husbands of Aristophanes, who look under the bed for *moichoi* and want to know where their wives have been, do not seem to act on the basis of a conviction that their wives spend all of their waking moments locked up in the women's quarters, 'ashamed to be seen even by their kinsmen', to quote Lysias again (III.6). It was precisely the autonomy of the women's sphere, and women's relative freedom within its boundaries,[39] which, together with the power of women to destroy the reputation of a lineage, fuelled male anxieties.

Combining this clarification of the meaning of separation of rôles and spheres with the point made above about the distinction between cultural ideals and social practices can do a great deal to illuminate the situation of women at Athens – these women who never cross the threshold yet somehow appear to participate in a wide range of activities and relationships. Women *should* not leave the house, but participation in their independent sphere of social, religious and economic activities requires that they do so. How is the

[37] Lloyd & Fallers 1976: 260.
[38] Pehrson 1971: 60. For just this reason, men in Athens are often portrayed as obsessed with the trustworthiness of their wives, the 'guardians of the house': see e.g. Xen. *Oec.* 4.
[39] As modern anthropological studies and the choruses from many ancient tragedies alike make clear, women are the primary agents of social control in ensuring that other women stay within those boundaries: see e.g. Eur. *Med.* 214–18.

conflict resolved? In fact, it is not resolved, but rather consciously manipulated in a serious game that is played according to a complex set of rules and prohibitions.[40] Some examples may help to clarify the point. Mothers in the Lebanese village of Harouch say of their daughters that they never leave the house. This is the cultural ideal dictated by the code of honour and shame, according to which the honour of a woman is measured by 'the closeness she keeps to her house and the distance she maintains towards strangers'. Thus one mother says, 'We are here in the house and we have nothing to do with anyone; we just stay in the house and see our neighbours.'[41] One wonders how the neighbours got there. As Bourdieu reports of Kabylia, the hour of *azal*, during the heat of the day, is a sort of 'dead' time. The streets are deserted, the men are resting where they work, and

No one can say whether the public space of the village belongs to man or to woman. So each of them takes care not to occupy it: there is something suspicious about anyone who ventures into the streets at that hour ... Furtive shadows slip across the street from one house to another: the women, equally unoccupied, take advantage of the limited presence of the men to meet together or visit one another.[42]

In practice, what statements to the effect that the women never leave the house in fact mean is that they never leave the house without a purpose, a purpose that will be regarded as legitimate in the eyes of the watchful community, for example, going to the fountain, going to work in the fields, visiting a neighbour, etc.[43] But, as Williams (1967: 77) notes of the girls of Harouch, 'I have watched our neighbour's daughter dump a full water jar behind the stables so that she can briskly set out for the tower while the boy she likes is on the road.' As another scholar puts it

The very fact that there is a well-recognized dividing line between the two sexes engenders an atmosphere of artful intrigue or flirtation in disguise, which in itself provides its own form of village recreation. Young men stand silently on the verandah and look down on the fountain where the girls lean to fill their pitchers. The young girls, in their turn, make more trips to the fountain than necessary.[44]

These descriptions recall the women of Athens described by Aristophanes: the wives in the *Ecclesiazusae* (520, 1008) and *Thesmophoriazusae* (414, 519, 785–800) whose husbands find them out of the house and want to know what they have been doing. The husbands know that they go out, but they should not *be found* to have been out, particularly not at an inappropriate time or without an appropriate purpose.[45] Or the woman in *Peace*, peeking out of the door to see the man she admires walking down the street (978–85); the young girl waiting at home for her lover while her mother is out (*Ecclesiazusae*,

---

[40] The strategic manipulation of such categories is one of the major themes of Bourdieu 1977; so too of Goffman's penetrating studies of social interaction (e.g. Goffman 1963; 1971).
[41] Williams 1967: 76–7.   [42] Bourdieu 1977: 161; cf. Du Boulay 1974: 190–200.
[43] Du Boulay 1974: 159, 191.
[44] Fuller 1961: 47.   [45] Cf. Bourdieu 1977: 160.

920); the man hanging around outside the house of a married woman waiting to catch another glimpse of her at the window (*Thesmophoriazusae* 840); or, finally, the daughter in *Acharnians* (253) on the way to a sacrifice with her mother and father but conscious that she is on display to prospective suitors.[46] These are examples from literature, of course, but, as Dover briefly notes, such women 'may be much nearer the norm of Athenian life than those cloistered ladies who were embarrassed by the presence even of a male relative'.[47] Because of their preoccupation with the lives of the wealthy, however, many scholars have not thought through the implications of such evidence for their general position on 'Athenian women'. In fact, such bits and pieces of evidence from Aristophanes offer better evidence of women's daily life than do the set-piece speeches of a Medea or Andromache, or Xenophon's idealised vision of gentry life. Of course such passages are part of a comedy, and of course they were written by a man. But a portrayal of women talking at the fountain in the morning is not a product of comic distortion, though some of their conversation, with its often grotesquely exaggerated sexual humour, may be. Moreover, vase paintings and comparative evidence support the accuracy of the description, which, though the product of a male imagination, derives much of its force from the plausibility and verisimilitude of its social setting. It bears repeating that Aristophanes' dramas are not an unthinking product of male ideologies, but rather a conscious manipulation and satire of them. The catalogue of women's treacherous ploys in *Thesmophoriazusai* (335–51, 383–432), for example, transparently functions in this way. In short, I would argue that Aristophanes offers considerable insight not only into Athenian sexual politics, but also into the perceived social practices that form the practical basis of such politics. Further, as this discussion shows, comparative evidence from modern Mediterranean communities can play a crucial rôle in distinguishing these types of social action.

The same duality, the same manipulation of categories and behaviour as described above for the social sphere also applies to economic and political activities. Bourdieu (1977: 39–51), for example, shows the way that among the Kabyle norms and definitions in the contexts of kinship, marriage alliances, legal disputes, and feuds are articulated in a rhetorical manner so as to meet the strategic exigencies of the occasion. Or, for example, in Lebanon,

---

[46] The dynamics of such behaviour are illuminated in the treatment of female modesty by Antoun (1968: 682–3): 'The abandonment of [a norm in] particular actions may be justified explicitly or implicitly by the realization of the same norm in a wider context. Thus, although girls are not allowed to look attractive for fear of tempting males, they are dressed up at an early age by their mothers until puberty "in order to attract attention to themselves and secure a husband" ... Here violation of the norm prohibiting adornment is in order to bring early marriage and in so doing avoid a much more serious breach of modesty.' The vocabulary of strategic manipulation of norms is preferable, but Antoun's example helps to explain the contradiction between the norm requiring the most extreme modesty for girls and the kind of behaviour Aristophanes portrays. Indeed, here again, Aristophanes derives his humour precisely from the exploitation of this normative conflict.

[47] Dover 1973: 69.

the women of Harouch claim that they only work in the house – a rare occurrence that is a great sign of status. But once Williams met one of the girls who had previously told her that she only worked in the house coming back from a day of labour in the fields: 'Before I even had a chance to speak, she hastened to explain that she had gone out to supervise the hired hands for an hour . . . She told me then as she had done many times before, that her work is "only in the house"' (1967: 67; cf. 79). Statements by authors like Xenophon about women's work being confined to the house should be taken in the same light. Indeed, Xenophon's description clearly applies to the wealthy family with a host of servants. Aristotle's statement that the wives of the poor *must* go out to work reveals the underlying economic necessity that touched the bulk of the population. That in Athens, too, status concerns were connected to such economic distinctions appears clearly enough from the law, alluded to above, that prohibited anyone from denigrating an Athenian man or woman for working in the market place. The social reality behind such legislation appears from Aristophanes' use of comic licence to deride Euripides because his mother sold produce in the agora (*Lysistrata* 560; *Thesmophoriazusae* 840).

A further way in which confusion as to the nature and meaning of separation has created problems in the understanding of Greek sexual rôles brings the discussion more directly back to adultery. Many classical scholars have assumed that, in this society where men and women led separate lives, the marital relation was viewed instrumentally as simply a means for producing legitimate children, involving little affection, let alone love or deep emotional attachment.[48] Sally Humphreys (1983b: 17), for example, asserts that in Athens friendship and romantic love are only found in male–male relationships. Or, as Flacelière says, 'It seems fairly clear that there was little intimacy, intellectual contact, or even real love between husband and wife in classical Athens.'[49] Such conclusions are not to be taken seriously, for there is abundant evidence from Aristotle, Xenophon, Isocrates, Aristophanes, and Lysias which makes clear that men were often both passionately enamoured of women and deeply emotionally and sexually attached to their wives. This explains why adultery is described in the sources as an offence which undermines the *philia* (love, friendship, attachment) between husband and wife (Xen. *Hiero* 3.4). Thus it is not only the external explanation provided by the code of honour and shame that accounts for the hatred directed to adulterers, but also the internal explanation that focuses upon the violation of the relationship of trust and affection between husband and wife.

This dual level of explanation may also be appropriate in understanding the motivation of the men who ran the risks which adultery entailed. The adulterer is a man of honour in the sense that he increases his own status, accentuates his masculinity, by dishonouring other men by seducing their women. Aristotle thus characterises adultery as typical of the hubristic *nouveaux-riches* (*Rhet.* 1391a19). This, as Pitt-Rivers has shown, is the

[48] E.g. Cantarella 1987: 39–51.   [49] Flacelière 1965: 55.

Spanish understanding of Don Juan, as a punctilious man of honour, interested only in the conquests which magnify his own stature and reputation.[50] The very seclusion of women that is designed to protect them is a sexual challenge to other men, who, in Athens as in other Mediterranean societies, were willing to run considerable risks to achieve their ends. On the other hand, this explanation is not the whole picture. Men did not become adulterers simply for sexual gratification; in Athens there was little need of this. But, on the other hand, because of the early age of marriage for girls, married women or widows were the only free women who were likely to be available for a relationship which did not have to be bought. This is still the case in many modern Mediterranean societies, where unmarried men often prefer to pursue relationships with young married women, for a variety of reasons.[51]

Likewise, for the many young women who were unfortunate enough to find themselves in marriages in which, because of differences in age and other problems associated with arranged marriages, *philia* was not a possibility, adultery might be the only opportunity they would ever have for a romantic–erotic attachment. Another related factor appears from the many references to the jealousy (and envy?) which women felt towards the sexual freedom of their husbands (evidence which has too often been ignored).[52] As Clytaemnestra says in Euripides' *Electra*, when 'a husband looks elsewhere and slights his lawful wife, she will copy him, and find herself another friend. And then the glance of public censure lights on us; the husbands are to blame but they are not concerned' (1036–40). In any society with arranged marriages, restricted courtship, and a double standard, adultery is a likely outlet for the emotional and sexual frustrations which such arrangements often produce. In Athens these various motivations were obviously strong enough to induce men to face torture or death, and women to risk major civic disabilities and social disgrace. The accepted notion of Athenian men as only interested in *hetairai* (courtesans) and boys, and Athenian women as isolated, passive, and uninterested in sexual attachments, requires serious rethinking.

The foregoing analysis, far from having exhausted its subject, has merely suggested some issues which future research might pursue. Indeed, I intended the discussion as much as a methodological excursus as a treatment of adultery itself. The point has not been to show that Athens was 'exactly the same' as modern traditional Mediterranean societies. It certainly was not. Rather, by focusing upon the particular examples of adultery and the 'confinement' of women, I have attempted to show the way in which models from contemporary societies, with similar patterns of social organisation in regard to sexuality and the family, can provide an analytical framework that

---

[50] See, e.g. Pitt-Rivers 1977: 23.
[51] This was also the preference of Samuel Pepys in seventeenth-century England; it avoided problems of pressure to marry and 'fatherless' pregnancy.
[52] See, e.g., Keuls 1985: ch. 4.

can assist both in sorting out the different views of women which the Athenian sources convey, and in understanding the contradictions which underlie every complex pattern of social practices.[53]

[53] I would like to thank Dr Peter Garnsey, Professors Gregory Vlastos, Dieter Simon, and Dieter Nörr, and the editors of this volume, for their helpful comments and criticisms.

8

Sale, credit and exchange in Athenian law and society

PAUL MILLETT

I

It is a commonplace that the exchange of goods and services lies at the heart of the economic process. Outside the textbook conditions of complete self-sufficiency, appropriate only to the make-believe world of Robinson Crusoe or the superhuman existence of the gods, some form of exchange is inevitable (Codere in *IESS* s.v. 'Exchange and display'; Aristotle, *Politics* 1253a25–9). The mechanisms whereby exchange occurs are, together with their associated attitudes, crucial to the understanding of any economy and society. Surveys of the scope of social anthropology show this to be as true of non-capitalist societies as of the capitalist world (Mair 1972: 179–94; Leach 1982: 149–75; Lewis 1985: 197–233). It is also presumably the case with the pre-capitalist economy and society of ancient Greece. The character of the ancient Greek economy has been the subject of a century-long debate that needs no detailed discussion here (Gernet 1933; Will 1954a; Pearson 1957; Humphreys 1970; Austin & Vidal-Naquet 1977: 1–8). And yet, in spite of its long life, the terms of reference of the debate have hardly moved away from those set down by the earliest participants: essentially, the production of goods and maritime trade (see the selection of essays reprinted in Finley 1979). With one major and a handful of minor exceptions, exchange seems to have been excluded from the agenda and gets no systematic or even incidental treatment in those standard texts of Greek economic history that have paralleled the discussion (Glotz 1926; Calhoun 1926; Michell 1957; Bolkestein 1958; Hopper 1979).[1]

This neglect of the exchanging process seems to stem, at least so far as the textbooks are concerned, from the widespread assumption that exchange of goods in classical Athens shared the pattern of the market economy with which

---

[1] For the major exception (Polanyi), see in the text below. Heichelheim (1958–70, II: 64–70, 190–3) lists earlier bibliography, including relevant encyclopaedia entries; Zimmern (1931: 279–85) has, as often, a few helpful pages. See also the standard treatments of Athenian 'social life' cited in n.3; lively enough, but low on analysis.

we are so familiar today (explicitly in French 1964: 128–31). Exemplifying the close identification of modern economy and market exchange is the tendency for the one to be defined in terms of the other. So Erich Roll, in his classic *History of Economic Thought* (1973: 371) regards the economic system as 'an enormous conglomeration of interdependent markets' and 'the central problem of economic enquiry' as 'the explanation of the formation of price'. The emphasis is almost everywhere on the naturalness and inevitability of market exchange, helping to account for the supposition that this must somehow be the system appropriate to classical Athens.[2]

The illusion of Athens as a market economy is heightened by the appearance in the ancient literature of the external trappings of market exchange. All texts having any connection with the 'everyday life' of classical Athens are more or less thickly studded with allusions to buying and selling.[3] By way of illustration, even a short work like the *Characters* of Theophrastos (less than twenty pages of Greek) contains more than thirty references to the sale or purchase of goods (Edmonds & Austen 1904: index s.v. 'Buying'). Prices in the *Characters* are presented as relatively high or low and therefore elastic (III.3, IX.6, X.4, XII.8, XVII.6, XXX.12); and, what is more, marketing activities are consistently connected with the Athenian *agora* (II.9, III.3, VI.9, XI.4, XXII.7). The existence in Athens of a focal area for all this buying and selling, policed by magistrates and regulated by law, only serves to strengthen the impression of a fully fledged market economy.[4] But the conclusions of (among others) Bohannan & Dalton (1962:1), in relation to modern African markets, suggest that the practice of buying and selling, even in the context of a market place, need not imply formal market exchange. The essence of the market principle lies in Roll's 'formation of price' *via* the interplay of supply and demand (Neale 1957). The part played by sellers' supplies and buyers' demands in the process of price-fixing in Athens remains obscure and unexplained. It is the theme of this paper that the surface phenomena of exchange in Athens, and the underlying laws and conventions relating to

---

[2] The passage from Roll is cited by Finley (1973: 22) as part of his attack on the application of market theory to the Graeco-Roman world. It has to be said that Finley offers no alternative explanation about how goods might have been exchanged in 'the ancient economy'. The formal correctness of Roll's definition can be confirmed by looking at the chapter headings of any standard textbook of economics, from Marshall (1890) to Lipsey (1963), Samuelson (1970) and beyond. Mention might also be made of the way in which non-traditional texts take trouble to spell out their unorthodoxy (Robinson & Eatwell 1974: 1–3; McCormick *et al.* 1977: 9–15).

[3] Appropriate passages from the ancient sources are strung together in modern compilations of the 'everyday life' genre: Becker 1866: 61–73, 277–92; Mahaffy 1890: 306–10; Tucker 1906: 120–5; Webster 1969: 54–62. The descriptions are often vivid but rather thin; slightly 'thicker' is Ehrenberg 1951: 113–36. Metaphorical use of the language of sale also implies familiarity: Epikharmos DK fr.36; Soph. *Ant.* 1165–71; Dem. XXIII. 201 (and many more).

[4] For the full range of *agora* references, see Edmonds & Austen 1904: index s.v. 'The Market Place'. That is, of course, an inadequate and misleading translation of *agora*, which embraced a whole range of non-commercial activities (see section IV below). The theory of Ste. Croix (1972: 267–9) that *agora* in the sense of 'market' had no topographical meaning in Athens is opposed (not quite decisively) by Stanley 1976: 35–43.

exchange, are best understood through an alternative type of analysis along non-market lines.[5]

Exchange is an area where, by comparison with advances in understanding the process in other periods and places, the ancient Greek world has been left behind. There is irony here in that the decisive contribution, opening up the whole field of comparative exchange relations, was the achievement of Karl Polanyi, who had an informed, professional interest in the economy and society of ancient Greece (Humphreys 1969; Garlan 1973). Although Polanyi was by no means the first to appreciate the qualitative differences between exchange in ancient and modern, pre-capitalist and capitalist societies, he established the problem as one of the preoccupations of modern anthropologists.[6] Specifically, he rejected the idea that contemporary economic theory, generated by and for the modern market economy, was helpful in the analysis of anything beyond a minority of recent societies, the creation of the Industrial Revolution or (as he termed it) *The Great Transformation* (1944). In opposition to the market principle, Polanyi identified two earlier modes of exchange (1957a; 1957c): *reciprocative* (reciprocal gift-giving) and *redistributive* (transfer of resources to, and their re-allocation from, a central repository or authority).

On the face of it, the variety and flexibility of this three-sided approach to exchange look attractive to the historian of ancient Greece; but progress in its application has been patchy and limited to the economies of the pre-classical period.[7] That Polanyi's approach should be ignored for the period for which our sources are relatively full, and its application potentially fruitful, is a paradox to be explained on two different but connected levels. In the first place, Polanyi's types of exchange were originally presented as mutually exclusive alternatives, lacking in flexibility. The impression was given that a society had to conform to one of the three modes, or at least be so heavily dominated by a single mode as to render the remaining two peripheral. The implication that the market mode of exchange could not easily co-exist with reciprocity and redistribution helps to account for the second part of the explanation. Polanyi himself seems to have been won over by the outward appearance of classical Athenian exchange (as detailed above) to see in Athens a partial exception to the pre-capitalist rule of non-market exchange. He devoted a whole paper (1957b) to presenting price-making markets, not as the heritage of early Mesopotamia, but as an invention of the Greeks; more precisely, the invention of the Athenians in the fourth century. This intrusion

---

[5] Listing of prices has, for some historians, acquired the status of a fetish: Heichelheim 1930; Frost 1987: 68–70; (more sensibly) Ehrenberg 1951: 219–26. But prices by themselves, divorced from the process of formation, have little to offer economic historians.

[6] Among the authors and works cited by Polanyi as predecessors are: Maine 1861; Tönnies 1887; Marx (see Elster 1985: 310–17); Malinowski 1922; Mauss 1925; and Thurnwald 1932.

[7] On the redistributive economy of the Mycenaean palaces: Polanyi 1960; Finley 1957; on the dark age and reciprocity: Finley 1955; 1978: 51–107; on the survival of reciprocal exchange into the Archaic period: Morris 1986.

of the market principle into an economy depending primarily on reciprocal and redistributive exchange resulted in an 'inevitable crisis of values', as reflected in Aristotle's normative distinction between natural and unnatural exchange (*Ethics* 1131a10–34a25).

It has to be conceded that there are difficulties about this paper by Polanyi. It leaves unclear, for example, what kind of exchange relationships are being replaced by price-making markets and the extent to which the change is taking place. Polanyi talks in vague terms about (65) 'Greece at the climactic point of her awakening from a heroic to a semi-commercial economy'. Empirical evidence for this 'awakening' is, however, decidedly thin: not much more than a reinterpretation of some of the most problematical passages in Aristotle's *Ethics* and *Politics*.[8] Later writings add little by way of clarification. His attempt, in a comparative study of economic institutions (1960: 333–40), to restrict the scope of the market principle in Athens is not without inaccuracies and inconsistencies (Humphreys 1969: 49). In a final, posthumous publication (1977: 159–87), Polanyi tried to account for the growth of the 'market habit' in Athens in terms of broad political developments. The wealth of empire, passed on to the citizens in the form of public pay, was seen as instrumental in sustaining the *agora* as a market for ready-cooked food: the contrast between the old and the new being exemplified by the contest between the redistributive behaviour of Kimon (Plutarch, *Kimon* x.1–3) and the policies of the market-oriented Pericles (Plutarch, *Pericles* xvi.4–5). Although not without insights, the theory is naive in formulation, depending on the selective citation of passages out of context. And yet, in spite of these and other imperfections, Polanyi's broad conception of a decisive shift towards market exchange in classical Athens seems to have found favour with historians who reject the crude, market-dominated approach to the whole of Greek history. And there the matter of exchange in classical Athens appears to rest.[9]

More recent research on contemporary non-capitalist societies has served to show up the limitations of Polanyi's rather rigid, tripartite analysis. Although it remains helpful in the preliminary stages of classification, the detailed (and

[8] The passages in question (*Ethics* 1131a10–34a25; *Politics* 1256b27–58a14) have been repeatedly re-examined; Finley (1970) gives a critical report on earlier work. It is the strength of Finley's analysis (and that of Will 1954b) that Aristotle's arguments are interpreted against the background of fourth-century economy and society. That is not the case with recent 'economic' interpretations of the texts (Lewis 1978: Lowry 1969, 1974, 1988, on which see Meikle 1989). All these items either ignore the socio-economic context or rely on inadequate and outdated secondary sources (see, for example, Wilson 1975: 61 n.21, where for 'Mickel' read 'Michell').

[9] Though there are differences of opinion over the precise period in which the development of market exchange began to have repercussions on society as a whole. For Starr (1977: 191) the process was well under way by 500; French (1964: 107–34) seems to favour the fifth century. Meikle (1979) follows Polanyi in so far as he takes Aristotle as evidence for a fourth-century transformation. To engage with this debate is beyond the scope of this paper, but some of the problems involved in identifying the 'rise of a money economy' were pointed out long ago by Postan (1944). On the critical question of the relationship between coinage and the ancient Greek economy, see Kraay 1964; Crawford 1982: 29–59.

conflicting) contributions of Bohannan & Dalton (1962), Dewey (1962), Belshaw (1965), Nash (1965), Sahlins (1974), Gregory (1982) and Hill (1986) all illustrate the complexity and subtlety of non-capitalist exchange.[10] Not only are the mechanisms of exchange mixed up and modified, there can also be a blending of the ideologies assumed by Polanyi to be appropriate to the different modes of exchange. So, in our own capitalist society, the 'moral economy' of gift-giving both parallels and impinges upon the 'political economy' of market exchange (Davis 1972; Cheal 1988). The result, therefore, may be compromise and control rather than the tension identified by Polanyi in fourth-century Athens.[11]

To apply this kind of post-Polanyian integrated analysis to the economy and society of classical Athens would be a massive undertaking, involving study of a range of different types of testimony: literary, epigraphic, numismatic, archaeological, iconographic and comparative. It is as a contribution towards such a comprehensive study that this paper is offered. Although a variety of source materials will necessarily be brought into play, the problem is approached obliquely by examining the complex of attitudes relating to the exchange of goods as mediated through laws and legal writings from Athens.[12]

II

Any attempt to grapple with the legal aspects of exchange in Athens must take as its point of departure Pringsheim's fundamental study of *The Greek Law of Sale* (1950). Since its appearance this has remained the standard work in the field and is the essential source for the few pages devoted to sale in more recent textbooks of Athenian law and legal theory (Jones 1956: 227–32; MacDowell 1978: 138–40). Pringsheim began the conclusion to his book by expressing the hope that new discoveries and better interpretations would lead to revision and correction of many of the statements and explanations it contained (502). He also stated his expectation that the two theses running through the book would remain unchallenged; namely, the notion of sale in the Greek world as sale for ready money, and the versatility with which the Greeks manipulated that simple concept to meet the requirements of an increasingly sophisticated economy and society. To date, both these predictions have proved correct.

---

10 Many of the works listed in the text (and plenty of others) are usefully summarised in the synoptic study by Hodges (1988); for a survey of the rôle of the market in earlier societies, see Rodinson (1973).

11 On the inadequacy of the original Polanyi paradigm as an explanation of exchange in the Graeco–Roman world, see Finley 1975: 177. Relevant here is the recent discovery amongst Finley's papers of the unpublished contribution that he withheld from the *Trade and Market* volume (Humphreys 1969: 42); the possibility of its publication is being discussed. It should also be noted that doubts have been expressed about Polanyi's presentation of marketless trading as the dominant form of exchange in the ancient Near East (Gledhill & Larsen 1982).

12 For the sake of brevity, the analysis that follows passes over the important questions of the relationship between maritime trade and retailing (Finley 1935) and the countryside as a source of supplies for the city (Osborne 1987a: 93–112). Also ignored is the exchange of services as opposed to goods (for the hiring of labour-services, see Fuks 1951, Mossé 1976).

Such amendments as have been offered involve only points of detail (Demeyere 1952, 1953; Gernet 1953; Wolff 1957; Kränzlein 1963: 76–82). But application to exchange of the broader approach outlined in the first part of this paper cuts across Pringsheim's analysis of sale, calling into question and in part modifying his twin themes of cash sale and consequent legal versatility.

The law of sale as conceived by Pringsheim provides an apparent exception to the rule (noted in the first section of ch.1 of this volume) that the study of the law in ancient Greece necessarily echoes the practice of Greek history in its Athenocentricity. The number of actual laws relating to sale surviving from Athens is small (Lipsius 1915: 738–49). There are several references (all from fourth-century sources) to a law forbidding deceit or misrepresentation in the *agora* (*apseudein en tei agorai*: Hyp. *Athenogenes* 14; cf. Dem. xx.9). The Hyperides passage is glossed by Harpokration in his late *Lexicon of the Ten Orators* as follows (s.v. *kata ten agoran apseudein*):

The law moreover requires honest dealing in the *agora*, and it was probably written to cover goods (*peri ton onion*). Theophrastos says in his *Nomoi* (*Laws* = Szegedy-Maszak 1981: fr.20) that the *agoranomoi* (market inspectors) must look after two things: good order in the *agora* and absence of deceit not only by the sellers but also by the buyers.

According to the Aristotelian *Constitution of the Athenians* (LI.1), there were ten of these *agoranomoi* appointed by lot, five each for the Peiraieus and the city of Athens: 'These are required by the laws to take responsibility for all goods that are on sale (*ton onion*), to ensure that what is sold is in good condition and genuine.' Hyperides (*Athenogenes* 15) also mentions a law that obliged anyone selling a slave to say if he had any physical defect; and Theophrastos in his *Nomoi* (Szegedy-Maszak 1981: fr.21.1) records that where real property was involved, the seller had to register the sale with a magistrate at least sixty days in advance of the transaction, and the buyer had to deposit one per cent of the purchase price. These, then, make up the total of known laws concerning the general conditions of sale in classical Athens.[13]

Although it cannot be assumed that this collection is complete, it is at least consistent in content. There is repeated emphasis on the avoidance of deceit (*apseudeia*) and, with the exception of the sale of real property and slaves, the scenario for this bad faith is the *agora* (see Ste. Croix 1972: 399). That association recalls the alleged gibe of the Persian King Cyrus that he could never fear a people like the Greeks, 'who have a place set apart in the centre of the *polis* where they cheat one another with oaths' (Hdt. 1.153; for the possible nature of these oaths, see the final section). The narrow range of Athenian laws about sale (at least, as they survive) is in striking contrast with the scope of modern law about sale. The standard exegesis of current English law

---

[13] On the duties of the *agoranomoi* see Stanley 1976: 197–297. I am less certain than Stanley (206–7) that their responsibilities included a law, known only from a fragment of fourth-century comedy (Athen. 225c), prohibiting salt-fish sellers from sluicing down their wares. On the law relating to the purchase of real property in Athens, see Schwahn 1934.

relating to the sale of goods (Atiyah 1980) involved the citation of over a thousand statutes and cases, and invites consideration of a wide range of concepts and problems, including definition and nature of the contract of sale, effects of the contract, duties of seller and buyer, and remedies open to them. The historian of Athenian law has to make do with a single law-court speech arising out of a sale transaction.[14]

As might be anticipated from the meagreness of the material, encyclopaedic treatments of Athenian law cover the law of sale in a handful of pages (Vinogradoff 1922: 259–65; Harrison 1968: 245, 1971: 25–7). By contrast, Pringsheim's treatment of the *Greek* law of sale rivals modern legal textbooks in its amplitude. What makes all this possible is the range of texts built into the survey: Pringsheim incorporates material from the world of Homer, through archaic and classical Greece, to Ptolemaic and even Roman Egypt, moving backwards and forwards across the Mediterranean world, through a thousand years of history. The methodological question raised by this aggregation of texts was one of the major themes of Finley's review (1951) of *The Greek Law of Sale* and it remains a matter for debate. Although some of the improbabilities inherent in Pringsheim's combining of texts across time and space will emerge below (and see Préaux 1961), that is not the aspect of his method under scrutiny in this paper, which is concerned with the wider problem of the choice of concepts and categories.[15]

In his Preface (1951: VIII), Pringsheim disclaims any intention of writing a systematic treatise on the Greek law of sale and presents his task in terms of the interpretation of texts. The texts are grouped under more than 180 subheadings, with an overall division between the history and theory (86–242), and the practice of sale (243–500). It is therefore appropriate that the chapter headed 'Conclusion' should open with the frank admission that a summary of conclusions is neither necessary nor possible (500). But in spite of the apparently unsystematic approach, there are underlying principles that give the book a definite shape. The aim of Pringsheim is not so much reconstruction of the individual laws and statutes encompassing sale in the Greek world, as elucidation of the broad legal doctrines that are presumed to underpin the mass of material he has collected. Where he differs fundamentally from his predecessors (Caillemer 1871, 1873; Beauchet 1897, IV: 104–56) is in consistently arguing against the crude assimilation of the Greek law of sale to its Roman equivalent. But in proving his point, Pringsheim paradoxically

---

[14] Hyperides, *Against Athenogenes*. On some of the legal implications of this speech, see Furkiotis 1956. One presumes that the great majority of disputes arising in the *agora* were settled summarily by the *agoranomoi* and never reached a court (Harrison 1971: 25–6). Pollux, in his *Onomastikon* or 'Wordbook' (x.177), glosses a line from Kratinos, the fifth-century comic playwright – 'With his neck in the pillory (*kuphon*)' – as follows: 'It must be supposed that this pillory was a device employed in enforcing the law of the *agora*, in which a person doing wrong in the *agora* was forced to put his neck for a beating.'

[15] For a critique of Pringsheim's book from a different perspective, see Gernet 1951. It may be added that Pringsheim's slightly earlier study of 'The Greek sale by auction' (1949) is also heavily dependent on the testimony of the papyri.

applies to the Greek material a system of categories and classification derived straight from Roman law, with the result that his analysis remains straitjacketed by inappropriate concepts. The summary that follows is, as far as possible, based on Pringsheim's own exposition (86–90).

In the simplest societies, sale is conceived of as an instantaneous affair with goods and money changing hands simultaneously. That is the process known to Roman law as a 'real contract', being validated by the actual exchange of goods and cash (Nicholas 1962: 167–71). Difficulties arise because of the inflexibility of such a simple system and its supposed inability to meet the sophisticated requirements of a more developed economy. The buyer may want to take the goods now but pay later (deferred payment or credit-sale) or the seller may want the money right away but hand over the goods only at a later date (deferred delivery). Either process is potentially awkward in that having an instantaneous contract of sale, validated on the actual exchange of goods and cash, there can be no legal sanction for enforcing delayed payment of purchase price or delivery of goods. The great achievement of Roman law in this regard was the development of the so-called 'consensual contract' (Nicholas 1962: 171–82). The crucial point about this type of contract was that a legal obligation could be established between buyer and seller by virtue of a mutual agreement. Once an agreement had been reached, the buyer was under an obligation to pay over the money and the seller to hand over the goods. Any delay in either paying over the purchase price or delivering the goods was irrelevant; as a contract was held to exist from the moment agreement was reached, completion of the process was legally enforceable. As a consequence, ownership of the goods in question was transferred along with the goods, independently of any payment of the purchase price. The buyer in a credit-sale agreement therefore became the owner of the goods as soon as they came into his possession.

Legal historians before Pringsheim had tended to see the Greeks as anticipating the Romans in arriving at the idea of the consensual contract with respect to sale transactions. Their conclusion was based on two assumptions: in the first place, that the Greek economy had, by the classical period, advanced beyond the stage at which its needs could be adequately met by simple cash sale (Hoetink 1929); secondly, that progress in Greek law was bound to prefigure later Roman developments. Such evidence as survives for the theory and practice of sale in mainland Greece was accordingly distorted to fit the Roman model (see for example Dareste 1893: 305–12). It was one of the achievements of Pringsheim to discredit the second assumption and show conclusively that consensual contract had no formal existence in the known law of any Greek *polis*. The weakness of his analysis lies in the failure to question the first assumption, supposing like his predecessors (and many of his successors) that the Greeks had a 'highly developed cultural *and commercial* civilization' (501, with my italics). This led in turn to the formulation of an alternative assumption: that there was still the need for some equivalent mechanism, corresponding to credit-sale and deferred delivery. The conclusion reached by Pringsheim was that the Greeks bridged the gap between the primitive principle of cash-sale and their growing economic sophistication by developing a set of devices or legal fictions that served as substitutes for the as-yet-uninvented consensual contract. So credit-sale was transformed into a fictitious loan transaction, with seller lending buyer the money needed to purchase the goods, thereby becoming his creditor. Should the debtor–purchaser subsequently refuse to pay up, the lender–seller could institute the usual proceedings for the recovery of the loan (244–7). Alternatively, the buyer could make a down-payment on the purchase price, for which the Greek term is *arrha* or *arrhabon* (translated as 'deposit', 'earnest money' or 'option'). That served as a reassurance that both parties were committed to the transaction and supplied an incentive to complete the sale at a later date (333–429).

Pringsheim sees in these and similar devices the true measure of Greek ingenuity in law. 'Certainly', he writes (243), 'the Greek genius used its versatility and freedom of thought for so shaping the rules of sale as to cope with the variety of daily life and the requirements of a high civilization.' That is a thread running through the book, which closes with a statement balancing the fertility of the Greek legal imagination against the Roman genius for jurisprudence (510–11). As we shall see, there is an element of truth in that comparison, though Athenian flexibility was not along the lines envisaged by Pringsheim. More specifically, his theory about compensatory devices taking the place of consensual contract can be challenged on two different fronts. Apart from the shadowy existence of the devices themselves (at least, in classical Athens), also open to objection is the underlying assumption that the devices were somehow indispensable to the development of the Athenian economy. Closer examination of these criticisms makes up the substance of the following section.

III

The infrequency with which the devices of deferred payment and *arrha* appear in Athenian sources was remarked on by Finley in terms that deserve greater prominence than the obscurity of an endnote (1952: 268 n.39). 'Because of their exclusive concern with legal problems, the jurists tend to ignore the question of the relative frequency and socio-economic significance of credit operations in real property transfers.' That observation, which could be applied to the study of many aspects of 'Greek law', is neatly exemplified by the institution of the *arrha*.[16]

---

[16] The jurists referred to by Finley are, of course, modern exponents of Greek law. As instances of misleading concentration on exceptional examples, at the expense of establishing the general pattern of sale, he cites the articles by Simonetos (1939) and Hellebrand (*RE* xviii: 417–37 s.v. *onē*).

The treatment of the *arrha* by Pringsheim gives sufficient indication of its limited relevance to the social and economic historian of classical Athens. In a chapter of almost one hundred pages (333–428), only one concrete example is drawn from Athens (370–2): a speech of Isaeus has a fleeting reference to an *arrhabon* given for some funerary equipment (VIII.23, with Wyse *ad loc.*). All other references to the *arrha* are indirect. The term occurs twice in a disputed passage from the *Nomoi* of Theophrastos (Szegedy-Maszak 1981: fr.5–6) and once in an anecdote preserved by Aristotle about the financial acumen of the early sixth-century sage Thales (*Politics* 1259a3–19). Neither text need have any direct bearing on the use of the *arrha* in Athens. Apart from an obscure gloss in the *Lexicon* of Harpokration (s.v. *bebaioseos*), *arrha* also appears in two plays by Plautus derived from Athenian originals (*Mostellaria* 637–8; *Rudens* 45–6, 860–2, 1281–3). Although this rag-bag of references confirms the existence of the *arrha* in Athens, it hardly appears as an institution crucial to the functioning of the Athenian economy.[17]

Much the same could be said about the other device singled out by Pringsheim: the legal fiction of having a loan contract stand in place of credit-sale. In light of Pringsheim's response to his critics, this calls for a more extended treatment. Restricting the field in the first instance to literary evidence, there are from Athens only two certain references to credit-sale being replaced by loans between buyers and sellers (Dem. XLI.8; Lyk. *Leok.* 23). Both cases will be discussed in the next section; as will two statements by Plato seeming to suggest that in his second-best state deferred payment for goods would be discouraged (*Laws* 849e, 915d–e). Finley objected that these examples, even when combined with doubtful cases and the evidence for the *arrha*, hardly supported the view that 'the concept of sale on credit was familiar to Greek law' (1952: 268 n.39, citing Pringsheim 1950: 247). The response from Pringsheim (1953) was a widening of the field to take in the testimony of inscriptions.

The argument revolves around a group of twelve so-called *horos*-inscriptions.[18] These were stelae bearing short, often roughly cut inscriptions,

---

[17] For possible interpretations of the Harpokration passage, see Reimer (1941); Gernet 1951: 213–22. Although the Plautine references to the *arrha* probably reflect Athenian usage (MacDowell 1978: 139; Lowe 1985), note the residual caution of Gernet 1951: 210. To the references in the text may be added the conjectural restoration of *arrhabon* in a battered inscription thought by Fine to be a *horos* (1951: no.28; see the sceptical comments by Finley 1952: no.114A); also, a comic fragment of the late fourth century, variously attributed to Python of Katana, Python of Byzantium and Alexander the Great (!), mentions metaphorically *hetairas arrhabon* – 'the deposit on a call-girl' (Athen. XIII.586d, 596a). Taking a wider view, Gofas (1982) sees in the *arrha* the legal device whereby merchants viewing samples of imported goods in the *deigma* or 'display area' in the Peiraieus were able to strike a binding agreement without cargo and purchase-price changing hands. But as the need for the mechanism is based on Pringsheim's thesis of real contract (126 n.29), the argument is circular. The bibliography on the *arrha* continues to grow; to the list given by Finley (1952: 268 n.39) add Talamanca 1953.

[18] What follows is a shortened and simplified version of the argument presented in Millett 1982: xiv–xviii. For details of the twelve *horoi* involved, see n.21 below.

placed on the boundaries of real property to indicate that the title of the party in possession was somehow compromised. The property might, for example, have been offered as security in a loan transaction.[19] The function of each individual *horos* is usually clear, though the terseness of the text can sometimes lead to ambiguity. That is the case with the twelve inscriptions under analysis: elliptical wording makes it possible to interpret them as indicating either loan transactions with the property acting as security (Finley), or sale of the property with deferred payment or deferred delivery (Pringsheim). An example may help to clarify the opposing views. One of the disputed *horoi* (Finley 1952: no.3) reads: 'In the archonship of Theophrastos (340/39 or 313/12 B.C.), *horos* of land for the price owed on it to Phanostratos of Paiania, 2,000 (drachmae).'[20] Finley assumes the omission (not unparalleled in these amateurish productions) of some phrase indicating a security operation, giving the sense: '*horos* of land (put up as security) for the price owing on it ...' The transaction therefore resembles the modern English mortgage, with the piece of property acting as security for its own purchase price. But, according to Pringsheim (1950: 163), such an interpretation was impossible, inasmuch as only the owner of a piece of property was in a position to offer it as security. If the full purchase price had not yet been paid, there could be no change of ownership, short of invoking the principle of consensual contract. 'All this would go against our thesis', admits Pringsheim (1950: 163). He therefore reinterpreted the *horos* as recording a credit-sale. Possession of the land had changed hands, but not ownership, because the purchase price was still owing to Phanostratos. The inscription, argued Pringsheim, was set up as a warning to any third party intending to buy the land or accept it as security that the occupier was not yet the owner. His translation of the *horos* would read: '*horos* of land on which the price is owing ...'

Taking a similar line with other *horos*-inscriptions with phrases indicating obligation or sale but not security, Pringsheim (1953) was able to construct two sub-categories of *horoi* apparently marking deferred payment of purchase price (three examples) and deferred transfer of property to the new owner (nine examples).[21] In the latter case, the *horos* was to be seen as a warning to third parties that ownership of the property no longer rested with the occupier. Again, this was in opposition to Finley's view that the inscriptions recorded more or less conventional security operations: 'If the *horoi* regularly recorded hypothecation, an occasional omission of a word or phrase would probably have gone almost unnoticed' (1952: 104). Although there were points to be made for and against each side in the argument, the rather rigid

---

[19] For a brief introduction to the *horoi* (unique to Athens and areas under Athenian control) and an estimate of their socio-economic significance, see Finley 1953.

[20] ἐπὶ Θεοφράστου/ ἄρχοντος ὅρος/ χωρίου τιμῆς/ ἐνοφειλομέν/ης Φανοστράτωι/ Παιαν(ιεῖ) xx. (Here, and in other texts quoted in the notes, I have not indicated restorations and corrections that may be considered certain.)

[21] Deferred payment: Finley 1952: nos.3, 18A, 114A; deferred delivery: 63, 66c, 85c, 101, 112, 113, 114, 114B, 115.

formalism of Pringsheim seemed to give the edge to Finley's more flexible interpretation (Millett 1982: xvi-xvii).[22] The subsequent discovery of a single *horos* would seem to have resolved the debate in Finley's favour.

The *horos* in question (Millett 1982: no.12A = *SEG* xxxiv, 1984: 167) may be translated as follows: '*horos* of land, house and gardens put up as security to Philon of Halai for the price owed on half the land: 3,000 (drachmae).'[23] Two explanations of the transaction behind this *horos* are possible. Either the unnamed debtor bought the land, house and gardens from Philon, offering him the property as security for the unpaid part of the purchase price; or the debtor bought the property from an unnamed third party, paying him in full by borrowing the price of half the land from Philon. Of the alternatives, the former is by far the more plausible and economical explanation of the text. The crucial point about this *horos* is the presence in the wording of a security element. As such, it indubitably contradicts Pringsheim's fundamental thesis that ownership of property could not change hands until the full purchase price had been paid. The borrower here had not yet paid over the full price to Philon, but was still able to offer the property as security and was presumably regarded as the effective owner.

The resolution to the problem offered above has a significance that is wider than the immediate point at issue. Although the Philon *horos* seems to subvert Pringsheim's theory of strict cash sale, it should not be read as support for the opposing principle of consensual contract. What is to be rejected is the mode of thinking by which all sales in Athens (still less the whole Greek-speaking world) have to be subsumed under some single, rigid principle that can be discovered by aggregating the appropriate texts. The decisive thing was that the parties to a transaction should be satisfied with the terms, which would be negotiated without much attention to legalistic niceties. The permissive character of Athenian legislation in this regard may be indicated by a law (cited in several sources) that mutual agreements should be binding on both parties.[24] Had the agreement behind the Philon *horos* resulted in a court case, it would presumably have been argued out along lines familiar from surviving forensic speeches, with rhetoric, emotion and appeals to justice well to the fore, and arguments based on law or legal principles kept in the background.

These are some of the things that mystify and occasionally scandalise the modern reader, coming to Athenian law-court speeches for the first time. The speakers cheerfully ignore, or treat lightly, legal technicalities and loopholes such as in our systems of justice would be deployed to block or evade the whole

---

[22] Certain aspects of Finley's reading of the *horoi* have been challenged in an important paper by Harris (1988; see n.29 below); but not in ways which compromise his position regarding Pringsheim.

[23] ὅρος χωρίου/ καὶ οἰκίας καὶ/ κήπων πεπραμ/ένων ἐπὶ λύσει/ Φιλίωνι ʿΑλαιεῖ/ τιμῆς ἐνοφει/λομένης τοῦ ἡ/μίσεος χωρίου/ xxx.

[24] Hyp. *Athenog.* 13; Dem. xlii.12, xlvii.77, lvi.2; Dein. iii.4; Plato, *Symp.* 196c. For the attempt by Pringsheim (1950: 34–43) to argue that this law need not indicate the existence of consensual contract, see Finley 1952: 297 n.23.

process. So the Athenian equivalent of a Statute of Limitations never appears as an absolute bar to an action (e.g. Dem. XXXVI.25; see Harrison 1971: 116–20). Rather, it is cited as an additional argument in support of pleas which turn out to be based primarily on appeals to fairness (*to epieikes*).[25] That is an extreme illustration of how laws in general are handled in the speeches; according to Aristotle's realistic classification, they were to be treated as a type of evidence, alongside and on a level with witnesses, documents, torture and oaths (*Rhetoric* 1375a24–6; see ch.2 above). The legal laxity with which litigants presented their cases was matched by the latitude allowed to (or assumed by) the jurors. Noisy interventions in the course of a speech are well attested (Bers 1985); in an extreme case, the jurors might actually howl down the speaker, bring the trial to a premature close, and find in favour of his opponent. Such was apparently the fate of Apollodoros in his suit against his stepfather, the banker Phormion (Dem. XXXVI). Appearing on a subsequent occasion (Dem. XLV.6), he described how his opponent, by speaking first and perjuring himself, made such an impression on the jurors that they refused to hear a single word from Apollodoros and fined him more than three talents.

There is a tendency to see in all this the deviation from an ideal, towards what Weber characterised as 'justice ... according to tears, flattery, demagogic invectives and jokes' (quoted by Finley 1985: 100). But that is to place a negative value on what, taking a wider view, was an integral part of the system. As touched on in the opening chapter of this volume (section III), the unspoken aim of the legal process in Athens was not primarily enforcement of the laws or even securing justice for the individual; rather, it was the settlement of disputes. And implicit here was the underlying notion that disputes were to be resolved in such a way as to preserve the *koinonia* or 'communality' of the *polis*. As Aristotle points out towards the beginning of his *Politics* (1253a37): 'Justice (*dikaiosunē*) is a feature of the *polis* (*politikon*); for judicial procedure (*dikē*), which is the decision of what is just (*dikaion*), is the regulation of the *koinonia* of the *polis*.' In the case of classical Athens, the *politeia* or 'polity' happened to be a democracy, with the jurors representing the interests of the democratic community (ch.1, section II).[26] That is presumably why litigants were unwilling to rely on technicalities as the basis of their cases; and it also explains why Apollodoros should have been shouted down, receiving thereby a stronger expression of communal disapproval than would have been possible through a formal vote of condemnation.[27]

A major consequence of the informality of the Athenian legal process was

[25] For the full range of references, see Isager & Hansen 1975: 126. On the rôle of *to epieikes* (only the loose equivalent of modern 'equity') in Athenian legal argument, see Jones 1956: 64–7; Dover 1974: 184–7.

[26] The Greek of the *Politics* is notoriously elusive and the translation given in the text is not intended as definitive; for *dikē* as 'legal procedure' see the note *ad loc.* in Sinclair & Saunders 1981. On the concept of the *koinonia* of the *polis*, see Mulgan 1977: 13–16.

[27] That Apollodoros was not discouraged by this display of popular disapproval says more about Apollodoros than the force of judicial opinion; for a survey of the career of this litigious Athenian, see Bonner 1927: 113–34.

the non-appearance in Athens of the professional jurists who were a characteristic of the Roman model (Frier 1985). It is therefore unfortunate that modern
writers on Greek law have tried to fill what they perceive as a gap in the
literature by promoting to the status of an ancient Greek jurist an essentially
philosophical writer like Theophrastos. Such interpretations are based on the
assumption that, as there are underlying principles of 'Greek law', so they
must somehow be recoverable from the fragments of the *Nomoi*. Their latest
editor (Szegedy-Maszak 1981: 72) concludes that the lengthy fragment
concerned with sale is 'invaluable for our understanding of the Greek law of
sale, because it provides a framework for the disparate bits of evidence that can
be culled from literary and epigraphical sources'. But Theophrastos was no
jurist nor was the *Nomoi* intended as a formal legal treatise. The long list of
works preserved as a part of Diogenes Laertios's *Life of Theophrastos*
(v.42–50; see Sollenberger 1985) gives some impression of his range of
interests, of which law made up only a minor part. As for the *Nomoi*, that work
is, as Pringsheim appreciated (1950: 137), 'a mixture of a treatise on actual
laws, a comparison with other, partly old, partly imaginary laws, and
philosophical remarks on the merits and faults of those laws. It contains gaps
and unanswered questions, and reports and criticisms are sometimes insepara-
bly intermixed.' And yet, in spite of this realistic assessment, Pringsheim
expects the contents of the *Nomoi* to conform to the principle of cash sale to the
extent of being seriously embarrassed when they do not (139–41).

If, as I have argued above, there is little evidence for deferred payment or
delivery in Athenian sources, why did Pringsheim assume that legal devices
would be needed to make them possible? The answer, which is my second and
deeper objection to Pringsheim's thesis, seems to lie in the evolutionary
conception of law and society which was a part of the intellectual tradition
within which he worked. Such a view is explicit in his assumption that legal
fictions were introduced in order to circumvent the limitations of cash sale in
Athens. The evolutionary interpretation of early law is most closely associated
with Henry Maine, with whom the doctrine reached its climax (Burrow 1966:
17–41; Stein 1980: 86–98; Kuper 1988: 17–41; Cocks 1988: 52–78). In his
massively influential *Ancient Law* (1861: 20–41; see ch. 1 section 1 above), legal
fictions are an early and indispensable part of the process whereby obsolete
restrictions of codes are by-passed, making progress possible. Pringsheim
seems to have held similarly progressivist views of developments in ancient
law, economy and society.[28] Although he never speaks in any detail in *The
Greek Law of Sale* about his conception of the economy in which sale transactions took place, there is always implicit the idea of increasing commercial
sophistication to which the law has to be adjusted. The clearest hint comes in
his statement that (86) 'Barter is the predecessor of sale. Therefore the legal

---

[28] See, for example, his paper (1955) on symbols and fictions in Greek and Roman law. It may be
significant that Maine, in explaining the failure of the Greeks to develop a sense of
jurisprudence, describes the 'mobility and elasticity' of their intellect in terms which anticipate
Pringsheim (Maine 1861: 72–3, with Cocks 1988: 58–9).

history of sale always begins with the conception of cash sale ... But the practical requirements of a developing economic life cannot for ever be satisfied with this simple sale for ready money.' Pringsheim's modification of cash sale to introduce an element of credit shows that he is thinking in conventional terms of a progression through time from primitive barter to the use of cash and finally credit.

That concept of barter, cash and credit as a hierarchy of increasingly sophisticated forms of exchange can be traced back beyond Adam Smith (Gras 1930). Though superficially attractive, such simple patterns of social and economic (and legal) evolution tend to distort the way in which we view the past. In order to highlight progress towards ever greater sophistication the past is negatively presented and typically labelled 'primitive'. But a major achievement of social and cultural anthropology has been to show how so-called 'primitive societies' invariably have their own complexity and sophistication. More insidiously, what we regard as 'primitive' tends to be mirrored through our own preconceived ideas about civilisation (see Diamond 1974; Kuper 1988). That is the mistaken attitude at the heart of the debate over the ancient economy referred to earlier (section 1). For the so-called 'modernists', who take capitalism as their measure of success, 'primitive' is a negative concept: a term of failure and almost abuse. Their reasoning (subconscious or otherwise) seems to be based on the assumption that the sophistication of the literary and visual culture of ancient Greece must have been matched by a sophisticated economy, which necessarily means capitalism – if only in its earlier stages. There has been a failure to appreciate that pre-capitalist economies can and do generate their own subtlety and complexity.[29]

With respect to the problem of sale, one way forward is through a passage from Mauss's *The Gift* (1925: 34–5), suggesting an alternative approach to the development of exchange in the ancient world:

Cuq could still say in 1910: 'In primitive societies, barter alone is found; in those more advanced, direct sale is practised. Sale on credit characterises a higher stage of civilisation; it appears first in an indirect manner, a combination of sale and loan.' In fact, the origin of credit is different. It is to be found in a range of customs neglected by lawyers and economists as uninteresting: namely the gift, which is a complex phenomenon ... Now a gift necessarily implies the notion of credit. Barter arose from the system of gifts given and received on credit, simplified by drawing together the moments of time which had previously been distinct.[30]

---

[29] The misapprehension persists among Greek legal historians; see, for example, Fine 1951: 93; Cohen 1973: 66 n.164. Says Harris (1988: 37 n.81): 'Even P. Millett, who takes a primitivist view of the Athenian economy, admits that "The easy availability of credit was essential to the smooth functioning of Athenian society; loan transactions of one type or another are a pervasive feature at all levels of Athenian life" (Millett 1983: 42).' But Harris has failed to appreciate that the credit relations embedded in ancient Athenian society were qualitatively different from those conventionally held to be characteristic of the capitalist economy.

[30] The quotation from Cuq, paralleling to perfection Pringsheim's idea of the evolution of Greek sale, is taken from a study of ancient Babylonian law. Cuq also enjoyed a reputation as a historian of Roman law.

This idea of reciprocal gift-giving takes us back to Polanyi, although it suggests a closer relationship between gift, sale and credit than he seemed to think possible. In the following final sections I will try to develop that relationship to hint at a more integrated approach to exchange in classical Athens.[31]

IV

The plausibility of a connection between sale and gift-exchange is enhanced by the Greek terminology of sale. Most striking is the direct link between *apodidomai*, one of the commonest words for 'sell', and *didomi*, 'to give'. According to LSJ, the compound form has the primary meaning of 'render what is due'. In a valuable study of Greek verbs for sale, Chantraine (1940) concluded that there was no word for 'sell' in classical Greek where sale was the original meaning. Apart from *apodidomai*, *pernemi* meant 'transport across the sea' (typically of slaves), while *poleō* had the sense of 'offer for sale'. Similarly, *onoumai*, the usual term for 'to buy', had the earlier sense of 'make an offer'. Although all these verbs came to have the accepted sense of buy and sell, the older meanings were preserved at least as late as Herodotus, who uses the words in both senses (Pringsheim 1950: 97–8); and, as Gernet remarked (1951: 204), the context is commonly that of gift-exchange. For Pringsheim this seems to have the status of a linguistic curiosity or an institutional survival. While agreeing that the concept of 'exchange' (here meaning barter) can be traced through the fifth and into the fourth century (101–2), he assumes that 'Exchange itself had almost disappeared in the Greek classical period with its developed commerce.'

Etymology alone can, of course, prove nothing; but there is a clear parallel for the gift-sale connection in the terminology of credit. Thanks to the detailed researches of Korver (1934), it can be shown that no familiar Greek word for 'lend' had that as its original meaning. The commonest term, *daneizein*, has close connections with *danos*, 'gift' (79–84); and other verbs, such as *kikhranai* (74–7), *proiesthai* (89–93) and *sumballein* (93–4), had the earlier sense of 'furnish' or 'supply' which survived as subsidiary meanings. The ambiguity inherent in this association of loan with gift seems to have resulted in the coining of the word *tokizein*, where the incorporation of *tokos* (interest) made the credit element explicit (97–9). From the side of sale, there is the analogous invention of the verbs *kapeleuein* and *agorazein*, referring almost unambiguously to selling and buying.[32]

---

[31] As often, the argument is anticipated by Gernet who, in his review of Pringsheim (1951: 211–13), pointed out that sale may be better understood as a development of gift-giving (cf. Gernet 1948: 111–46, 1948–9: 146–72, 1956: 226–31). I must here acknowledge much helpful discussion with Sitta von Reden, who is at present preparing a wide-ranging study of Greek exchange along the lines indicated in the text.

[32] For a secondary sense of *agorazein*, see n.39 below. The ambiguity of words connected with sale is also found in *empolein* which, according to Chantraine (1940: 21–4), has the underlying

What is more, it can be demonstrated in the case of credit that connections with gift-giving go deeper than terminology.[33] There survives from Athenian sources a mass of material relating to lending and borrowing that makes overall sense only if viewed from the perspective of the gift-exchange relationship identified by Mauss. In simple terms, it is possible to identify for fourth-century Athens two types or systems of credit relations. One system involved loans that were interest-free and without formality. This type of credit is close to gift and may be exemplified by the *eranos* or reciprocal loans that were a feature of mutual support within the *koinonia* of the *polis*.[34] By contrast, the second type of loan carried interest, along with associated formalities including witnesses (or written agreement) and security. Where ancient theoretical writers comment explicitly on the relationship between the two types they stress the gulf between them and are invariably hostile to the interest-bearing variety. The strictures of Plato (*Laws* 742c, 921c) and Aristotle (*Politics* 1258b5) against the taking of interest are well known. But, as will be suggested below, that negative attitude may be attributed to their ideological stance, which inadequately reflects the realities of Athenian society. An alternative assessment, concentrating on the practice and pattern of lending and borrowing in Athens, brings out the integration of the two systems of credit.

Different conditions of credit were appropriate to the varying degrees of intimacy between the people who made up the *polis*. For those regarded as *philoi* (friends, relatives, neighbours and associates), the kind of borrowers with whom close reciprocal relationships might be established, loans without interest were appropriate.[35] Where the association between lender and borrower was more distant and a reciprocal favour seemed unlikely, it was legitimate to charge interest and require security. An interest-free loan implied the expectation of mutual assistance at some future date; receipt of interest took the place of a future favour and closed the account. On these terms, an individual could simultaneously lend (or borrow) money both with and without interest. So the father of Demosthenes had at the time of his death about a talent lent out in interest-free *eranos* loans of between two and three hundred drachmae, in addition to a talent lent at interest (Dem. xxvii.9,11).[36] The analogy between gift and loan, and gift and sale should be clear. To

sense of 'exchange' and can mean either 'buy' or 'sell' according to the context. This apparent imprecision in the terminology of buying and selling (and see n.54 below) is in agreement with the looseness detected in the terminology of credit by Korver (1934: 144–6) and of banking by Bogaert (1968: 59–60).

33 In what follows, I draw on the detailed documentation of my forthcoming book, *Lending and Borrowing in Ancient Athens*.

34 On the role of *eranos* credit in Athenian society and its basis in reciprocity, see the brief account by Gernet 1948–9: 155–9.

35 Although *philos* and *philia* are conventionally rendered as 'friend' and 'friendship', the correspondence is not complete. Briefly, a *philos* was anyone with whom one enjoyed a relationship that was mutually beneficial; affection need not be involved. See Goldhill 1986: 79–107.

36 The model outlined in the text is in part derived from Sahlins (1974: 185–275), with his concept of 'kinship distance' replaced by the broader idea of 'social distance' based on *philia*.

people who were close, either physically or metaphorically (or both), one gave and at some future date received something back in return. But as social distance between individuals increased, so it became unrealistic to hope for a future return. The return therefore became instantaneous and gift was transformed into sale. An important aspect of reciprocal giving is the strengthening of relationships which are to be continued into the future. It is therefore beneficial for both parties if an exact balance cannot be struck: a guarantee that the association will continue. Sale, by contrast, is a more impersonal transaction that need have no implications for the future, making it crucial that both sides be satisfied with the exchange. That may help to explain the importance of cash in sale transactions, facilitating some kind of balance between what is given and received in a way not easy or possible with straight barter.[37]

Whereabouts in terms of social distance an individual drew the line between gift and sale would depend on a combination of social convention and personal judgement. The sheer size of the population of Athens made it inevitable that citizens who were unconnected by ties of *philia* would have at least occasional dealings with one another. As with Demosthenes' father and his loan at interest, no shame was attached to selling rather than giving, provided it was not habitual and the bounds of *philia* were not transgressed. To return to a text introduced earlier (and to which we will refer again), the *Characters* of Theophrastos commonly sell things on a casual, private basis (I.5, XII.8, XV.5, XVIII.9, XXII.4, XXIII.9). By itself, this is unexceptionable: criticism comes only when a Character illegitimately combines *philia*, gift and sale. That is the speciality of the 'Man who thrives on sordid gain (*aiskhrokerdeia*)' (XXX). He sells watered wine – even to his *philoi* (5); having claimed his share of gifts (*xenion*) on an embassy, he sells them (7); and, after persuading a *philos* to sell him something cheaply, he immediately re-sells it at a profit (12).[38]

[37] The impersonal overtones of sale may help to explain the insistence of the Corinthians in the early fifth century that the Athenians pay five drachmae for each of the twenty ships that they gave (*didousi*) to help Athens in her war against Aegina. 'This was', says Herodotus (VI.89), 'because according to their *nomos*, they were not allowed to give them as a gift.' As noted by Salmon (1984: 251 n.41), *nomos* may here have the sense of either formal law or custom. But by taking a price for the ships, the Corinthians could pass off the transaction as 'impersonal', not necessarily implying any bond of *philia* between the two *poleis* that might continue into the future.

[38] As often in the *Characters*, the status and precise meaning of the text are here (XXX.12) unclear, but the general drift is unmistakable; see Ussher 1960: *ad loc*. Comparable is the behaviour of the 'Mean Man' (*aneleutheros*), who sells off the meat from a sacrifice he is obliged to perform rather than give it away (XXII.4). Other passages from classical texts juxtapose sale with reciprocity: Isoc. II.54; Plato, *Laws* 727e–28a; cf. Dem. LVI.1 where a loan of 3,000 drachmae is weighed sarcastically against the scrap of paper worth two coppers (*khalkoi*) given as a receipt. Also relevant is the tendency for words meaning 'buy' and 'sell' to be combined with *argurion*, 'money' or 'silver'. This idea of buying or selling 'for money' suggests that money could itself be seen as an object of exchange: see Kraay 1964: 90; for a modern African parallel, Bohannan & Dalton 1961: x. Appropriate texts are collected by Pringsheim (1950: 100–1), who interprets the phrasing as emphasising 'actual sale for ready money'.

These and other passages all testify to the lively existence and appreciation of the concept of

Also under suspicion are those who sell on a more-than-casual basis, making a living out of buying and selling (*kapeleia*). Again, credit provides a parallel with the popular mistrust of professional money-lenders, as indicated by attacks on them in the courts (Dem. xxxvii.52–4; xlv.69–70). Alleged grounds are the way in which professional lenders make their living through the systematic exploitation of other people's misfortunes. With professional retailers (*kapeloi*), suspicion seems to have arisen out of the obligation imposed on them by their occupation to buy cheap and sell dear. It was assumed that without links of *philia* to restrain them they would incline towards deceit and misrepresentation. Some of the stock accusations made against retailers in Athens are given below; but mention might be made of the shame apparently felt by a citizen in being associated with the business-end of the *agora* (Dem. lvii.30–6), and the unpleasant associations of some *agora*-words.[39]

The healthy suspicion with which market traders were regarded in Athens should not be confused with the downright hostility and even contempt they meet with in the pages of Plato and Aristotle. Both identify sale with exchange (*allagē, allaktikē*; refs. in Pringsheim 1950: 99) and are highly sensitive to the way in which exchange in pursuit of increased wealth, rather than for the sake of self-sufficiency, is liable to abuse, disrupting the *koinonia*. This is the basis of Aristotle's notorious distinction between exchange that is 'natural' and 'unnatural' (*Politics* 1258a39–b2). But in what follows, the emphasis will be on Plato's presentation of the problem of retail trade in the *polis*, arguing by reference to empirical evidence for exchange that he (and Polanyi) underestimated the scope for integration between *philia* and exchange in the *agora*.

In Plato's *Sophist* (223c–d), exchange (*allaktikē*) is agreed to be of two kinds: gift (*doretikon*) and sale (*agorastikon*). It is further agreed that exchange-by-sale can be further subdivided into 'selling one's own products' (*autopolikē*) and 'selling what others produce' (*metabletikē*), which in the city is called 'retailing' (*kapelikē*). In the *Politicus* (260c–d), Plato reveals his relative disapproval of *kapelikē*: kings and their heralds are metaphorically and respectively compared with *autopoloi* and *kapeloi*; and in the *Republic* (371c) disapproval is absolute, with *kapeloi* presented as weaklings, fit only for hanging around the *agora*, exchanging goods for money. That is the more immediate background for Plato's treatment of retailing in the *Laws*, where a

reciprocal gift-giving right through classical Athens (and beyond). When Demosthenes advised the Athenians to accept Halonnesos from Philip only if he gave it *back* (*apodidomi*) and not merely offered to *give* it (*didomi*), he was not just quibbling over syllables as Aeschines argued (iii.83). A gift implied a counter-gift in a way that the restoration of a former possession did not. See also the catalogue of passages with the same motif collected by Athenaeus 223d–224b.

39 For example, *agoraios* and *agorazein* in the sense of lounging around in the *agora*, with implications of inferior status. On the derogatory overtones of *kapelos*, see Ehrenberg 1951: 113–15.

comprehensive programme for its control verges on suppression.[40] There are detailed regulations for holding markets for specified products on fixed days with separate markets for citizens and non-citizens (849a–d). Within the market itself, pitches are to be marked out and allocated by the *agoranomoi* in conjunction with other officials (849e); selection of these market inspectors has already been carefully described (763e–764b). Regulations relating to pricing and adulteration are listed (916d–918a); and, after a remarkable tirade against the anti-social behaviour of *kapeloi* and *pandokeis* (innkeepers), laws are set down forbidding any citizen to act as *kapelos*, with imprisonment for one year as the punishment for a first offence (918a–920b). The conditions of sale prescribed by Plato are as follows (915d–e; cf. 849e):

When one person makes an exchange (*allattetai*) with another by buying or selling, the transfer shall be made by handing over the article in the appointed part of the *agora* and nowhere else, and by receiving the price on the spot; and no delay (*anabolē*) in sale or purchase is allowed. If a person exchanges (*diameibeitai*) something in any other place or under any other agreement, trusting (*pisteuon*) the other party to the exchange, he must do so on the understanding that there is no legal redress regarding things not sold according to the laws set down.

Although apparently straightforward, the interpretation of this passage has proved problematical. For Pringsheim in particular it presents a stumbling-block as he tries to read into the text Plato's reassertion of the principle of strict cash sale, outlawing the device of the fictitious loan contract. As the motive behind this he identifies Plato's antipathy towards credit transactions (130), based on a broader hostility towards capitalism (129).[41] But a problem remains for Pringsheim in Plato's treatment of credit-sale operations in which the buyer fails to hand over the purchase price. By denying the seller any right to legal redress, he seems to be supporting the idea that ownership of an article (or, at least, its unassailable possession) could be transferred without the purchase price having to change hands. That apparently secure interpretation of the text – and it was so understood by Theophrastos in his *Nomoi* (Szegedy-Maszak 1981: fr.21.7) – is rejected by Pringsheim as having consequences that are (140) 'incompatible with the Greek law of ownership'. 'Moreover', he says, 'they violate the first principle of the Greek law of sale, that ownership passes only if the price is paid, a principle emphasized by Plato himself who wishes to restore pure cash sale.'

There is more than a hint of circularity in Pringsheim's reasoning, hemmed in as he is by preconceived notions about the primacy of cash sale and Plato's dislike of credit. Clarification of Plato's attitude towards sale and credit seems

---

[40] For a full discussion of Plato's laws relating to the marketplace and a comparison with Athenian legislation, see Stanley 1976: 33–57.

[41] 'We may say with some confidence that Plato disliked credit transactions and in this respect was in accord with the popular and deep-rooted feelings of many contemporaries as well as those of the old poetry' (131). But the references supplied to a law ascribed to Zaleukos (see n.42 below) and a passage from Theognis (283) are poor evidence on which to base such a sweeping statement.

to come from the continuation of the passage from the *Laws* cited above. In what at first looks like an aside, Plato concedes that (915e), 'Concerning *eranos* loans, whoever wishes may collect them as a *philos* among *philoi*. But if any dispute arises involving the raising of *eranos* loans, he must act on the understanding that in regard to these matters no legal actions are possible.' Plato cannot intend the lack of legal redress as a disincentive to *eranos* credit, which, with its closeness to gift, reinforces the ideal of mutual support within the community encouraged elsewhere in the *Laws* (e.g. 738d–e). Rather, he regards legal sanctions as inappropriate in loans between *philoi*: an attitude that is echoed in the law codes of other *poleis*.[42] Plato's aim in making loans at interest non-recoverable at law was presumably to buttress the gift-associations of credit (*Laws* 742c, 921c). By his pessimistic reckoning, offering the opportunity to default on repayment to borrowers not bound to lenders by ties of *philia* would effectively suppress this branch of interest-bearing credit.[43] Plato's attitude towards sale seems to be similar. He regards the transaction (especially in the *agora*) as being between non-*philoi* and therefore open to fraud. Although he seems to envisage the bare possibility of trust (*pistis*) between buyer and seller (see the passage quoted above), the implication of his comments is that abuse is liable to break in. That is why he seeks to minimise the opportunity for fraud by insisting on instantaneous exchange where non-*philoi* are involved.[44]

An examination of the empirical evidence for sale and credit sale in Athens suggests that Plato's pessimism was misplaced. It was argued above (III) that formal examples of credit sale were few and far between. Where cases can be identified, they typically involve substantial purchases of real property or slaves.[45] The relative rarity of credit-sale agreements may be explained in

[42] The fullest statement comes from Aristotle (*Ethics* 1162b21–63a6), who, in a discussion of the difference between personal and impersonal relationships, notes that in some places legal redress is not allowed in agreements based on trust (*pistis*). Along these lines, Zaleukos, the early seventh-century lawgiver of Locri, is reputed to have established a law forbidding the use of written agreements in loan transactions (Zenobius, *Prov.* v.4). In fourth-century Athens the position was reversed, with disputes arising out of *eranos* loans having the privileged status of 'monthly suits' (*Ath.Pol.* LII.2; see Cohen 1973: 12–20).
    Other authors follow Pringsheim in apparently extending Plato's opposition to interest-bearing loans to all branches of credit (e.g. Nicolet 1971: 1204 n.1, 'Le prêt à intérêt, donc l'usage du crédit, sont condamnés'). Szegedy-Maszak (1981: 72) avoids that error but appears to be under the impression that even interest-free credit was required for commercial purposes.

[43] Pringsheim seems to envisage three types of loans in the society behind the *Laws*: interest-bearing, interest-free, and *eranos*; of which only the interest-free variety was protected by law (130). But that introduces an anomaly into the analysis that can be avoided by accepting that Plato assumed all interest-free loans would be of the *eranos* type.

[44] Interestingly enough, it is Theophrastos' 'Mistrustful Man' (*apistos*) who insists on immediate payment from a purchaser who will not tolerate any delay (XVIII.9). These nuances escape Beauchet (1897, IV: 126), who ascribes Plato's provisions concerning credit sale to his awareness of the proverbial bad faith of his fellow-Greeks!

[45] Finley 1952: no.3 (land), Millett 1982: no.12A (land, house and gardens); see above, section III. Dem. XLI.8 and Lyc. *Leok.* 23 both involve the purchase of slaves using the device of a loan as described by Pringsheim. In both cases the transaction was arranged along semi-formal lines with interest-charge and use of either witnesses or written agreement.

terms of the networks of interest-free credit available to most citizens. Again, straight credit provides a parallel, with borrowers seeking to replace interest-bearing loans from professional lenders with interest-free credit from *philoi* (e.g. Dem. LIII.4–13). By an analogous process, obligations owed by *philoi* could be deployed as a way of avoiding liabilities arising out of dealings with *kapeloi*. This mechanism can be seen at work in a letter on lead from Attica, dated to the early fourth century:[46]

Carry to the Potters' Market (*ton keramon*), and deliver to Nausias or Thrasykles or my son. Mnesiergos sends his greetings to all at home and hopes this may find them as well as it leaves him. Please send me a rug, either a sheepskin or a goatskin, as cheap as you can get it, and not with hairs on, and some strong shoe leather. I will pay you when a chance arises.

The pattern of that relationship appears elsewhere, in contexts from which the underlying ethical norm can be inferred. In Aristophanes' *Plutus* (380–1) there is a sarcastic allusion to expending three minas on behalf of a *philos* and then billing him for ten: and the 'Skinflint' (*mikrologos*) of Theophrastos (x.4) complains to a person who buys something on his behalf at a bargain price that it is still too expensive.[47]

Texts like these suggest sets of relationships on a different plane from the formal contracts and agreements that are the concern of legal historians. That is why so much that is written on Greek law has about it an air of unreality when viewed from the perspective of the socio-economic historian. The contrast can be made more starkly through rival readings of the long fragment of Lysias' speech *Against Aiskhines the Socratic* preserved by Athenaeus (XIII.611d–12f = Gernet & Bizos 1955–9, II: fr.XXXVIII). The unnamed speaker was trying to get Aiskhines, a former pupil of Socrates, to repay a debt. As part of his attempt at character-assassination he presents a black picture of his opponent's habit of borrowing without repaying: how his neighbours have been forced to abandon their houses and rent others far away; how he refuses to repay his *eranos* loans, with the result that those who helped him out are themselves ruined; how there are so many people standing outside his house at dawn, demanding repayment, that passers-by think it's his funeral and the crowd is waiting for the corpse to be carried out. The speaker

---

[46] The text as restored by Wilhelm (1904) reads: φέρεν ἰς τὸν κέραμ/ον τὸγ χυτριόν·/ ἀποδόναι δὲ Ναυσίαι/ ἢ Θρασυκλῆι ἢ θ' υἱῶι·/ Μνησίεργος/ ἐπέστελε τοῖς οἴκοι/ χαίρεν καὶ ὑγιαίνεν/ καὶ αὐτὸς οὕτως ἔφασκε ἔχεν·/ στέγασμα εἴ τι βόλεστε/ ἀποπέμψαι ἢ ὦας ἢ διφθέρας/ ὡς εὐτελεστάτας καὶ μὴ σισρωτὰς/ καὶ κατύματα: τυχὸν ἀποδώσω. See the brief comments by Zimmern 1931: 284–5, whose translation (with minor alterations) is given in the text.

[47] Although the text of the Theophrastos passage is uncertain, the general meaning is clear (see n.38 above). Also tempering sale with *philia* (though in a different way) the prospective purchaser of a slave boy, as described in Hyperides' *Against Athenogenes* (1–5), used as a go-between a third party known to both buyer and seller. If the speaker can be believed, the scheme backfired; which is why we hear about it. When Theophrastos' 'Inopportune man' (*akairos*) acts as go-between, he brings a buyer prepared to offer more just after the deal has been clinched (XII.8).

also alleges that: 'the *kapeloi* who live near him, and from whom he received advances (*prodoseis*) without making repayments, have shut their shops (*kapeleia*) and gone to law with him.'

For Pringsheim (1950: 372) this last accusation presents an interesting legal problem. He considers the possibility that Aiskhines might have taken an *arrha* for the delivery of some goods (assumed to be wine) which he subsequently failed to produce. As an alternative, he wonders whether the *kapeloi* had sold Aiskhines some wine on credit. This second suggestion involves Pringsheim in a solemn discussion as to whether Aiskhines gave the *kapeloi* a 'deed of loan' for the price of the wine, or whether they sued Aiskhines for the return of the *arrha*. He ends by admitting that no firm conclusion can be drawn from the passage. And yet, when considered in the context of economic rather than formal legal institutions, the meaning of the fragment seems clear. If a clue is needed, it can be found in the *Onomastikon* of Pollux (VII.194): 'Hermippos [a comic poet of the later fifth century] uses the phrase "to drink on credit (*prodosin pinein*)" of wine got from the inn (*ek kapeleiou*) without payment.' The supplying of goods by shopkeepers 'on tick' is so familiar as to need hardly any explanation (de Vessilitsky & Bulkley 1916; Roberts 1976: 22–3). Although the social significance of these 'credit sales' may have been considerable, their petty commercial level renders a juristic analysis inappropriate. The only 'contract' needed was a piece of slate on which to record the customer's name and the sum owed. The idea that debts run up in this way by a single customer like Aiskhines should cause shopkeepers to close down and resort to the law is a piece of humorous exaggeration that appears to have escaped Pringsheim.

One detail of the attack on Aiskhines hints at a way in which *philia* and sale might be drawn together to produce an element of personal integration in apparently impersonal exchange relations. The *kapeloi* who have put up their shutters to go to law with Aiskhines are those 'who live near him'. The implication that their neighbour Aiskhines was a regular customer suggests a more-than-casual relationship between buyer and seller. The connection is made by Leach (1982: 152–3) who, in his discussion of gift-giving, points out that the label 'regular customer' really means 'a customer who has the potential to go into debt'. That raises the possibility of enduring relationships between buyers and sellers in which, after the fashion of gift-exchange, an exact balance might be struck only intermittently or momentarily.

It is not hard to imagine how lasting links between drinkers and innkeeper might develop at the neighbourhood *kapeleion*, itself a focus of social interaction. In a fragment from a lost comedy by the fourth-century play-wright Antiphanes (Athen. x.441b), a female character praises the local *kapelos* as being the only person who knows how to mix wine to her taste. More problematical is the possibility of blending *philia* with sale in the *agora*. The marketplace is singled out by Polanyi as the area in which exchange is at its most random and impersonal, with buyer and seller bonded only by the cash-nexus (Polanyi, Arensberg & Pearson 1957: viii–ix). But the Athenian *agora* was only in part given over to buying and selling; its other functions as a centre of political, judicial and religious activities are too well known to need detailed documentation. In this broad and literal sense, the economic aspect of the *agora* was, to use Polanyi's term, 'embedded' in a range of social and political institutions.[48] And there were narrower ways in which personal associations interpenetrated even the commercial side of the *agora*. It was the rule that shops and stalls selling similar sorts of commodities were gathered together in the same general areas in or around the market-place.[49] These collections of *kapeloi* also acted as informal social centres for groups of people who were not necessarily interested in buying. Texts repeatedly refer to groups congregating at the cobbler's, barber's, perfumer's, metalworker's, wreathmaker's and moneychanger's.[50]

All the indications point towards stability in these groups of bystanders, with people habitually gathering at some favoured place. We are told specifically by Lysias (XXIII.3) that men from the outlying deme of Dekeleia tended to gather at the barber's in the street of the Herms, hard by the *agora*. Individuals also had their favourite haunts. The speaker, again in a speech by Lysias (XXIV.20), reminds the jurors how 'Each of you is in the habit of frequenting some place: a perfumer's, a barber's, a cobbler's or wherever it might happen to be; and the greatest number visit those who are nearest the *agora* ... you are all in the way of paying a call and passing the time at some place or other.' Xenophon (*Mem.* IV.2.1) tells how Socrates discovered that the young intellectual Euthydemos 'did not enter the *agora* owing to his youth, but if he wanted to get anything done, he would be found sitting in a leather-worker's shop (*heniopoieion*) near the *agora*'. Euthydemos was presumably able to find older friends there who would enter the *agora* on his behalf. It is just possible that this leather-worker's is to be identified with the workshop belonging to Simon, the philosophically inclined shoemaker, where Socrates allegedly went to meet and talk with his companions (Diog. Laert. II.122). Although onlookers presumably doubled up as purchasers at the shops and stalls they frequented, Socrates can hardly have ranked among Simon's best customers.[51]

---

[48] For a chronological summary of the development of the *agora* in relation to recent excavations, see Camp 1986; literary and epigraphical testimonia are collected by Wycherley (1957). Evidence for the commercial function of the *agora* is presented by Wycherley 1956, 1978 and Thompson 1971. For the emergence of the commercial aspect of the *agora* in the sixth and fifth centuries, see Martin 1951 (cf. Spahn 1984: 309–13). The arguments of Stanley (1976: 12–33) for the appearance of the *agora* as a centre of exchange as early as the *Odyssey* are inconclusive.

[49] See Wycherley 1956: 5–9; Stanley 1976: 47–50. For an impression of the range of goods on offer, see the testimonia collected by Wycherley 1957: 193–206.

[50] Refs. in Wycherley 1956: 3; for the moneychangers add Plato, *Apol.* 17c, *Hippias Min.* 368b; Theoph. *Charact.* v.7.

[51] A shoemaker's workshop, right against a boundary stone of the *agora*, is plausibly identified as Simon's (Camp 1986: 145–7). As often in Athens (Young 1951; Bettalli 1985), the workshop seems to have served as shop and house, cutting across Weber's observation that (1958:

This broadening of the rôle of the marketplace to encompass a range of social functions is not in any way peculiar to Athens. Bohannan & Dalton (1961: 15) introduce their material on modern African markets by remarking how 'Market places can be utilized for almost every conceivable purpose that requires a large number of people brought together in a controlled situation.' More specifically, a study of social relations in a Philippine market (Davis 1973: 211–19) shows in detail how buyers try to establish personal relationships with stallholders, acquiring thereby the status of 'privileged customers'. A similar pattern of behaviour can be traced in the Athenian *agora*, where links between *kapeloi* and at least some of their customers seem to have gone beyond the cash-nexus. So a fishmonger in a fragment from a comedy by Antiphanes (Athen. VIII.338e–9b) knows his higher-spending customers by name and earmarks special fish for them as he sets out his wares. From the other side of the counter, as it were, the 'Rustic' (*agroikos*) among the *Characters* of Theophrastos (IV.15) announces to anyone he meets on the road his intention, on arriving in the city, of buying some salt-fish from Arkhias. Other Characters hint at how these relationships might be built up and exploited. The 'Abominable Man' (*bdeluros*) contrives to 'chat up' the sellers of nuts, myrtle berries and fruit, nibbling away at their stock all the while (XI.4). The 'Shameless Man' (*anaiskhuntos*) has a well-developed technique: 'When he's out shopping, he reminds the butcher of any service he may have done him and, standing next to the scales, tosses on some meat if he can or, failing that, a bone for making soup. If he gets away with it, he is well pleased; if not, he grabs a piece of tripe off the table and laughs as he hurries away' (IX.4).[52]

The idea that the creation of a personal bond between buyer and seller might prove beneficial to both parties reintroduces a question posed at the beginning of this essay: the problem of price-formation in the Athenian *agora*. Although a comprehensive attempt at an answer would call for a full-length study, we are now at least in a position to see some way forward. An outline of the possible forces involved in the forming of prices in Athens brings the paper to a close.

V

In the world of pure theory, forces of demand and supply interact to establish the price for a commodity at the level that will just clear the market. Whether that is by itself an adequate account of price-formation in the modern,

---

33), 'City production is for the market, for completely unknown consumers who will never enter the producer's actual field of vision.'

52 He also has the nerve to ask a person who has bought something cheaply to give him a share (6). In the passage quoted in the text, the element of shamelessness seems to lie in reminding the *kapelos* of non-existent favours. This could explain the duty placed on the *agoranomoi* of suppressing deceit on the part of both sellers *and* buyers (though Stephen Todd reminds me that buyers' deceit might include the passing of bad coin).

capitalist economy is open to doubt; as an explanation of price in ancient Athens it is demonstrably false. There is, to be sure, abundant evidence in our texts for price fluctuations, and fixed or administered prices were the exception.[53] And yet, it seems likely that prices in Athens were determined by a complex of factors, with longer-term shifts compounded by fluctuations from day to day and even from customer to customer. To calculate in quantitative terms the degree to which the various forces offset each other in the process of price fixing is beyond the capabilities of the ancient evidence; but it may be possible to isolate the factors involved and locate them in their appropriate social context.

Description of prices by our sources as being relatively high or low implies some standard of comparison: a norm (however notional) from which actual prices were thought to deviate.[54] The implied comparison seems to be conceived in terms of an underlying or customary price. That distinction between customary and actual price is clearest in the case of grain (*sitos*). Grain is in many ways exceptional among the commodities on sale in Athens. Indicators include extensive state intervention to secure adequate supplies of imports (Garnsey 1988: 137–42), special arrangements for unloading and storage of grain as distinct from other cargoes (Stanley 1976: 153–5), large numbers of officials concerned with grain distribution (Gauthier 1981), and the existence of partial price controls, regulating retailers' profits (Seager 1966; Figueira 1986). The reason for all this is beyond any doubt Athenian dependence on large-scale importation and day-to-day distribution of grain supplies (Garnsey 1988: 90–109). This overwhelming importance of grain is reflected in its sensitivity of price to changes in supply. As the demand for grain was barely elastic, so any shortfall in supply (real or imagined) would result in a disproportionately steep increase in price. That is the background to the numerous comments about the price of grain surviving from fourth-century sources; far more than for any other commodity. Speeches from the Demosthenic *corpus* mention grain increasing in price in the Peiraieus (L.6), grain being sold for three times its former price (XLIII.31), and the arrival of a shipment of grain causing the price to fall (LVI.9). When the 'Chatterer' (*adoloskhes*) of Theophrastos remarked inconsequentially on the cheapness of wheat in the *agora*, he was presumably stating what was obvious to everyone (III.3).[55]

---

53 The idea of administered prices may lie behind an otherwise obscure passage in Plato's *Laws* (920b–c). From Athens, there is the restriction on the profits of those retailing grain (Lys. XXII.5, 8), a limit on the price of hiring flute-girls (Hyp. *Euxen.* 3), and a bare hint of controlling the price of silphium (Ar. *Knights* 893–5). There is nothing here to support the statement by Harrison (1971: 25; cf. Szegedy-Maszak 1981: 56) that the *agoranomoi* administered a section of the market law (*nomos agoranomikos*) fixing certain prices. The testimony of Aeneas Tacticus (X.12) suggests that price controls were seen as extraordinary measures, appropriate to cities under siege.

54 The terminology of price (*timē*) would possibly repay further study, recalling in its ambiguity (*axios* can mean either 'cheap' or 'expensive') the vocabulary of sale (n.32 above).

55 Although the basic relationship between demand, supply and price was understood (e.g. Dem. X.49; Xen. *Poroi* IV.36), its wider ramifications may have been only imperfectly appreciated. In the 330s Kleomenes, Alexander's governor of Egypt, organised an information

Even with the sale of grain, where prices were undeniably sensitive to shifts in demand and supply, there was still the concept of a customary price. In a speech attributed to Demosthenes (XXXIV.39), the litigant tries to curry favour with the jurors by reminding them how, 'When grain earlier increased in price and reached sixteen drachmae, we imported more than 10,000 *medimnoi* of wheat, and measured it out to you at the normal price (*tes kathestekuias times*) of five drachmae a *medimnos*.' The figure of five drachmae as an appropriate price for a *medimnos* of wheat appears in at least two inscriptions from the same period, honouring merchants selling subsidised grain in time of shortage.[56]

Grain was probably exceptional in the extent to which customary and actual prices tended to diverge; with other, less essential items, the discrepancy might be negligible. But there was also an intermediate range of commodities (almost exclusively foodstuffs) for which demand was relatively inelastic and supply less than certain. There was nothing necessarily predictable about the produce brought to market by peasants from the surrounding countryside (Osborne 1987a: 93–112), or by fishermen dependent on the daily catch (Gallant 1985). Under these circumstances, prices for particular commodities could vary from day to day, oscillating around what was regarded as the customary price. That is presumably why Theophrastos' 'Rustic', as he approaches the city, interrogates passers-by about the price of hides and salt-fish (IV.15). It may also be the explanation behind Plato's concession that prices charged in his near-ideal market may be changed from one day to the next – a response to the realities of supply (*Laws* 917b–c). But that is in the context of a law that effectively forbids haggling in the market and also prohibits the *kapeloi* from 'praising up (*epainos*)' their wares and taking oaths as to their quality. All this is fully in line with Plato's poor opinion of *kapeloi*, but in sharp contrast with the practices prevailing in the Athenian *agora*.[57] The implication, that the process of haggling will degenerate into a deceitful and unpleasant confrontation, anticipates Polanyi (1957c: 255), who sees antagonism as the inevitable consequence of 'higgling-haggling'. And yet, it is paradoxically the process of bargaining between buyer and seller that enables personal relationships to intrude into the otherwise impersonal operation of

service, dispatching grain ships to where prices were reported to be high. But this apparently legitimate response to market forces was roundly denounced in an Athenian court as a conspiracy against Athens and the other Greek states (Dem. LVI.7–8, with Garnsey 1988: 152).

[56] *IG* II² 360, 1–10; *IG* II² 408, 14; for the context, see Garnsey 1988: 156–62. Opposed to the *kathestekuia timē* was the *huparkhousē timē* which, in the Demosthenic speech *Against Lakritos* (XXXV.12), plainly refers to the sale of grain at the current or actual price. But my interpretation of the *kathestekuia timē* as the customary price is not unassailable (Humphreys 1969: 280 n.86; cf. Dem. LVI.8), and the whole subject needs more detailed study. For a hint of the idea of a customary price for barley ('mostly – *malista* – four drachmae per measure'), see the quotation from Strattis, a comic poet of the late fifth century, preserved by Pollux (IV.168).

[57] Bargaining scenes are a common comic motif: Ar. *Frogs* 167–79, *Peace* 1197–264, *Acharnians* 863–928 (see further n.59 below). Plato's banning of oaths calls to mind the taunt of the Persian King as reported by Herodotus (section II above).

sale. Reminding the seller of one's status as a privileged customer, like the 'Shameless Man' at the butcher's, opens the way to a range of possible benefits. The buyer who is well known to the seller may get his goods at a bargain price, or more for the same price, or goods of a better quality or a combination of all these advantages. So haggling appears as a third factor affecting overall price: a 'personal price' to be set against considerations of customary and actual prices.[58]

Comparative studies confirm the positive potential of haggling, provided both sides behave according to established rules of etiquette (Uchendo 1967). Far from the opposing positions of buyer and seller representing real antagonism, the confrontation has about it an air of posturing or play-acting. Adding to the impression of 'sale as theatre' is the presence of an audience in the shape of bystanders and prospective customers. All this etiquette of haggling can be read into surviving accounts of behaviour in the Greek *agora*. Athenaeus (vi.228e) notes the existence of a book called *The Art of Provisioning* by the late-fourth-century figure Douris of Samos. Written for one of his friends who was inexperienced at buying, its advice included coping with a fishmonger who refused to lower his prices, by running down his wares in a loud voice. 'For', says Douris (Athen. vii.313f–14a), 'you will scare away many customers and bystanders, and by doing that force him to accept the price that seems right to you.' Awkwardness or animosity occurred only when one or other of the parties broke the unwritten rules. Such is the fault of Theophrastos' 'Unco-operative Man' (*authades*) who, when he has something to sell, won't name a price, but leaves his buyers guessing (xv.5).[59]

The theme of this paper has been the integration of different types of exchange in the Athenian economy. Implicit in that process has been the search for a further form of integration: finding an appropriate context within which to assess the laws relating to sale. Much remains to be done, but I have tried to suggest how, in the absence of a juristic framework, the law and custom of sale (*nomos* in both senses) may be combined, and then viewed in relation to the economy and society in which they were embedded.

[58] Conditions of sale in the marketplace gave plenty of scope for bargaining about the quality of goods on sale. Not for nothing was a taste of the wine on offer regarded as a necessary preliminary to the purchase (Eur. *Cyclops* 150). Comedy has plenty of the tricks (legal and otherwise) practised by market traders: dressing up meat in the way a whore tarts herself up (Athen. xiii.568d); placing sound figs on the top of the basket, masking the bad ones underneath (Athen. ii.76d); taking payment in the heavier coins of one state and giving as change the lighter coinage of another (Athen. vi.225b).

[59] And also the fault of a fishmonger condemned in a fragment of fourth-century comedy (Amphis in Athen. vi.224d–e). He refuses to engage with his customers, at first ignoring their enquiries as to price, and then giving out his answers in a dismissive way. For further examples of banter between bargainers, see Athenaeus iii.84b, vi.224c, vii.309d, xiii.580c.

References

ADCOCK, F. E. (1923) rev. of Vinogradoff 1922, *Cambridge Law Journal* 1: 388–91

ADKINS, A. W. H. (1960) *Merit and Responsibility: A Study in Greek Values.* Oxford (repr. Chicago 1975)

(1972) *Moral Values and Political Behaviour in Ancient Greece from Homer to the End of the Fifth Century.* London

(1976) '*Polupragmosunē* and "minding one's own business": a study in Greek social and political values', *CPh* 71: 301–27

(1978) 'Problems in Greek popular morality', *CPh* 73: 143–58 (review-article of Dover 1974)

ALTORKI, S. (1986) *Women in Saudi Arabia.* New York

AMPOLO, C. (1984a) 'Il lusso funerario e la città arcaica', *AION* 6: 71–102

(1984b), 'Il lusso nelle società arcaiche', *OPVS* 3: 469–76

ANDREADES, A. (1933) *A History of Greek Public Finance* (trans. Brown, C. N.). Cambridge, MA (repr. New York 1979)

ANTOUN, R. (1968) 'On the modesty of women in Arab villages', *American Anthropologist* 70: 671–97

ATIYAH, P. S. (1980) *The Sale of Goods.* Oxford

AUBERT, V. (1969), ed., *Sociology of Law: Selected Readings.* Harmondsworth

AUSTIN, M. M. and VIDAL-NAQUET, P. (1977) *Economic and Social History of Ancient Greece: An Introduction.* London (corr. and augmented trans. of 2nd French edn, Paris 1972)

BADIAN, E. (1987) 'The Peace of Callias', *JHS* 107: 1–39

BAITER, J.G. and SAUPPE, H. (1839–50), eds., *Oratores Attici.* 2 vols. Zürich

BALDWIN, J. and BOTTOMLEY, A. K. (1978), eds., *Criminal Justice: Selected Readings.* London

BARKAN, I. (1936) 'Imprisonment as a penalty in ancient Athens', *CPh* 31: 338–41

BATEMAN, J. J. (1966) rev. of Lavency 1964, *Gnomon* 38: 800–4

BEAUCHET, L. (1897) *Histoire du droit privé de la république athénienne.* 4 vols. Paris (repr. Amsterdam 1969)

BECKER, W. A. (1866) *Charicles, or Illustrations of the Private Life of the Ancient Greeks* (trans. Metcalfe, F.). London (German original, Leipzig 1840)

196   *References*

BEHREND, D. (1975) 'Die ἀνάδιϰος δίϰη und das Scholion zu Plato *Nomoi* 937d', in Wolff 1975a: 131–56

BELSHAW, C. (1965) *Traditional Exchange and Modern Markets*. Englewood Cliffs, NJ

BERNEKER, E. (1968), ed., *Zur griechischen Rechtsgeschichte*. Darmstadt

BERS, V. (1985) 'Dikastic *thorubos*', in Cartledge & Harvey 1985: 1–15

BETTALLI, M. (1985) 'Case, botteghe, *ergasteria*: note sui luoghi di produzione e di vendita nell' Atene classica', *OPVS* 4: 29–42

BISCARDI, A. (1979), ed., *Symposion 1974: Vorträge zur griechischen und hellenistischen Rechtsgeschichte*. Cologne & Vienna
    (1982) *Diritto greco antico*. Milan

BLASS, F. (1887–98) *Attische Beredsamkeit*. 2 vols. 2nd edn. Leipzig (repr. 1962)

BOECKER, H. J. (1980) *Law and the Administration of Law in the Ancient Near East and the Old Testament*. London (German original, Neukirchen 1976)

BOGAERT, R. (1968) *Banques et banquiers dans les cités grecques*. Leiden

BOHANNAN, P. (1957) *Justice and Judgement among the Tiv*. Oxford

BOHANNAN, P. and DALTON, G. (1962), eds., *Markets in Africa*. Evanston, IL

BOISACQ, E. (1950) *Dictionnaire étymologique de la langue grecque*. 4th edn. Heidelberg

BOLKESTEIN, H. (1958) *Economic Life in Greece's Golden Age* (trans. Jonkers, E. J.). Leiden (Dutch original, Haarlem 1923)

BONAMENTE, M. (1980) 'Leggi suntuarie e loro motivazioni', in *Tra Grecia e Roma. Temi antichi e metodologie moderne*, 251–60. Rome

BONNER, R. J. (1905) *Evidence in Athenian Courts*. Chicago
    (1906) 'Did women testify in homicide cases at Athens?', *CPh* 1: 127–32
    (1912) 'Evidence in the Areopagus', *CPh* 7: 450–6
    (1927) *Lawyers and Litigants in Ancient Athens. The Genesis of the Legal Profession*. Chicago (repr. New York 1969)

BONNER, R. J. and SMITH, G. (1930–8) *The Administration of Justice from Homer to Aristotle*. 2 vols. Chicago (repr. New York 1970)

BOSSY, J. (1983), ed., *Disputes and Settlements: Law and Human Relations in the West*. Cambridge

BOURDIEU, P. (1977) *Outline of a Theory of Practice*. Cambridge

BOURRIOT, F. (1976) *Recherches sur la nature du génos: étude d'histoire sociale athénienne*. Diss. Lille

BRAND, G. (1979) *The Central Texts of Wittgenstein*. Oxford

BREMEN, R. VAN (1983) 'Women and wealth', in Cameron & Kuhrt 1983: 223–42

BROWN, P. (1975) 'Society and the supernatural: a mediaeval change', *Daedalus* 104: 33–51 (repr. in Brown, *Society and the Holy in Late Antiquity*, London 1982, 302–32)

BURROW, J. W. (1966) *Evolution and Society: A Study in Victorian Social Theory*. Cambridge

BURY, J. B. and MEIGGS, R. (1975) *History of Greece*. 4th edn. London

BUXTON, R. G. A. (1982) *Persuasion in Greek Tragedy. A Study of Peitho*. Cambridge

CAILLEMER, E. (1865–72) *Études sur les antiquités juridiques d'Athènes* (ten pamphlets, separately published). Paris (repr. in 1 vol., New York 1979)
    (1870–1) 'Le contrat de vente à Athènes', *Revue de législation*: 631–71

(1873) 'Le contrat de vente à Athènes', *Revue de législation*: 5–41

(1879) *Le Droit de succession légitime à Athènes*. Paris

CALHOUN, G. M. (1913) *Athenian Clubs in Politics and Litigation*. Austin (repr. Rome 1964)

(1919) 'Oral and written pleading in Athenian courts', *TAPA* 50: 177–93

(1926) *The Business Life of Ancient Athens*. Chicago (repr. New York 1968)

(1927) *The Growth of the Criminal Law in Ancient Greece*. Berkeley & Los Angeles

(1944) *Introduction to Greek Legal Science*, ed. F. de Zulueta. Oxford

CALHOUN, G. M. and DELAMERE, C. (1927) *A Working Bibliography of Greek Law*. Cambridge, MA (repr. Amsterdam 1968)

CAMERON, A. and KUHRT, A. (1983), eds., *Images of Women in Antiquity*. London

CAMP, J. M. (1986) *The Athenian Agora. Excavations in the Heart of Classical Athens*. London & New York

CAMPBELL, J. K. (1964) *Honour, Family and Patronage. A Study of Institutions and Moral Values in a Greek Mountain Community*. Oxford (repr. New York 1974)

CANTARELLA, E. (1983) 'Spunti di riflessione critica su *hybris* e *timē* in Omero', in Dimakis 1983: 85–96

(1987) *Pandora's Daughters*. Baltimore

CARAWAN, E. M. (1984) '*Akriton apokteinai*: execution without trial in fourth-century Athens', *GRBS* 25: 111–21

CAREY, C. (1988) 'A note on torture in Athenian homicide cases', *Historia* 37: 241–5

CAREY, C. and REID, R. A. (1985), eds., *Demosthenes. Selected Private Speeches*. Cambridge

CARTER, L. B. (1986) *The Quiet Athenian*. Oxford

CARTLEDGE, P. A. (1986) rev. of MacDowell 1986, *LCM* 11: 142–4

(1987) *Agesilaos and the Crisis of Sparta*. London & Baltimore

(1988) rev. of Garner 1987 and Strauss 1986, *Hermathena* 144: 105–10

CARTLEDGE, P. A. and HARVEY, F. D. (1985), eds., *CRUX. Essays in Greek History Presented to G. E. M. de Ste. Croix on his 75th Birthday*. Exeter & London

CAWKWELL, G. L. (1963) 'Eubulus', *JHS* 83: 47–67

CHANTRAINE, P. (1940) 'Conjugaison et histoire des verbes signifiant vendre', *RPh* 14: 11–24

(1968) *Dictionnaire étymologique de la langue grecque*. 2 vols. Paris

CHEAL, D. (1988) *The Gift Economy*. London & New York

CHELHOD, J. (1971) *Le Droit dans la société bédouine*. Paris

CHRISTIE, G. C. (1982) *Law, Norms and Authority*. London

CLARK, M. (1983) 'Variations on themes of male and female: reflections on gender bias in fieldwork in rural Greece', *Women's Studies* 102: 117–33

CLEMENTE, G. (1981) 'Le leggi sul lusso e la società romana tra III e II secolo A.C.', in Giardina, A. and Schiavone, A., eds., *Società romana e produzione schiavistica*, 1–14. Rome

COCKS, R. S. J. (1988) *Sir Henry Maine: A Study in Victorian Jurisprudence*. Cambridge

COHEN, D. (1982) 'Theft in Plato's *Laws* and Athenian legal practice', *RIDA* 29: 121–43 (incorporated, in revised form, in Cohen 1983)
    (1983) *Theft in Athenian Law* (Münchener Beiträge zur Papyrusforschung und Antiken Rechtsgeschichte 74). Munich
    (1984) 'The Athenian law of adultery', *RIDA* 31: 147–65
    (1987) 'Law, society and homosexuality in Classical Athens', *Past & Present* 117: 3–21
COHEN, E. E. (1973) *Ancient Athenian Maritime Courts*. Princeton
COLE, S. G. (1984) 'Greek sanctions against sexual assault', *CPh* 79: 97–113
CONNOR, W. R. (1971) *The New Politicians of Fifth-Century Athens*. Princeton
COPE, E. M. (1877), ed., *Aristotle's Rhetoric with a Commentary by E. M. Cope*, ed. J. E. Sandys. 3 vols. Cambridge
CORNISH, W. R. (1968) *The Jury*. London
COZZOLI, U. (1980) 'La tryphè nella interpretazione delle crisi politiche', in *Tra Grecia e Roma. Temi antichi e metodologie moderne*, 133–45. Rome
CRAWFORD, M. H. (1982) *La moneta in Grecia e a Roma*. Rome
CRAWLEY, L. W. A. (1970) 'Graphe sykophantias', in Harris, B. F., ed., *Auckland Classical Essays presented to E. M. Blaiklock*, 77–94. Auckland & Oxford
CROSS, R., WILKINS, N. and TAPPER, C. F. H. (1986) *Outline of the Law of Evidence*. 6th edn. London
CUTILEIRO, J. (1971) *A Portuguese Rural Society*. Oxford
DAREMBERG, C. V. and SAGLIO, E. (1875–1919), eds., *Dictionnaire des antiquités grecques et romaines d'après les textes et les monuments*. 9 vols in 5. Paris
DARESTE, R. (1893) *La Science du droit en Grèce. Platon, Aristote, Théophraste*. Paris (repr. New York 1976)
DAVIES, J. K. (1971) *Athenian Propertied Families 600–300 B.C.* Oxford
    (1981) *Wealth and the Power of Wealth in Classical Athens*. New York
DAVIES, W. and FOURACRE, P. (1986), eds., *The Settlement of Disputes in Early Medieval Europe*. Cambridge
DAVIS, J. (1971) *Land and Family in Pisticci*. New York
    (1972) 'Gifts and the UK economy', *Man* 7: 408–29
    (1977) *People of the Mediterranean*. London
DAVIS, N. Z. (1983) *The Return of Martin Guerre*. Cambridge, MA (repr. Harmondsworth 1985)
DAVIS, W. G. (1973) *Social Relations in a Philippine Market: Self-Interest and Subjectivity*. Berkeley
DEMEYERE, J. (1952) 'La formation de la vente et le transfert de la propriété en droit grec classique', *AHDO-RIDA* 1: 215–66
    (1953) 'La formation de la vente en droit grec classique: les obligations des parties', *AHDO-RIDA* 2: 197–228
DERRETT, J. D. M. (1968), ed., *An Introduction to Legal Systems*. London
de STE. CROIX, G. E. M.: see STE. CROIX, G. E. M. de
de VESSILITSKY, V. and BULKLEY, M. E. (1916) 'Money-lending among the London poor', *The Sociological Review* 9: 129–38
DEVLIN, LORD (1979) *The Judge*. London
DEVONS, E. (1978) 'Serving as a juryman in Britain', in Baldwin & Bottomley 1978: 154–63
DEWEY, A. G. (1962) *Peasant Marketing in Java*. New York

References 199

DIAMOND, A. S. (1971) *Primitive Law Past and Present*. London
(1974) *In Search of the Primitive: A Critique of Civilization*. New Brunswick
DIMAKIS, P. (1983), ed., *Symposion 1979: Vorträge zur griechischen und hellenistischen Rechtsgeschichte*. Cologne & Vienna
DOVER, K. J. (1950) 'The chronology of Antiphon's speeches', *CQ* 44: 44–60 (repr. with additional note, in Dover 1989: 13–35)
(1968a), ed., *Aristophanes, Clouds*. Oxford
(1968b) *Lysias and the Corpus Lysiacum*. Berkeley, Los Angeles & London
(1972) *Aristophanic Comedy*. Berkeley, Los Angeles & London
(1973) 'Classical Greek attitudes to sexual behaviour', *Arethusa* 6: 59–73 (repr. in English in Siems, A. K., ed., *Sexualität und Erotik in der Antike*, Darmstadt 1988, 264–81)
(1974) *Greek Popular Morality in the Time of Plato and Aristotle*. Oxford
(1978) *Greek Homosexuality*. London & Ithaca
(1986) 'Ion of Chios: his place in the history of Greek literature', in Boardman, J. and Vaphopoulou-Richardson, C. E., eds., *Chios: a Conference at the Homereion in Chios 1984*, 27–37. Oxford (repr., with additional notes, in Dover 1989: 1–12)
(1989) *The Greeks and their Legacy. Collected Papers Volume II: Prose Literature, History, Society, Transmission, Influence*. Oxford
DRIVER, G. R. and MILES, SIR JOHN (1952–5), eds., *The Assyrian Laws*. 2 vols. Oxford
DUBISCH, J. (1986), ed., *Gender and Power in Rural Greece*. Princeton
DU BOULAY, J. (1974) *Portrait of a Greek Mountain Village*. Oxford & New York
DU CANN, R. (1964) *The Art of the Advocate*. Harmondsworth
DUE, B. (1980) *Antiphon. A Study in Argumentation (Opuscula Graecolatina 17)*. Copenhagen
EDMONDS, J. M. and AUSTEN, G. E. V. (1904), eds., *The Characters of Theophrastus*. London
EDWARDS, M. and USHER, S. (1985), eds., *Greek Orators I*. Warminster
EHRENBERG, V. (1951) *The People of Aristophanes. A Sociology of Old Attic Comedy*. 2nd edn. Oxford (repr., slightly augmented, New York 1962)
(1973) *From Solon to Socrates. Greek History and Civilization during the Sixth and Fifth Centuries B.C.* 2nd edn. London
ELSTER, J. (1985) *Making Sense of Marx*. Cambridge
ENGLAND, E. B. (1921), ed., *The Laws of Plato*. 2 vols. Manchester
ERBSE, H. (1956) 'Über die Midiana des Demosthenes', *Hermes* 84: 135–51
FEAVER, G. (1969) *From Status to Contract: A Biography of Sir Henry Maine, 1822–88*. London
FERNEA, E. (1969) *Guests of the Sheik*. New York
FIGUEIRA, T. J. (1986) '*Sitopolai* and *sitophylakes* in Lysias' "Against the Graindealers": governmental intervention in the Athenian economy', *Phoenix* 40: 149–71
FINE, J. V. A. (1951) *Horoi: Studies in Mortgage, Real Security and Land Tenure (Hesperia* Supp. 9). Princeton
FINLEY (FINKELSTEIN), M. I. (1935) '*Emporos, naukleros* and *kapelos*: prolegomena to the study of Athenian trade', *CPh* 30: 320–36

FINLEY, M. I. (1951) 'Some problems of Greek law' (review-article of Pringsheim 1950), *Seminar* 9: 72–91 (repr. in part in Finley 1986: 147–52)

(1952) *Studies in Land and Credit in Ancient Athens*. New Brunswick (repr., with Millett 1982 as new introduction, 1985)

(1953) 'Land, debt and the man of property in classical Athens', *Political Science Quarterly* 68: 249–68 (repr. in Finley 1981: 62–76)

(1955) 'Marriage, sale and gift in the Homeric world', *RIDA* 2: 167–94 (repr. in Finley 1981: 233–45)

(1957) 'Mycenaean palace archives and economic history', *Economic History Review* 10: 128–41 (repr. in Finley 1981: 199–212)

(1962) 'Athenian demagogues', *Past & Present* 21: 3–24 (repr., in somewhat revised form, in Finley 1974: 1–25 and Finley *Democracy Ancient and Modern*, 2nd edn, London 1985, 38–75)

(1970) 'Aristotle and economic analysis', *Past & Present* 47: 3–25 (repr. in Finley 1974: 26–52)

(1973) *The Ancient Economy*. London & Calif. (2nd edn, 1985)

(1974), ed., *Studies in Ancient Society*. London & Boston

(1975) 'Anthropology and the Classics', in *The Use and Abuse of History*, 102–19. London (repr. in Finley 1986)

(1976) 'The freedom of the citizen in the Greek world', *Talanta* 7: 1–23 (repr. in Finley 1981: 77–94)

(1978) *The World of Odysseus*. 2nd edn. London & New York

(1979), ed., *The Bücher-Meyer Controversy*. New York

(1980) *Ancient Slavery and Modern Ideology*. London (repr. Harmondsworth 1983)

(1981) *Economy and Society in Ancient Greece*, ed. Shaw, B. D. and Saller, R. P. London (repr. Harmondsworth 1983)

(1985) *Ancient History. Evidence and Models*. London

(1986) *The Use and Abuse of History*. 2nd edn. London

FISHER, N. R. E. (1976a) '*Hybris* and dishonour I', *G&R* 23: 177–93

(1976b), ed., *Social Values in Classical Athens*. London & Toronto

(1979) '*Hybris* and dishonour II', *G&R* 26: 32–47

(1988) 'Greek associations, *symposia* and clubs', in Grant & Kitzinger 1988, II: 1167–97. New York

(forthcoming) *Hybris*. Warminster

FLACELIÈRE, R. (1965) *Daily Life in Ancient Greece*. London

FREEMAN, K. (1946) *The Murder of Herodes and other Trials from the Athenian Law Courts*. London

FREEMAN, S. (1970) *Neighbors*. Chicago

FRENCH, A. (1964) *The Growth of the Athenian Economy*. London

FRIEDRICH, C. J. (1934) 'Separation of powers', in *ESS* XIII: 663–7

FRIER, B. W. (1985) *The Rise of the Roman Jurists: studies in Cicero's pro Caecina*. Princeton

FRISK, H. (1960–72) *Griechisches etymologisches Wörterbuch*. Heidelberg

FROST, F. J. (1987), ed., *Greek Society*. 3rd edn. Lexington, MA

FUKS, A. (1951) '*Kolonos misthios*: labour exchange in classical Athens', *Eranos* 49: 171–3 (photostatically repr. in Fuks, *Social Conflict in Ancient Greece* [1984] 303–5. Jerusalem & Leiden)

FULLER, A. (1961) *Portrait of a Lebanese Muslim Village*. Cambridge, MA

FURKIOTIS, C. (1956) 'Aus dem attischen Recht: die ΔΙΚΗ ΑΝΑΓΩΓΗΣ', in Paoli 1956: 323–31

FUSTEL DE COULANGES, N. D. (1864) *La cité antique*. Paris (Small, W., trans., *The Ancient City: A Study on the Religion, Laws and Institutions of Greece and Rome*, 1873, repr., with a new foreword [= Momigliano & Humphreys 1983], Baltimore & London 1980)

GABBA, E. (1983), ed., *Tria Corda. Scritti in onore di Arnaldo Momigliano*. Como

GABRIELSEN, V. (1987) 'The *Antidosis* procedure in classical Athens', *C&M* 38: 7–38

GAGARIN, M. (1973) '*Dikē* in the *Works and Days*', *CPh* 68: 81–94
(1979) 'The Athenian Law against *Hybris*', in Bowersock, G. W., Burkert, W., and Putnam, M. C. J., eds., *Arktouros: Hellenic Studies presented to Bernard Knox*, 229–36. Berlin & New York
(1986) *Early Greek Law*. Berkeley & Los Angeles

GALLANT, T. W. (1985) *A Fisherman's Tale: An Analysis of the Potential Productivity of Fishing in the Ancient World* (Miscellanea Graeca 7). Gent

GARLAN, Y. (1973) 'L'Oeuvre de Polanyi: la place de l'économie dans les sociétés anciennes', *La Pensée* 171: 118–27

GARNER, R. (1987) *Law and Society in Classical Athens*. London & Sydney

GARNSEY, P. D. A. (1988) *Famine and Food Supply in the Graeco-Roman World: Responses to Risk and Crisis*. Cambridge

GAUTHIER, Ph. (1981) 'De Lysias à Aristote (*Ath. Pol.* 51.4): le commerce de grain à Athènes et les fonctions des sitophylaques', *RDFE* 59: 5–28

GERNET, L. (1917a) *Platon, Lois IX, Traduction et Commentaire*. Diss. Paris
(1917b) *Recherches sur le développement de la pensée juridique et morale en Grèce*. Paris
(1923), ed., *Antiphon* (Budé edn). Paris
(1927) 'La diamartyrie, procédure archaïque du droit athénien', *RHD* 6: 5–37 (repr. in Gernet 1955: 83–102)
(1933) 'Comment caractériser l'économie de la Grèce antique?', *Annales d'histoire économique et sociale* 2: 561–6 (repr. in Gernet 1983: 193–200)
(1937) 'Sur la notion du jugement en droit grec', *AHDO* 1: 111–44 (repr. in Gernet 1955: 61–81)
(1938a) 'Introduction à l'étude du droit grec ancien', *AHDO* 2: 261–92
(1938b) 'Sur les actions commerciales en droit athénien', *REG* 51: 1–44 (repr. in Gernet 1955: 173–200)
(1939) 'L'institution des arbitres publics à Athènes', *REG* 52: 389–414 (repr. in Gernet 1955: 103–19)
(1948) 'La notion mythique de la valeur en Grèce', *Journal de Psychologie* 41: 415–63 (trans. as, and cited from, '"Value" in Greek myth', in Gordon, R. L., ed., *Myth, Religion and Society: Structuralist Essays*, Cambridge & Paris 1981, 111–46)
(1948–9) 'Droit et prédroit en Grèce ancienne', *L'Année sociologique*, ser. 3: 21–119 (trans. as, and cited from, Gernet 1981: 143–215)
(1950) 'Aspects du droit athénien de l'esclavage', *AHDO* 5: 159–87 (repr. in Gernet 1955: 151–72)

(1951) 'Le droit de la vente et la notion du contrat en Grèce d'après M.
    Pringsheim', *RDFE* 29: 560–84 (repr. in Gernet 1955: 200–24)
(1953) 'Sur l'obligation contractuelle dans la vente hellénique', *RIDA* 2: 229–47
    (repr. in Gernet 1955: 225–36)
(1955) *Droit et société dans la Grèce ancienne*. Paris (repr., with bibliographical
    notes by Imbert, J. and Modrzejewski, J., 1964)
(1956) 'Le temps dans les formes archaïques du droit', *Journal de Psychologie
    normale et pathologique* 53: 379–406 (trans. as, and cited from, 'The concept
    of time in the earliest forms of law', in Gernet 1981: 216–39)
(1959a), ed., *Démosthène: Plaidoyers civils* (Budé edn). Vol. 3 (of 4). Paris
(1959b) 'Note sur la notion de délit privé en droit grec', in *Mélanges Lévy-Bruhl
    (Droits de l'antiquité et sociologie juridique)* = Publications de l'Institut de
    droit Romain de l'Université de Paris, XVII, 393–405. Paris
(1981) *The Anthropology of Ancient Greece*, trans. Hamilton, J. and Nagy, B.
    Baltimore & London (French original, Paris 1968)
(1983) *Les Grecs sans miracle*, ed. R. Di Donato. Paris
GERNET, L. and BIZOS, M. (1955–9), eds., *Lysias: Discours* (Budé edn). 2 vols.
    Paris
GERST, K. (1963) *Die allgemeine Anklagebefugnis in der attischen Demokratie*.
    Diss. Erlangen/Nürnberg
GIDDENS, A. (1984) *The Constitution of Society*. Berkeley
GLEDHILL, J. and LARSEN, M. (1982) 'The Polanyi paradigm and a dynamic
    analysis of archaic states', in Renfrew, C., Rowlands, M. J. and Segraves,
    B. A., eds., *Theory and Explanation in Archaeology*, 197–229. New York &
    London
GLOTZ, G. (1904) *La Solidarité de la famille dans le droit criminel en Grèce*. Paris
    (repr. New York 1973)
(1906) *Études sociales et juridiques sur l'antiquité grecque*. Paris
(1926) *Ancient Greece at Work* (trans. Dobie, M. R.). London (French original,
    Paris 1920)
(1928) *La Cité grecque*. Paris (repr., with supplementary bibliography, Paris
    1968)
GLUCKMAN, M. (1955) *The Judicial Process among the Barotse of Northern
    Rhodesia*. Manchester
GOFAS, D. C. (1982) 'La vente sur échantillon à Athènes d'après un texte
    d'Hypéride', in Modrzejewski & Liebs 1982: 121–9
GOFFMAN, E. (1963) *Behavior in Public Places*. Glencoe, IL
(1971) *Relations in Public*. New York
GOLDHILL, S. D. (1986) *Reading Greek Tragedy*. Cambridge
GOMME, A. W., ANDREWES, A. and DOVER, K. J. (1945, 1956, 1956, 1970, 1981),
    eds., *A Historical Commentary on Thucydides*. 5 vols. (I–III by Gomme
    alone). Oxford
GOODY, J. (1976) *Production and Consumption. A Comparative Study of the
    Domestic Domain*. Cambridge
GOODY, J. and WATT, I. (1968) 'The consequences of literacy', in Goody, J., ed.,
    Literacy in Traditional Societies, 27–68. Cambridge
GOULD, J. (1980) 'Law, custom and myth: aspects of the social position of women
    in classical Athens', *JHS* 100: 38–59

GRANT, M. and KITZINGER, R. (1988), eds., *Civilisation of the Ancient Mediterranean*. 3 vols. New York

GRAS, N. S. B. (1930) 'Stages in economic history', *Journal of Economic & Business History* 2: 395–418

GREER, D. S. (1978), 'Anything but the truth', in Baldwin & Bottomley 1978: 164–81

GREGOR, T. (1985) *Anxious Pleasures*. Chicago

GREGORY, C. A. (1982) *Gifts and Commodities*. London & New York

GROTE, G. (1846–56) *History of Greece*. 8 vols (repr. in 12 vols., 1862). London

HAMNETT, I. (1977), ed., *Social Anthropology and the Law*. London

HANDMAN, M. (1983) *La Violence et la ruse: hommes et femmes dans un village grec*. Aix-en-Provence

HANSEN, M. H. (1974) *The Sovereignty of the People's Court in Athens in the Fourth Century B.C., and The Public Action against Unconstitutional Proposals*. Odense

(1975) *Eisangelia. The Sovereignty of the People's Court in Athens in the Fourth Century B.C. and the Impeachment of Generals and Politicians*. Odense

(1976) *Apagōgē, Endeixis and Ephegesis against Kakourgoi, Atimoi and Pheugontes: A Study in the Athenian Administration of Justice in the Fourth Century B.C.* Odense

(1981) 'Initiative and decision: the separation of powers in fourth-century Athens', *GRBS* 22: 345–70

(1983a) *The Athenian Ecclesia. A Collection of Articles 1976–1983*. Copenhagen

(1983b) 'The Athenian "politicians", 403–322 B.C.', *GRBS* 24: 33–55

(1983c) 'Political activity and the organization of Attica in the fourth century B.C.', *GRBS* 24: 227–38

(1983d) '*Rhetores* and *Strategoi* in fourth-century Athens', *GRBS* 24: 151–80

(1986) 'The origin of the term *demokratia*', *LCM* 11: 35–6

(1987) *The Athenian Assembly in the Age of Demosthenes*. Oxford

HARE, R. M. (1952) *The Language of Morals*. Oxford

HARRIS, E. M. (1988) 'When is a sale not a sale? The riddle of Athenian terminology for real security revisited', *CQ* 38: 351–8

HARRISON, A. R. W. (1957) 'Aristotle's *Nicomachean Ethics*, Book V, and the law of Athens', *JHS* 77: 42–7

(1968–71) *The Law of Athens*. 2 vols. [I.] *The Family and Property*. [II.] *Procedure*, ed. D. M. MacDowell. Oxford

HART, H. L. A. (1961) *The Concept of Law*. Oxford

HARVEY, F. D. (1966) 'Literacy in the Athenian democracy', *REG* 79: 585–635

(1985) '*Dona ferentes*: some aspects of bribery in Greek politics', in Cartledge & Harvey 1985: 76–117

HASLUCK, M. (1954) *The Unwritten Law in Albania*. Cambridge

HAVELOCK, E. A. (1978) *The Greek Concept of Justice: from its Shadow in Homer to its Substance in Plato*. Cambridge, MA

HAZARD, J. N. (1970) *Communists and their Law*. Chicago

HEADLAM, J. W. (1891) *Election by Lot at Athens*. Cambridge (2nd edn., ed. MacGregor, D.C., 1933)

(1893) 'On the *proklesis eis basanon* in Attic law', *CR* 7: 1–5

(1894) 'Slave-torture in Athens', *CR* 8: 136–7

HEHN, V. (1911) *Kulturpflanzen und Hausthiere in ihrem Übergang aus Asien nach Griechenland und Italien sowie in das übrige Europa*. 8th edn. Berlin

HEICHELHEIM, F. M. (1930) *Wirtschaftliche Schwankungen der Zeit von Alexander bis Augustus*. Jena (repr. New York 1979)

(1958–70) *An Ancient Economic History from the Palaeolithic Age to the Migrations of the Germanic, Slavic and Arabic Nations* (trans. Stevens, J.). 3 vols. Leiden (German original 1938)

HEITSCH, E. (1984) *Antiphon aus Rhamnus*. Wiesbaden (Akad. Mainz)

HENDERSON, J. (1975) *The Maculate Muse*. New Haven

HERFST, P. (1922) *Le Travail de la femme dans la Grèce ancienne*. Paris

HERMAN, G. (1987) *Ritualised Friendship and the Greek City*. Cambridge

HERZFELD, M. (1980) 'Honour and shame: problems in the comparative analysis of moral systems', *Man* 15: 339–51

HIGGINS, W. E. (1977) *Xenophon the Athenian: The Problem of the Individual and the Society of the Polis*. Albany, NY

HIGNETT, C. (1952) *A History of the Athenian Constitution*. Oxford

HILL, G. F. (1951), ed., *Sources for Greek History between the Persian and Peloponnesian Wars*. 2nd edn. by Meiggs, R. and Andrewes, A. Oxford

HILL, P. (1986) *Development Economics on Trial: The Anthropological Case for a Prosecution*. Cambridge

HIRZEL, R. (1902) *Der Eid. Ein Beitrag zu seiner Geschichte*. Leipzig (repr. New York 1979)

HITZIG, H. (1907) *Iniuria*. Leipzig

HODGES, R. (1988) *Primitive and Peasant Markets*. Oxford

HOETINK, H. P. (1929) 'Quelques remarques sur la vente dans le droit grec', *Tijdschrift voor Rechtsgeschiedenis* 9: 253–70

HOFSTETTER, J. (1978) *Die Griechen in Persien: Prosopographie der Griechen im persischen Reich vor Alexander*. Berlin

HOLLADAY, A. J. (1986) 'The détente of Kallias?', *Historia* 35: 503–7

HONORÉ, T. (1981) 'The primacy of oral evidence', in Tapper, C. F. H., ed., *Crime, Proof and Punishment: Essays in Memory of Sir Rupert Cross*, 172–92. London

HOPKINS, K. (1983) *Death and Renewal* (Sociological Studies in Roman History 2). Cambridge

HOPPER, R. J. (1979) *Trade and Industry in Classical Greece*. London & New York

HORNBLOWER, S. (1983) *The Greek World 479–323 B.C.* London (corr. impr. 1985)

HORSLEY, G. R. H. (1982) 'Aristophanes' *Wasps*', in Horsley, ed., *Hellenika. Essays on Greek History and Politics*, 69–96. North Ryde, NSW

HUMPHREYS, S. C. (1969) 'History, economics, and anthropology: the work of Karl Polanyi', *H&T* 8: 165–212 (repr. in Humphreys 1978: 31–75)

(1970) 'Economy and society in classical Athens', *ASNP²* 39: 1–26 (repr. in Humphreys 1978: 136–58)

(1978) *Anthropology and the Greeks*. London & Boston

(1983a) 'The evolution of legal process in ancient Attica', in Gabba 1983: 229–56

(1983b) *The Family, Women and Death: Comparative Studies*. London & Boston

(1985a), ed., *The Discourse of Law = History and Anthropology* 1.2. London

(1985b) 'Law as discourse', in Humphreys 1985a: 241–64
(1985c) 'Social relations on stage: witnesses in classical Athens', in Humphreys 1985a: 313–69
(1986) 'Kinship patterns in the Athenian courts', *GRBS* 27: 57–91
HUNT, A. S. and EDGAR, C. G. (1932–4), eds., *Select Papyri*. 2 vols. London & Cambridge, MA
IMHOOF-BLUMER, F. and KELLER, O. (1889) *Tier- und Pflanzenbilder auf Münzen und Gemmen des klassischen Altertums*. Leipzig
ISAGER, S. and HANSEN, M. H. (1975) *Aspects of Athenian Society in the Fourth Century B.C.* Odense
JAMESON, M. H. (1971) 'Sophocles and the Four Hundred', *Historia* 20: 541–68
JOHNSON, C. (1984) 'Who is Aristotle's citizen?', *Phronesis* 29: 73–90
JONES, A. H. M. (1957) *Athenian Democracy*. Oxford
JONES, C. P. (1987) 'Stigma: tattooing and branding in Graeco-Roman antiquity', *JRS* 77: 139–55
JONES, J. W. (1956) *The Law and Legal Theory of the Greeks*. Oxford
JORDAN, D. P. (1985) 'A survey of Greek *defixiones* not included in the special corpora', *GRBS* 26: 151–98
KELLER, O. (1913) *Antike Tierwelt*. Vol. 2. Leipzig
KENNEDY, C. R. (1888, 1894), trans., *The Orations of Demosthenes*. Vols. 4 and 3. London
KENNEDY, G. (1963) *The Art of Persuasion in Greece*. Princeton
KENNY, A. J. P. (1975) *Wittgenstein*. Harmondsworth
KEULS, E. (1985) *The Reign of the Phallus*. New York
KIENAST, D. (1973) 'Presbeia', in *RE* Supp. XIII, 429–68
KNOCH, W. (1960) *Die Strafbestimmungen in Platons Nomoi*. Wiesbaden
KOCH-HARNACK, G. (1983) *Knabenliebe und Tiergeschenke. Ihre Bedeutung im päderastischen Erziehungssystem Athens*. Berlin
KORVER, J. (1934) *De terminologie van het crediet-wezen in het Grieksch*. Amsterdam (repr. New York, 1979)
KRAAY, C. M. (1964) 'Hoards, small change and the origins of coinage', *JHS* 84: 76–91
KRÄNZLEIN, A. (1963) *Eigentum und Besitz im griechischen Recht des fünften und vierten Jahrhunderts v. Chr.* Berlin
KROLL, J. H. (1972) *Athenian Bronze Allotment Plates*. Cambridge, MA
KUPER, A. (1988) *The Invention of Primitive Society: Transformations of an Illusion*. London
LÄMMLI, F. (1938) *Das attische Prozessverfahren in seiner Wirkung auf die Gerichtsrede*. Paderborn
LANE FOX, R. J. (1985) 'Aspects of inheritance in the Greek world', in Cartledge & Harvey 1985: 208–32
LANZA, D. (1979) *Lingua e discorso nell' Atene delle professioni*. Naples
LATTE, K. (1931) 'Beiträge zum griechischen Strafrecht', *Hermes* 66: 30–48, 129–58 (repr. in Berneker 1968: 263–314 and in Latte 1968)
(1968) *Kleine Schriften*. Munich
LAVENCY, M. (1964) *Aspects de la logographie judiciaire attique*. Louvain
LEACH, E. R. (1982) *Social Anthropology*. London
LEISI, E. (1907) *Der Zeuge im attischen Recht*. Frauenfeld

LE ROY LADURIE, E. (1975) Original French edn of *Montaillou: village occitan de 1294 à 1324* (Paris). (Abridged English trans. 1978). London

LEVY, E. (1980) 'Cité et citoyen dans la Politique d'Aristote', *Ktema* 5: 223–48

LEWIS, I. M. (1985) *Social Anthropology in Perspective*. 2nd edn. Cambridge

LEWIS, N. (1982) '*Aphairesis* in Athenian law and custom', in Modrzejewski & Liebs 1982: 161–78

(1983) *Life in Egypt under Roman Rule*. Oxford

LEWIS, T. J. (1978) 'Acquisition and anxiety: Aristotle's case against the market', *The Canadian Journal of Economics* 11: 69–90

LIPSEY, R. G. (1963) *An Introduction to Positive Economics*. London

LIPSIUS, J. H. (1905–15) *Das attische Recht und Rechtsverfahren*. 3 vols in 4. I. *Gerichtsverfassung*; II.1. *Öffentliche Klagen*; II.2. *Privatklagen*; III. *Prozessgang*. Leipzig (repr. Darmstadt 1966, Hildesheim 1984)

LLEWELLYN, K. and HOEBEL, E. A. (1941) *The Cheyenne Way: Conflict and Case-Law in Primitive Jurisprudence*. Oklahoma

LLOYD, A. and FALLERS, M. (1976) 'Sex roles in Edremit', in Peristiany, J. G., ed., *Mediterranean Family Structures*, 243–60. Cambridge

LLOYD, G. E. R. (1979) *Magic, Reason and Experience. Studies in the Origins and Development of Greek Science*. Cambridge

LOFBERG, J. O. (1917) *Sycophancy in Athens*. Chicago

LONIS, R. (1983) '*Astu* et *polis*. Remarques sur le vocabulaire de la ville et de l'état dans les inscriptions attiques du Ve au milieu du IIe s. av. J.-C.', *Ktema* 8: 95–109

LOWE, J. C. B. (1985) 'Plautine innovations in *Mostellaria* 529–857', *Phoenix* 39: 6–26

LOWRY, S. T. (1969) 'Aristotle's mathematical analysis of exchange', *History of Political Economy* 1: 44–66

(1974) 'Aristotle's "Natural Limit" and the economics of price regulation', *GRBS* 15: 57–63

(1988) *The Archaeology of Economic Ideas: The Classical Greek Tradition*. Durham, NC

LUKES, S. and SCULL, A. (1983) *Durkheim and the Law*. Oxford

MACCORMICK, N. (1981) *H. L. A. Hart*. London

MCCORMICK, B. J. *et al.* (1977) = McCormick, B. J., Kitchen, P. D., Marshall, G. P., Sampson, A. A., and Sedgwick, P., *Introducing Economics*. 2nd edn. Harmondsworth

MACDOWELL, D. M. (1963) *Athenian Homicide Law in the Age of the Orators*. Manchester

(1971), ed., *Aristophanes Wasps*. Oxford (repr. 1988)

(1976) '*Hybris* in Athens', *G&R* 23: 14–31

(1978) *The Law in Classical Athens*. London

(1984) rev. of Cohen 1983, *CR* 34: 229–31

(1986) *Spartan Law*. Edinburgh

(1988) 'Greek law', in Grant & Kitzinger 1988, 1: 589–605. New York

(1989) 'The *oikos* in Athenian law', *CQ* 39: 10–21

MACKENZIE, M. M. (1981) *Plato on Punishment*. Berkeley

MACLEOD, C. W. (1978) 'Reason and necessity: Thucydides III. 9–14, 37–48', *JHS* 98: 64–78 (repr. in Macleod, *Collected Essays*, ed. Taplin, O., Oxford 1983, 88–102)

MAHAFFY, J. P. (1890) *Social Life in Greece from Homer to Menander.* 7th edn. London

MAHER, V. (1974) *Women and Property in Morocco.* Cambridge

MAIDMENT, K. J. (1941), ed., *Minor Attic Orators* (Loeb edn.) Vol. 1. Cambridge, MA & London

MAINE, H. S. (1861) *Ancient Law: Its Connexion with the Early History of Society, and its Relation to Modern Ideas.* London (repr. Tucson, ARIZ 1986)

(1871) *Village-Communities in the East and West.* London

(1875) *Lectures on the Early History of Institutions.* London

(1883) *Dissertation on Early Law and Custom.* London

(1885) *Popular Government.* London

MAIO, D. P. (1983) '*Politeia* and adjudication in fourth-century B.C. Athens', *American Journal of Jurisprudence* 28: 16–45

MAIR, L. (1972) *An Introduction to Social Anthropology.* 2nd edn. Oxford

MALINOWSKI, B. (1922) *Argonauts of the Western Pacific.* London

(1926) *Crime and Custom in Savage Society.* London

(1929) *The Sexual Life of Savages.* New York

MANVILLE, P. B. (1980) 'Solon's Law of *stasis* and *atimia* in Archaic Athens', *TAPA* 110: 213–21

MARASPINI, A. (1968) *The Study of an Italian Village.* Paris

MARKLE, M. M. III (1985) 'Jury pay and Assembly pay at Athens', in Cartledge & Harvey 1985: 265–97

MARR, J. L. (1983) 'Notes on the pseudo-Xenophontic *Athenaion Politeia*', *C&M* 34: 45–53

MARSHALL, A. (1890) *The Principles of Economics.* London

MARTIN, R. (1951) *Recherches sur l'agora grecque. Études d'histoire et d'architecture urbaines.* Paris

MAUSS, M. (1925) *Essai sur le don.* Paris (cited from Cunnison, I., trans., *The Gift. Forms and Functions of Exchange in Archaic Societies.* London 1954)

MEIER, M. H. E. and SCHÖMANN, G. F. (1824) *Der attische Prozess.* 2 vols. Halle

MEIER, M. H. E., SCHÖMANN, G. F. and LIPSIUS, J. H. (1883–7) *Der attische Prozess.* 2 vols. 2nd edn. Berlin

MEIKLE, S. (1979) 'Aristotle and the political economy of the polis', *JHS* 99: 57–73

(1989) 'Et in Arcadia Chicago', *Polis* 8: 25–34 (review-article of Lowry 1988)

MEYER-LAURIN, H. (1965) *Gesetz und Billigkeit im attischen Prozess.* Weimar

MICHELL, H. (1957) *Economics of Ancient Greece.* 2nd edn. Cambridge

MICKWITZ, G. (1939) 'Zum Problem der Betriebsführung in der antiken Wirtschaft', *Vierteljahrschrift für Sozial- und Wirtschaftsgeschichte* 32: 1–25

MILES, D. P. (1987) 'Forbidden pleasures: sumptuary laws and the ideology of moral decline in Ancient Rome' (unpublished diss. London)

MILLETT, P. C. (1982) 'The Attic *horoi* reconsidered in the light of recent discoveries', *OPVS* 1: 219–49 (repr. as, and cited from, introduction to 1985 repr. of Finley 1952)

(1983) 'Maritime loans and the structure of credit in fourth-century Athens', in Garnsey, P., Hopkins, K. and Whittaker, C. R., eds., *Trade in the Ancient Economy*, 36–52. London

(1989) 'Patronage and its avoidance in Classical Athens', in Wallace-Hadrill, A. F., ed., *Patronage in Ancient Society*, 1–33. London

MITTEIS, L. (1891) *Reichsrecht und Volksrecht in den östlichen Provinzen des römischen Kaiserreichs*. Leipzig

MODRZEJEWSKI, J. (1983) 'La structure juridique du mariage grec', in Dimakis 1983: 39–71

MODRZEJEWSKI, J. and LIEBS, D. (1982), eds., *Symposion 1977: Vorträge zur griechischen und hellenistischen Rechtsgeschichte*. Cologne & Vienna

MOMIGLIANO, A. D. (1971) *The Development of Greek Biography*. Cambridge, MA

MOMIGLIANO, A. D. and HUMPHREYS, S. C. (1983) 'Fustel de Coulanges, *The Ancient City*', in Humphreys 1983b: 131–43 [*see also* Fustel de Coulanges, N. D. (1864)]

MOORE, B., jr (1984) *Privacy. Studies in Social and Cultural History*. New York & London

MOORE, S. F. (1978) *Law as Process: An Anthropological Approach*. London & Boston

MORRIS, I. M. (1986) 'Gift and commodity in archaic Greece', *Man* 21: 1–17

MORROW, G. R. (1939) *Plato's Law of Slavery in its Relation to Greek Law*. Urbana, IL

(1960) *Plato's Cretan City*. Princeton

MOSSÉ, Cl. (1976) 'Les salariés à Athènes au IVᵉ siècle', *DHA* 2: 97–101

MUIR, J. V. (1982) 'Protagoras and education at Thurioi', *G&R* 29: 17–24

MULGAN, R. G. (1977) *Aristotle's Political Theory*. Oxford

MURPHY, P. (1988) *A Practical Approach to Evidence*. London

MURRAY, O. (1983) 'The Greek symposion in history', in Gabba 1983: 257–72

(1985) 'Symposium and genre in the poetry of Horace', *JRS* 75: 39–50

(1990), ed., *Sympotica. Proceedings of a Symposium on the Symposion September 1984*. Oxford

(1990a) 'The affair of the Mysteries: democracy and the drinking group', in Murray (1990)

NADER, L. and TODD, H. F. (1978), eds., *The Disputing Process: Law in Ten Societies*. New York

NASH, M. (1965) *Primitive and Peasant Economic Systems*. San Francisco

NEALE, W. C. (1957) 'The market in history', in Polanyi, Arensberg & Pearson 1957: 357–72

NEIL, R. A. (1901), ed., *The Knights of Aristophanes*. Cambridge

NICHOLAS, B. (1962) *An Introduction to Roman Law*. Oxford

NICOLET, C. (1971) 'Prix, monnaies, échanges: les variations des prix et la "théorie quantitative de la monnaie" à Rome, de Cicéron à Pline l'Ancien', *Annales (ESC)* 26: 1203–27

OSBORNE, R. G. (1985a) *Demos. The Discovery of Classical Attika*. Cambridge

(1985b) 'Law in action in Classical Athens', *JHS* 105: 40–58

(1987a) *Classical Landscape with Figures: The Ancient Greek City and its Countryside*. London

(1987b), rev. of Garner 1987, *Cambridge Law Journal* 46: 526–8

OSTWALD, M. P. (1969) *Nomos and the Beginnings of the Athenian Democracy*. Oxford

(1982) *Autonomia: Its Genesis and Early History*. Philadelphia

(1986) *From Popular Sovereignty to the Sovereignty of Law: Law, Society and Politics in Fifth-Century Athens*. Berkeley, Los Angeles & London

PANNICK, D. (1987) *Judges*. Oxford
PAOLI, U. E. (1933) *Studi sul processo attico*. Padua
(1956) *Studi in onore di Ugo Enrico Paoli*. Florence
PARKER, R. (1983) *Miasma: Pollution and Purification in Early Greek Religion*. Oxford
PARTSCH, J. (1909) *Griechisches Bürgschaftsrecht*, vol. I. Leipzig & Berlin
(1920) 'Die alexandrinischen *Dikaiomata*', *APF* 6: 34–77
PEARL, D. S. (1979) *Muslim Law*. London
PEARSON, H. W. (1957) 'The secular debate on economic primitivism', in Polanyi, Arensberg & Pearson 1957: 3–11
PEHRSON, R. (1971) *The Social Organization of the Marri Beluch*. Chicago
PELLIZER, E. (1990) 'Outlines of a morphology of sympotic entertainment', in Murray 1990
PENDRICK, G. (1987) 'Once more Antiphon the Sophist and Antiphon of Rhamnus', *Hermes* 115: 47–60
PERISTIANY, J. G. (1966), ed., *Honour and Shame*. Chicago
PERLMAN, S. (1963) 'The politicians in the Athenian democracy of the 4th century B.C.', *Athenaeum* 41: 327–55
PHIPSON, S. L. and ELLIOT, D. W. (1987) *Manual of the Law of Evidence*. 12th edn. London
PIÉRART, M. (1973) *Platon et la cité grecque*. Brussels
PITT-RIVERS, J. (1958), ed., *Mediterranean Countrymen*. Paris
(1971) *The People of the Sierra*. 2nd edn. Chicago
(1977) *The Fate of Shechem*. Cambridge
POLANYI, K. (1944) *Origins of our Time: The Great Transformation*. New York
(1957a) 'Marketless trading in Hammurabi's time', in Polanyi, Arensberg & Pearson 1957: 12–26
(1957b) 'Aristotle discovers the economy', in Polanyi, Arensberg & Pearson 1957: 64–94
(1957c) 'The economy as instituted process', in Polanyi, Arensberg & Pearson 1957: 243–69
(1960) 'On the comparative treatment of economic institutions in antiquity, with illustrations from Athens, Mycenae and Alalakh', in Kraeling, C. H., and Adams, R. M. (1960), eds., *City Invincible: An Oriental Institute Symposium*, 329–50. Chicago
(1977) *The Livelihood of Man*, ed. H. W. Pearson. New York, San Francisco & London
POLANYI, K., ARENSBERG, C. M., and PEARSON, H. W. (1957), eds., *Trade and Market in the Early Empires: Economies in History and Theory*. Glencoe, IL
POLLARD, J. T. (1948) 'The *Birds* of Aristophanes – a source book for old beliefs', *AJPh* 69: 353–76
(1977) *Birds in Greek Life and Myth*. London & New York
POLLOCK, F. and MAITLAND, F. W. (1968) *The History of English Law before the Time of Edward I*. Vol. 1 (of 2). 2nd edn. Cambridge
POSTAN, M. M. (1944) 'The rise of a money economy', *EconHistRev* 14: 123–34
POWELL, C. A. (1988) *Athens and Sparta. Constructing Greek Political and Social History from 478 B.C.* London

POWELL, E. (1989) *Kingship, Law and Society. Criminal Justice in the Reign of Henry V.* Oxford

PRÉAUX, C. (1961) 'De la Grèce classique à l'Égypte hellénistique: les formes de la vente d'immeuble', *CE* 36: 187–95

PRINGSHEIM, F. (1949) 'The Greek sale by auction', in *Scritti in onore di Contardo Ferrini.* Vol. IV: 284–343 (repr. in German in Pringsheim 1961, II: 262–329)

(1950) *The Greek Law of Sale.* Weimar

(1951) 'Le témoinage dans la Grèce et Rome archaïque', *AHDO* 6: 161–75 (repr. in Pringsheim 1961, II: 330–8)

(1953) 'Griechische Kauf-Horoi', in *Festschrift Hans Lewald*, 143–60. Basel (repr. in Pringsheim 1961, II: 354–68)

(1955) 'Symbol und Fiktion in antiken Rechten', in *Studi de Francisci.* Vol. IV: 211–36 (repr. in Pringsheim 1961, II: 382–400)

(1961) *Gesammelte Abhandlungen.* 2 vols. Heidelberg

RAEPSAET, G. (1973) 'A propos de l'utilisation de statistiques en démographie grecque. Le nombre d'enfants par famille', *AC* 42: 536–43

RANKIN, H. D. (1983) *Sophists, Socratics, and Cynics.* London & Canberra

RAZ, J. (1980) *The Concept of a Legal System: An Introduction to the Theory of a Legal System.* 2nd edn. Oxford

REDFIELD, J. M. (1975) *Nature and Culture in the Iliad: The Tragedy of Hector.* Chicago

REIMER, P. J. (1941) 'Zur δίκη βεβαιώσεως bei Harpokration', *Mnem.* 9: 153–6

RHODES, P. J. (1970) 'Ephialtes and the achievement of Athenian democracy', in *Essays Presented to C. M. Bowra*, 39–49. Oxford

(1972) *The Athenian Boule.* Oxford (repr., with addenda and corrigenda, 1985)

(1979) 'ΕΙΣΑΓΓΕΛΙΑ in Athens', *JHS* 99: 103–4

(1980) 'Athenian democracy after 403 BC', *CJ* 75: 305–23

(1981) *A Commentary on the Aristotelian* Athenaion Politeia. Oxford

(1984), trans., *Aristotle: The Athenian Constitution.* Harmondsworth

ROBERTS, J. T. (1982) *Accountability in Athenian Government.* Madison

ROBERTS, R. (1976) *A Ragged Schooling.* Manchester

ROBERTS, S. (1979) *Order and Dispute: An Introduction to Legal Anthropology.* Harmondsworth

(1983) 'The study of dispute: anthropological perspectives', in Bossy 1983: 1–24

ROBINSON, J. and EATWELL, J. (1974) *An Introduction to Modern Economics.* London

ROBINSON, O., FERGUS, T. D., and GORDON, W. M. (1985) *An Introduction to European Legal History.* Abingdon

ROBINSON, R. E. (1954) *Definition.* Oxford

RODINSON, M. (1973) 'Preface', in Chalmeta Gendron, P. *El 'señor del zoco' en españa: edades media y moderna, contribución al estudo de la historia del mercado*, xv–lxix. Madrid

ROLL, E. (1973) *A History of Economic Thought.* 4th edn. London

ROMILLY, J. de (1988) *Les Grands Sophistes dans l'Athènes de Périclès.* Paris

ROUSE, W. H. D. (1898–9), ed., *Plutarch's Lives Englished by Sir Thomas North.* 10 vols. London

ROUSSEL, D. (1976) *Tribu et cité.* Montpellier

RUSCHENBUSCH, E. (1965) '*Hybreos graphē*: ein Fremdkörper im athenischen Recht des 4. Jahrhunderts v. Chr.', *ZSS* 82: 302–9

(1966) *ΣΟΛΩΝΟΣ ΝΟΜΟΙ*. (*Historia* Einzelschrift 9). Wiesbaden

(1968) *Untersuchungen zur Geschichte des athenischen Strafrechts*. Cologne

(1969) 'Δίκη κατά τινος und πρός τινα', *ZSS* 86: 386–94

(1978) *Untersuchungen zu Staat und Politik in Griechenland vom 7.-4. Jh. v. Chr.*. Bamberg

(1984) rev. of Cohen 1983, *HZ* 239: 397–9

SAHLINS, M. (1974) *Stone Age Economics*. London

STE. CROIX, G. E. M. de (1970) 'Some observations on the property rights of Athenian women', *CR* 20: 273–8

(1972) *The Origins of the Peloponnesian War*. London & Ithaca

(1981) *The Class Struggle in the Ancient Greek World*. London & Ithaca (corrected impression 1983)

SALMON, J. B. (1984) *Wealthy Corinth: A History of the City to 338 B.C.* Oxford

SAMUELSON, P. (1970) *Economics*. 11th edn. New York

SAUNDERS, T. J. (1963) 'Two points in Plato's penal code', *CQ* 13: 194–9 [Note i, on 728bc, = note 23 in Saunders, *Notes on the Laws of Plato* (*BICS* Supp. 28, London 1972).]

(1968) 'The Socratic paradoxes in Plato's *Laws*: a commentary on 859c–864b', *Hermes* 96: 421–34

(1970), trans., *Plato, The Laws*. Harmondsworth

(1984), 'Plato, *Laws* 728bc: a reply', *LCM* 9: 23–4

SAWER, G. (1965) *Law in Society*. Oxford

SCHAPS, D. M. (1977) 'The woman least mentioned: etiquette and women's names', *CQ* 27: 323–30

(1979) *The Economic Rights of Women in Ancient Greece*. Edinburgh

SCHNEIDER, J. (1971) 'Of vigilance and virgins: honour, shame, and access to resources in Mediterranean societies', *Ethnology* 10: 1–24

SCHOFIELD, M. S. (1986) '*Euboulia* in the *Iliad*', *CQ* 36: 6–31

SCHÖPSDAU, K. (1984) 'Zum Strafrechtsexkurs in Platons *Nomoi*', *RhM* 127: 97–132

SCHULHOF, E. and HUVELIN, P. (1907) 'Loi régulant la vente du bois et du charbon à Délos', *BCH* 31: 46–93

SCHWAHN, W. (1934) 'Der Hauskauf in Athen', *Hermes* 69: 119–20

SEAGER, R. J. (1966) 'Lysias against the corndealers', *Historia* 15: 172–84

(1967) 'Alcibiades and the charge of aiming at tyranny', *Historia* 16: 6–18

SEALEY, R. (1987) *The Athenian Republic: Democracy or the Rule of Law?* Philadelphia & London

SELLAR, W. C. and YEATMAN, R. J. (1930) *1066 and All That*. London

SHACKLETON, R. (1961) *Montesquieu: A Critical Biography*. Oxford

SHIPLEY, G. (1987) *A History of Samos 800–188 B.C.* Oxford

SIMONETOS, G. (1939) 'Das Verhältnis von Kauf und Übereignung in altgriechischen Recht', in *Festschrift Paul Koschaker*, III: 172–98. Weimar

SINCLAIR, R. K. (1988) *Democracy and Participation in Athens*. Cambridge

SINCLAIR, T. A. and SAUNDERS, T. J. (1981) *Aristotle: The Politics*. Harmondsworth

SMITH, W. (1848) *A Dictionary of Greek and Roman Antiquities*. 2nd edn. London

SOLLENBERGER, M. G. (1985) 'Diogenes Laertius 5.36–57: the *Vita Theophrasti*', in Fortenbaugh, W. W., ed., *Theophrastus of Eresus, On his Life and Work*, 1–62. New Brunswick

SOMMERSTEIN, A. H. (1980), ed., *Aristophanes: Acharnians*. Warminster (1981), ed., *Aristophanes: Knights*. Warminster (1983), ed., *Aristophanes: Wasps*. Warminster (1987), ed., *Aristophanes: Birds*. Warminster

SOUBIE, A. (1973–4) 'Les preuves dans les plaidoyers des orateurs attiques', *RIDA* 28: 171–253; 29: 77–134

SPAHN, P. (1984) 'Die Anfänge der antiken Ökonomik', *Chiron* 14: 301–23

STANLEY, P. V. (1976) 'Ancient Greek market regulations and controls' (unpublished Diss. Berkeley)

STARR, C. G. (1977) *The Economic and Social Growth of Early Greece 800–500 B.C.* New York & Oxford

STEIN, P. G. (1980) *Legal Evolution: The Story of an Idea*. Cambridge

STIRLING, P. (1966) *Turkish Village*. New York

STONE, L. (1987) *The Past and the Present Revisited*. London & Boston

STOREY, I. C. (1987) 'Old Comedy 1975–1984', *EMC/CV* 6: 1–46

STRAUSS, B. (1986) *Athens after the Peloponnesian War: Class, Faction and Policy 403–386 B.C.* London & Sydney

STROUD, R. S. (1968) *Drakon's Law on Homicide*. Berkeley & Los Angeles (1985) rev. of Biscardi 1982, *Gnomon* 57: 377–8

SZEGEDY-MASZAK, A. (1981) *The Nomoi of Theophrastos*. New York (repr. Salem 1987)

TAILLARDAT, J. (1965) *Les Images d'Aristophane: études de langue et de style*. Paris

TALAMANCA, M. (1953) *L'arra della compravendita in diritto greco e in diritto romano*. Milan

TECUŞAN, M. (1990) '*Logos sympotikos*: patterns of the irrational in philosophical drinking', in Murray (1990)

THIEL, J. H. (1966) rev. of Turasiewicz 1963, *Mnem.* 19: 312–13

THOMAS, J. A. C. (1968) 'Roman law', in Derrett 1968: 1–27

THOMAS, R. (1989) *Oral Tradition and Written Record in Classical Athens*. Cambridge

THOMPSON, C. V. (1894) 'Slave-torture in Athens', *CR* 8: 136

THOMPSON, D. B. (1971) *An Ancient Shopping Center. The Athenian Agora*. Princeton (Agora Picture Book No. 12)

THOMPSON, H. A. and WYCHERLEY, R. E. (1972) *The Agora of Athens. The History, Shape and Uses of an Ancient City Center* (*The Athenian Agora* XIV). Princeton

THOMPSON, W. E. (1972) 'Athenian marriage patterns: remarriage', *CSCA* 5: 211–25

THOMSON, J. A. K. (1935) *The Art of the Logos*. London

THÜR, G. (1977) *Beweisführung vor den Schwurgerichtshöfen Athens: die Proklesis zur Basanon*. Vienna (1983) 'Bemerkungen zum Zeugenbeweis im Rechtshilfe-vertrag aus Stymphalos (*IG* 5/2, 357)', in Dimakis 1983: 329–42

THURNWALD, R. (1932) *Economics in Primitive Communities*. Oxford

TODD, S. C. (1990a, forthcoming) 'The use and abuse of the Attic orators', *G&R* 37
  (1990b, forthcoming) rev. of Gagarin 1986, *Polis*
TÖNNIES, F. (1887) *Gemeinschaft und Gesellschaft*. Leipzig (trans. as *Community and Association*, London 1955)
TUCKER, T. G. (1906) *Life in Ancient Athens. The Social and Public Life of a Classical Athenian from Day to Day*. London
TUPLIN, C. J. (1985) 'Imperial tyranny: some reflections on a classical Greek metaphor', in Cartledge & Harvey 1985: 348–75
TURASIEWICZ, R. (1963) *De servis testibus in Atheniensium iudiciis saec. V et IV a. Chr. n. per tormenta cruciatis*. Warsaw
TYRRELL, W. B. (1984) *Amazons: A Study in Athenian Mythmaking*. Baltimore
UCHENDO, V. (1967) 'Some principles of haggling in peasant markets', *Economic Development and Cultural Change* 16: 37–50
USSHER, R. G. (1960), ed., *The Characters of Theophrastus*. London
VAN BREMEN, R.: *see* BREMEN, R. VAN
VELLACOTT, P. (1975) *Ironic Drama*. Cambridge
VERING, C. (1926) *Platons Gesetze: Die Erziehung zum Staate*. Frankfurt/Main
VICKERS, B. F. (1988) *In Defence of Rhetoric*. Oxford
VICKERS, M. J. (1984, publ. 1988) 'Demus's gold *phiale* (Lysias 19.25)', *AJAH* 9: 48–53
VINOGRADOFF, P. (1909) *Roman Law in Mediaeval Europe*. Oxford
  (1920) *Outlines of Historical Jurisprudence* I. *Introduction: Tribal Law*. Oxford
  (1922) *Outlines of Historical Jurisprudence* II. *The Jurisprudence of the Greek City*. Oxford
VLASTOS, G. (1946) 'Solonian justice', *CPh* 41: 65–83
WADE-GERY, H. T. (1958) *Essays in Greek History*. Oxford
WALCOT, P. (1970) *Greek Peasants Ancient and Modern*. Manchester
  (1984) 'Greek attitudes towards women: the mythological evidence', *G&R* 31: 37–47
WALTMAN, J. L. and HOLLAND, K. M. (1988), eds., *The Political Role of Law Courts in Modern Democracies*. London
WANKEL, H. (1976) *Demosthenes: Rede für Ktesiphon über den Kranz*. Heidelberg
WATSON, A. (1974) *Legal Transplants: An Approach to Comparative Law*. Edinburgh
WEBER, M. (1958) *The City* (Martindale, D. and Neuwirth, G., trans.). Chicago (originally 'Die Stadt', *Archiv für Sozialwissenschaft und Sozialpolitik* 47 [1921] 621–772)
WEBSTER, T. B. L. (1969) *Everyday Life in Classical Athens*. London
WEISS, E. (1933) 'Greek law', in *ESS* IX: 225–9
WELSKOPF, E. C. (1985), ed., *Soziale Typenbegriffe. Belegstellenverzeichnis altgriechischer sozialer Typenbegriffe von Homer bis Aristoteles*. Vol. 1. Berlin
WHITEHEAD, D. (1977) *The Ideology of the Athenian Metic* (*PCPhS* Supp.4). Cambridge
  (1980) 'The tribes of the Thirty Tyrants', *JHS* 100: 208–13
  (1983) 'Competitive outlay and community profit', *C&M* 34: 55–74
WHITEHEAD, T. and CONAWAY, M. (1986), eds., *Self, Sex, and Gender in Cross-cultural Fieldwork*. Urbana, IL

WIESEHÖFER, J. (1980) 'Die "Freunde" und "Wohltäter" des Grosskönigs', *Studia Iranica* 9: 7–21

WILHELM, A. (1904) 'Der älteste griechische Brief', *JOAI* 7: 94–105

WILL, ED. (1954a) 'De l'aspect éthique des origines grecques de la monnaie', *RH* 212: 209–31

(1954b) 'Trois quarts de siècle de recherches sur l'économie grecque antique', *Annales (ESC)* 9: 7–22

WILLIAMS, J. (1967) *The Youth of Harouch*. Cambridge, MA

WILSON, G. W. (1975) 'The economics of the just price', *History of Political Economy* 7: 57–74

WITTGENSTEIN, L. (1958) *Philosophical Investigations*. Oxford

WOLFF, H.-J. (1946) 'The origin of judicial litigation among the Greeks', *Traditio* 4: 31–87

(1951) *Roman Law: An Historical Introduction*. Norman, OK

(1957) 'Die Grundlagen des griechischen Vertragsrechts', *ZSS* 74: 26–72

(1975a), ed., *Symposion 1971: Vorträge zur griechischen und hellenistischen Rechtsgeschichte*. Cologne & Vienna

(1975b) 'Juristische Gräzistik: Aufgaben, Probleme, Möglichkeiten', in Wolff 1975a: 1–22

(1975c) 'Greek legal history: its functions and potentialities', *Washington University Law Quarterly* 1975: 395–408

(1979) *Das Problem der Konkurrenz von Rechtsordnungen in der Antike*. Heidelberg

WOODHEAD, A. G. (1981) *The Study of Greek Inscriptions*. 2nd edn. Cambridge

WOODRUFF, P. (1982), ed., *Plato's Hippias Major*. Oxford

WROTTESLEY, F. J. (1910) *The Examination of Witnesses in Court*. London (2nd edn. 1926)

WYCHERLEY, R. E. (1956) 'The market of Athens: topography and monuments', *G&R* 3: 2–23 (repr. in shortened form in Wycherley 1978: 91–103)

(1957), ed., *Literary and Epigraphical Testimonia (The Athenian Agora* III). Princeton

(1978) *The Stones of Athens*. Princeton

WYSE, W. (1904) *The Speeches of Isaeus, with Critical and Explanatory Notes*. Cambridge (repr. Hildesheim 1967)

(1916) 'Law', in Whibley, L., ed., *A Companion to Greek Studies*, 461–90. 3rd edn. Cambridge

YOUNG, R. S. (1951) 'An industrial district of ancient Athens', *Hesperia* 20: 135–288

ZIMMERN, A. E. (1931) *The Greek Commonwealth*. 5th edn. London

Glossary–Index

This glossary is intended to fulfil several functions. Its primary duty is to provide a summary of the technical or semi-technical terms used throughout the book (most but by no means all of them Athenian legal terms); this has enabled us to avoid over-burdening the text with repeated explanations, while at the same time ensuring that the book is accessible to the non-specialist. We have also included within the glossary frequent page-references to the text of the book, so that the glossary can serve in place of an index of the major themes discussed. We hope finally that the glossary may perform one further function independent of the rest of the book: to provide a convenient (and sorely needed) way into the terminology of Athenian law for readers who are approaching the subject from outside; for this reason a number of terms are included here because they are important, even though they are not (as it happens) discussed by any of the contributors to the book. For cross-reference within the glossary, an asterisk is used to mark terms which are themselves the subject of an independent entry.

adjective law   See *sv*. procedural* law.
adversarial   An adversarial system of justice is one in which a criminal trial is constructed as a dispute between two sides, with the judge/jury acting as umpire. The aim of the trial is not to discover the truth (though it may be hoped that this will occur incidentally), but to determine whether the side charged with the burden of proof (pp. 20–1: in this context normally the prosecution) has demonstrated its case. See for contrast *sv*. inquisitorial* system. English criminal law operates under the adversarial system; but Athenian justice took it to extremes: the court's rôle was to decide not whether a burden of proof had been sustained, but which of two general theses was preferable, that of the prosecutor or that of the defendant.
agnate   In Roman law, blood-relations in the male line (i.e., where there is a relationship to a common ancestor which can be traced through males alone): to an English reader, agnates are perhaps best described as the people who share one's surname. See for contrast *sv*. cognate*.
agon   Lit. 'contest' of any kind: especially a lawsuit, or an athletic or dramatic competition (p. 55).
agora   The civic centre and market-place of a Greek *polis** (pp. 10, 41, 49, 87, 93 n.31, 156, 163, 167–94 *passim*, esp. 189–91).

agoranomos, pl. *agoranomoi*   Lit. '*agora**-regulator(s)': public officials attested in a large number of Greek *poleis**; their duties consisted of supervising the commercial aspects of the *agora* (pp. 172–3, 186, 191 n.52).

aidesis   Because homicide in Athenian law was a matter for private prosecution (cf. *sv. phonou**, *dikē*), the relatives of the dead man, as prosecutors, were under certain circumstances permitted or expected to grant pardon (*aidesis*: p. 68) to his killer. Once this had been done, the killer was immune from further prosecution. (The derivation of the term is unclear: it is certainly connected with the verb *aideomai* 'to feel shame, awe or respect'; LSJ notes that the verb can be used to mean 'to respect another's misfortune' and thus 'to be reconciled to him'; but unlike English 'reconciliation', *aidesis* is only used to denote the action of the wronged party.)

aikia (sometimes *aikeia*)   'Injury' or 'assault' (pp. 126, 128, 131, 141): a general term, without the further implications of *hubris**.

(*dikē**) *aikias*   A private indictment concerning assault (*aikia**): pp. 126 with n.12, 133.

alien   See *svv. metic**, *xenos**.

anakrisis   A preliminary hearing before the public official within whose court a case will later be heard (for the rôle of the presiding official within a lawcourt, see *sv. arkhon**). Lit., 'examination', but it should not be equated with the inquisitorial* *instruction* of civil-law* systems: an Athenian public official had very restricted discretion; and unlike an arbitrator (see *sv. diaitetes**), his function was not to settle the case.

antidosis   Lit. 'a giving in exchange'. A man who was nominated to perform a liturgy* could avoid this duty if he could name another citizen who was richer and better-qualified to perform the task. If the man challenged agreed that he was richer, he had to take over the liturgy; if he claimed to be poorer, then the challenger could insist on an exchange of all their property to test the claim – in which case the challenger would himself perform the liturgy as the new owner of the (putatively) greater estate. This process of exchange was called *antidosis* (pp. 92, 99). The advantage of the system from the viewpoint of the democracy was that it encouraged the rich to be suspicious of each other, instead of being hostile towards the state; but although we know of several challenges, there is no attested case in which the exchange was completed.

antitimesis   See *sv. timē** (3).

antomosia   See *sv. diomosia**.

apagogē, pl. *apagogai*   Lit. 'dragging away', i.e., to the appropriate magistrate* (pp. 31 n.19, 76). Summary arrest was permitted against certain categories of criminal, such as thieves and highwaymen, if they were caught *ep' autophoroi** ('red-handed', but see further *sv.*): pp. 73 n.39, 106 with n.16, 147. If the accused admitted his guilt before the magistrate he was promptly executed; only if he claimed to be innocent was he put on trial (p. 80 n.71). See also *svv. endeixis**, *ephegesis**, *ep' autophoroi**, and *kakourgos**.

apeleutheros, pl. *apeleutheroi*   A 'freedman' (ex-slave). References to freedmen are far less common in Athenian sources than in Roman texts.

aphanes ousia   Lit. 'non-visible property': a category which roughly corresponded to English personal* property (i.e., everything except land and houses, which are described in Athens as *phanera** *ousia* and in English law as real* property). In Athenian law however, the distinction seems to have been social rather than legal:

extant uses of the terms concern the relative ease with which the two types of wealth can be hidden in disputes over taxation (see svv. *eisphora**, liturgy*), rather than (as in English law) the different way in which the two types of property are treated in sale or inheritance.

apographē   Lit. 'a (written) list': a catalogue of some or all of the property of a man in debt to the state. The state took no initiative in the confiscation of property: this was left either to private individuals or else, it appears, to local deme* officials (demarkhs*). The term *apographē* is used to describe the list itself, the process of denunciation, and any judicial hearing arising out of the case (pp. 39 n.35, 57–8 with p. 57 n.66, 87 n.16, 92). See also *sv. phasis **.

apophasis   Lit. 'a showing forth, declaration'. A procedure newly instituted around the middle of the fourth century: either on the invitation of the *ekklesia** or on its own initiative, the Areiopagos* could investigate any matter involving public security and present a report (*apophasis*) to the *ekklesia*, recommending particular action, for instance the prosecution of a named individual (p. 31, cf. p. 39).

apotimema   See *sv. horos**.

appeal   See *sv. ephesis**.

apragmon, pl. *apragmones* (adj.); *apragmosunē* (abstract noun)   Lit. 'one who does not conduct business': a person who refrains from taking part in public affairs (pp. 99 n.47, 116, 117). It can be either a positive or a negative characteristic, depending on the attitude of the speaker ('philosophical contemplation' or 'political irresponsibility'). For the opposite characteristic, see *sv. polupragmon**.

(*graphē*) *aprostasiou*   See *sv. prostates**.

arbitration   See *sv. diaitetes**.

Areiopagos   The ancient and originally aristocratic council of Athens (p. 100 n.50); its membership comprised those who had completed a term as one of the nine arkhons*. Its powers had been severely restricted by the democratic reforms of Ephialtes in the 460s B.C., which left it as little more than the main court for cases of homicide; in the fourth century however other powers were added, most notably *apophasis**.

arkhē, pl. *arkhai* (noun)   Lit. 'rule' or 'authority' (the term is often used for instance to describe the fifth-century Athenian empire). Originally an abstract noun, but often used in a concrete sense, as a general term to describe any public office or official (pp. 16 with n.33, 117); the term was probably used to include the *boulē**, but this has been contested. Unlike *arkhon**, the word *arkhē* is not normally restricted to one of the nine arkhonships. With a few exceptions, most notably the generalship (see *sv. strategos**), public offices at Athens were filled not by election but by lot*.

Note: The English term 'magistrate' is often used to translate the Greek *arkhē*; this should be understood in a Roman or Shakespearean sense, to denote a public official with some judicial duties, rather than (as today) to mean a part-time lay judge: p. 43.

arkhon, pl. *arkhontes* (participle acting as a noun), Eng. archon or arkhon   Lit. 'one who is in authority'. Used in three senses: loosely, to refer to any Athenian public official; more strictly (usually a collective plural) to describe the 'nine arkhons'; specifically, as the title of the senior of the nine arkhonships. These were still the titular chief magistrates of Athens, but their real authority had been severely restricted ever since they began to be appointed by lot, apparently in the 480s. They retained however an honorific position, particularly in the administration of justice: for instance, former arkhons became members of the Areiopagos* for life; and during their year of office they processed the litigation presented to the most important of the *dikasteria**, and presided over trials held there, although in this capacity they were by now little more than non-voting (and non-speaking) chairmen. The three senior arkhons each had a specific title and competence: the *arkhon* (the eponymous official of Athens who gave his name to the civil year) heard cases involving family and inheritance matters of citizens; the *arkhon basileus* (lit. 'king arkhon': p. 88) presided over religious matters, including sacrilege and homicide; the *polemarkhos* (lit. 'war arkhon', but by now all his military functions had been handed over to the *strategoi**) dealt with family and inheritance cases involving metics*, and apparently cases involving certain other privileged foreigners also. The other six arkhons were called *thesmothetai* (sing. *thesmothetes**: originally perhaps 'establisher of judgements' rather than 'maker of laws'); they heard those public cases, and perhaps also some private ones, which did not fall within the competence of the three senior arkhons or of other named officials. For the *thesmothetai*, see pp. 123, 145.

arrest, summary   See *sv. apagogē**.

arrha (or *arrhabon*)   A word of Semitic origins used by the Greeks to indicate the deposit paid over to secure an option on the purchase of particular goods or services: pp. 175–6 with p. 176 n.17, 189.

(*graphē**) *asebeias*   A public action against somebody who has allegedly committed impiety or sacrilege (*asebeia*: pp. 64, 66, 69): in Athenian eyes, impiety was essentially a matter of actions rather than thoughts, but words spoken in certain situations or in certain places could themselves become impious actions, as Socrates found out to his cost.

assembly   See *ekklesia**.

astunomos, pl. *astunomoi*   Lit. 'one who regulates (affairs within) the *astu* (the built-up area of Athens)'. A board of public officials charged with the general supervisory duties which we associate with the police. Unlike the police, however, they did not undertake the investigation of crime. Nor were they much concerned with the arrest or punishment of accused or convicted criminals: this rôle was played by the Eleven*. For the *astunomoi*, see p. 143 n.14.

Ath.Pol.   Two separate texts bear the title *Athenaion Politeia* (lit. 'Constitution of the Athenians'). One is a short work of anti-democratic polemic, wrongly attributed in antiquity to the historian Xenophon. It is the earliest surviving work of Attic prose literature, dating probably from the 420s B.C. Its date and opinions have earned for the unknown author the conventional title of the 'Old Oligarch'; but since this description conjures up pictures of an angry old man, a less misleading description may be '[Xen.] *Ath.Pol.*'. The more famous *Athenaion Politeia*, however, is the monograph on constitutional history written either by Aristotle or by a pupil, probably between 332 and 322 B.C. (pp. 13–14). Throughout this book, the title of *Ath.Pol.* without qualification refers to the Aristotelian text.

atimetos   See *sv. timē** (3).

atimia (abstract noun)   Lit. 'loss of *timē** (2), honour'. In early archaic Athens, *atimia* seems to have meant outlawry, the total deprivation of all rights, such that a citizen could kill an *atimos* (pl. *atimoi*: person suffering from *atimia*) without committing an offence or apparently incurring blood-guilt. Well before the classical period, however, *atimia* had already been restricted in its scope to mean the loss of some or all of a man's active rights as a citizen. Such *atimia* could be partial or total; it could be imposed permanently by a court, or it could be the (theoretically) temporary result of an unpaid debt to the state, a condition which would automatically terminate if the debt were ever paid off. A man subject to total *atimia* could not appear in certain public places, could not take part in public life, and could not appear in court. If he broke any of these bans, he was liable to *apagogē** and death. But he did retain his private rights as a citizen: to kill him would be murder; he was not formally exiled; and he continued to own his property – though his lack of the capacity to sue may have made it difficult procedurally to defend these rights, and many may have found life under such restrictions so intolerable that voluntary exile seemed preferable. A man subject to partial *atimia* lost either a particular right or rights, or else the power to exercise his rights in a particular situation: for instance, the ability to bring certain types of prosecution. For *atimia*, see pp. 25 n.10, 37 n.33, 78 n.64, 106 n.11, 125, 127, 131, 134, 139–41 and esp. 140 n.3; for its position within Athenian penology, see *sv.* penalty*, *sv. timē** (3).

basileus   See *sv. arkhon**.
(*dikē**) *blabes*   A private action for damages: the concept of *blabē* is broad, and seems to have covered any physical or material loss suffered by the plaintiff as a result of action or inaction on the part of the defendant. For its use in one particular set of circumstances, see p. 25.
boulē   Lit. 'council'. The democratic council of 500 men, appointed annually by lot* from among citizens aged at least thirty, and with severe restrictions on repeated membership. Its chief function was to prepare the agenda for meetings of the *ekklesia**, and to undertake certain routine administrative duties, in particular that of co-ordinating the activities of numerous boards of minor officials; but it had also certain independent judicial powers, mainly but not only in cases of limited importance: in some cases of *eisangelia**, the *boulē* could decide whether to refer the trial to the *ekklesia** or to a *dikasterion**. See generally pp. 16 n.33, 87 n.15, 100 n.51, 101, 117 n. 46, 118 n. 50; and for the rôle of the *boulē* in *eisangelia*, see p. 78 n.64.
(*ho*) *boulomenos*   Lit. 'anyone who wishes' (pp. 83, 103–5, 107, 123–4, 132). Whereas prosecution in a *dikē* could only be brought by the aggrieved party, in a *graphē* or other public case it could be brought by any qualified person (which normally meant any Athenian citizen who was not himself *atimos**).

challenge   See *sv. proklesis**.
citizen   See *svv. politeia**, *polites**; and for contrast, *svv. nothos**, metic*.
civil law   A civil-law system today is one which derives from the *ius civile* ('law pertaining to citizens') of classical Rome. Such systems are used throughout much of continental Europe (pp. 2–4, 20, 22–3).
cognate   In Roman law, all blood-relations; but the term is often used more narrowly to mean those who are not agnates*. According to this usage, cognates are blood-relations in the female line (i.e., where there is a relationship to a common ancestor, but this cannot be traced entirely through males).
coinage   Athenian monetary terms originally referred not to denominations of coin but to weights of uncoined metal. Indeed, even in the classical period, only the

smaller denominations (obol, drachma) existed as coins in their own right; the larger (mina, talent) were simply convenient forms of reckoning for large sums of money. The following table shows the relative values of Athenian monetary terms:

    6 obols = 1 drachma

    100 drachmae = 1 mina

    6,000 drachmae = 100 minas = 1 talent

(There were also a number of non-Athenian coins, such as the stater of Kyzikos and the Persian daric, which were virtually legal tender in Athens.) Equivalent values in modern currencies are impossible to give: calculations based on silver content are useless; and any fixed estimate rapidly gives way before the impact of inflation; moreover, we would tend to pay proportionally more for some things (such as houses) and less for others (such as food) than the Athenians did – even if we take account of the fact that many citizens will have lived as part of a substantially non-monetised subsistence economy. But for what it is worth, a day's wages for a skilled labourer seem to have risen gradually throughout the fourth century B.C. from roughly one to roughly two or even two-and-a-half drachmae.

collateral   A term used in English law to describe people who share the same ancestry, but not necessarily (indeed not normally) the same line of descent: for instance the descendants of brothers or sisters.

common law   A common-law system today is one which has developed out of the common law (i.e., the law that is the same throughout the kingdom) of medieval England (pp. 2–3, 20–2). English law is a common-law system; and so is the law of these countries which have derived their legal system from it, such as the USA and much of the Commonwealth.

compurgator   See sv. oath-helper*.

consensual contract   A contract in which the agreement ('consent') of the parties involved is considered binding, without the necessity of goods and purchase price changing hands (as is the case with a 'real contract'): on both terms, see pp. 174, 177–8.

council   See svv. Areiopagos*, boulē*.

court-fees   Several words for court-fee are attested in our sources: for instance epobelia, parakatabolē, parastasis and prutaneia. These various fees seem to have been payable normally by the plaintiff but in different categories of procedure: in some cases they were clearly a straight fee paid to the court; in others they were apparently more in the nature of a deposit, to be returned in the event of a successful prosecution; in yet other cases they seem to have been closer to the English system of awarding costs, payable to a successful defendant rather than to the state. The precise interpretation of each type of fee however is obscure, not least because on the rare occasions when payments are mentioned, the individual terms do not appear to be used in any precisely consistent fashion.

demagogos, pl. demagogoi   Etymologically this term has the neutral meaning 'leader of the people', and it could therefore be used to describe any democratic political leader. But it was commonly used like the English 'demagogue' in a pejorative sense ('mis-leader of the people', 'rabble-rouser') in the mouths of the traditional aristocracy, to describe those whom they regarded as upstarts, the new-style political leaders of the late fifth century; these were wealthy men such as Kleon, Hyperbolos and Kleophon, whose wealth was however derived from sources less respectable than land-owning (pp. 52 with n.47, 58 with n.69, 60, 95 n.38, 99 with n.48, 107 with n.19, 118 with n.49).

demarkh, Gk. *demarkhos*   See *svv. apographē**, deme* (2).

demos, pl. *demoi* (use of Eng. deme is confined to sense (2) below)   This is a term used in two radically different senses, and with significant further shades of meaning within at least one of the two.

(1)   It can mean 'the people of Athens', either the whole citizen population or else the common people as contrasted with the rich. In the first sense (1a) it is commonly used especially in official documents as a virtual synonym for the *ekklesia**; the second sense (1b) is implicit behind hostile interpretations of the term *demokratia**.

(2)   But *demos* is also used to denote the *c.* 140 villages or civil parishes (Eng. 'demes') into which Attica (including the city of Athens) was divided; shortly before 500 B.C. the reforms of Kleisthenes had organised these demes into the ten 'tribes' (*phulai*), which for many purposes became the electoral districts of Athens. It is in this sense that for instance demarkh* comes to mean an official of the local deme rather than of the whole state.

For *demos* in sense (1a), see pp. 43, 48, 50, 52, 54, 55, 57–8, 96; in sense (1b), see pp. 118, 133, 137 with n.41 and n.42, 141, 143, and possibly 105 n. 9; and in sense (2), see pp. 96, 110 n.25, 118. The name Demos (pp. 44–6) may be a play on both (1a) and (1b).

demokratia   'Sovereign authority (*kratos*) of the people', either in the interests of the state as a whole (*demos* (1a) above), or else serving the narrow interests of the common people rather than those of the rich (*demos* (1b) above), depending on the prejudices of the speaker (pp. 43, cf. 48 and 50, 45 n. 17).

diadikasia   Lit. 'judgement (contested) between': a dispute between two people who each claim the same thing, in particular a contested inheritance (p. 37 n.32). Compare *sv. epidikasia**, and see further *sv.* inheritance*.

diaitetes, pl. *diaitetai*   An arbitrator. Throughout the history of Athenian law, it had always been open for litigants to arrange arbitration (*diaita*) on a private basis: in theory, the decision of a private arbitrator was binding, presumably because the litigants had voluntarily contracted to accept it. There was also, however, a system of public arbitration, introduced *c.* 400 B.C.: every hoplite (or possibly every citizen), in the year that he ceased to be eligible for military service at the age of 59, had to serve as public arbitrator; and every *dikē** (private dispute) was allocated by lot to one of them for an attempt at preliminary resolution. In such cases arbitration was compulsory (litigants were obliged to attend) but it was not binding (a dissatisfied litigant could refuse to accept the verdict: see *sv. ephesis**). According to Aristotle, the job of the arbitrator (private or public) is unlike that of the *dikastes** in several respects: he should try to reconcile the parties before imposing a solution; he has the discretion to bring in a decision mid-way between the demands of the litigants (contrast *sv. timē** (3)); and in his judgement he should look to *epieikeia** ('equity', but see further *sv. epieikeia*) rather than to *dikē** ('justice'). See generally pp. 16–17, 35 n. 29, 55.

diamarturia   A formal presentation of a witness (*martus**) whose evidence serves to compel the public official before whom it is presented either to act in a certain way, or (more commonly) to desist from so acting. As a result of the introduction of *paragraphē** around 400 B.C., the scope of *diamarturia* was soon rapidly restricted: after 380 B.C., its only attested use is in inheritance* cases, where a legitimate son could have a claim by a more remote relative quashed on the grounds that the case was not actionable; to re-open the case, the rival claimant would have successfully to prosecute the witness by *dikē pseudomarturion**. For *diamarturia* as an institution, see p. 30; for discussion of an early case, see p. 89.

(the) Digest   A compilation of authoritative excerpts from the works of earlier jurists, issued at the command of the Emperor Justinian in the early sixth century A.D. as the chief part of his codification of Roman law: pp. 2, 143.

dikastai kata demous   See *sv.* Forty*, the.

dikastes, pl. *dikastai*; Eng. dikast(s)   A man who served on an Athenian *dikasterion**, fulfilling the functions both of a modern juror and of a modern judge (pp. 19, 44, 95 n.38, 100 with n.50). As in the case of the *boulē** and many other public offices, the position was restricted to citizens who had reached the age of thirty.

dikasterion, pl. *dikasteria*; Eng. dikastery/ies   One of the numerous People's Courts of Athens, to be contrasted with those special courts which were not manned by *dikastai**, such as the Areiopagos*. The typical *dikasterion* consisted of 200–500 *dikastai**, selected by lot* (see also *svv.* kleroterion, pinakion**). See generally pp. 19, 42, 44, 48, 50, 59, 95, 96 n.41.

dikē, pl. *dikai*   A concept of wide scope: 'justice', 'good order', 'judgement' (p. 13). But it can also refer to the process by which a just settlement is determined, thus 'a lawsuit', 'a trial', and even 'the case which one pleads' or 'the penalty which one has to pay'. In the sense of 'lawsuit', *dikē* can be used either generically, to refer to any type of indictment, or else (more commonly) in a semi-technical sense, to denote the older 'private suit' (which only the aggrieved party or his immediate personal representatives could bring) as opposed to the newer 'public suit' (*graphē**), which could be brought by any citizen in good standing; it should however be noted that the category of public procedure was broader than that of *graphē*, and included a number of extraordinary procedures which were not themselves *graphai* (p. 57): see for instance *svv. apagogē**, *apophasis**, *eisangelia**, *euthunai**, *phasis**. For *dikē* in the sense of 'private suit', see pp. 55, 84 n.3, 92, 94, 96, 125, 133, 138 n.44; aspects of the *dikē/graphē* distinction are discussed on pp. 37 n.33, 55–7, 69 n.21, 91–3 with 93 n.30, 98, 139.

Note: It seems that these indictments in Athenian law were only allowed if use of the *dikē* or *graphē* procedure against a particular offence was authorised by statute; whether the defendant's alleged behaviour fell within the terms of this offence could of course be a matter for debate. An indictment was normally described as a *dikē* (or *graphē*, as appropriate), qualified by the name of the offence, usually in the genitive case: thus *graphē hubreos*, a public indictment for *hubris*. For convenience in this glossary, procedures discussed are listed alphabetically under the title of the offence rather than under *dikē* or *graphē*.

diobelia   The 'two-obol fund', instituted apparently by Kleophon during the latter stages of the Peloponnesian War; its function was to give grants to poor citizens, presumably as war-relief, but the details of the distribution and of the fund itself are obscure (p. 97).

diomosia   A special oath taken in cases of homicide: in all other cases the litigants alone swore the *antomosia* (lit. 'oath [of two people] against each other'); in homicide cases all the witnesses had to join in the oath of their principals, which was for this reason known as the *diomosia* (lit. 'oath between [more than two people]'): p. 36. See further *sv.* oath*, *sv. phonou**, *dikē*.

disfranchisement   See *sv. atimia**.

dokimasia, pl. *dokimasiai*   An investigation held either by the *boulē** or in a court, to test whether a man was formally qualified either to hold the public office to which he had been appointed or else to exercise a privilege to which he was laying claim. *Dokimasiai* were of various types, and were for the most part held in advance: no public official, whether elected or appointed by lot*, could hold office without having passed his *dokimasia*; and newly enrolled citizens, whether by birth or by naturalisation (uncommon), were among those similarly tested. In these cases a man who was rejected suffered disqualification but no further penalty; a public speaker however (see *sv. rhetor**) could be challenged to undergo a retroactive *dokimasia* before a court, and this had more of the nature of a regular trial, in that if convicted he would apparently be punished.

drakhmē, pl. *drakhmai*; Eng. drachma   See *sv.* coinage*.

ecclesia   See *sv. ekklesia**.

eisangelia, pl. *eisangeliai*   Lit. 'public announcement, laying of information': a form of public indictment broadly corresponding to impeachment in the USA. It was available for use against any public official during or after his term of office (he would normally be suspended from office for the duration of the trial) or against any political leader who had made a public proposal. It seems that the case could be brought either directly to the *ekklesia** or else to the *boulē**, and that the final hearing would take place either before the *ekklesia* or (more commonly, and in every known case after 360 B.C.) before a *dikasterion**. See pp. 31, 39, 80, 106 with n.15, 111, and for detailed discussion 78 n.64.

eisphora, pl. *eisphorai*   An occasional tax on property (unlike modern taxes, which are usually charged on income), levied at Athens at times of financial shortage. It was imposed on the richer citizens, apparently as a fixed (i.e., non-progressive) percentage of their total wealth. The total number liable at any time is unknown, but may have been several thousand; at any rate, considerably more were liable to pay this tax than to undergo liturgies*.

ejectment   See *sv. exoules**, *dikē*.

ekdosis   Lit. 'giving forth': the ceremony at which the *kurios** of a betrothed bride gave her into the hand of her new husband. Marriage* in Athenian law took one of two forms, either by *enguē** and *ekdosis* or else (if a man died leaving his daughter with no *kurios* to give her away, and no heir to his property) by the *epidikasia** of the *epikleros**, for which see further *sv.* inheritance*.

ekklesia   The public assembly of Athens, held usually on the Pnyx*, at which all adult male citizens were formally entitled to attend, vote and speak (pp. 16 n.33, 50, 55, 78 n.64, 95 with n.38, 96 n.41).

(the) Eleven; Gk. *hoi hendeka*   A board of public officials responsible for the state prison of Athens. The majority of *apagogai** were brought before them, and they were in charge of all executions. See p. 76.

emmenos dikē, pl. *emmenoi dikai*   Lit. 'monthly case': for the meaning of 'monthly' here, see *sv. emporikē** *dikē*.

emporikē dikē, pl. *emporikai dikai*   A case involving *emporoi*, traders who import goods (especially the extra grain which was needed to feed the population of Attica). Because of the urgency of the trade, such cases had rapid and privileged access to the courts; but it is not clear whether the term *emmenos*, commonly used to describe them, should be interpreted to mean that the case must be completed within a month (the traditional view), or (as has recently been argued) that there was an opportunity every month to initiate such cases; it is uncertain also whether such litigation could take place only during the summer months or only during the winter months. It is possible that other special rules may have applied in these cases: see pp. 26 n.12, 29 n.15, 32 n.23, 187 n.42.

endeixis, pl. *endeixeis*   A procedure closely related to *apagoge**. The precise significance of the term is disputed: traditionally it was thought to be a denunciation made before a public offical who would then himself arrest the culprit; but it may instead have been used by the plaintiff in some cases as a voluntary preliminary to *apagoge*. See further pp. 39 n.35, 92, 106 with n.16.

engue, pl. *enguai*; *enguetes*   A surety: the *engue* is the thing which is pledged as security, and the *enguetes* the person who pledges or commits himself as a pledge. Such sureties were used in a range of legal contexts: to guarantee the payment of a fine or the appearance of a defendant (particularly a foreigner) in court; and as a deposit payable by those who contracted from the state the right to collect taxes or to operate mining-concession (see *sv. poletai**). But the most notable use of *engue* was as the necessary prelude to *ekdosis** in the regular Athenian form of marriage*, corresponding to (but much stronger than) the modern engagement.

enktesis   Tenure of land by a person who is not a citizen of the community in which he holds it. It was one of various privileges (see also *sv. isoteleia**) which could be granted at Athens to individual metics*. Surviving inscriptions record grants of 'enktesis of land' or 'of a house' or 'of land and a house', but it is not known whether the three categories are legally distinct, or simply the product of casual draughtsmanship.

ep' autophoroi   Catching the culprit 'red-handed' was a necessary preliminary to *apagoge** and summary execution (pp. 65, 76). It is not wholly certain however whether *ep' autophoroi* meant 'caught in the act (of theft, for instance)' or (more probably) 'caught in such circumstances as to make denial of the offence impossible'.

ephebos, pl. *epheboi*; Eng. ephebe(s)   An adolescent who is on the threshold of adulthood. The early history of the institution (*ephebeia*) is obscure: it may possibly have derived from primitive *rites de passage* (rituals of transition from boyhood to adulthood); in the later fourth century however the *ephebeia* was formalised (at least for those of hoplite* status and above), so that young men at the age of (probably) eighteen had to undergo two years of compulsory military service before being admitted to the full exercise of their rights as citizens. But the term is used widely well before this time to refer to (rich) young men (p. 140).

ephegesis, pl. *ephegeseis*   A procedure closely related to *apagoge** and *endeixis**, the characteristic feature of *ephegesis* is that the arrest is made not by the complainant but by a public official acting upon his denunciation (p. 75 n.52).

ephesis   Refusal to accept the decision of an official or a court of first instance, combined with a demand for the dispute to be resolved by a higher authority. For instance, Solon in the 590s B.C. is said to have introduced '*ephesis* to the *dikasterion**' as a curb on the summary jurisdiction of public officials; and from their introduction in *c.* 400 B.C., the decisions of public arbitrators (see *sv. diaitetes**) were similarly subject to *ephesis*. *Ephesis* is conventionally translated 'appeal', but this can have misleading connotations. An appeal in English law is brought on the initiative of a dissatisfied litigant (in criminal cases, a convicted defendant) after the court of first instance has decided against him/her; it is his/her duty to persuade the appellate court to reverse this decision, and s/he becomes in a sense the plaintiff in this process. In Athens, there were at least some situations in which *ephesis* could take place before the lower authority had reached a decision; it was the duty of the original plaintiff, not of the dissatisfied litigant, to persuade the court to act (that is, the court was re-trying the case from scratch and not reviewing a decision already made); and it is possible that in the case of Solonian *ephesis*, this referral was automatic and did not depend on an initiative taken by one of the two litigants.

epidikasia   Lit. 'a judgement (awarded) to': an uncontested claim to the estate of a dead man; if the claim was contested, it gave rise to a *diadikasia**. See further *sv*. inheritance*.

epieikeia   Aristotle says that it is the function of the *dikastes** (juror/judge) to judge according to *dikē** ('justice'), but that the *diaitetes** (arbitrator) should make his decision according to *epieikeia*. It is conventional therefore to translate *epieikeia* as 'equity', since this is a standard and convenient way to describe 'fairness' or 'natural justice' as opposed to the strict application of legal rules. There are however certain problems here. Equity in English law can mean simply 'fairness', but it is also the name given to the system of law developed originally by the Court of Chancery (the Lord Chancellor's court), to provide relief in cases where to apply the rules of the common* law would have seemed manifestly unfair. 'Equity' in this sense is itself a body of rules; it is found only in countries which base their legal system on the common law; and it is clearly not what Aristotle is talking about. It should indeed be noted that Aristotle's statement of theory receives little acknowledgment in Athenian practice: when a litigant in an extant speech pleads for the application of natural justice in his favour, he characteristically describes this as *dikē* and not as *epieikeia*. See further p. 179 with n.25.

epikleros (fem. adj. acting as noun), epiklerate (abstract noun)   An *epikleros* was the daughter of a man who died leaving no male heir; she was not his heiress, but possession of his estate went together with her hand in marriage. This system of inheritance is described as the epiklerate: for further details, see *sv*. inheritance*; and for comparison, see *sv. enguē** and *sv. ekdosis**. (The etymology of *epikleros* is unclear: it may possibly mean 'one to whom the property pertains', but more likely is 'one who pertains to the property'.)

epobelia   See *sv*. court-fees*.

equity   See *sv. epieikeia**.

eranos   A word with a cluster of meanings, having in common the idea of shared and reciprocal contributions (e.g., to a common meal). In legal contexts, *eranos* commonly refers to the contributions supplied by a number of lenders to a *philos* (friend or associate) who was in financial difficulties. The size of the individual contributions varied according to the means of the lender and the needs of the borrower, but tended to be small in scale. *Eranos*-loans were interest-free, and were given on the understanding that repayment would be made as soon as the borrower was in funds. See generally pp. 183 with n.34, 187, 188.

euthunē, normally pl. *euthunai*   Lit. 'the action of setting straight'. Every public official at Athens had to undergo at the end of his term an examination of his conduct in office. If he had handled public money, he had to present his accounts (*logoi*, pl.); in all cases he had to seek approval of the way he had used his powers (*euthunai* properly so called, but the term *euthunai* came also to be applied to the whole process of audit, *logoi* included). The examination was conducted by boards of *logistai* (pl.) and *euthunoi* (pl.), as appropriate; but any private citizen could bring a charge at any stage during the proceedings. For *euthunai* see pp. 31, 39, 78, 79 n.67; for the *euthunoi* see p. 65.

euthunoi   See *sv. euthunē**.

execution   For execution in the sense of capital punishment, see *sv.* penalty*, and for summary execution in this sense see *sv. apagogē**. The term 'execution' however is more often used by lawyers to mean execution of judgement: if the court decides in favour of the plaintiff and awards him either damages or some other recompense at the hands of the defendant, how does the plaintiff get his hands on what he is now entitled to? In Athenian law, execution of judgement was left almost entirely in the hands of the individual, with minimal assistance from the state: see further *sv. exoules**, *dikē*.

exegetes, pl. *exegetai*   Lit. 'interpreter'. A group of officials who expound the proper procedure in situations which raise unusual questions of religious law. Their activity is attested in several cases, all of homicide; and in each case they are responding to an enquiry by an individual rather than as expert witnesses before a court. In one case they offer also to advise a litigant, implying that this was something more than their regular function of interpreting the law.

exomosia   Lit. 'an oath rejecting (something)': an oath denying knowledge of a fact, taken by a man who was unwilling to act as witness when challenged; the precise significance of the procedure is discussed on pp. 24–5, 36. See also *sv. lipomartu-riou**, *dikē*.

(dikē*) exoules   A possession-order: a private indictment designed to eject the holder from a piece of real* property claimed by the plaintiff. The *dikē exoules* could only be brought if the plaintiff had one of several statutorily privileged rights to the property in question, the most significant of which was that it had already been adjudicated to him by a previous court-hearing. This procedure therefore played a major rôle in the execution* of judgement, because in Athenian law it was the responsibility of the successful plaintiff in any action to collect whatever damages he had been awarded: if the defendant proved unable or unwilling to pay, the plaintiff could bring a *dikē exoules* against him, which would then entitle him to seize property in payment of the debt. Although the state took no active part in the seizure, a plaintiff armed with a *dikē exoules* became in a sense the state's agent: he was licensed to use any necessary violence, and to resist him was to commit the serious offence of *hubris**.

fine   See *sv.* penalty*.

(the) Forty   A board of public officials in the fourth century, whose duties were entirely judicial. They took over the functions of the earlier *dikastai kata demous* or 'judges in the demes' ('deme' here is used in *demos** sense (2)): but the latter term continued to be used loosely to describe the new board, even though the Forty unlike their predecessors did not go out on circuit. They were organised on a tribal basis, with four allocated to each of the ten tribes (not their own): they received those private cases (see *sv. dikē**) which did not fall within the competence of other magistrates, a group of cases which corresponded closely if not exactly to those which were subject to public arbitration. Cases were submitted to one (probably) of the judges allocated to the defendant's tribe: if the sum at issue were very small (less than ten *drakhmai*: see *sv.* coinage*), he could decide it summarily; otherwise he was obliged to refer it to a public arbitrator, and only in case of appeal would he bring it before a court (see *svv. diaitetes**, *ephesis**).

freedman See *sv. apeleutheros**.

graphē, pl. *graphai* Lit. 'a writing'; hence 'a written indictment', cf. Eng. 'writ'. This was the name given to the new 'public' form of ordinary prosecution introduced apparently by Solon in the 590s. Its characteristic was that the indictment could be brought by any qualified citizen (*ho boulomenos**), whereas the older *dikē** procedure could be brought only by the injured party. *Graphai* and other public procedures appear to have given rise to higher penalties, and thus to have rewarded a successful plaintiff much more heavily than did *dikai*; but they were also considerably more risky: a plaintiff in a public suit who failed to obtain 20 per cent of the votes of the jury could expect to suffer a heavy fine and possibly also other penalties (e.g. at least partial *atimia**). See further pp. 29 n.15, 56–7, 69 n.21, 92–3, 95 n.38, 106 with n.12 and n.13, 111, 123–4, 125, 132–4; and for the naming of the various *graphai*, see the note *sv. dikē** above.

(*hoi*) *hendeka* See *sv.* Eleven, the*.

hetaira, pl. *hetairai* Lit. 'female companion': the normal Greek word for a courtesan, call-girl or high-class prostitute (pp. 133 n.29, 135, 137 n.41, 145, 164, 176 n.17), which can be confusing for a modern reader (compare *hetairos**).

hetaireia, pl. *hetaireiai* A term used to describe aristocratic drinking-clubs, which might or might not have political in addition to their social aims (pp. 52 with n.47, 143). See also *sv. sunomosia**.

hetairos, pl. *hetairoi* Lit. 'comrade(s), drinking-companion(s)': member(s) of a *hetaireia** (pp. 45 n.19, 54, 93 n.33).

hierosulia Temple-robbery (pp. 70 with n.27, 73 n.39): a particularly blatant form of *asebeia**.

ho boulomenos See *sv. boulemenos**, *ho*.

hoi hendeka See *sv.* Eleven*, the.

homicide See *sv. phonou**, *dikē*.

hoplite Heavy-armed infantryman. Greek armies were essentially citizen militias, and it was customary for soldiers to provide their weapons. (Sparta may have been an exception in this respect, as in so many others.) As a result in late fifth- and in fourth-century Athens the cavalry was the preserve of the upper classes (probably no more than the richest 5 per cent of the citizen-body); the hoplites will have comprised perhaps the next 30–40 per cent. These figures are of course no more than plausible guesses.

horos, pl. *horoi* Lit. 'boundary': by extension, inscribed stones, marking the boundary of a piece of property; by further extension, applied to inscriptions placed on the boundary of the property to warn third parties that the person in possession did not have the unencumbered right to dispose of it (e.g., because he had offered the property as security for a loan: pp. 176–8). Three types of transaction are recorded on extant *horoi*: *hupothekē*, *prasis epi lusei*, and *apotimema*; but the precise nature of the distinction between these terms is unclear (see further p. 178).

(*graphē**) *hubreos* A public indictment concerning *hubris** (pp. 123–45 *passim*).

hubris   The core-concept of *hubris* is disputed: it is probably an action which intentionally causes damage to the *timē** of the person suffering it (p. 126). See generally pp. 123–45, and also 158 with n.31.

hubristes   A person who commits *hubris** (pp. 131, 132, 135, 139).

hupothekē   See *sv. horos**.

imprisonment   See *sv.* penalty*.

inheritance   The inheritance regulations of classical Athens were very distinctive. If the deceased left a direct heir or heirs in the male line, then he had in effect no powers to make a will; and immediately, without the need for a court hearing, the inheritance passed to the heir(s) (see *sv.* partible* inheritance). If however the deceased had no male heir but left a daughter, she became an *epikleros**: that is, she was not herself the heiress, but possession of the property was vested in her. The man who married her took the estate, but apparently only as a trustee: when the sons of this marriage reached adulthood, the property reverted to them. The function of this institution is disputed: was it intended (as has traditionally been believed) to provide an heir for a household that would otherwise lack one? or was the aim (as has recently been suggested) to protect the interests of the propertied woman in a society where she had no real control over her property and her marital prospects, by ensuring that an unscrupulous male next-of-kin did not seek to keep her unmarried in the eventual hope of inheriting her property? A man who had no direct male heir did have the power to make a will: its purpose would be primarily to fill the absence of an heir, normally by posthumously adopting a male relative or close friend as son, or marrying him to the testator's daughter, or both; if the deceased died without heir and intestate*, then his relatives in a set order of kinship had the right to claim the hand of the *epikleros*, or if there was no *epikleros* to claim the estate in their own right. But whether or not there was a will, the destination of such an estate had to be confirmed by a *dikasterion** presided over by the *arkhon**, a hearing at which anybody might submit a claim. An uncontested claim was known as an *epidikasia**; if there was a dispute between two or more claimants, the hearing was called a *diadikasia**. It was notorious that Athenian *dikastai** tended to rank the claims of relatives ahead of the intentions of the testator.

inquisitorial   An inquisitorial system of justice (p. 23) is one in which the judge in a criminal trial is charged with discovering the truth: he will normally direct proceedings, deciding what witnesses to call and examining them in person. This is the basis of the system of criminal justice that operates in most civil-law* countries. See for contrast *sv.* adversarial* system.

intestacy (noun); intestate (adj.)   In English law, intestacy is the condition of dying without leaving a will; a person who does this is described as intestate. Athenian regulations for inheritance are summarised *sv.* inheritance*.

isoteleia   Lit., 'equality of taxation': one of a number of privileges granted by individual decree to particularly favoured metics*; the privilege in this case was exemption from the *metoikion**, the regular direct tax to which all metics were otherwise liable. For other similar privileges, see *sv. enktesis**.

judge   See *sv. dikastes**

jury   See *sv. dikastes**.

(*dikē**) *kakegorias* Lit. '(prosecution concerning) evil-speaking': a private indictment concerning slander (p. 133). It is not clear whether any allegedly false statement was actionable, or only certain phrases or statements made in certain situations.

(*dikē**) *kakotekhnion* Lit. '(prosecution concerning) wrongful plotting': a private indictment brought against a man who had suborned a false witness (p. 36 n.31).

kakourgos, pl. *kakourgoi* Lit. 'evil-doer', 'malefactor'. *Kakourgoi* caught red-handed could be arrested by means of *apagogē**, but it is not certain whether this procedure could be used against any criminal so caught, or whether for the purpose of *apagogē* the term *kakourgos* acquired a semi-technical meaning to denote certain offences specified by statute: the latter seems more likely. See p. 147.

kalos kagathos, pl. *kaloi kagathoi* Lit. 'attractive and honourable', or 'handsome and virtuous', thus 'gentleman': a self-approbatory term used by the Athenian aristocrat to describe himself and his fellows (pp. 100–1 with 100 n.51, 104 n.2, 116, 128).

khoregos, pl. *khoregoi* 'Leader or producer of a chorus': the term refers not to a member of the chorus in a drama nor to a playwright, but to the impresario who has to undertake as his liturgy* the *khoregia*; that is, paying for the production of a play at one of the annual dramatic festivals organised either by the *polis** or by one of the demes* (p. 134).

klepsudra Lit. 'water-stealer'. A water-clock, used to regulate the length of proceedings in legal cases. It consisted of a bowl of water with a small hole near the base, such that the hole could be stopped or opened as desired: normally two such bowls were used, the one being allowed to empty its contents into the other, and then *vice versa*, to measure the passage of time. In any category of case, a set number of bowls-full was allocated to each speaker, but the flow of water was stopped for the reading of laws and the testimony of witness.

kleros, pl. *kleroi* Originally 'the action of casting lots'; hence 'that which is allotted', often 'a man's landed property'; and thus 'an estate which is to be inherited'. *Logoi klerikoi*, speeches concerning *kleroi* (inheritance disputes), were a recognised category of forensic oratory; but there is no evidence for a *dikē** or a *graphē* kleron* (see further pp. 36–7 with 37 n.32); instead, inheritance disputes were normally dealt with by means of *diadikasia**.

kleroterion A machine used in the fourth century B.C. to allocate *dikastai** to lawcourts: see further *svv.* lot*, *pinakion**.

kleter, pl. *kleteres; kleteusis* Lit. 'one who calls', etc. *Kleteusis* is the action of summoning either a defendant or a witness to court. The significance of the rules for the *kleteusis* of witness is discussed on pp. 24–5. In the case of a defendant, on the other hand, it is the plaintiff's job to enforce the summons; and he would take one or more *kleteres* (summons-witness: p. 37 n.33) with him. If the defendant failed to attend and the court was satisfied by the *kleteres* that he had been properly summoned, the verdict would be delivered against him automatically; if subsequently he wished to contest this, he had to claim that the summons had never been served, by convicting the witness of lying (see *pseudokletias**, *graphē*).

klopē Theft (pp. 63–82 *passim*). Very unusually, this was an offence which could be prosecuted by both *dikē** and *graphē**. It is however possible (though not certain) that the latter was reserved for cases of embezzlement or theft from public sources.

(*dikē**) *klopes* See p. 75 with n.48 and n.52, 76 with n.57, 79 with n.67, and also *sv.* *klopē** above.

(*graphē**) *klopes*   See pp. 56 n.61, 75 n.49, 79 n.67, and also *sv. klopē** above.
kratos   Power or authority: see *sv. demokratia**.
krisis   A judgement or decision: the word is used to describe all forms of decision-making, but particularly that of a court: p. 43.
kurios   Lit. 'master', 'lord', or in certain contexts 'sovereign'. An Athenian woman had to be represented in legal transactions by a male relative, who was described as her *kurios*: in the case of an unmarried girl or a widow who had returned to the house of her family, this would normally be her father or (failing him) her brother or paternal uncle, but it could even be her adult son. A married woman was represented by her husband, but it appears that her agnatic* *kurios* did retain certain rights: for instance, the reversion of her dowry. Confusingly, the term *kurios* was also used to denote the owner of property or master of a household, and there are contexts in which the two uses might conflict: a married son, for instance, would be *kurios* of his wife; but his father may still be *kurios* of his household.

law-making   See *sv. nomothesia**.
legislation   See *sv. nomothesia**.
(statute of) limitations   See *sv. prothesmia**.
(*dikē**) *lipomarturiou*   A private indictment against a man who refuses to witness: the precise constituents of the offence are discussed on p. 25 with n.11. See also *sv. exomosia**.
liturgy; Gk. *leitourgia*, pl. *leitourgiai*   Much of Athenian public expenditure was met, not by the state paying out money which it had collected as taxes, but in the form of compulsory public service imposed on rich individuals (mostly citizens, but for some tasks metics* were included). The tasks in question were called *leitourgiai* ('works for the people'), conventionally transliterated as 'liturgies', but with none of the ecclesiastical overtones of the English term. These *leitourgiai* included the *khoregia** (paying for the production of a play at a dramatic festival) and the trierarkhy* (paying for the crew and the upkeep of a warship for a year). There was of course an element of competitive outlay implicit in this system: an impressively-performed liturgy stood to win great prestige for its performer, and this could be exchanged into political currency (*kharis*: p. 54). There were also possibilities of tax-fraud and under-declaration of wealth: hence the need for the *antidosis**. The number of men liable to undertake liturgies at any one time is unknown, but was probably no more than 300–400, at least if we exclude the trierarkhs (p. 53 n.53) – considerably fewer and considerably richer than those liable to pay *eisphorai**, because the sums in question stood to be much larger. For liturgies, see pp. 45, 53, 96, 137 with n.42.
logistai, (pl.)   See *sv. euthunai**.
logographia   The art of the *logographos**: p. 51.
logographos, pl. *logographoi*   Lit. 'speech-writer': specifically, a professional writer of speeches for litigants to deliver in court. It has recently been argued that the *logographos* did not normally write the speech so much as help the litigant to prepare it, but this view is contested. For the career of Antiphon, the first *logographos* whose work has survived, see pp. 48–52 (esp. p. 49 n.34), 60 n.79.
logoi, (pl.)   See *sv. euthunai**.
lot   The majority of public offices at Athens were filled not by election but by casting lots, on the ground that this was more democratic: elections, as Aristotle observed,

favour the well-known. A similar system was used in the daily allocation of *dikastai**
to lawcourts, although here the rationale was apparently to prevent jury-'nobbling':
see further *svv. kleroterion**, *pinakion**. For the details of selection for various
offices, see p. 117 n.46.

magistrate   See *sv. arkhē**.
marriage   For the two alternative types of marriage in Athenian law, see (for the
regular form) *svv. enguē** and *ekdosis**, and (for the procedure in the case of an
*epikleros**) *sv. epidikasia** and (for the implications of this) *sv*. inheritance**. For
Plato's suggestions, see p. 69 n.20.
martus, pl. *martures*   A witness: discussed in detail on pp. 19–35 *passim*, cf. also
p. 183.
marturia, pl. *marturiai*   The testimony of a *martus**: e.g. p. 31.
metic; Gk. *metoikos*, pl. *metoikoi*   A non-citizen resident more or less permanently in
a Greek *polis** (metics are attested in more than 70 *poleis*, but in so little detail that
virtually all our information derives from Athens): pp. 27 n.14, 53, 73, 94 n.37, 106
n.13. Metics at Athens were subject to considerable restrictions; for instance, they
were obliged to pay a special *metoikion** or metic-tax, and to register the name of a
citizen as their *prostates**, and they were not entitled to own land: see for contrast
*svv. enktesis**, *isoteleia**.
metoikion   Lit., 'metic-tax': see *sv*. metic**. Only a tyrant, in Greek political thought,
imposed regular direct taxation on his subjects; it is notable that all citizen taxes at
Athens were either irregular (like the *eisphora**) or indirect (like liturgies** or
harbour dues): even though the tax itself may not have been financially crippling
(our sources suggest a rate of one drachma per month for men, and half this for
women), to impose a direct regular tax on metics was nevertheless a potent statement
of their subordinate status.
mina; Gk. *mna*   See *sv*. coinage**.
misthos   Pay for holding public office: Greek political theory regarded this as one of
the distinguishing features of a democracy. At Athens the *dikastai** were paid for
attendance from the 450s (p. 44), and the members of the *ekklesia** from approximately 400 (p. 50 with n.42). Public officials were certainly paid during the late fifth
century, and in both fifth and fourth centuries they received *sitesis* (probably meals
at public expense, rather than an allowance in lieu); but it is disputed whether they
received *misthos* during the fourth century.
mna; Eng. mina   See *sv*. coinage**.
moikheia   Adultery: discussed in detail in pp. 147–65 *passim*.
moikhos   One who commits *moikheia**.
money   See *sv*. coinage**.
monthly case   See *sv. emmenos** dikē.

natural law   See *sv*. positive** law.
(*graphē**) *nomon mē epitedeion theinai*   See *sv. paranomon**, graphē.
nomos, pl. *nomoi*   Lit. a 'norm', in the sense both of 'custom' and of 'law' (pp. 11–12,
142, 184 n.37, 194). *Nomos* is often contrasted, especially in fifth-century Greek
thought, with *phusis* (lit. 'nature'); the latter represents underlying reality, and the
former denotes the patterns by which men try to shape this. In this sense *nomos* is
normally translated 'convention'.

Nomos was also, at least after 500 B.C., the normal word for 'a law' in the sense of 'a statute' (e.g. p. 143 n.14); before this, the word *thesmos* had been preferred, and the change is surely significant: 'that which is laid down (by the gods?)' has given way to 'the order that men impose'; for various interpretations of the significance of the change, see p. 12 n.23. In classical usage, a distinction should be drawn between *nomos* (sing.), meaning 'a law' in the sense of a particular statute, and *nomoi* (pl.), meaning 'law' or 'the law' in the sense of 'the constitution' or perhaps even 'the legal system'.

One additional contrast should be noted, that between *nomos* and *psephisma** (lit. 'decree'). In the fifth century there was no difference in law between these two forms of statute; any decision of the *ekklesia** could be described either as a *nomos* or as a *psephisma*. From 403 B.C., however, a formal distinction was drawn: the *ekklesia* continued to pass *psephismata*, but this term was confined either to temporary rules or to those which applied only to named individuals; the passing (though not the proposing) of *nomoi*, rules which were intended to be of general and permanent validity, was taken out of the hands of the *ekklesia*. This served to enhance legal stability, and to prevent the overthrow of the *nomoi* ('constitution') in the way that was felt to have occurred too easily during the oligarchic revolution of 411 B.C.: it became much more difficult to change a *nomos* (for details see *sv. nomothesia**); and it was illegal for any proposed *psephisma* to contravene a *nomos*. See further *sv. paranomon**, *graphē*.

nomothesia; *nomothetes*, pl. *nomothetai*   *Nomothesia* is the process of enacting laws (of general and/or permanent validity: see *sv. nomos**). After 403 B.C., this was taken out of the hands of the *ekklesia** and given to the *nomothetai*, in order to provide a check on the passage of reckless legislation. The precise arrangements for the process seem to have been revised several times during the fourth century; but it is notable that the *nomothetai* were a body selected by lot* from among the panel of eligible *dikastai**. Their function was to hear in detail (but not apparently to discuss) the arguments for and against any proposed legislative change, and to make a final and authoritative decision. They could however only act when requested to do so on the initiative of the *ekklesia*.

nothos, pl. *nothoi*   Lit. 'a bastard'. In the classical period, Athenian citizenship was confined to those born of citizen parents on both sides. The child of an unmarried union between citizen and non-citizen was clearly illegitimate, and had rights neither of inheritance nor of citizenship. The status of the child of unmarried citizen parents is less clear: such a person was clearly a *nothos* without rights of inheritance, but it is disputed whether s/he was or was not a citizen. It is possible, though less certain, that the word *nothos* was used to describe the child of a mixed marriage even in those contexts (e.g. before 450 B.C.) where such a marriage was legally permissible, even though such a child might have full rights to inheritance as well as to citizenship.

oath   The use of the oath in Athenian law was very different from its use in a modern English court. Witnesses* were not normally required to swear, except in cases of homicide, where they had to join in the oath regularly sworn by the litigants (see *sv. diomosia**). Women however, who could not be witnesses, could in principle swear an oath, provided this was done with the agreement of both litigants: for the sole attested case, see p. 35; for the procedure, see pp. 26, 28, 33, 35 n.29, and also *sv. proklesis**; for the use of oaths in the *agora**, see pp. 172, 193 n.57.

oath-helper   A medieval witness who swears not to the truth of a fact but in support of the 'cleanness' of his principal's oath (p. 30). Sometimes known as a 'compurgator'.

obol   See *sv*. coinage*.

oikos   A household (p. 130): the word can be used to describe people or family property or a building, or all three together. The term is rarely used in the formulation of Athenian statutes, but the concept seems to play an important rôle not only in family but in citizenship law: see *svv*. *kurios**, marriage*, *nothos**; and compare the discussion of the epiklerate *sv*. inheritance*.

Old Oligarch   See *sv*. *Ath.Pol**.

ostracism   Every year the Athenian *ekklesia** had the right to decide whether to hold an ostracism, a ballot in which any citizen could vote against one political leader. If a quorum of 6,000 voted, the man with the most votes was exiled for ten years, but with no further penalty. The institution was frequently used in the first half of the fifth century; but it apparently fell into abeyance (apart from a single occasion probably in 417) after 443 B.C. A vote was cast by scratching a name on an *ostrakon* (a piece of broken pottery): hence the name of the procedure. See pp. 58, 94 n.37.

ostrakon, pl. *ostraka*   A vote in an ostracism*: several thousands of these *ostraka* have now been discovered, some bearing offensive personal remarks about the man named: p. 59 n.74.

paragraphē   A counter-indictment, in which the defendant charges the plaintiff with bringing an illegal prosecution (pp. 89, 92). The procedure was invented (or possibly re-organised) around 400, to help those threatened with charges which broke the Amnesty: the latter had been imposed under Spartan supervision to protect former supporters of the Thirty Tyrants, the oligarchic junta of 404/3 which had been overthrown by the democratic restoration of 403/2. *Paragraphē* however rapidly extended its scope: for the defendant, it seems to have had the advantage that it was itself a prosecution; whereas the older procedure of *diamarturia** simply served to block a particular claim by the plaintiff, *paragraphē* enabled the defendant to turn the tables, becoming himself the prosecutor and (if successful) imposing a penalty on his opponent.

parakatabolē   See *sv*. court-fees*.

(*graphē**) *paranomon*   A public indictment against the proposer of a new *psephisma** (decree), charging that his proposal is unconstitutional (lit. 'against the law'): pp. 31, 90, 95 n.38. One of the most extensively documented of all Athenian legal procedures, and one of the most overtly political: the prosecutor might claim for instance that the bill had been proposed without the necessary formalities; but many of the extant *graphai paranomon* are directed against honorary decrees, and in these the prosecutor regularly bases his case on the claim that the honour is itself undeserved. See also *sv*. *nomos**.

The procedure could be employed against proposals both before and after they had been voted on by the *ekklesia**. Until 403 B.C., it was apparently used without discrimination against both *nomoi* (laws) and *psephismata*; but in that year a formal distinction was for the first time drawn between the two types of statute (see *sv*. *nomos**). The old procedure of *graphē paranomon* was retained for use against *psephismata*; but a new parallel procedure, the *graphē nomon mē epitedeion theinai*, was felt to be required for use against unconstitutional (lit. 'inexpedient') *nomoi*: for the latter, see p. 31.

parastasis   See *sv.* court-fees*.

partible inheritance   The custom of dividing the estate of a dead man equally among his legitimate sons. This system obtained at Athens (p. 48), as presumably throughout the Greek world: for details on the Athenian system see *sv.* inheritance*. English land law however has traditionally rested on an assumption of primogeniture* (where everything passes to the eldest son), but this has now been abolished.

patriline   A man's relatives in the male line, particularly in a context of descent or inheritance (p. 46).

penalty   The penalties imposed by Athenian courts could affect either the person of the defendant (execution*, *atimia**) or else his property (either by fine or by confiscation, for which see *sv. apographē**). Imprisonment however was uncommon, at least as a penalty: it could be used for remand, particularly to ensure that a foreign defendant did not abscond before trial. In the case of fines, it is sometimes difficult to see whether the money is strictly a penalty (payable to the state) or damages (payable to the plaintiff): for the latter, see further *sv. exoules**, *dikē.*

personal property   English law classifies property as either 'real*' (broadly speaking, land and houses) or 'personal' (everything else: pp. 167–94 *passim*). The law treats the two categories of property in different ways, particularly in cases of intestate* inheritance. For the significance of a superficially similar distinction in Athenian law, see *sv. aphanes* ousia*.

phanera ousia   Lit. 'apparent or visible property': a category which roughly corresponded to English real* property (i.e., land and houses). For the contrasting term, and the significance of the contrast, see *sv. aphanes* ousia*.

phasis   Lit. 'a showing forth, declaration': denunciation of a man who is illegally withholding property which belongs to the state (pp. 57–8 with n.66 and n.68, 87 with n.11 and n.13, 90, 95 n.38, 106 with n.14, 111). Unlike the related (and much better attested) procedure of *apographē**, *phasis* was apparently directed against the person rather than the property.

(dikē) phonou*   A private indictment concerning murder, or more generally homicide: p. 33 n.24. In striking contrast to contemporary practice both in civil*-.and common*-law systems, homicide in Athenian law was normally dealt with by means of a *dikē*: in other words, only the immediate relatives of the deceased had the right (and duty) to bring an action. Homicide cases were heard by one of a number of courts, among which the Areiopagos* was only the most notable: the choice of court seems to have been determined both by the details of the charge (was the deceased a citizen, or a metic* or slave?) and also by the nature of the defendant's plea (claims of justifiable homicide for instance were heard by a special court). Procedure in homicide cases was in a variety of ways different from that of other cases: see *sv. diomosia**.

pinakion, pl. *pinakia*   Identity tokens, made of wood or bronze (several hundred of the latter have been discovered), used when lots were cast for the appointment of public officials or the selection of *dikastai** to hear a case: for the latter, see p. 43. For the process of casting lots, see also *svv. klēroterion**, lot*.

pistis, pl. *pisteis*   Lit. 'that which creates trust'. Traditionally translated 'proof' or 'evidence', but the term is used generally by ancient rhetorical theorists to describe all forms of supporting argument (pp. 32–3, 50, 179). For the distinction between *pisteis entekhnoi* and *pisteis atekhnoi*, see p. 32.

plethos   Lit. 'a mass of people' (p. 52 n.48): the term has a range of meanings similar to *demos** (1). It can be used by public speakers in a favourable or neutral sense to mean virtually 'your democracy' (unlike *demos* however the word itself is not found in this sense in official Athenian documents); or it can be used by hostile critics to mean 'the mob' or 'the rabble'.

pnyx   The hill on which meetings of the Athenian *ekklesia** were held (pp. 49, 50).

polemarkhos   See *sv. arkhon**.

poletai   Lit., 'sellers'. A board of public officials whose principal duty was to sell state property by auction. Since there was no state administration capable of handling it, confiscated property (see *sv. apographē**) was normally sold at the earliest possible opportunity; but the *poletai* also leased out concessions to operate the silver-mines (things underground, in Athenian law, remained the inalienable property of the state) and to collect taxes (there was no Inland Revenue, at Athens as at Rome: once again, this was beyond the administrative capabilities of the state).

polis, pl. *poleis*   Conventionally if awkwardly translated 'city-state', but for that reason perhaps better transliterated. The typical constitutional unit of the classical Greek world: an independent self-governing community, made up of both urban centre (*astu*) and rural hinterland (*khora*). Two striking characteristics of the classical *polis* should be noted: first, they were generally very small geographical units and there were a lot of them; secondly, the hinterland was surprisingly free from domination by the urban centre. For the *polis* as a place, see p. 57 with n.67; for the *polis* as an ideal or a concept, see pp. 10 with n.19, 95, 96, 99, 101, 117, 126, 142, 144, 145, 172, 174, 179, 183, 184 n.37.

politeia (abstract noun derived from *polis**)   A word with a cluster of meanings, most notably 'constitution' (as in the title *Athenaion Politeia*, or 'Constitution of the Athenians': see *sv. Ath.Pol.**), and 'citizenship' (in the sense of the status or privilege of being a citizen).

polites, pl. *politai*   A member of a *polis**; hence, a (male) citizen as opposed to metic* or a slave: p. 43. The word 'politics' (*ta politika*: 'things pertaining to the *polis*') was a classical Greek invention.

(*hoi*) *politeuomenoi* (pl. participle)   Lit. 'those who (regularly) take part in the affairs of the *polis**': p. 118 n.50. In the fifth century, a would-be political leader aimed ideally to hold public office, for instance as *strategos**; in the fourth century this was no longer the norm. This change had effects on the vocabulary of politics: the normal way to describe active politicians in the fourth century became '*rhetores** and *politeuomenoi*' rather than holders of specific offices.

polupragmon, pl. *polupragmones* (adj.); *polupragmosunē* (abstract noun)   Lit. 'one who conducts much business', i.e. 'too much'. Usually pejorative in the eyes of the speaker. The fifth-century Athenian empire was according to its opponents the product of corporate Athenian *polupragmosunē*; on an individual level (p. 110), the term has the overtones of 'officious' and 'busybody'. For comparison, see *sv. apragmon**.

positive law   Law seen as the creation of a human source and for a human context. The term is associated most notably with the name of the early nineteenth-century jurist John Austin, who put it forward as an alternative to the natural* law theory developed by Thomas Aquinas, the thirteenth-century theologian and philosopher. For Aquinas the existence of law is embedded within God Himself, and all law therefore necessarily has a moral content. For Austin and other positivists, law is a human creation; and although it may have a moral content, it need not. In Austin's thought, what gives positive law (which he regarded as identical to 'law strictly so called') its authority is that it is the command of a political superior; this is the essence of his so-called 'command' theory of law. There are however, other positivists, such as the contemporary jurisprudent Sir Herbert Hart, who regard law as a human creation but do not share Austin's 'command' theory.

prasis epi lusei   See *sv. horos**.

primogeniture   The system of inheritance whereby the whole estate descends to the eldest son to the exclusion of sisters and younger brothers. It was characteristic of Norman and English feudalism, and appears to have been attractive because it kept military fiefs intact. It applied only to real* property; and even here, its rigidity was in practice softened by rules granting a life-interest in a proportion of the estate to the widower or widow of the deceased. It was important in medieval English land law because the law severely restricted the freedom of testators to devise landed property by will. In the seventeenth century, however, these restrictions were substantially abolished: since then, primogeniture has applied only in cases of intestate* succession; its application here was further restricted by a series of nineteenth-century statutes, and it was finally abolished in 1926. For the normal practice of Athenian law, see *sv*. partible* inheritance.

probolē, pl. *probolai*   Lit. 'a throwing forward'. A preliminary accusation, which an intending plaintiff could bring before the *ekklesia** rather than directly to a *dikasterion**. This vote of the *ekklesia* had no formal effect: it did not bind a successful plaintiff to continue his action in court, nor apparently did it prevent him from so doing if unsuccessful; it imposed no penalty either on plaintiff or on defendant. It did however strengthen the hand of the successful plaintiff: after the manner of a straw poll, it showed which way the wind was blowing. We hear of *probolē* being used in disputes which arise at festivals (pp. 125, 134–8); and also against sykophants* (pp. 94 n.37, 106 with n.13) and against political leaders (presumably) who have allegedly deceived the people with false promises.

procedural law   That part of a legal system which answers the question, 'how do I go about exercising my rights?' (p. 5). See for contrast *sv*. substantive* law. Procedural law has by tradition held a relatively low status within modern legal thought; this is illustrated by the use of the term 'adjective* law' as a synonym: 'adjective' in grammar as elsewhere is that which serves merely to qualify 'substantive'.

proklesis   Lit. 'challenge': certain categories of evidence (notably statements given on oath* or under torture*) could only be admitted in an Athenian court with the consent of both sides; any litigant could challenge his opponent to accept such evidence, but the challenge was in practice regularly rejected, for reasons discussed on pp. 33–6.

prostates   'Patron' or 'protector': widely used to describe various types of formal or informal guardianship. Metics* were obliged to register under a citizen as their *prostates*; and if they failed to do this they could be prosecuted by *graphē aprostasiou* (public indictment for failure to have a *prostates*) in which the penalty was sale into slavery outside the *polis** of Athens.

prothesmia   A statute of limitations, making it impossible to bring a charge once a set time has passed after the action which forms the basis of the case (p. 179). The majority of prosecutions had to be brought within five years of the alleged offence, but in certain categories of case (such as homicide) we are told that there was no such limit; in a *graphē paranomon**, on the other hand, a proposal could be annulled at any time, but its proposer could only be punished if the action was brought within a single year.

prutaneia   See *sv*. court-fees*.

psephisma, pl. *psephismata*   A decree of the *ekklesia**. Lit., 'that which is resolved by *psephos*' (voting-pebble: i.e., by secret ballot); but in practice secret ballot at Athens was reserved for votes of the *dikasteria**, and voting in the *ekklesia* was normally conducted by show of hands (*kheirotonia*). See further *sv*. *paranomon**, *graphē*; and, for the fourth-century distinction between *nomos* and *psephisma*, see *sv*. *nomos**.

(*graphē**) *pseudokleteias*   Lit. '(prosecution concerning) false summons': a public action brought by a litigant who has been convicted in his absence against a summons-witness, alleging that the summons had never in fact been delivered: p. 37 n.33. See further *sv*. *kleter**.

(*dikē**) *pseudomarturion*   Lit. '(prosecution concerning) false witness': a private indictment against a *martus**. This is by its nature a secondary action, brought against a man who has been a witness in previous legal proceedings, and charging him with having given a false or illegal testimony (pp. 19–39 *passim*, esp. 28 and 36–8, 92).

real contract   See p. 174, and also *sv*. consensual* contract.

real property   Broadly speaking, land and houses, which in English law are treated differently from 'personal*' property (everything else): p. 172 n.13.

Reception   The process by which classical Roman law was 'received' (accepted) in place of local customary law as the basis for the legal system of most of the continental countries of medieval Europe (pp. 2–3).

rhetor, pl. *rhetores*   An orator. The word can mean simply 'public speaker' or 'writer of speeches', or perhaps 'teacher of rhetoric': thus some of the 'Ten Orators' canonised by later Greek rhetorical theory did not themselves normally speak in public (cf. *sv*. *logographos**). But it can also mean 'public speaker' in the sense of 'political leader' (pp. 48, 95 n.38); this is particularly true in the fourth century at Athens, when it had become normal for political leaders not to hold any public office (see *sv*. *politeuomenoi**). Of course the same man may be a *rhetor* in both senses, as Demosthenes was.

self-help   Taking the law (legitimately) into one's own hands. The use of officially-sanctioned aggression or violence as a way of defending one's rights; in particular, the use of summary arrest against certain categories of criminal (pp. 56 n.61, 76). The term 'self-help' is a somewhat awkward literal translation of the German *Selbsthilfe*: the concept is influential in both German and Athenian legal thought, but not in English law.

sophistes, pl. *sophistai*; Eng. sophist(s)   Lit. 'practitioner of wisdom'. The sophists were professional teachers of *sophia* ('wisdom'), which included not simply 'philosophy' (*philo-sophia*, 'love of wisdom') in the modern sense of the word, but also such topics as natural science and in particular rhetoric. The sophistic movement was not a philosophical school; what united them was not shared doctrines but similarity of method: in particular, considerable intellectual sophistication combined with a flair for marketing at a high price their abilities as teachers. See pp. 50 with n.40, 107 with n.19.

stasis   Lit. 'taking up a position': thus 'the taking up of partisan positions', culminating in revolution or civil war: pp. 54 n.55, 95, 100, 118 with n.49, 124 n.5, 130.

statute of limitations   See *sv. prothesmia**.

strategos, pl. *strategoi*   A board of ten generals, the senior military officials of Athens in the classical period (pp. 117, 118). They differed from almost all other officials in two respects: they were elected rather than appointed by lot*; and although their term of office was a single year, there were no limits on re-election. As a result, the generalship became a position of considerable political importance, particularly during the second half of the fifth century: it was the prize for which intending political leaders would strive. In the fourth century, however, increasing military specialisation tended to divide political from military leadership: fourth-century politicians were for the most part private citizens rather than office-holders. See also *svv. arkhon**, *rhetores**, *politeuomenoi**.

subpoena   Lit. 'under (threat of) penalty': in English and American law, the court will at the request of the litigants summon compellable witnesses to attend and give evidence; if they refuse, they will be committing an offence and are liable to be punished for it. This summons is descibed as a *subpoena* (pp. 24–5).

substantive law   That part of a legal system which answers the question, 'what are my rights and my duties?' (pp. 5, 20). See for contrast *svv.* procedural* law.

sukophantes, pl. *sukophantai* (noun); *sukophantein* (verb)   A term of disputed etymology (p. 105 with n.6) and disputed meaning (pp. 52, 56 with n.63, 83–121 *passim*, 133), used pejoratively to describe an officious litigant. Conventionally transliterated as 'sycophant' or 'sykophant', but the English adjective 'sycophantic' derives from a later, post-classical development in the meaning of the word. (To avoid anachronistic confusion, we transliterate the classical term as 'sykophant', etc.) For the verb *sukophantein* 'to be a sykophant', see pp. 28, 83–121 *passim*, esp. 110.

(*graphē**) *sukophantias*   A public indictment which charges the defendant with being a *sukophantes**: pp. 37, 107 n.18.

summary arrest   See *sv. apagogē**.

summary execution   See *sv. apagogē**.

sumposion, pl. *sumposia*; Eng. symposion or symposium   Lit. '(the action of) drinking together': a general term for upper-class ritualised drinking-parties, common even in classical Greece among the wealthy leisured élite, but particularly important in the archaic period (pp. 129 n.19, 135, 139–45 *passim*); the English adjective 'sympotic' is used to mean 'pertaining to the *sumposion*' (pp. 52, 128).

sundikos, pl. *sundikoi*   Lit. '(one who is) together (with somebody) in justice'. The title of a little-known board of public officials; but the term is more often used as a virtual synonym for *sunegoros** to mean a supporting speaker, whether appointed by the state or acting on behalf of a private individual.

sunegoros, pl. *sunegoroi*   Most commonly, a person who appears in court to speak on behalf of a litigant (pp. 24, 32, 56). Lit. 'speaker together with', thus at least in theory preserving the rule that litigants could not be represented by advocates: the *sunegoros* was officially a supporting speaker. The word is also used to describe a speaker appointed to represent the state, normally as prosecutor; but the overwhelming majority even of public prosecutions were brought by private individuals.

sunomosia (or *xunomosia*)   Lit. 'a joint swearing of an oath', hence 'a group of men bound together by such a mutual oath'. Used as the equivalent of *hetaireia**, but with a stronger emphasis on the political or conspiratorial overtones (p. 52 with n.47).

surety   See *sv. enguē**.

sykophant   See *sv. sukophantes**.

talent   See *sv.* coinage*.

thesmothetes   The title of the six junior arkhons*: pp. 123, 145.

timē   (1) The value, honour or respect which an individual enjoys or believes that he ought to enjoy: pp. 55 with n.57, 60, 126, 129 n.20, 139–45 *passim*, esp. 140–2. To attack a man's *timē* was probably the essential constituent of *hubris**. The word can also be used in an economic sense to mean 'price': pp. 192–3, esp. 192 n.54.

(2) To deprive a man of his *timē* is to make him *atimos*, subject to the condition of *atimia** (see *sv.*).

(3) *Timē* in the sense of 'evaluation' lies at the root of *timesis**, the system by which the penalty was fixed for the majority of offences. A few procedures laid down statutory penalties: such a process was *atimetos** (pl. *atimetoi*), 'not subject to *timesis*'. The vast majority of procedures however were *timetoi**: in these, assuming that the defendant was convicted, both litigants had to propose alternative penalties, the proposal of the plaintiff being the *timema** and that of the defendant the *antitimema**; the *dikastai** would then vote for a second time, and they were obliged to choose one or other proposal. Like the system of 'pendular arbitration' which is occasionally used in modern industrial disputes (whereby employers and trade unions agree to binding arbitration on condition that the arbitrator will decide wholly in favour of one or other side), this tended to discourage flippant proposals; but the example of Socrates (whose failure to propose a serious alternative provoked the jury at his trial into voting for the death-penalty proposed by the prosecution) shows that it did not always succeed. See further p. 76 n.57.

timema, timesis (nouns); *timetos* (adj.)   See *sv. timē** (3).

torture   Athenian citizens were exempt from judicial torture, but it could be applied under certain circumstances to metics* and other foreigners. In the case of slaves, indeed, their evidence was not admissible in court except under torture (p. 26); but such torture could only be administered with the consent of both litigants, on the basis of a *proklesis** or challenge, which was (it appears) always refused: the rationale of the system is discussed on pp. 33–6.

(*dikē**) *traumatos ek pronoias*   A private indictment concerning attempted murder or (lit.) 'wounding with intent (to kill)': p. 133. It was closely related to the *dikē phonou* (see *sv. phonou**, *dikē*), and was subject to many of the same procedural peculiarities.

trierarkhos, Eng. trierarkh   The trierarkhy was one of the most important and expensive liturgies*: the man who undertook it had to pay for the manning and the upkeep of a warship (trireme) for a year. He was expected, at least in theory, to command the ship in person: hence the title trierarkh ('commander of a trireme'). It is very difficult to calculate the numbers of trierarkhs required, even if we assume (as seems probable) that the size of the Athenian navy never exceeded 400 ships. This was a maximum figure, reached only in the late fifth century; and even then, some at least of these ships remained in the dockyards as a reserve. On the other hand, there were periods especially during the fourth century when the trierarkhy was shared between several individuals, presumably because the burden was proving too onerous.

usufruct   A term of Roman law, used to denote the right (usually as a life-interest) to use and enjoy the fruits or profits of another person's property, but without being allowed fundamentally to alter that property. There is one attested example of a bequest in an Athenian will on broadly similar terms; but the absence of the clearly-defined Roman doctrines of property at Athens makes it dangerous to speak of 'usufruct in Athenian law'.

water-clock   See *sv. klepsudra**.
witness   See *sv. martus**.

xenia   Lit. 'being a *xenos**'. The term means generally 'outsider', 'foreigner', but is particularly used of the formalised hereditary friendships between members of different *poleis** or between Greeks and non-Greeks (pp. 45 n.20, 59 n.74). Such links were common among the aristocracy, and formed much of the practical basis for international dealing and diplomacy.

(*graphē) *xenias***   A public indictment brought against a foreigner who is allegedly pretending to be a citizen (pp. 33 n.24, 36–7 with 37 n.32, 39 n.35, 133); the penalty was sale into slavery outside the *polis** of Athens. See *sv. xenos**.

xenos, pl. *xenoi*   Lit. 'stranger' or 'outsider'. Either 'a foreigner' (as in *graphē xenias**) or else 'a foreigner with whom one has entered into a relationship as guest or host' (as in *xenia**). In the latter sense, see pp. 53, 59.

xunomosia   See *sv. sunomosia**.